PERFORMANCE
AND CULTURAL POLITICS

This ground-breaking collection gathers together some of the foremost scholars of performance studies to examine the historical and cultural territories of performance.

"'Culture'" in the twentieth century, says ethnographer James Clifford, "is not an object to be described, neither is it a unified corpus of symbols and meanings that can be definitively interpreted. Culture is contested, temporal, and emergent." The essays in this exciting volume explore performance – encompassing theater, performance art, dance, music, and photography – as a vital component of this hybrid, contested culture.

The contributors to this landmark volume focus on topics varying from Oscar Wilde to Milli Vanilli; the Rose Theatre to U.S. Holocaust museums. They provide new interpretations of performance and its relation to issues of history, memory, mourning, racism, homophobia, and performativity. Performance artist Robbie McCauley concludes with a practitioner's perspective on art-making and politics which offers fresh insights into questions raised in the other essays of the volume.

Performance and Cultural Politics is interdisciplinary, thought-provoking and rich in new ideas. It is essential reading for students and scholars of performance studies.

Elin Diamond is Associate Professor of English at Rutgers University.

PERFORMANCE AND CULTURAL POLITICS

Edited by Elin Diamond

London and New York

First published 1996
by Routledge
11 New Fetter Lane, London EC4P 4EE

Simultaneously published in the USA and Canada
by Routledge
29 West 35th Street, New York, NY 10001

Typeset in Garamond by
Florencetype Ltd, Stoodleigh, Devon

Printed and bound in Great Britain by
Biddles Ltd, Guildford and King's Lynn

British Library Cataloguing in Publication Data
A catalogue record for this book is available from the British
Library

Library of Congress Cataloguing in Publication Data
A catalogue record for this book has been requested

ISBN 0-415-12767-X
ISBN 0-415-12768-9 (pbk)

CONTENTS

Part III Moving/Seeing: Bodies and technologies

Part IV Identity Politics: Law and performance

Part V Performer/Performance

LIST OF ILLUSTRATIONS

To our students

NOTES ON CONTRIBUTORS

Emily Apter is Professor of French and Comparative Literature at UCLA. She is the author of *Feminizing the Fetish: Psychoanalysis and Narrative Obsession in Turn-of-the-Century France* (Cornell University Press 1991) and co-editor of *Fetishism as Cultural Discourse* (Cornell University Press 1993). She is currently completing a book on "Colonial Subjects/Postcolonial Seductions".

Philip Auslander is Associate Professor in the School of Literature, Communication and Culture of the Georgia Institute of Technology. He is the author of *New York School Poets as Playwrights* (1989) and *Presence and Resistance: Postmodernism and Cultural Politics in Contemporary American Performance* (University of Michigan Press 1992).

Herbert Blau is Distinguished Professor of English and Comparative Literature at the University of Wisconsin–Milwaukee. His most recent books are *The Eye of Prey: Subversions of the Postmodern* (Indiana University Press 1987), *The Audience* (John Hopkins University Press 1990) and *To All Appearances: Ideology and Performance* (Routledge 1992).

Ed Cohen teaches Gender and Cultural Studies at Rutgers University. He is the author of *Talk on the Wilde Side* (Routledge 1993) as well as a number of articles on the history of male sexualities. He is currently working on a book about autoimmunity called *The Body Is Not a Defensible Boundary*.

Elin Diamond is Associate Professor of English at Rutgers University. Author of *Pinter's Comic Play*, she has written articles on feminist and theater theory for *TDR*, *Theatre Journal*, *Discourse*, and *The Kenyon Review*, among others. She is completing her book *Unmaking Mimesis* for Routledge (1996).

Glenda Dicker/sun is Professor and Chair of Drama and Theater at Spelman College. She has directed extensively, both on and off Broadway, and has created a number of original scripts, most recently *Re/Membering Aunt Jemima: An Act of Magic*. Her many credits and awards include an Emmy nomination for her television production of *Wine in the Wilderness* (1972). Her articles have appeared in *Theatre Journal* and in *Upstaging Big Daddy: Directing Theater As If Gender and Race Matter*, edited by Ellen Donkin (University of Michigan Press 1993).

Susan Leigh Foster, choreographer, dancer, and writer, is author of *Reading Dancing: Bodies and Subjects in Contemporary American Dance* (University of California Press 1986), *Storying Bodies: Ballet's Choreography of Narrative and Gender* (Indiana University Press 1996), and is the editor of *Choreographing History and Corporealities* (Routledge 1995). She is a member of the Department of Dance at the University of California, Riverside.

Lynda Hart is Associate Professor of English and Theatre Arts at the University of Pennsylvania. She is the author of *Fatal Women: Lesbian Sexuality and the Mark of Aggression* (Princeton University Press and Routledge 1994), and co-editor with Peggy Phelan, of *Acting Out: Feminist Performances* (University of Michigan Press 1993).

Robbie McCauley started her performance work in 1979 and in 1989 became a core member of the American Festival Project, a collection of artists who develop work with local communities throughout the country. She is now creating the Stories Exchange Project with Romany and Czech citizens in the Czech Republic.

Vivian Patraka, Professor at Bowling Green State University, has published in *Theatre Journal, Modern Drama, Discourse, The Kenyon Review*, among others. Her book, *Spectacular Suffering: Theatrical Representations of the Holocaust and Fascism*, will be published by Indiana University Press.

Peggy Phelan is Chair of the Department of Performance Studies, Tisch School of the Arts, New York University. She is the author of *Unmarked: the Politics of Performance* (Routledge 1993) and co-editor with Lynda Hart of *Acting Out: Feminist Performances* (University of Michigan Press 1993).

Joseph Roach is Professor of English at Tulane University. His recent publications include *Critical Theory and Performance* (University of Michigan Press 1992), co-edited with Janelle Reinelt, and *Sacrifice and Circum-Atlantic Performances* (Columbia University Press 1996).

Amy Robinson is Assistant Professor of English at Georgetown University where she teaches Cultural Studies. Her work has appeared in *Critical Inquiry* and *Feminist Studies* and in *Acting Out: Feminist Performances*, edited by Lynda Hart and Peggy Phelan.

Rebecca Schneider is Visiting Assistant Professor of Drama at Dartmouth College. She is contributing editor to *The Drama Review* and has published in various journals and in *Acting Out: Feminist Performances*, edited by Lynda Hart and Peggy Phelan. She is currently working on a book to be titled *The Explicit Body* for Routledge.

1

INTRODUCTION

In our simplest references, and in the blink of an eye, performance is always a doing and a thing done. On the one hand, performance describes certain embodied acts, in specific sites, witnessed by others (and/or the watching self). On the other hand, it is the thing done, the completed event framed in time and space and remembered, misremembered, interpreted, and passionately revisited across a pre-existing discursive field.[1] Common sense insists on a temporal separation between a doing and a thing done, but in usage and in theory, performance, even its dazzling physical immediacy, drifts between present and past, presence and absence, consciousness and memory. Every performance, if it is intelligible as such, embeds features of previous performances: gender conventions, racial histories, aesthetic traditions – political and cultural pressures that are consciously and unconsciously acknowledged. Whether the performance of one's gender on a city street, an orientalist impersonation in a Parisian salon, or a corporation-subsidized, "mediatized" Broadway show, each performance marks out a unique temporal space that nevertheless contains traces of other now-absent performances, other now-disappeared scenes.[2] Which is to say – and every essay in this anthology offers a compelling version of this saying – it is impossible to write the pleasurable embodiments we call performance without tangling with the cultural stories, traditions, and political contestations that comprise our sense of history.

Yet to invoke history, and to propose a "drift" between presence and absence, is not to hitch performance to an old metaphysics of presence – the notion that an absent referent or an anterior authority precedes and grounds our representations. In their very different ways the contributors to this anthology take up the postmodern assumption that there is no unmediated real and no presence that is not also traced and retraced by what it seems to exclude.[3] Indeed, postmodern notions of performance embrace what Plato condemned in theatrical representation – its non-originality – and gesture toward an epistemology grounded not on the distinction between truthful models and fictional representations but on different ways of knowing and doing that are constitutively heterogeneous, contingent, and risky. Thus while

1

a performance embeds traces of other performances, it also produces experiences whose interpretation only partially depends on previous experience. This creates the terminology of "re" in discussions of performance, as in *re*embody, *re*inscribe, *re*configure, *re*signify. "Re" acknowledges the preexisting discursive field, the repetition – and the desire to repeat – within the performative present, while "embody," "configure," "inscribe," "signify," assert the possibility of materializing something that exceeds our knowledge, that alters the shape of sites and imagines other as yet unsuspected modes of being.

Of course, what alters the shape of sites and imagines into existence other modes of being is anathema to those who would police social borders and identities. Performance has been at the core of cultural politics since Plato sought to cleanse his republic of the contamination of histrionic display, from both performers and spectators. But contestations over censorship are just one manifestation of cultural politics. The essays in this book explore performances as cultural practices that conservatively reinscribe or passionately reinvent the ideas, symbols, and gestures that shape social life. Such reinscriptions or reinventions are, inevitably, negotiations with regimes of power, be they proscriptive conventions of gender and bodily display (see Apter, Foster, Cohen, Schneider) or racist conventions sanctioned by state power (see Robinson, Dicker/sun, Roach, McCauley, Patraka). Viewing performance within a complex matrix of power, serving diverse cultural desires, encourages a permeable understanding of history and change. As Joseph Roach puts it, the "present" is how we nominate (and disguise) "the continuous reenactment of a deep cultural performance." Critique of performance (and the performance of critique) can remind us of the unstable improvisations within our deep cultural performances; it can expose the fissures, ruptures, and revisions that have settled into continuous reenactment.

PERFORMANCE/THEATER

Because performance discourse, and its new theoretical partner, "performativity," are dominating critical discussion almost to the point of stupefaction, it might be helpful to historicize the term (and this book) in relation to debates with clearly defined ideological investments. Since the 1960s performance has floated free of theater precincts to describe an enormous range of cultural activity. "Performance" can refer to popular entertainments, speech acts, folklore, political demonstrations, conference behavior, rituals, medical and religious healing, and aspects of everyday life. This terminological expansion has been produced and abetted by a variety of theorists whose critique of the Enlightenment cogito as fully self-present cause them to view their own critical acts as performative – as indeterminate signifying "play" or as self-reflexive, non-referential "scenes" of writing. Moreover, because it appears to cut across and renegotiate institutional boundaries, as well as those of race,

2

gender, class, and national identity, performance has become a convenient concept for postmodernism. It has also become a way for skeptics of postmodernism to excoriate what Raymond Williams has called our "dramatized" society, in which the world, via electronics, is recreated as a seamlessly produced performance.

This focus on performance has produced provocative debates among theater theorists about the political status of theater in relation to performance.[4] Among early experimental groups like Beck and Malina's Living Theater, Joseph Chaikin's The Open Theater, Ed Bullins's and Robert Macbeth's New Lafayette Theater, Richard Schechner's The Performing Garage, Richard Foreman's Ontological-Hysteric Theater, Barbara Ann Teer's National Black Theater; in journals like *TDR* (*The Drama Review*, formerly *Tulane Drama Review*) and *Performing Arts Journal*; and in mid-1960s poststructuralist theorizing (Barthes on Brecht, Derrida on Artaud), performance came to be defined in opposition to theater structures and conventions. In brief, theater was charged with obeisance to the playwright's authority, with actors disciplined to the referential task of representing fictional entities. In this narrative, spectators are similarly disciplined, duped into identifying with the psychological problems of individual egos and ensnared in a unique temporal-spatial world whose suspense, reversals, and deferrals they can more or less comfortably decode. Performance, on the other hand, has been honored with dismantling textual authority, illusionism, and the canonical actor in favor of the polymorphous body of the performer. Refusing the conventions of role-playing, the performer presents herself/himself as a sexual, permeable, tactile body, scourging audience narrativity along with the barrier between stage and spectator.[5] Theater collectives of the 1960s were greatly influenced by Artaud and by experimentation across the arts. They and their enthusiastic theorists believed that in freeing the actor's body and eliminating aesthetic distance, they could raise political consciousness among spectators and even produce new communal structures. In performance theory of the late 1970s, the group affirmation of "being there" tends to celebrate the self-sufficient performing instant. In performance theory of the 1980s, consciousness-raising drops away (totalizing definitions of consciousness are, after all, suspect).[6] In line with poststructuralist claims of the death of the author, the focus in performance today has shifted from authority to effect, from text to body, to the spectator's freedom to make and transform meanings.

Feminist performance criticism has been vitally sensitive to both sides of this debate. Feminists have wondered whether performance can forget its links to theater traditions, any more than, say, deconstruction can forget logocentrism. As Brecht understood, theater's representation apparatus – with its curtains, trapdoors, perspectives, exits and entrances, its disciplined bodies, its illusorily coherent subjects, its lures to identification – might offer the best "laboratory" for political disruption, for refunctioning the tools of class and gender oppression.[7] But feminists also know that highly personal, theory-sensitive performance art, with its focus on embodiment (the body's social text), promotes a heightened awareness of cultural difference, of historical specificity, of sexual preference, of racial and gender boundaries and transgressions. This dialectic has been a focusing element for performers and theorists who want both political consciousness-raising and "erotic agency," the pleasure of transgressive desire.[8] Without resolving this dialectic, we might observe that if contemporary versions of performance make it the repressed of conventional theater, theater is also the repressed of performance. Certainly powerful questions posed by theater representation – questions of subjectivity (who is speaking/acting?), location (in what sites/spaces?), audience (who is watching?), commodification (who is in control?), conventionality (how are meanings produced?), politics (what ideological or social positions are being reinforced or contested?) – are embedded in the bodies and acts of performers. To study performance is not to focus on completed forms, but to become aware of performance as itself a contested space, where meanings and desires are generated, occluded, and of course multiply interpreted. Such discussion helps situate this anthology's relation to "performativity" and to cultural studies.

PERFORMATIVITY/PERFORMANCE

Poststructuralist conceptions of the human subject as decentered by language and unconscious desire, and postmodern rejections of foundational discourses (especially totalizing conceptions of gender, race, or national identity) have all made performance and performativity crucial critical tropes, whose relatedness I want briefly to explore. In a runner-up article to her ground-breaking *Gender Trouble*, Judith Butler uses performance to underscore the fictionality of an ontologically stable and coherent gender identity. Gender is rather a "*stylized repetition of acts* . . . which are internally discontinuous . . . [so that] the *appearance of substance* is precisely that, a constructed identity, a performative accomplishment which the mundane social audience, including the actors themselves, come to believe and to perform in the mode of belief."[9] Butler's point is not that gender is just an act, but that gender is materially "performative": it "is real only to the extent that it is performed."[10] Performativity derives from J.L. Austin's concept of the performative utterance which does not refer to an extra-linguistic reality but rather enacts or produces that to which it refers. This anti-essentialism pushes past constructionism. It's not just that gender is culturally determined and historically contingent, but rather that "it" doesn't exist unless it's being done. And yet the intractable existence of the cultural ideologies of gender is marked by Butler in the word "repetition"; gender is the "stylized *repetition* of acts . . ." Or, put another way, the "act that one does, the act that one performs is, in a sense, an act that has been going on before one arrived on the scene."[11] Gender, then, is both a doing – a performance that puts a conventional gender attributes into possibly disruptive play – and a thing done – a pre-existing oppressive category. It is a cultural apparatus that coerces certain social acts and excludes others across what Butler calls "culturally intelligible grids of an idealized and compulsory heterosexuality."[12]

When being is de-essentialized, when gender and even race are understood as fictional ontologies, modes of expression without true substance, the idea of performance comes to the fore. But performance both *affirms and denies this evacuation of substance.* In the sense that the "I" has no interior secure ego or core identity, "I" must always enunciate itself: there is only performance of a self, not an external representation of an interior truth. But in the sense that I do my performance in public, for spectators who are interpreting and/or performing with me, there are real effects, meanings solicited or imposed that produce relations in the real. Can performance make a difference? A performance, whether it inspires love or loathing, often consolidates cultural or subcultural affiliations, and these affiliations might be as regressive as they are progressive. The point is, as soon as performativity comes to rest on *a* performance, questions of embodiment, of social relations, of ideological interpellations, of emotional and political effects, all become discussable.

Interestingly, in Butler's more recent *Bodies That Matter*, performativity moves closer to Derridean citationality, operating within a matrix of discursive norms, and further from discrete performances that *enact* those norms in particular sites with particular effects. For Butler, "cultural norms" materialize sex, not the body of a given performer, even though she wishes at the outset to pose the problematic of agency. Noting that performativity in *Gender Trouble* seemed to instantiate a humanist subject who could choose her gender and then perform it, Butler is careful here not to personify norms, discourse, language, or the social as new subjects of the body's sentencing. Rather she deconstructively elaborates a temporality of reiteration as that which instantiates gender, sex, and even the body's material presence. "There is no power that acts, but only a reiterated acting that is power in its persistence and instability,"[13] and again, "performativity is thus not a singular 'act,' for it is always a reiteration of a norm or set of norms, and to the extent that it acquires an act-like status in the present, it conceals or dissimulates the conventions of which it is a repetition."[14] Performance, as I have tried to suggest, is precisely the site in which concealed or dissimulated conventions might be investigated. When performativity materializes as performance in that risky and dangerous negotiation between a doing (a reiteration of norms) and a thing done (discursive conventions that frame our interpretations), between someone's body and the conventions of embodiment, we have access to cultural meanings and critique. Performativity, I would suggest, must be rooted in the materiality and historical density of performance.

PERFORMANCE AND CULTURAL STUDIES

Performance as rite, ritual, specialized play has always been a privileged locus of anthropological investigation. In this discourse, culture complexly enunciates itself in performance, reiterates values, reaffirms community, and creates, in Victor Turner's words, sites of "liminality" with which to broach and resolve crises.[15] In Turner's concept of the "social drama" (encompassing breach–crisis–redress–outcome) and in Richard Schechner's performance models, liminality both interrupts and sustains cultural networks, tending to reaffirm an organic model for the understanding of culture.[16] Postmodern skepticism about all totalizing metanarratives challenges such descriptions. In the words of contemporary ethnographer James Clifford: "Twentieth-century identities no longer presuppose continuous cultures or traditions. Everywhere individuals and groups improvise local performances from (re)collected pasts, drawing on foreign media, symbols, and languages"; and again, "'culture' is not an object to be described, neither is it a unified corpus of symbols and meanings that can be definitively interpreted. Culture is contested, temporal, and emergent."[17] Performance as I have been developing it in this introduction – performance with its representational and ideological traces remembered – is an important component of culture so defined. In performance, and in the developing field of Performance Studies (see Roach for an excellent discussion), signifying (meaning-ful) acts may enable new subject positions and new perspectives to emerge, even as the performative present contests the conventions and assumptions of oppressive cultural habits. As Stuart Hall puts it, cultural practices (such as performance) are "interwoven with all social practices; and those practices, in turn, [with] sensuous human praxis, the activity through which men and women make their own history."

In British cultural studies (from its emergence at the University of Birmingham Centre for Contemporary Culture in 1964), the analysis of cultural texts, was conceived as both historically specific and interventionist. Taking culture as the struggle for meaning in class-bound industrial societies, the work of Raymond Williams, Stuart Hall, John Fiske, and Angela McRobbie was, in its Marxian negotiations, avowedly political.[18] Cultural analysis might not only read "general causes" and "broad social trends" behind the practices of everyday life, it could *produce* consciousness, make meanings, provoke contestation. "Social relations," notes Stuart Hall, "require meanings and frameworks [cultural arrangements] which underpin them and hold them in place."[19] Cultural studies seeks to link the humanities, social sciences, arts, and political economy. It ranges from early study of working-class culture and popular traditions, through work on subcultures and media studies, to work on racism, hegemony, and feminist revisioning of earlier subcultural work, and on to (on both sides of the Atlantic), work on representation, postcolonial identity, difference, "othering," and the AIDS crisis. As Renato Rosaldo puts it, "Whether speaking about shopping in a supermarket, the aftermath of nuclear war, Elizabethan self-fashioning, or ritual among the Ndembu of central Africa, work in cultural studies sees human worlds as constructed through historical and political processes, and not as brute timeless facts of nature."[20]

In the United States, where academics on the left have long been divorced from public traditions of progressive social practice, cultural-studies battles have recently been waged around the question of interdisciplinarity in universities. Cultural studies has come to mean not just the reading of popular culture texts and practices in relation to structures of power, but a resistance to institutional boundaries and hierarchies. (Charges of "political correctness" reflect the wish to prohibit this putative politicization of – and the exposure of political processes at work in – academic departments and institutions.) Cultural studies is at the heart of such contestations (at the time of this writing, such *losing* contestations), not only because it questions traditional canons and disciplinary formations, but because it causes scholars on the left to evaluate what they are doing and why. As bell hooks reminds us, cultural studies in U.S. universities might become a crucial site of vigilance against the vagueness of "multiculturalism." The attempted shifts in curricular direction (for example, literature syllabi including works by people of color) will, she notes, "transform the academy only if they are informed by non-racist perspectives, only if these subjects are approached from a standpoint that interrogates issues of domination and power."[21] This underscoring of relations between pedagogy and cultural politics was a motivation in the making of this book.

PERFORMANCE AND CULTURAL POLITICS

It is no coincidence that debates about cultural studies arise at about the same time that "performance" gains critical currency; indeed performance in all its hybridity would seem to make the best case for interdisciplinary thinking.[22] And yet, while Michel Benamou named "performance" the "unifying mode of the postmodern," the early texts of cultural studies have focused more on mass media's invasion of the cultural, and, as a political response, on resistant styles, subcultures or rituals that introduce "noise" in the hegemonic status quo. The recent *Cultural Studies* (Routledge 1992) and *The Cultural Studies Reader* (Routledge 1993) generally blindside performance as a slightly less significant cultural practice.

In planning this book, I wanted performance critics and artists to move beyond explicit theater contexts and confront performance issues within structures of power. In other words, I sought to stage a dialogue between performance and cultural studies. Despite differences in subject matter and style, and with varying degrees of intensity, these essays exemplify what I understand to be basic to a cultural-studies (or indeed a performance-studies) project. One, a concern with the historical, cultural, and political specificity of the object of study. Two, a corollary concern with authorial performance – what

Rebecca Schneider calls the subject/writer's *complicity* with her object: an engagement with her own embodied specificity, her habits of seeing and desiring. Here the critique of performance merges with the performance of critique as a deliberate project of self-reflexiveness, projection, and fantasy (see especially Dicker/sun, Schneider, Foster, Phelan, and Blau). Three, a reflection on identity and difference as politically inflected but mobile terms that make space for, rather than close off, new critical territories.

In Part I, "Re-sexing Culture: Stereotype, Pose, and Dildo," Emily Apter and Ed Cohen each take issue with Butler's concept of performativity, not by returning to the "truth-regime[s]" of sex and gender, but by exploring the interplay between subjectivity, artifice, and cultural history. In Apter's "Acting Out Orientalism: Sapphic Theatricality in Turn-of-the-Century Paris," the stereotype not only functions as a form of outing in specific lesbian sub-cultures, it labors theoretically as "the Achilles heel of performativity . . . a kind of psychic ossification that reassimilates subjective novelties into the doxa." In Cohen's "Posing the Question: Wilde, Wit, and the Ways of Man," posing is "an embodied question" that dangerously disturbs late-Victorian doxa on masculinity while allowing Wilde to live out, and temporarily market, the social contradictions of his sexuality. In Lynda Hart's "Doing It Anyway: Lesbian Sado-Masochism and Performance," the dildo not only poses a question to gender ontology, it introduces and eroticizes a "representational crisis" in the lesbian imaginary, for the phallus (and the symbolic order it maintains) is, Hart notes, "never where it appears." Cited by Apter, but threading through all three essays, is the late Craig Owen's important formulation on posing: "the subject poses as an object in order to be a subject." In transgressive sexualities, acts of self-objectification may be one complex yet pleasurable way of "pretending an identity into existence."

I noted at the outset that performance, as a doing and a thing done, drifts between past and present, presence and absence, consciousness and memory. In Part II, "Grave Performances: The Cultural Politics of Memory," Peggy Phelan, Vivian Patraka, and Glenda Dicker/sun, show us that memory performed is an occasion for national and cultural mythmaking. In Phelan's "Playing Dead in Stone, or, When is a Rose not a Rose?," more is dug up than the remains of the Rose Theatre at a commercial site on London's South Bank. In her "psychoanalysis of excavation," Phelan performatively reads the signs of cultural homophobia in parliamentary posturing. Stalking the Rose are the ghosts not only of Oscar Wilde and Christopher Marlowe, but of gay men dying of AIDS. Dennis Hollier's notion (paraphrased by Phelan) that "the invention of architecture was motivated by a desire to forestall and forget death" might serve as an epigraph to Patraka's "Spectacles of Suffering: Performing Presence, Absence, and Traumatic History at U.S. Holocaust Museums." The Washington and Los Angeles museums, in their fundraising, in their appeal to democratic institutions, in their very design, attempt to re-member the dead by stimulating or constraining acts of memory in their visitors. Patraka's essay deploys a series of fascinating contrasts – between, for example, de Certeau's concept of space and place, between a room of disintegrating shoes taken from concentration-camp victims and a room of computer-synchronized exhibits that attempt to "manage" mass annihilation. In Glenda Dicker/sun's "Festivities and Jubilations on the Graves of the Dead: Sanctifying Sullied Space," unmarked graves are again disturbed, but this writer's "hovering" ghosts are the defiled and forgotten drylongso (ordinary) citizens of cultural memory, the lost black communities she summons and re-embodies in three performances crafted from oral histories: a "live oak drama" on St. Simons Island, a "living portrait" in Setauket, N.Y., and a "play scrap" in Newark, N.J. Seeking space for the "uppity Black woman," Dicker/sun is a self-conscious secular charismatic, sanctifying what racism has sullied. Yet to sanctify is to lose nothing of the history that has dirtied her ancestors. Rather she re-inhabits that history, walking with Langston Hughes on the northbound road, making legible and visible a cultural imaginary that is still effaced in official discourse.

Part III, "Moving/Seeing: Bodies and Technologies," explores the viscera of performance, its corporeal and visual pleasures. Foster's "Pygmalion's No-Body and the Body of Dance" treats the three ballet versions of the Pygmalion story and finds in the reigning corporeal conventions a subterranean narrative of pre- and post-Revolutionary subjectivity. This narrative includes the signifying of interiority, of gender idealizations, and culminates, in the nineteenth century, in stereotypic marketed displays, in which the body was divorced from emotional expressivity. In the original performance of this piece, at an MLA panel in 1992, Foster danced her essay; here italics dance with conventional typeface as the critic seeks to embody her long-dead choreographers without "fixing a body of facts like Milon's immovable Galathea." In "After Us the Savage Goddess: Feminist Performance Art of the Explicit Body Staged, Uneasily, Across Modernist Dreamscapes" Rebecca Schneider finds herself in the eye of the hurricane and imagines new feminist configurations of Yeats's millenial modernist prophecy (upon seeing Jarry's excretory surrealist *Ubu Roi*): "after us the savage god." For Schneider, feminist performance art, from Carolee Schneeman's vaginal scrolls to Annie Sprinkle's cervical peep-show, presents a cultural politics that refigures modernism's traditional whore/objects. Writing herself into community with these performers, Schneider revises the end of Bataille's *Eye/Body* as "perspectivalism on the flip." While photography is Herbert Blau's technology of choice, "Flat-Out Vision" works dialectically with Schneider's essay in its eulogy to modernist seeing: the flat-out vision that, like Ibsen's "devastating realism," eludes the mediations of political captioning or, as Blau puts it, the "vanities of critique." Where Schneider finds in the explicit body a means of reversing the dissecting modernist gaze, Blau argues that the image, far from framing and occluding the body (or object), can be neither fixed nor read; its details constantly recede in the "viscissitudes of light." Philip Auslander's "Liveness: Performance and the Anxiety of Simulation" reminds us that in our technoculture, performance's corporeality, like the difference between seeing and not-seeing or "perspectivalism on the flip," may just be as an effect of "mediatization." Using Milli Vanilli and Eric Clapton on MTV's "Unplugged" as studies in the political operations of capital and simulation, Auslander dissects and extends Baudrillard's theories, showing that "liveness," performance's most precious commodity, need have nothing to do with the living.

In Part IV, "Identity Politics: Law and Performance," performance abets the making of racist traditions and legal history. Joseph Roach's "Kinship, Intelligence, and Memory as Improvisation: Culture and Performance in New Orleans" offers a rich genealogy of performance studies linked to an investigation of the Mardi Gras krewes of late-nineteenth-century New Orleans. Roach demonstrates how the krewes' rites of passage produced a ludicrous but deadly serious performance of identity. In hybrid societies like that of New Orleans, performance becomes the "principle mode whereby cultures produce themselves in the face of those whose exclusion defines by contrast the status of the elect." Roach cites and Amy Robinson focuses on *Plessy versus Ferguson*, the case in which a performance of deliberate passing intended to challenge Louisiana's Jim Crow accommodations law allowed the Supreme Court, in 1896, to make "separate but equal" official U.S. law. In her "Forms of the Appearance of Value: Homer Plessy and the Politics of Privacy," Robinson argues that when Plessy's lawyer claimed that Plessy's "whiteness" was his property, and thus constitutionally protected, he misunderstood "the performative logic of the pass" – the Justices decided that Plessy was stealing. From this she suggests that the right-to-privacy concept in gay-rights advocacy commits a besieged community to the same flawed Lockean notion of identity as property. The natural rights of a self-owning subject, Robinson argues, have never protected those whom dominant culture has deemed "unnatural."

Placing the reflections of a "real" performance artist at the end of the book gives Robbie McCauley, in "Thoughts on My Career, *The Other Weapon*, and Other Projects," the elect and lonely status of sharing the rubric, "Performer/Performance," with no one. It's not that McCauley's brilliant work on stage makes her unique, but that her own selective oral history helps recapitulate the ways in which performance, as one crucial practice in the making of culture, is inseparable from politics and history. As narrator of her "performance-theater" career, McCauley is both actor and director, doer and namer, a performer of personal tales in self-consciously politicized spaces.

Always a master of the "talkback," McCauley helps me close with some reflections on intratextual talkback in this anthology, beyond the connections I have indicated above. Not only are racist and homophobic logics deconstructed through most of these essays, there are quieter echoings. The artifacts of veneration in Dicker/sun's Setauket piece, the "photographs, paintings, family Bibles . . ." seem to redeem the artifacts of mourning, the "photographs, eyeglasses, shoes" in the Holocaust museum (Patraka), and the "coins, jewelry, shoes, and hazelnut shells" in the ruins of the Rose (Phelan). Similarly, survivor testimony in Patraka's essay speaks to Dicker/sun's gathering of communal voices and to McCauley's after-show discussions. Affixing a caption in Blau resonates with "fixing" the pose in Cohen and "the real" in Hart; and Auslander's discussion of mediatized performance glosses Patraka's analysis of simulated histories. Apter joins Foster, Schneider, Roach, and Robinson in providing a cultural panorama for performances of identity and difference. Dicker/sun and McCauley give two versions of making performances, McCauley and Auslander offer different perspectives on post-1960s acting, and McCauley guides us back to Apter: "Rather than avoid stereotypes, I study them."

Intratexual dialogue is of course one of the pleasures of reading a text of many voices. It is my hope the reader will carry on making these connections, in which case *Performance and Cultural Politics* will be both a doing and a thing done.

NOTES

1 See *The American Heritage Dictionary* definition for performance: "1. The act of performing . . . and 5. Something performed: an accomplishment; a deed."

2 The notion that historical memory is embedded in the performative present is a constant theme in Herbert Blau's work. See, for example, "Universals of Performance," in *The Eye of Prey* (Bloomington and Indianapolis: Indiana University Press, 1987): "So long . . . as there is performance to be referred to *as such* it occurs within a circumference of representation with its tangential, ecliptic, and encyclical lines of power. What blurs in the immanence of seeing are the features of that power. . . ."

3 See Henry Sayre's discussion of "presentness" in *The Object of Performance: The American Avant-Garde since 1970* (Chicago: University of Chicago Press, 1989), p.9 ff. For a different perspective, see Peggy Phelan's "The Ontology of Performance," in *Unmarked: The Politics of Performance* (London: Routledge, 1993), pp. 146–66.

4 The performance/theater inquiry has been a thematic in Blau's writing since *Blooded Thought: Occasions of Theater* (Performing Acts Journal Publications, 1982). For a recent look at these issues in the academy, see Jill Dolan, "Geographies of Learning: Theater Studies, Performance, and the 'Performative,'" *Theater Journal*, 45. 4 (Dec. 1993): 417–41. Much of what Dolan envisions for a reconfigured "Theater Studies" is compatible with my sense of a performance criticism that attends to the specificity of theater. For an earlier brief discussion of theater as a discipline in the postmodern academy, see Sue-Ellen Case's introduction to *Performing Feminisms* (Baltimore: Johns Hopkins University Press, 1990), pp.1–13.

5 Consider the early work of performance artists Carolee Schneemann, Valie Export, Linda Montano, Eleanor Antin, Chris Burden, Vito Acconci, among others. For an influential articulation of the postmodern body in performance, see Josette Féral, "Performance and Theatricality: The Subject Demystified," *Modern Drama* 25.1 (1982): 170–81. See David Roman's recent discussion of Feral's piece in "Performing All Our Lives: AIDS, Performance, Community,"

in Janelle G. Reinelt and Joseph R. Roach, *Critical Theory and Performance* (Ann Arbor: University of Michigan Press, 1992), pp. 208–21.

6 See Bonnie Marranca on "being there" in *Theatre of Images* (New York: Drama Book Specialists, 1977), p. xii.

7 See Sue-Ellen Case, *Feminism and Theatre* (London: Routledge, 1988), p.132. See also my "Brechtian Theory/Feminist Theory: Toward a Gestic Feminist Criticism," *The Drama Review (TDR)*(Spring 1988): 82–94.

8 Jeannie Forte's phrase in "Focus on the Body: Pain, Praxis, and Pleasure in Feminist Performance," in Roach and Reinelt's *Critical Theory and Performance*, pp. 248–62. Consider the work since the 1980s of Karen Finley, Holly Hughes, Split Britches (Lois Weaver, Peggy Shaw, Deb Marolin), among others.

9 Judith Butler, "Performative Acts and Gender Constitution: An Essay in Phenomenology and Feminist Theory," in Case, *Performing Feminisms*, pp. 270–1.

10 Ibid., p. 278.

11 Ibid., pp. 270, 277.

12 Judith Butler, *Gender Trouble: Feminism and the Subversion of Identity* (London: Routledge, 1990), p. 135.

13 Judith Butler, *Bodies That Matter: On the Discursive Limits of "Sex"* (London: Routledge, 1993), p. 9.

14 Butler, *Bodies That Matter*, p. 12.

15 See Victor Turner, *From Ritual to Theatre: The Human Seriousness of Play* (Performing Arts Journal Publications, 1982).

16 See Richard Schechner, "Towards a Poetics of Performance," in *Essays on Performance Theory* (New York: Drama Book Specialists, 1977), pp. 120 ff., and in *The End of Humanism: Writings on Performance* (PAJ, 1982). For a good discussion of Schechner's anthropological convergences, see Susan Bennett, *Theatre Audiences* (London: Routledge, 1990), pp. 133 ff.

17 James Clifford and George E. Marcus, eds., *Writing Culture: The Poetics and Politics of Ethnography* (Berkeley and Los Angeles: University of California Press, 1986), p. 19. See the important work on performance written in the context of postmodernism and the new ethnography, under the rubric "Cultural Studies," in Roach and Reinelt, *Critical Theory and Performance*, including Roach's introduction. See especially Sandra Richards's "Under the 'Trickster's' Sign: Toward a Reading of Ntozake Shange and Femi Osofisan," in which she theorizes a "diaspora literacy" (66) in our reception of Shange's appropriation of Yoruba traditions of divination.

18 For his initial ambivalence about marxism, see Stuart Hall, "Cultural Studies and its Theoretical Legacies," in Lawrence Grossberg, Cary Nelson, Paula Treichler, *Cultural Studies* (London: Routledge, 1992), pp. 279 ff.

19 Cited in Dick Hebdige, *Subculture* (London: Methuen, 1979), p. 7.

20 Renato Rosaldo, *Culture and Truth: the Remaking of Social Analysis* (Boston: Beacon Press, 1989).

21 bell hooks, "Culture to Culture: Ethnography and Cultural Studies as Critical Intervention," in *Yearning: Race, Gender, and Cultural Politics* (Boston: South End Press, 1990), p. 131.

22 Martin Barker and Anne Beezer's *Reading Into Cultural Studies* (London: Routledge, 1992) expresses dissatisfaction with current cultural-studies projects based on ethnographic studies of audience, and the concomitant move away from text-based ideology and class critique of the Williams and Hall variety. This coincides with the terminological expansion of performance, and its drift away from theater. The political inflections of this volume come from queries into representation as well as demonstrations of performativity. See, for example, Emily Apter's discussion of the stereotype in Chapter 2.

Part I

RE-SEXING CULTURE
Stereotype, pose, and dildo

2

ACTING OUT ORIENTALISM

Sapphic theatricality in turn-of-the-century Paris[1]

Emily Apter

In briefly considering the status of Orientalism as a theatrical conceit in turn-of-the century feminist performance, I want to situate recent discussions surrounding performativity and the stereotype which in their turn beg certain questions about the appointment and settling of identity. It has struck me that in the concern to escape stale gender epistemologies, with their hetero-sexist contraries, psychosexual clichés, and *doxa* of "difference," a frangible alternative rhetoric has been ushered in figuring sexual identity as a conditional performativity that leaves only a ghostly and sometimes ghastly trace of the stereotype behind in the wake of its performances. Mutable sexualities, body parts semiotically open to erotic opportunity, sexed bodies recast as morphologically plastic and phantasmatically unbound – such parsings, grafted from the language of Judith Butler's chapter on "The Lesbian Phallus and the Morphological Imaginary" in *Bodies That Matter*, while eschewing an outright utopianism of gender possibility, nevertheless rekindle great expectations for a genuinely gender-troubled future.[2]

There has been considerable confusion surrounding the status of the term "performativity" in Butler's work. Despite its celebrity in relation to her writing, the term, interestingly enough, does not even figure in the index of *Gender Trouble*, where "parody" is the preferred word and does much of performativity's work. On one level, performativity emerges as a concept coinciding with the French sense of "une belle performance," that is, an obtained result, an act accomplished on bodies in readiness (and here agency seems psychoanalytically curtailed, as it is in poststructuralism). On another level, performativity refers to the contractual conditions of signification developed by the ordinary language philosopher, J. L. Austin. Austin employs the term to restrict the force-field of signification: locutionary exchanges are driven by circumstantial motivations and intentions, and within these rather strict conditions, speech-acts either misfire or hit their mark. Implicitly transposing these rules of language to gender, Butler, it seems, wants to preserve the framework of discursive constraint on meaning-production (where constraints are produced by normative prohibitions and the Law), while steering clear of a full-blown rehabilitation of subjective agency and intentionality.

Of course, the immediate purchase of the term performativity is on the realm of theatricality, but recently Butler has been concerned to take the performance out of the performative:

> In no sense can it be concluded that that part of gender that is performed is therefore the "truth" of gender; performance as bounded "act" is distinguished from performativity insofar as the latter consists in a reiteration of norms which precede, constrain, and exceed the performer and in that sense cannot be taken as the fabrication of the performer's "will" or "choice"; further, what is "performed" works to conceal, if not to disavow, what remains opaque, unconscious, unperformable. The reduction of performativity to performance would be a mistake.
>
> (B 234)

This critique of literalized theatricality echoes throughout the recent work. Performativity is linked to the "citationality" of cultural norms and practices, and to the psychic prohibitions and exclusions that regulate the normative visibility of the symbolic order; its connection to "living theater" is more or less disavowed, except in the arena of queer politics where "theatrical rage" is recognized as a vital strategy deployed against the "the killing inattention of policy-makers on the issue of AIDS" (B 233).

Though Butler's reservations toward theatricality make perfect sense in the context of a rigorous argument seeking to avoid the "adopt-a-gender" model of identity that has become the bane of 1990s gender theory, I am nonetheless struck by what seems to be her almost phobic disinterest in theater history and dramatic art. Part of my concern in this discussion will be to try to assert a place for performance within the theory of gender performativity without resorting to philosophies of reified truth-value (enshrined within the culture of compulsory heterosexuality).

In her discussion of queer performativity in Henry James, Eve Kosovsky Sedgwick also disallows the term's narrow theatrical application. Elaborating a notion of performativity that underscores "the obliquities among *meaning, being* and *doing*," Sedgwick warns against the domestication of the term through reductive determinations of

> whether particular performances (e.g. of drag) are really *parodic and subversive* (e.g. of gender essentialism) or just *uphold* the status quo. The bottom line is generally the same: kinda subversive, kinda hegemonic. I see this as a sadly premature domestication of a conceptual tool whose powers we really have barely yet begun to explore.[3]

With this caveat against taming the mental constructs for thinking sexuality Sedgwick ups the ante in the intellectual quest for alternatives to exhausted dyads and oppositionalities. But in dismantling historically resilient gender ontologies with an eye to accomplishing more than a simplistic resistance to gender essentialism and less than a naively redemptive vision of sexual polysemy, Sedgwick, like Butler, still leaves open the question of the hinge that keeps identity signification in place. A nagging anxiety about how referents ultimately come to bear meaning (which follows learning of the arbitrariness of signifiers or the non-originary nature of the Transcendental Signified), accompanies the prospect of reading sexual semiotics adrift in psychic prohibitions and identifications. The materialist grounding of phantasmatic signification – acknowledged as essential by Butler and Sedgwick alike – often remains elusive on the level of interpretative history.

My hypothesis in this essay is that part of what allowed turn-of-the-century French gay and lesbian sexual identity to perform itself along Sedgwick's axis of "meaning, being, and doing," was its mediation by the culturally exotic stereotype. Psychoanalytically, the stereotype is akin to Freud's notion of "character types," assigned explicit importance in the essays: *Psychopathic Characters on the Stage* (1905–6), *Character and Anal Eroticism* (1908), *Some Character-Types Met with in Psychoanalytic Work* (1916), and *Libidinal Types* (1931). In the second of these essays he wrote:

> Among those whom one tries to help by means of psychoanalytic treatment, one very often meets with a type of character in which certain traits are strongly marked, while at the same time one's attention is arrested by the behaviour of these persons in regard to a certain bodily function and of the organ connected with it during their childhood. I can no longer say on what precise occasion I first received the impression that a systematic relationship exists between this type of character and the activities of this organ, but I can assure the reader that no theoretical anticipations of mine played any part in its production.[4]

In this account, the character-type makes itself embarrassingly evident. Undoubtedly sensitive to antisemitism's strategic use of physiognomical stigmas and types, Freud is understandably wary of legitimizing facile conjugations of bodily feature with personality trait. But the character-type, like some unsuccessfully disavowed manifestation of the unconscious, refuses, as it symptomatically does, to go away.

A rather underrated staple of critical discourse that may be ripe for theoretical revisitation, the stereotype, as we all know, is a term deriving from the history of printing, referring to the metal plate made from a mold of composed type. An early example of technology's impact on textual representation, the stereotype retains the semantic residue of the materiality of its origin even within its more figurative usage as a synonym for the commonplace, hackneyed, or conventionally "settled in form." The notion of *imprinting*, whether visual or discursive, remains a key to understanding the negative reputation of the stereotype as that which stamps the complex subject with the seal of reductive caricature and/or bad habit. It was in this way that Oscar Wilde employed the term in his bitter reproach to Lord Alfred Douglas.

"My habit," he wrote in *De Profundis*, "– due to indifference chiefly at first – of giving up to you in everything had become insensibly a real part of my nature. Without my knowing it, it had *stereotyped* my temperament to one permanent and fatal mood."[5] The association of the stereotype with "permanence" and "fatality" implies that the stereotyped character is flawed, even deviant, insofar as it contains a groove of moral decadence veering toward the death drive.

Wilde's reference to his "stereotyped temperament" encapsulates a drama of ego destitution and volitional subjugation. In an essay concentrating on the way in which stereotypes are "intercepted" in the graphic, slogan-slashed art of Barbara Kruger, the late Craig Owens also reminds us that "to imprint (stereo-*type*) the image directly on the viewer's imagination, to eliminate the need for decoding" is tantamount to visual "subjection."[6] A tool of paranoid surveillance, the stereotype, according to Owens's Foucauldian ascription, emerges as:

> A form of symbolic violence exercised upon the body in order both to assign it a place and to keep it in place, the stereotype works less through persuasion (the goal of traditional rhetoric: ideological adherence, consent) than through deterrence – what Jean Baudrillard calls "dissuasion." It promotes passivity, receptivity, inactivity – docile bodies. This effect is achieved primarily through intimidation: the stereotype poses a threat.
>
> (BR 194)

Though this passage calls for a nuanced reading of the stereotype's moral and physical damage to the subject, what I would like to pick up on here is not so much the repressive effect of the stereotype's over-legibility (explored in interesting ways by Roland Barthes in terms of how stereotypical iterations, conceived as deadening repetitions of intellection, "repress" and thereby produce textual bliss), but rather, on the problematics of *posing* implicit in Owens's assertion that the "stereotype poses a threat." Inadvertently or not, Owens signals the performativity of the stereotype; its theatrical flair for striking a pose, assuming a guise, pretending an identity into existence. As Owens observes in another essay dedicated explicitly to the problem of posing, "the subject poses as an object *in order to be a subject*" (BR 215). This formulation, it would seem, lies at the heart of the essentialism-versus-parodic-gender-performance debate insofar as it illustrates the lack of clear boundaries between the two camps. Though essentialism in feminist theory privileges crystallized, transcendent stereotypes, while its performative counterpart supposedly emphasizes typological dissolution and resignification, the two discourses are, so to speak, joined at the hip by their mutual reliance on a subject that makes itself *be* by enacting objectification.

The enactment of objectification can be seen at work quite self-consciously in the way in which French feminism mobilized Orientalist stereotypes to fashion "new" sexual identities that functioned as props on which to hang a pose. "Monstrous superhuman figures" to borrow Mario Praz's terms, were excavated from cultural history; women such as Sémiramis, Thaïs, and Cleopatra, whose erotic appetites were legendarily matched to their thirst for political authority. Sémiramis was an Assyrian queen who rebuilt Babylon with fortresses, fabulous palaces, and suspended gardens. She became famous in ancient history for her successful military campaigns throughout Asia and the Middle East. Revived in the eighteenth century as the subject of plays by Crébillon and Voltaire, celebrated as a romantic heroine in Rossini's opera of 1823, Sémiramis, not surprisingly, re-surfaced at the turn of the century in a 1904 dramatic production written by the decadent author Joseph Peladan (famous for his *fin de siècle* taste for androgyne and lesbian protagonists), which received ecstatic reviews in women's journals of the period, such as *Fémina*. Like Peladan's *Sémiramis*, Anatole France's *Thaïs*, first published in 1890 and adapted for the immensely popular opera by Jules Massenet in 1894, played on the hieratic, historic grandeur of the female stereotype by exploiting the full regalia of Orientalist decor. In this kitsch anticlerical conversion story about a fourth-century Egyptian courtesan and a hypocritical holy man who falls under her spell while diverting her from the path of sin, Thaïs is featured as an actress, seducing her riveted audience on the Alexandrian stage. Clothed in heavy gems, and presented to the viewer as an image graven in stone, she embodies the stereotype made pure performative: at once fetishized and mobilized in conceptual and visual space.

The immense prestige of the historical stereotype embodied in these Orientalist phallic women made them ripe for feminist re-appropriation. In Britain, for example, a feminist Thaïs emerged in suffragette circles in the 1910s and 1920s with the revival and retranslation of *Paphnutius*, a medieval play written by Hrotsvit von Gandersheim, "the first known women playwright of written texts," according to Sue-Ellen Case.[7] As emblems of national character, these stereotypes conferred the ideological adhesive of nationalism on to a nascent women's movement built on fragile coalitions and disparate class interests. In the context of Parisian identity politics, where the political was defined more personally and the salon or stage prevailed as the chosen arena of activism, Orientalist stereotypes were used as a means of partially or semi-covertly outing sapphic love. Colette's outing of her erotic partnership with the Marquise de Belboeuf in *Rêve d'Egypte* may be seen, in this regard, as of a piece with Mikhail Fokine's choreographed renditions of *Cléopâtre* (based on Théophile Gautier's short story "Une Nuit de Cléopâtre") and *Shéhérazade* in 1908 and 1910 respectively for the Ballets Russes. (Figure 2.1) Both productions featured the celebrated lesbian performer Ida Rubenstein in the major role.[8] Rubenstein's exotic features (she was Russian Jewish), great height, thin, androgynous body, and imperious manner made her a favorite for Orientalist roles in which sado-masochistic scenarios prevailed. Peter Wollen has traced the origin of her Orientalist mystique to the beginnings of her acting career in St. Petersburg, "where she was first introduced to Fokine by Bakst because she wanted dance lessons in order to play the part of Salome in her own production of Oscar Wilde's play."[9] He also notes that she eventually would perform Salome's Dance of the Seven Veils when it was transposed to *Cléopâtre*, making her entrance "on the shoulders of six slaves," and removing each veil (increased to twelve) in an elaborate striptease. What is particularly interesting in the case of Rubenstein and Colette is the use of Orientalism as an erotic cipher, a genre of theatricality in which acting "Oriental" becomes a form of outing, and outing is revealed to be thoroughly consonant with putting on an act (each flips into the other unpredictably).

An important *fin-de-siècle* paradigm for this acting/outing slippage may be found in Pierre Loti's colonial novel, *Aziyadé* (1879). Though dated, the work provides a prime example of Orientalist decadence revolving around the treacly romance of a British naval officer whose heart is stolen by a Circassian slave. The *mise-en-scène* is formulaically embellished with *turqueries*, just as his Far Eastern novel, *Madame Chrysanthème*, avails itself of stylistic *japonisme*, or *Le Roman d'un Spahi* of a black African fetish discourse. *Aziyadé* is the earliest of his colonial novels, earning him the dubious title, "Pimp of the Sensation of Difference," by his revisionist successor in the aesthetics of tourism, Victor Segalen. Set in Salonika and Istanbul during the waning of the Ottoman empire, *Aziyadé* is suffused with an atmosphere of imperial belatedness; what Mario Praz in *The Romantic Agony* characterized as "the long Byzantine twilight, that gloomy apse gleaming with dull gold and gory purple, from which peer enigmatic faces, barbaric yet refined, with dilated neurasthenic pupils . . . a period of anonymous corruption, with nothing of the heroic about it, . . . devoid of any virile element."[10] Like Remy de Gourmont's *Lettres à l'Amazone* (written for that leading figure of lesbian salons in Paris, Natalie Clifford Barney), and Pierre Louÿs's "Chansons de Bilitis" (poems about a Turkish high priestess of Lesbos), *Aziyadé* functioned as an underground script for the initiate, interpreted improvisationally in salon skits and "real life," as when two western-educated Turkish women, Nouryé and Zennour Noury-Bey, purportedly snared Loti in his own sequel by posing as Aziyadé reincarnations, returned in the flesh from a fictional tomb. (Loti went along with the ruse, half believing in the revisitation of his dead mistress, and using the episode to great effect to structure his subsequent Turkish harem novel *Les Désenchantées.)*

Just as it would be for Parisian sapphic circles, the art of cultural camouflage was important to Loti's self-fashioning as both textual and (auto)-biographical figure. A naval officer from Brittany, he was famous for having himself photographed in the local costumes, both masculine and feminine, of the foreign territories he visited, including China, Japan, the South Sea

Figure 2.1   Sarah Bernhardt as Cleopatra (Victoria & Albert Museum)

Islands, North Africa, West Africa, and the Middle East. He even extended this fascination with exoticist drag to the Moorish interior of his own home at Rochefort, transformed into a kind of domestic stage-set modelled after the Turkish apartment that *Aziyadé*'s central character appoints for himself in the Istanbul casbah. Loti also gave vent to theatricalized Orientalism when, in order to gain his idol Sarah Bernhardt's attention, he "had himself carried in to Sarah, as Cleopatra was carried in to Caesar, wrapped in a carpet."[11] Not only was Sarah Bernhardt celebrated for her role in Victor Sardou's *Cléopâtre* – which she played into her seventies – but she, like Loti, had herself photographed in character, stretched out on a divan with jewelled girdle and arm-bracelets, an adoring female attendant at her knee. One could say that Loti's grand gesture, his trying to "be" Sarah, by "being" Sarah Bernhardt "being" Cleopatra, embodied a kind of portmanteau Orientalism crossing bisexual and bicultural identifications.

The histrionic quality of Orientalist posing, common to art and life in Loti's case, points to a performative reading of *Aziyadé* in which the narrative is read as a scenography written in order to be acted out. Each diegetic sequence is built up around visually suspended tableaus, thrown up like so many expendable scrims and flimsily interconnected by diacritical ellipses. A sense of theater is also given characterological specificity through the conceit of a central narrator whose name is shared by the author (Loti was the pen name of Julien Viaud), and the protagonist, who "passes" as a Turk under the alias Arif-effendi. The dissolution and fragmentation of authorial and characterological integrity lends the novel a modernist aspect: there is no essentialist core to Loti's persona. In fact he continually refers to the emptiness within, to a self filled up with *eski*, the Turkish word for existential vacuity and ennui. Loti's protagonist clings to seeming Turkish so as to avoid the more difficult metaphysic of "being" nothing, nothing that is but a fleeting coalescence of what Alan Sinfield has termed "expressivity effects." In his social deconstruction of Shakespearean character criticism Sinfield writes,

> I have been trying to exemplify a way of reading in which speech and action in a fictional text may be attributed to characters – understood not as essential unities, but as simulated personages apparently possessing adequately continuous or developing subjectivities. But, beyond that, the presentation of the dramatis personae must be traced to a textual organization in which character is a strategy, and very likely one that will be abandoned when it interferes with other desiderata. To observe this is important, not just as a principle of literary criticism, but because it correlates with a repudiation of the assumption that reality, in plays or in the world, is adequately explained by reference to a fixed, autonomous, and self-determining core of individual being. Rather, subjectivity is itself produced, in all its complexity, within a linguistic and social structure.[12]

Sinfield signals the extent to which the very notion of character, like its more degraded cousin, the stereotype, is a fixing in flux; a stamp of the real flimsily appended to strategic, contingent, semiotic subjectivities. Character itself emerges as stereotype in drag, ethnically, socially, and culturally gender-imitative.

In addition to pointing to the ontological tenuousness of character, Loti's sham Turkishness highlights the theatrics of passing crucial to the performance of national and sexual identity, as well as to the idea of performance *as* identity. In the novel, the protagonist wavers between the successful cultural plagiarist traveling through the casbah unremarked, to the unauthentic native who, on catching sight of himself in a mirror, perceives a risible figure resembling "a young tenor, ready to break into a passage of Auber" (A 102). This failed cultural pass is intertwined with the failed heterosexual pass. When Loti tries to test Aziyadé's love by "playing the sultan," forcing her to suffer his liaison with another Turkish women, his cultural masquerade backfires as he finds himself rendered impotent by the courtesan's Europeanized dress. This masculinist demise, coinciding as it does with his inability to carry off the part of despotic pasha, implies that Arif-effendi's staged harem is really a convenient disguise for Loti's homo-erotic closet. Aziyadé herself, childlike and subservient, emerges as the travestied stand-in for Loti's young servant Samuel, with whom he savors "the vices of Sodom" in the brothels of the red-light district. Falling asleep on a boat with Samuel by his side, Loti floats into a wet dream punctuated by the sudden eruption of enemy fire. This fantastic episode, along with several others in the book in which veiled allusions to cruising, trysting, and the procurement of boys are coyly disavowed, add up to what Roland Barthes, borrowing Loti's phrase, characterized as the novel's element of "pale debauchery." "Pale outing," may in fact be the more appropriate expression, particularly insofar as it shadow-plays what Barthes himself is doing through his reading of Loti. Famous for his reticence on the subject of his own sexuality, Barthes came as close to publicizing his open secret by "bringing out" (in D. A. Miller's words) the gay innuendoes of Loti's writing and culturally staged persona. Queered in this way, Loti's Turkophilia (acted "out" in real life, so to speak, through his propensity for cultural transvestism) gives a new twist to Said's characterization of the colonial traveler's perception of the Orient as a "living tableau of queerness."[13]

By emphasizing Barthes's interpolation of the queer signals in *Aziyadé* I do not mean to imply that Loti's Turkish act was merely a decoy for that which was erotically not quite "out" (after all, Loti was perhaps only acting "out," that is, not really outing himself, but only appearing to do so), but rather that acting and outing are mutually implicated in exaggerated truth claims, claims to being "true to type." Acting and outing, as ontological strategies, commonly rely on essentialist typologies of enacted being that are thrown into definitional crisis by the wild mimeticism of affect. Perhaps it is this inflation of affect that helps to explain why campy Orientalist scenarios have always been and continue to be good value within gay drama;

their over-acted quality points to the way in which nonconformist sexual identity must perform itself into existence, more often than not through the transformation of originally conservative models.

Orientalism, as a nexus of extravagant psychic investments and layered semblances of the type, evolved into feminist and lesbian camp for a number of other more obvious reasons. Not only were women empowered or accorded sexual license through association with the dominatrix characterologies attached to exemplary princesses, queens, seductresses, or women leaders of the East, but, more interestingly, their agency was enhanced by "being" these avatars both on stage and off.[14] Ida Rubenstein, Sarah Bernhardt, Mata Hari, Colette, Lucie Delarue Mardrus, Renée Vivien and others expanded the performative parameters of the historic stereotype by moving their larger-than-life thespian personas into the choreography of erotic everyday life.

In the case of Renée Vivien (Pauline Tarn), the author of several lesbian cult books and translations of Sappho, whose short life was mythically commemorated by Nathalie Barney and Colette among others, the art of "being" Sappho seems to have done as much for the legendary quality of her persona as anything she wrote or transposed.[15] Her Sappho, according to Jean-Paul Goujon, was "Asiatic" and exotic, inhabiting a Lesbos that never forgot its contiguity to Smyrna.[16] This conflation of Greece and the Orient was of course particularly common in turn-of-the-century art, literature, opera, dance, and theater; syncretistic otherness was the fashion, spawning a wild hybridity of styles – Egypto-Greek, Greco-Asian, Biblical-Moorish – that would eventually be taken over by Hollywood. The particularism of the Orientalist stereotype was important nonetheless. In Vivien's case, a "real," living Turkish woman anchored her exoticist fantasies. Goujon has recently unearthed evidence of her epistolary (and ultimately consummated) romance with Kérimé Turkhan-Pacha, an "emancipated" woman from Constantinople who had originally written to Vivien as a literary fan. Erected as the prover-bial "Captive Princess" on the shores of the Bosphore in Vivien's prose fragment *Le Jardin Turc* (1905–6), and apostrophied as the "brown Mistress" and "My Sultana" in subsequent love poems, Kérimé, according to Goujon, played Orientalist double to Natalie Barney in Vivien's erotic pantheon. The heady mix of fantasy and tourism which sealed the Vivien–Kérimé love affair spilled over into Vivien's financial sponsorship of Nouryé and Zennour Noury-Bey, the same Turkish women who had pretended to incarnate Aziyadé in the hopes of enlisting Loti's help in evading their respective harems. Informed by Kérimé of their escape from Constantinople and their struggle to survive in Paris, Vivien furnished them with an apartment and living allowance, thereby earning a place for herself as a character in the as-yet-unwritten sequel to Loti's *Désenchantées*.

In addition to allowing Vivien to extend her fanciful construction of a Hellenic Paris-Lesbos into the psychoterritory of the Orient, Kérimé may have also played a central role in the Barney–Vivien quest for the "gynan-dromorph," defined by Barney's feminist biographer Karla Jay as "a higher, more perfect being, which would re-establish the principle of Femaleness in the universe."[17] In Natalie Barney's fantastic, rhetorically extra-terrestrial "biography of a soul," *The One Who is Legion, Or A.D.'s After-Life*, the gynan-dromorphic principle is ethereally manifest in a succession of what Terry Castle has identified as "apparitional lesbians."[18] Identities "on loan," persons whose posthumous correspondences are retrieved from the "dead-letter office" in the hopes of constituting a "herstory," these transubstantiated shadow women form a great chain of being whose essence approximates an androgyny purged of its diametric opposition to masculinity. At one point in the novel the problem of how to generate a feminocentric characterology that eschews singular, individual identities is fascinatingly considered; diverse theoretical gambits are themselves performed in an invocatory, interrogative voice:

> Put down every wanderer found in our catacombs, fix them by some familiar trait, and so learn to know and govern our ghosts, our lovers, our low-characters, our martyrs and saints, and any that we might encounter in this journey through ourselves. Surprised that authors had established no manner of dealing with even their fictitious personages, should we not definitely adopt the play-writer's method of giving a name to each *dramatis persona* – the drama here consisting in their divergences and conflicts – their combined chemistries. But what of their simultaneous claims and antagonisms?[19]

The response to this incredulous question is negative; there is no fixing trait or character-name adjudicating among "simultaneous claims and antago-nisms." When alternative systems for classifying the multivalent female soul are tested – musical composition, color-codes, orthography – the confusion only worsens. In the end the narrator reverts to a composite of stereotypes including the siren, the sphinx, and St. Joan, to be appointed communal "sponsor" or surrogate for the soul after "she" has committed suicide.

Barney's phantasmatic, Swedenborgian soul-mate appears in hindsight to be a precursor of the transcendental female subject invested by Luce Irigaray – contradictorily essentialist and anti-essentialist, singular and multiple, at one and the same time. In this light, it is all the more interesting that Barney resurrects the stereotype at the end of her novel as an antidote to the complete derealization of character attempted at the outset; anti-essentialism is thus curtailed by the return of the type.

In a more materialistic vein, Cléo de Mérode's memoir, *Le Ballet de ma vie*, charts the predication of the feminine subject on the exotic stereotype and its subsequent fanning out into exorbitant character. Cléo's improbable name helped to overdetermine the mythic creature she became; christened "Cléopâtre-Diane," she joined Orientalism to Hellenism in her stage craft and publicity images. A celebrated Belle Epoque *cocotte* whose erotic incli-nation, like that of her famous rival Liane de Pougy, was deeply feminocentric,

Cléo began her career as a precocious star of the Paris Opera ballet corps. The winner of *l'Illustration's* beauty contest, her image was mass-reproduced everywhere. In the realm of high art she became a favorite model for painters, sculptors, and photographers (Nadar among them). It was costumed as an Egyptian dancer in *Aida*, so the legend goes, that she seduced Leopold II, King of Belgium. In 1900 she clinched the Orientalization of her performance profile (much like Ida Rubenstein and Ruth St. Denis), with "la danse Cambodgienne," the hot attraction of the Exposition Universelle's *Théâtre Asiatique*. Toward the end of World War I, she amplified her Orientalist repertory with the role of "the Sulamite" in Charles Cuvillier's *Judith courtisane*. Here she performed an "Egyptian" dance with hieratic steps against a black decor, dressed in a dramatic gold tunic and black velvet cape designed by Paul Poiret.

Following the narrative accents of her autobiography, her own signature performance as the Cambodian dancer was intended to rival Sibyl Sanderson's interpretation of Thaïs, witnessed by Mérode early on in her career while a "rat d'Opéra" on the set. Sanderson's rendering of Thaïs exfoliated around her, emerging in Mérode's account as a kind of "primal scene" of Orientalist characterology. There is a ripple effect to her definition of the courtesan/actress identity: each gesture "plays" as a form of literal instruction in theatricality, exoticism, and the art of love. In the choreography, the pairing of roses with the mask of comedy points to the kind of punned relationship between performance and sex already evident in the acting/outing paradigm:

> Still a child but already tall, I also appeared in *Thaïs*, where I danced a decorative intermezzo with some of my companions. We played the part of novice actresses, following the courtesan, and we balanced ourselves around her waving roses in one hand and a mask in the other. [. . .] And Thaïs was Sibyl Sanderson! The beauty of her plasticity, the shapeliness of her postures, the powerful charm that exuded from her person and her act, attracted the admiration of all.[20]

In this picture of young dancers impersonating the role of courtesans' disciples in anticipation of the courtesan's role that many of them would eventually play in "real life," character is enhanced by the infectious medium of admiration. Admiration, rapture, the thrill of bodily proximity to the diva – these hyperbolic tropes of feminine enthusiasm are transmitted "fem-to-fem," generating waves of affect that would, for many, translate into the sapphic bonds of the Parisian city of women. Cléo's ties to Paris-Lesbos were guaranteed by the presence of her life-long companion Marie Briot, a retired theater professional who had been part of the circle of Louise Balthy, a celebrated lesbian *demimondaine* known for her "ugly" chic.

Cléo de Mérode was constructed by her era as one of the "new" feminine stereotypes of Paris 1900, a stereotype compiled in large measure from the performances of famous actresses: Sarah Bernhardt's Cleopatra, Sibyl

Sanderson's Thaïs, Rose Caron's Salammbô, Madame Héglon's Delila, Loïe Fuller's pseudo-eastern veil dance, Sada Yacco's Japanese dances. A transferential identification with these female icons was reinforced by the hallowed ritual of torch-passing whereby the novice agreed to introject the stereotype of the big, exotic, feminine Other offered to her via the diva.

The expanded notion of performativity and performance that emerges from early feminist theater history has been recognized recently by a number of critics, most notably Sue-Ellen Case, who sees Natalie Barney as a pre-eminent forerunner of the contemporary woman performance artist. Barney, Case observes,

> invented the practice of women performing for women, which was to become important in feminist theater in the 1970s; she introduced images of lesbian sexuality; she conceived of improvisatory performances relating to the talents of women performers; and she created theatricals which occurred in her private, domestic space, but which were intended as formal, aesthetic works and even found their way into published dialogues. The personal theater of the salons and private theatricals paved the way for a new art form in this century, which has created an important intersection of feminism and theater – women in performance art.
>
> (FT 53)

Case's concern to develop a feminist history of performance, while highly useful, presents in this particular instance an unproblematized view of role-playing, role models, and feminist identifications with the "enabling" stereotype. In his psychoanalytic dissection of the colonial stereotype, Homi Bhabha argues that "the point of intervention should shift from the *identification* of images as positive or negative, to an understanding of the *processes of subjectivication* made possible (and plausible) through stereotypical discourse."[21] Though it is not entirely clear what these "processes of subjectivication" fully entail, it seems that for Bhabha, the stereotype, like the fetish, embodies a *doxa*, an image-repertoire of deadening repetitions (around, say, race or gender) that ultimately produces alienation from the psychically surinvested system of representations within which it is codified. Bhabha recoups the stereotype as the bad object of colonial mimicry by allowing it to return as a good object of subjectification, shattering politically fixed colonial subjects into a multitude of refractive, potentially emancipatory subject positions.

Bhabha's complication of the identification paradigm as applied to race and cultural identity lines up well in many respects with Judith Butler's performative reading of gender-imitation within the morphological Imaginary, but both theorists avoid fully recognizing the psychic recalcitrance of the stereotype as a constricting component of gender and cultural identity. Disavowed, the stereotype rebounds re-avowed, as that upon which gender destabilization pins itself as a point of departure or referent of resignification. The irrepressible coherence of characterology embedded in the stereotype introduces a kind of psychic ossification that re-assimilates subjective novelties into the *doxa*. The stereotype, I would maintain, is the Achilles' heel of performativity, or better yet, the "Cleopatra's nose" (to use Lacan's Pascalian trope for "le je ne sais quoi" in "The Freudian Thing") of historical subjectification.[22]

How then do we escape the prison-house of stereotypes in the field of identity politics? I don't think we can, but it is perhaps the desire to do so that motivates one of the more astonishing episodes in feminist performance history – the acting out of what I will call the "Isabelle Eberhardt complex." In looking at this complex, I will argue, subjectification occurs not so much, as Bhabha affirms, through a "shift *from* identification," but rather *through* a radical identification *with* nothing, nothing but the stereotype drained of its recognizable identity markers: its "Europeaness," its "femme-ness," its metaphysics of presence.

Eberhardt's larger-than-life biography, modeled quite self-consciously by Isabelle herself after Loti's Orientalist fictions, exerted and has continued to exert an extraordinary hold on the Occidental feminist imaginary. Her life-story, recounted first by executors and would-be publishers, Victor Barrucand, Robert Randau, and René-Louis Doyen, and emphatically retold in more recent times by Rana Kabbani, Annette Kobak, Denise Brahimi, Edmonde Charles-Roux, Leslie Blanch, and Paul Bowles, illustrates a compulsion to repeat symptomatic of the stereotype. Eberhardt was the illegitimate daughter of a slavic anarchist named Alexander Trophimowsky, who had an affair with Isabelle's mother after he was hired as the family tutor. Gifted in Oriental languages and fascinated by Islam, he taught Isabelle and her brothers Arabic. From 1897 on, Eberhardt traveled to North Africa, eventually adopting the name Si Mahmoud Essadi, converting to Islam, and getting herself inducted into the Sufi brotherhood of the Qadriya.[23] Cross-dressing as an Arab man, she pursued the rough pleasures of nomadic travel, casual sex, and drugs. A self-destructive streak matched the dark flashes in her destiny. Though her short stories and newspaper articles in the Algerian press garnered her a following in North Africa and abroad, she also enraged local *colons*, who were probably behind an assassination attempt that she survived (but not without an augmented sense of morbidity), only to die in 1904 in a freak desert flood at the age of twenty-seven.

One could say that Isabelle Eberhardt fell masochistically in love with death. In one tale, an anonymous male character sings "an ancient song in which the word for *love* alternated with the word for *death*" ("The Rival," p. 60). A beautiful Jewess is impaled in the street after falling prey to the charms of a cruel Sidi in "The Magician"; a dancer, abandoned by a French conscript, turns to self-wasting alcoholism and prostitution in "Achoura"; a young woman commits suicide when forced into a repulsive arranged marriage in "Taalith"; and throughout her journals, a solitary global adventuress restlessly moves on from shelter to shelter, "vagabonding" in body and spirit. "Vagrancy is deliverance," she wrote. "To be alone, to be *poor in needs*, to be ignored, to be an outsider who is at home everywhere, and to walk, great and by oneself, toward the conquest of the world" ("Pencilled Notes," p. 68). In virtually all her stories, women bind themselves as she did, to a nihilistic credo of addiction, moral abnegation, and poverty. Here one could say that the degree-zero stereotype performed by Eberhardt – that of a gender-dispossessed, deculturated woman inserted into the violent landscape of colonial history – fulfilled the Wildean ascription of "bad habit" or fatal groove.

Eberhardt's biography has been acted out by successive generations of feminists. In the 1920s and 1930s Lucie Delarue-Mardrus not only paid tribute to Isabelle's memory through a visit to her grave in Ain-Sefra, but she also "interpreted" the Eberhardt script in her self-staging as "la Princesse Amande." Immortalized in the memoir of her amanuensis Myriam Harry (written in what Wayne Koestenbaum would call "diva prose," a writing at once "florid, self-aggrandizing, imperial, amusing, banal, pathetic, full of trashy cadences"), Lucie is introduced in Harry's *Mon amie Lucie Delarue-Mardrus* in a Carthaginian amphitheater, overseeing the rehearsal of one of her own plays.[24] Interestingly it is the off-stage theatricality of her Orientalist identity performance that upstages an account of her play:

> The actors from the French theater, beturbaned and draped in Tunisian fabric, in keeping with their instinct for the stage, were smoking, like Oriental gentlemen, narguileh pipes, svelte as jets of water. Lucie Delarue-Mardrus – baptized "the Almond Princess" by her husband – came and went, hieratic and silent on the arm of Jeanne Delvaire, inspecting, with her discerning eye, the little kingdom of Shéhérazade.[25]

Alternatively cast in the part of Shéhérazade and Salammbo, sporting an opal ring, "set à la byzantine," which had been worn by Sarah Bernhardt in *Cleopatra* and *Lorenzaccio*, Lucie arouses awe and jealousy of her seductiveness in her self-appointed scribe. Throughout her life, as recounted by Harry, Lucie continued to play the role of Orientalized doyenne of the lesbian elite. She organized parties and *tableaux vivants* drawing on her husband's acclaimed erudition as an Arabic scholar (he translated *Mille et Une Nuits* and published a popular study of the Queen of Sheba); she authored Egyptophilic texts constructed around morbid *femmes fatales* (the novel *Amanit*); and dedicated verse to Eberhardt evoking her "bedouin coat" as a kind of sacred mantel of transvestism sanctioning future feminist explorations into the shadowy regions of bisexual biculturalism.[26]

The "Eberhardt complex" was similarly at work in Henriette Célarié's visit to Eberhardt's final dwelling. As soon as she crossed the threshold of the narrow barrack, stooping under a hand of Fathma, Célarié started to "be" Eberhardt, "imagining" herself "leaning on the parapet, awaiting the hour when the local mullah would announce that the sun had disappeared on the horizon and that the fast could be broken." Eberhardt's ghost – a fantasm of Islamic melancholia – inhabits Célarié, and though she tries to snatch at the reassuring real, asking her guide "the typical woman's question, was she pretty?", she is left overpowered by a sense of Eberhardt's "anguished, demoralized spirit," "tortured by piteous regrets," and the vagaries of her "savage and unsatisfied heart."[27]

The dark epiphanies of the Eberhardtian lady traveler also informed the biography and writings of the Australian journalist Ernestine Hill written about by Meaghan Morris. In Hill's death-driven panoramas, typically found in her travel narrative *The Great Australian Loneliness* (1937), Morris has determined that,

> a very strong relation is established in these texts between death and the historical mission of travel-writing (narration as well as description). This is partly a matter of their chosen "landscape": death is a dominant figure in the scenic history of a colonizing struggle to conquer the land, the sea, and the natives. In their expansionist commitment to Australia's brave white future, Hill's texts are not apparently concerned with any intimations of an absolute "death of history" – except for Aborigines. They are histories of death: not only because of the colonial scene, but because "history" is conventionally represented as a narrative of the dead (the past, or the passing).[28]

Whether it is Hill's desolate outback or Paul Bowles's "sheltering Moroccan sky," (in which Bowles, who translated Eberhardt into English, psychically augured the suicide of his wife, the lesbian writer Jane Bowles), there is a drama of ego destitution expressed through Eberhartian mimesis. *The Sheltering Sky* (1949) contains a kind of rewriting of the Eberhardt legend in the key of existentialist colonialism. When Port, the principal male character, dies mid-novel of the plague, his beautiful American widow, Kit, is abducted by a caravan of camel-drivers. Like Eberhardt, Kit dons the costume of an Arab youth, and like Eberhardt, she learns to "love rape" at the hands of her captors within a landscape of masochism.

Whatever the reason (the trope of female bondage?), Eberhardt's cult status has been firm in feminist and lesbian circles and continues to this day, rendered most interestingly by Leslie Thornton's art-house video *There Was an Unseen Cloud Moving* (1987).[29] Thornton takes the miraculous bones of Eberhardt's story and splices it with sepia-toned stills from the colonial archive, both then and now. North African wonders such as the Casbah, Mecca, or desert dunes are intercalated with early cinema clips of flying carpets and exotic dancing, creating the impression of "an unruly fetishism of the exotic object," to borrow Mary Ann Doane's terms in relation to another ironic Orientalist film by Thornton, *Adynata* (1983).[30] In this feminist *vita nuova* writ large, vignettes of Isabelle's unconventional upbringing, sex and drug exploits, and religious mysticism (played by different actresses with an East Village look) alternate with excerpts from educational films (with their inimitable acoustic cues) featuring camel convoys and geography maps. The net effect is a performative history, both personally and politically regressive to an age of innocence, in which bits of intentionally stilted acting thwart viewer identification with a "role model." The various Isabelles fall in and out of character, tugging blasphemously at their veils, improvising hippy dialogue, declaiming their passions with camp exaggeration. In this way, the avant-garde techniques of disjunction, dissociation, and disavowed seduction function, to borrow Craig Owens's phrasing, "to mobilize the spectator against the immobility of the pose."[41] The plurality of Eberhardts together with the displacement of the body by a visual shorthand of the colonial unconscious, serves, moreover, to undermine character essence. Like Lady Macbeth in Alan Sinfield's reading, Eberhardt is "compounded of contradictory stereotypes" and therefore becomes "a character who is not a character."[32]

This "character who is not a character," this stereotype which is a virtual subject stymied in its ideological "prise" by the mobilized spectator, is nonetheless residually and resiliently a cultural referent that "passes" for itself through a history of what Butler, in her phenomenological vein, referred to as "essence fabrication," "sedimented acts," and "corporeal stylizations."[33] Stereotypes,both cultural and erotic, are generated by and through the frozen inventory of gestures constitutive of theatrical meaning. Though the sheer performativity of this inventory can serve to unsettle identity (easily unmasked as "nothing but an act"), the rehearsed cultural referentialism of the performed type, together with its excessive affect, function to create politically strategic points of semantic connectivity among the blurred procedures of *acting, outing, being, doing, passing*, and *meaning*. Simultaneously subversive and hegemonic, unfixing and status quo, stereotypes render sexual identity politics legible through adhesive, situationally motivated fictions of culture.

NOTES

1   The ideas for this essay were worked out while I was a fellow at the Cornell Society for the Humanities. My thanks to Jonathan Culler for his intellectual presence during my stay. Many people offered vital readings and suggestions: Elin Diamond, Ali Behdad, Meaghan Morris, John Tagg, Amelia Jones. I am especially grateful to Janet Wolff and Michael Ann Holly for inviting me to develop a version of the piece for the Susan B. Anthony lecture at the University of Rochester. An abridged version of this text appeared in a special issue of *Esprit Créatur* on "Orientalism after *Orientalism*," guest-edited by Ali Behdad, 34. 2 (Summer 1994): 102–16.
2   Judith Butler, "The Lesbian Phallus and the Morphological Imaginary," in *Bodies That Matter: On the Discursive Limits of "Sex"* (New York: Routledge, 1993), pp. 57–92. All further references to this work will appear in the text abbreviated B.
3   Eve Kosovsky Sedgwick, "Queer Performativity: Henry James's *The Art of the Novel*," in *Gay and Lesbian Quarterly* 1. 1 (1993): 15.
4   Sigmund Freud, "Character and Anal Eroticism" (1908), in *Character and Culture*, ed. Philip Rieff (New York: Macmillan Publishing Company, 1963), p. 27.

5   Oscar Wilde, *De Profundis*, in *Oscar Wilde, The Soul of Man and Prison Writings*, ed. Isobel Murray (Oxford: Oxford University Press, 1990), pp. 46–7.

6   Craig Owens, "The Medusa Effect, or, The Specular Ruse," in *Beyond Recognition: Representation, Power and Culture*, eds. Scott Bryson *et al.* (Berkeley and Los Angeles: University of California Press, 1992), p. 195. All further references to this book of essays will appear in the text abbreviated BR.

7   Case informs us that "Hrotsvit did enjoy a certain popularity in London during the years of the suffragette movement. The first major production of *Paphnutius* was directed by Edith Craig (daughter of Ellen Terry and sister of Gordon) in London in 1914. The play was staged by Edith Craig's own ensemble, the Pioneer Players, with Ellen Terry as Thaïs."

8   Nineteenth-century Cleopatras were legion: there were particularly celebrated versions by Delphine de Girardin, Arsène Houssaye, Pushkin, Swinburne, and Théophile Gautier, Rider Haggard, and countless others.

9   Peter Wollen, "Fashion/Orientalism/The Body," in *New Formations* (Spring 1987): 18–19.

10 Mario Praz, *The Romantic Agony*, trans. Angus Davidson (Oxford: Oxford University Press, 1970), p. 397.

11 Lucy Hughes-Hallet, *Cleopatra: Histories, Dreams and Distortions* (New York: Harper and Row, 1990), p. 280.

12 Alan Sinfield, *Faultlines: Cultural Materialism and the Politics of Dissident Reading* (Berkeley and Los Angeles: University of California Press, 1992), p. 78.

13 Edward Said, *Orientalism* (New York: Vintage, 1979), p. 103.

14 A Lacanian version of the Oriental "woman with a phallus" theme may be found in a gloss on Lacan's article on the signification of the phallus by Mikkel Borch-Jacobson. In pointing out that Lacan never fully explains why the phallus is expressive of masculine power, Borch-Jacobson refers to the fact that Cleopatra and Semiramis have historically wielded the phallic scepter. Citing Lacan, who states in his article that "It is therefore because it is also the scepter that the phallus prevails," Borch-Jacobson remarks: "This amounts to saying that we will never know why the 'scepter' is phallic: masculine in fact, it is not so by right (the scepter, as the 'signifier of power,' can legitimately be held by a Cleopatra or a Semiramis)." See Mikkel Borch-Jacobson, *Lacan: The Absolute Master*, trans. Douglas Brick (Stanford: Stanford University Press, 1991), pp. 213–14.

15 Joan de Jean cites François-Jean Desthieux's 1937 *Femmes damnées*, where he insists that "Renée Vivien didn't only imitate Sappho: she certainly believed herself to be Sappho reincarnate." See Joan de Jean, *Fictions of Sappho 1546–1937* (Chicago: University of Chicago Press, 1989), p. 283.

16 On the issue of Sapphism's relation to Orientalism, Jean Goujon writes in his postface to Renée Vivien, *Le Jardin Turc: Prose inédite suivi de dix lettres à Kérimé* (Paris: A L'Ecart, 1982), p. 34: "Kérimé rapidly became the romantic 'love from afar' that Vivien had dreamed of for so long, while at the same time symbolizing this Orient that had already fascinated the entire 19th century, from Chateaubriand to Nerval, and from Flaubert to Loti. To object to Mytilène, would be to lose sight of the fact that, beyond the necessary references and pilgrimages, Sappho's island, far from being for Vivien a bastion of hellenism, took the form of a door opening onto an Orient of love and pleasure."

17 Karla Jay, *The Amazon and the Page: Natalie Clifford Barney and Renée Vivien* (Bloomington and Indianapolis: Indiana University Press, 1988), p. 100.

18 Terry Castle's resonant notion of the "apparitional lesbian" is broadly applied to the preponderance of lesbian novels whose plots involve "fantastical" settings or female phantoms. See Terry Castle, *The Apparitional Lesbian* (New York: Columbia University Press, 1993).

19 Natalie Barney, *The One Who is Legion or A.D.'s After-Life* (Orono, Maine: The University of Maine Printing Office, 1987), p. 97.

20 Cléo de Mérode, *Le Ballet de ma vie* (Paris: Editions Pierre Horay, 1955), pp. 46–7.

21 Homi Bhabha, "The Other Question: Colonial Discourse and the Stereotype," in *The Politics of Theory*, ed. Francis Barker (Colchester: University of Essex, 1983), p. 18.

22 Lacan ventriloquizes Cleopatra's nose in "La chose freudienne," to emphasize contingency. If Cleopatra's nose had been slightly shorter, according to the Pascalian lesson, the course of human history would have been different. Antony would not have fallen in love with her, and the Roman Empire would have maintained its control over Egypt. Lacan writes: "In any case, it is not enough to judge of your defeat to see me escape first from the dungeon of the fortress in which you are so sure you have me secured by situating me not in you your-selves, but in being itself? I wander about in what you regard as being the least true essence: in the dream, in the way the most far-fetched conceit, the most grotesque nonsense of the joke defies sense, in chance, not in its law, *but in its contingence, and I never do more to change the face of the world than when I give it the profile of Cleopatra's nose*" [my emphasis].

23 In an interesting article entitled "Isabelle Eberhardt: Portrait of the Artist as a Young Nomad," Hedi Abdel-Jaoud discusses Eberhardt's enactment of the Islamic doctrine of the *hejra*, defined as "a radical departure from beliefs of the past." In *Yale French Studies* 83. 2 (1993): 93–117.

24 Wayne Koestenbaum, *The Queen's Throat: Opera, Homosexuality, and the Mystery of Desire* (New York: Poseidon Press, 1993), pp. 84–5.

25 Myriam Harry, *Mon amie Lucie Delarue-Mardrus*, (Paris: Ariane, 1946), pp. 8–9.

26 On Orientalist cross-dressing see Marjorie Garber's chapter, "The Chic of Araby: Transvestism and the Erotics of Appropriation," in *Vested Interests: Cross-dressing and Cultural Anxiety* (New York: Routledge, 1992), pp. 304–52.

27 Henriette Célarié, *Nos sœurs musulmanes: Scènes de la vie du désert* (Paris: Hachette, 1925), p. 207.

28 Meaghan Morris, "Panorama: The Live, the Dead and The Living," in *Island in the Stream: Myths of Place in Australian culture*, ed. Paul Foss (Sydney: Pluto Press, 1988), p. 173.

29 Leslie Thornton has recently completed a feature-length film of Eberhardt's biog-raphy entitled *The Great Invisible* which I have unfortunately not yet had the opportunity to view.

30 Mary Ann Doane, see her chapter entitled "The Retreat of Signs and the Failure of Words: Leslie Thornton's *Adynata*" in her *Femmes Fatales: Feminism, Film Theory, Psychoanalysis* (New York: Routledge, 1991), p. 178.

31 I am paraphrasing Owens here. The exact quote and its context are from the essay on Barbara Kruger entitled "The Medusa Effect," p. 199. The passage reads as follows: "Kruger's work, then, engages in neither social commentary nor ideological critique (the traditional activities of politically motivated artists: consciousness-raising). Her art has no moralistic or didactic ambition. Rather, she stages for the viewer the techniques whereby the stereotype produces subjec-tion, interpellates him/her as subject. With one crucial difference: in Kruger's double inversion, the viewer is led ultimately to reject the work's address, this double postulation, this contradictory construction. There is a risk, of course, that this rejection will take the form of yet another gesture – a gesture of refusal. It can, however, be an active renunciation. Against the immobility of the pose, Kruger proposes the *mobilization* of the spectator."

32 Sinfield, *Faultlines*, p. 78.

33 Judith Butler, "Performative Acts and Gender Constitution: An Essay in Phenomenology and Feminist Theory," in *Performing Feminisms: Feminist Critical Theory and Theater*, ed. Sue-Ellen Case (Baltimore: Johns Hopkins University Press, 1990), pp. 270–82.

3

POSING THE QUESTION
Wilde, wit, and the ways of man

Ed Cohen

To be natural . . . is such a difficult pose to keep up.
Oscar Wilde, *An Ideal Husband*

You hold yourself like this [attitude]
You hold yourself like that [attitude]
By hook or crook
You try to look
Both angular and flat.

Gilbert and Sullivan's *Patience*

Among his many memorable distinctions, Oscar Wilde is one of the few people ever to have been legally declared a poseur. In the Spring of 1895, in a cramped, crowded courtroom at the Old Bailey, it was determined to be both legally true and published for the public benefit that the famous nineteenth-century litterateur and provocateur had "pos[ed] as a somdomite [*sic*]." Though the circumstances of this finding are convoluted, a brief summary will suffice here to suggest their poignancy: On 28 February 1895 Oscar Wilde arrived at his club, the Albemarle, after an absence of several weeks and was presented with an envelope containing the Marquis of Queensberry's calling card. On the back of the card were scrawled the words: "For Oscar Wilde Posing as a Somdomite [*sic*]." As the culmination of months of harassment by the Scottish aristocrat – who objected to Wilde's intimacy with his youngest son, Lord Alfred Douglas – the short text so incensed Wilde that it incited him to instigate legal action against its author. Filing charges under the 1843 Criminal Libel Act (6 and 7 Vict. I, c. 96), Wilde asked the court to interpret the marquis's text as a verbal attack upon his person and to hold its author criminally responsible for the consequences of his writing. Unfortunately for Wilde, the statute invoked on his behalf allowed the accused party a unique form of rejoinder: the defendant could assert his innocence by offering a competing interpretation of the alleged libel – known as a "plea of justification" – which sought to prove that the offending statement was both "true" and "published for the public benefit." If the court verified that *both*

35

these conditions obtained, then the defendant would be deemed innocent of the charge and the libel found to be legally substantiated. Needless to say, the Marquis of Queensberry quickly countercharged that such was the case. This defense tactic effectively transformed the legal proceeding in *Wilde v. Queensberry* into an interpretive contest that sought both to determine the "true" meaning of the Marquis's text and to assess its social significance. Hence, what was at stake in the proceedings of *Wilde v. Queensberry* was not simply whether or not the writing on the Marquis of Queensberry's card constituted a libel against Wilde, but just as notably what it meant "to pose as a sodomite," whether Wilde had done so, and if publishing the knowledge of such a "pose" was in the public interest.

Framed by the tenor of these questions, the trial necessarily foregrounded the specificity of the phrase "posing as a sodomite." Indeed, since the contested statement did not actually accuse Wilde of "sodomy" – or of *being* a sodomite – for which a strict standard of legal proof (i.e., proof of penetration) would have been required, the defense sought instead to show that Wilde was the kind of person – or at least that he had *represented himself as* the kind of person – who would be *inclined* to commit sodomy. Throughout the two-and-a-half days of the trial, then, the Marquis of Queensberry's barrister, Edward Carson, undertook to impress upon the court *not* that Wilde had engaged in any specific sexual acts with the men listed in the plea, but rather that Wilde, in both his life and in his writings, had demonstrated a "tendency" toward "indecent" relationships with other men. Hence, when Wilde's barrister, Sir Edward Clarke, rose in the midst of the opening speech for the defense to ask the court's permission to withdraw the prosecution against Queensberry, he did so by referring only to the imputations made against Wilde's writing – albeit in order to circumvent the defense's introduction of evidence about his client's sexual practices. Unfortunately by interrupting their prosecution to protect Wilde from the incriminating testimony that the defense appeared to have gathered against him, Wilde and his legal representatives effectively forced the court to find in the Marquis of Queensberry's favor. The short text scrawled on the back of the marquis's calling card, therefore, precipitated a legal contest that ended not only by affirming that Queensberry's words, "For Oscar Wilde Posing as a Somdomite," were both "true" and "published for the public benefit," but also by culling enough evidence to indict and ultimately convict Wilde, with a sentence of two years' imprisonment with hard labor.[1]

While this essay will return to the questions – and the threats – which Wilde's "pose" posed to late-Victorian concepts of normative masculinity, I would like to detour briefly from this historical consideration to introduce some theoretical implications that the late-Victorian evocation of "posing" might have for contemporary discussions of social embodiment. Recently, a number of theoretical works, written largely within a Lacanianly-inflected purview, have begun to foreground the "performativity" – if not the theatricality – of those constructs that we have come to know as human gender and sexuality. Most prominent among these has been the inspiring work of Judith Butler, who in her books *Gender Trouble* and *Bodies That Matter* tries to clarify this mortal play of power/knowledge, arguing that

> the very formation of subjects, the very formation of persons, *presupposes* gender in a certain way – . . . gender is not to be chosen and . . . "performativity" is not radical choice and it's not voluntarism. . . . Performativity has to do with repetition, very often with the repetition of oppressive and painful gender norms to force them to resignify. This is not freedom, but a question of how to rework the trap that one is inevitably in.
>
> (*Artforum*, 32.3 [Nov. 1992]: 84)

Following Butler, there has been a move, which I very much support, to query the constrained iterability of those affects, sensations, pleasures, knowledges, desires, relationships, fantasies, intensities, disciplines, regulations, and violence that congeal to produce the effects of stable or "naturally" sexed bodies. However, since this inquiry largely takes place within a psychoanalytic frame, it often tends to bracket the historical situations within which such iterations occur. As a result, it often becomes difficult to specify the pre-conditions for or consequences of the transformational work that Butler calls "resignification." Indeed, as the trope for change itself, resignification comes to foreground the effects of textual technologies while bracketing the contextual conjunctures which organize these technologies into meaningful and powerful social structures.

The limits of this particular formulation of performativity can be located throughout *Bodies That Matter*, especially as Butler directly responds to the arguments that her earlier work provoked. Attempting to assuage those critics who challenge her, on the one hand, for being too deterministic (social practices as mere repetitions of what always already has been), or on the other for being too volunteristic (individual acts of mimicry and impersonation as the radical edge of social change), Butler elaborates her thinking about the subject of performance in the introduction to her new book under the rubric "performativity as citationality." With this enticing metaphoric equivalence, Butler seems to circumscribe performativity "as" a form of textual practice whose disembodied domain operates by virtue of a linguistic – if not rhetorical – "compulsion." Not surprisingly, then, the text follows Lacan's linguistic bent at this point, inquiring into the "law" which renders "the forcible production of 'sex'"(12). However, unlike Lacan, Butler does not assume the structural inevitability of this law, arguing instead that the law itself is the accretion of its instantiations, or as she puts it: "the citational accumulation and dissimulation of the law that produces material effects" (12). With this gesture, Butler seeks to drag history into the Lacanian schema – or perhaps even to reconcile Lacan with Foucault – but even as she does so she frames it as an impossible undertaking:

Performativity is thus not a singular "act," for it is always a reiteration of a norm or set of norms, and to the extent that it acquires an act-like status in the present, it conceals or dissimulates the conventions of which it is a repetition. Moreover, this act is not primarily theatrical; indeed, its apparent theatricality is produced to the extent that its historicity remains dissimulated (and, conversely, its theatricality gains a certain inevitability given the impossibility of a full disclosure of its historicity).[2]

Locating the inevitable trace of "theatricality" as the foreclosed possibility of a "ful[ly] disclosed . . . historicity" (whatever that might be), Butler seeks to turn our attention towards a more language-based notion of performativity derived largely from the Derridean critique of speech act theories. Thus, she repeatedly invokes Derrida's meditation on "citation" in his seminal essay "Signiture, Event, Context" to rebut those who criticize her for romanticizing the radical effects of performance as self-theatricalization. Instead she argues that since citationality is the necessary (only?) conduit for normative power, performativity commands the "imaginary morphology" of sexed bodies: "the norm of sex takes hold to the extent that it is 'cited' as such a norm, but it also *derives its power* through the citations that it compels" (13, my emphasis). Even if we accept Butler's assertion here about the "compelling" power of citation, however, we need to recognize that it is at best a necessary – though not sufficient – characterization of the operations of power. For what Butler means by the notion that a "norm . . . derives its power" from and through its citation is manifestly circular: if a norm both compels its citation and derives its power from that citation then what sets this reiterating engine in motion and what fuels its pistons?

   In her subsequent discussion, Butler evades her discussion of this inertial problem by deftly shifting the ground of her consideration back to the epistemological terrain charted by psychoanalysis. Citation thus becomes interpellated into the theoretical "space" mapped by the Lacanian subject, where it becomes the primary mechanism of (re)production, even "producing" – by way of the citationality embedded in Lacan's famous discussion of identification in "The Mirror Stage"[3] – the "imaginary morphology" which we know as our bodies. As Butler moves quickly and elusively away from a more "sited" (i.e., historically and spatially localized) consideration of the particularities through which power is exercized over, within, and as the putatively stable forms of human embodiment,[4] she shifts her attention to a consideration of the Lacanian "symbolic" wherein "the law" is "assumed":

   The force and necessity of these norms ("sex" as a symbolic function is to be understood as a kind of commandment or injunction) is thus functionally *dependent* on the approximation and citation of the law; the law without its approximation is no law or, rather, it remains a governing law only for those who would affirm it on the basis of religious faith. (14, original emphasis)

While this dismissal of "faith" as a critical factor in promulgating the social contexts through which "the law" operates might itself bear further consideration,[5] what seems more relevant to my concerns in this essay is that, for Butler, law in its "governing" aspect appears as an iterating agency that remains structurally exterior to, but determinant of, the sited individual: "[T]he law is no longer given in a fixed form *prior* to its citation, but is produced through citation as that which preceded and exceeds the mortal approximations enacted by the subject" (14, original emphasis). The reason I have belabored my own citation of Butler's Lacanisms here is to trouble the notion that "the law" is "produced through citation," since such a formulation seems to bracket a more situated consideration of the law as it is perhaps more familarly understood, i.e., as that which regulates, consolidates, and legitimates the power of the state. Indeed, I have no wish to argue with Butler's psychoanalytic elaboration of "law of sex" as "a series of normativizing injunctions that secure the borders of sex through the threat of psychosis, abjection, psychic unlivability." Rather I want to suggest that the normativity compelled by the law is also historically situated and specified in particular cases – such as Wilde's conviction and imprisonment, but also more generally – by legal interventions that may indeed provoke "the threat of psychosis, abjection, psychic unlivability," but only after they have violently and yet legitimately been brought to bear on the body of an individuated, sexed, legal subject. In other words, by circumscribing the citational effects of performativity Butler's theorizations bracket the domain of social forces as they come to organize both the compulsions of and the resistances to the law. And in regard to "posing" as it emerged across the field of performed masculinities during the last decades of the nineteenth century, this is a telling omission. What I'd like to consider for the next few pages, then, is how Wilde's subversive repetitions, that is, his multiple, self-conscious, and self-marketing "poses," interrupted the prevailing ideological patternings of masculinity or "manliness" to such a degree that they provoked a legal struggle orchestrated precisely to "fix" male gender by "fixing" him.

So what is "posing" anyway? Well, according to the *OED*, "to pose" as a transitive verb means "to place in a specified situation or condition; to suppose or assume for argument's sake; to lay down, put forth (an assertion, allegation, claim, instance, etc.), or to propound, propose (a question or problem); and to place in an attitude (as an artist's model or sitter, etc.)." As an intransitive verb, on the other hand, it signifies "assum[ing] a certain attitude" or "plac[ing] oneself in position, especially for artistic purposes" or "presenting oneself in a particular character (often implying that it is assumed," that is "set[ting] up *as*, giv[ing] oneself out *as*," or briefly "attitudiniz[ing]." Augmenting these definitions there follows another sense of "pose", meaning "to examine by questioning, [to] question, [to] interrogate," "to place in a difficulty with a question or problem; to puzzle, confuse, perplex, nonplus," "to do that which puzzles (another)." A pose, then, refers to an "attitude or posture of the body, or of a part of the body, especially one deliberately assumed, or in which a figure is placed for effect, or for artistic purposes," and has become synonymous in this case with "air, affectation, and mannerism." As this definitional discourse suggests, what is ultimately at stake in the placement or presentation that constitutes "posing" in this last sense is the artifice or fictionality of "position," understood simultaneously as a social and spatial location of embodiment. In this way a pose unwittingly exposes the fabrication of personhood as a disposition insofar as it makes explicit that one can "present oneself in a particular character (often implying that it is assumed)," that is "set up *as*, give oneself out *as*," other than what one "is." Indeed, although its transitive and intransitive forms might at first seem contradictory, it is because "posing" undermines the ontological ground upon which the putative stability – if not "naturalness" – of positionality is predicated that it comes to question and/or threaten. Hence, if a pose "places [us] in a difficulty, with a question or a problem," if it "puzzles, confuses, perplexes or nonpluses" us, it does so by revealing the mutability of the "attitude" that represents itself as "natural." Thus, what posing foregrounds is the imbricated but usually concealed work of representation that (re)produces those mimetic effects which are habitually dis-posed as "the real." All of which Wilde, with his usual aphoristic flair, declares much more succinctly: "To be natural . . . is such a difficult pose to keep up."

In Wilde's case, the force of both his pose and his prose was directed towards the ideologically inscribed and socially privileged position known colloquially as the "middle-class Englishman." Or, to adapt Butler's rhetoric of performativity, Wilde's posing was a form of iteration that disclosed the aesthetic shapings of those symbolic positions which congealed in and as the always, already sexed body, a practice of resignification that made evident the imaginary work through which such distinctions were (re)produced. Thus, more than just another version of *épater les bourgeois*, Wilde's personal/aesthetic practice interrupted the unmarked elision between the signifiers of class, nation, and gender condensed in the familiar nomination "middle-class Englishman," thereby challenging the privilege accorded to the limited number of embodied subjects who could occupy this position. Yet, as thoroughgoing as I believe his embodied critique of bourgeois male subjectivity was, Wilde was also clearly interested in procuring some of this privilege for himself. And here again posing served his purpose. For to the extent that Wilde's attitudes and behaviors could be determined to be simply part of his pose – that is, part of his aesthetically rendered self (re)presentation – they could be accepted as insignificant or even "trivial" (to use Wilde's own characterization) and therefore humorous or even delightful. Ironically it was only after Wilde was legally determined to have been posing that the heretofore unexamined effects of his poses began to be taken seriously, whereupon the questions and threats they proffered could no longer be contained and so instead Wilde himself was – for two years with hard labor.

Consider then the narrative of Wilde the poseur: From the moment when he left Oxford (in 1879) and went down to London, where due to his father's death and the ensuing familial insolvency, he was forced for the first time to earn his income, Wilde had self-consciously marketed himself as a liminal figure within British society. His highly publicized tour of America in 1881 as the frontman for Richard D'Oyly Carte's U.S. production of the Gilbert and Sullivan operetta *Patience* not only established him as an iconic embodiment of the "aesthetic" type that the operetta parodied, but also demonstrated his ability *to sell* his association with this stylistic critique of bourgeois respectability – and especially male respectability – as a cultural commodity in its own right. In her book, *Idylls of the Marketplace: Oscar Wilde and the Victorian Public*, Regenia Gagnier forcefully argues that Wilde's self-positioning as a "dandy" represented a highly developed critique of the social articulation of middle-class ideologies and particularly those for male gender identity. She contrasts the figure of "the dandy" to that of "the gentleman," and his prototype "the public school boy," in order to illustrate that Wilde's personal aesthetic constituted an embodied challenge to the social and cultural – if not the economic – hegemony of the Victorian bourgeoisie.

While I heartily concur with Gagnier's assessment of Wilde's aesthetic as both personal and political practice, it is important to note that Wilde's "pose" was not entirely his own. In fact, his emerence into the metropolitian imaginary was (re)produced by and through those representations that identified Wilde with the "aesthetic" sensibility cultivated by the pre-Raphaelite Brotherhood – or more presisely, through the caricatures of that sensibility, especially as they appeared in the pages of *Punch*. The cartoons that depicted the male aesthete are consistent in their portrayal of this character as a "poseur" who is both recognizable and lamentable by virtue of his inability to maintain somatic rectitude. For example, in a series of three drawings that appeared on 20 December 1879 under the rubric "Nincompoopiana" – part of a larger series of the same name featured from late 1879 to 1880 – the artist depicts a number of langorously longhaired men who have self-consciously if not decoratively arranged themselves in their environments. One panel juxtaposes the image of a posturing dimunitive young man, set between a background screen decorated with lilies on one side and a mirror on the other, to a married couple comprised of a balding, barrel-chested bear of a man and his equally statuesque wife. Another confronts a slouching bespectaled male in evening dress with a frighteningly erect, fully bustled member of the opposite sex. The third reveals a drawing room full of such attitudinizing men most of whom seem so spineless that they are about to slide off their chairs. Across these three panels we discern the development of a particular iconography through which the "aesthetic" ideology that these men are held to represent comes to be embodied by them. Thus, their

41

physical bodies both manifest and reveal the "Nincompoopiana" that despoils the putatively common-sensical characteristics of their gender precisely insofar as the male body becomes purposefully mannered. These representations suggest that by lampooning those "poses" which render the male body "Aesthetic," this iconography locates aesthetic practice entirely on the side of the poseur, thereby masking its role in the production of normative masculinity itself.

In Wilde's case, the iconography of the pose became the medium through which he attained a cultural visibility which until his literary successes of the 1890s was crucial to his ability to earn a living. Beginning with George Du Maurier's 1881 cartoon of the physically convoluted "Maudle" proposing to the prosaic "Mrs. Brown" that she allow her "consummately lovely son" to become an artist, Wilde's recognizable visage was attached to many a languishing body. Indeed, these depictions so often foreground Wilde's body as an entirely aesthetic location that it is at times entirely derealized – most famously in the Punch "Fancy Portrait – no. 37" (Figure 3.1) . While such figurative representations consituted the body Wilde as an artifact rather than as the natural object male bodies were – both scientifically and popularly – taken to be, it was this very objectification that opened up Wilde's first big career opportunity. When Richard D'Oyly Carte wanted to bring Gilbert and Sullivan's *Patience* to the U.S., he realized that there would be a problem in translation: the aesthetic type that the operetta parodied was an English phenomenon for which there was not a ready American equivalent. Recognizing Wilde's potential as an aesthetic poster boy, D'Oyly Carte hired him to undertake a lecture tour of America in order to make the caricature familiar so that *Patience*'s humor would sell there. In other words, D'Oyly Carte paid Wilde to tour North America posing as the poseur he was supposed to be in order that the parody poseurs of *Patience* should pay off. Needless to say, Wilde's lecture itself was almost beside the point, a mere accessory that completed the Wildean ensemble. As the widely reproduced 1882 photographs by Napolean Sarony of Wilde in costume illustrate, Wilde was quite adept at assuming the pose – in fact, we might say that it was to prove his *métier*.

Yet posing, for Wilde, was not an innocent play. I'd like to suggest that perhaps what was most radical – and most threatening – about Wilde's engagements with and against the verities of late-Victorian English life were the ways in which he consistently sought to utilize the possibilities of "posing" *strategically* in order to interrupt social and philosophical "truths," or indeed, in order to interrupt the possibility of predicating social "truth" *per se*. In fact, I would argue, this practical aesthetic project is especially significant precisely because Wilde was so profligate in proffering his aesthetic critiques to as many audiences as he could. Writing in more genres than most of us would imagine possible, Wilde produced lyrics, ballads, narrative poems, prose poems, comedies, tragedies, political dramas, fairy tales, philosophical,

Figure 3.1 Oscar Wilde, Punch's Fancy Portraits
– no. 37, by Edward Sambourne,
Punch, June 25, 1881

political, and aesthetic essays, book reviews, art criticism, lectures, at least one "straight" novel if not also another pornographic one, a *faux* literary history, and aphorisms galore, in addition to voluminous letters including one to Alfred Douglas so long that it became a volume unto itself. Moreover, these texts appeared in more contexts than seems possible, ranging from the *Pall Mall Gazette*, to *Queen*, to *The World*, to *Woman's World*, to the *Irish Monthly*, to *The Court and Society Review*, to *Fortnightly Review*, to *Blackwood's Edinburgh Magazine*, to *Lippencott's Monthly Magazine*, to the *Chameleon*, in addition to the many volumes, plays, and lectures which appeared under his own name. In all these various texts and contexts, Wilde seems to have undertaken a consistent (though by no means unified) inquiry into the efficacy which the assumption of different aesthetic attitudes, or what I would call dispositions, afforded him in moving both with and athwart the ideological givens of his day. For even as Wilde was invested in contesting the limitations upon what it was possible to imagine and articulate – let alone enact or embody – in late-Victorian culture, he was even more invested in making his income from doing so: an ambitious, if contradictory, undertaking at best; a dangerous and self-destructive one at worst. Unfortunately for him, Wilde was often at his worst when he was at his best.

Elsewhere I have tried to explore this Wildean dilemma in relation to *The Picture of Dorian Gray* by asking how it was that from the moment of its publication and subsequently through a century of critical reception, this book has been branded as "homosexual" although it does not contain even one representation of physical intimacies between men. Or to phrase it more succinctly, how did Wilde write a novel "about" homosexuality in which no body came? In attempting to answer this question I was forced to recognize that rather than *being* a novel about "homosexuality," Wilde's novel was an integral part of the *processes whereby "homosexuality" came to be*. Writing in 1890, several years before the translation of Krafft-Ebing's *Psychopathia Sexualis* would make the words "homosexual" and "heterosexual" current in English usage, Wilde fashioned a text that crystallized the multiple currents whereby the context of "masculinity" (or "manliness," as it was more often called then) was made meaningful.[6] By playing upon the "pleasures" of the aesthetic, Wilde effectively engendered the highly ironic and unstable signifieds of his sexually marginal, subcultural experience so that the text necessarily articulates – if only *sotto voce* – the counterpoint between the incessant reproduction of hegemonic sexual positionings and the painful-yet-pleasurable emergence of that soon-to-be "other," the male homosexual. However, we do not have to look to such a marked and complex text as *The Picture of Dorian Gray* in order to observe the ways in which Wilde used his aesthetic both to articulate and ambiguate his disposition towards late-Victorian social and sexual norms.

"In matters of grave importance, style, not sincerity is the vital thing," says Gwendolyn in *The Importance of Being Earnest*, and it is a dictum which Wilde undoubtedly cherished. If we think for a moment about the aphorisms, such as this one, for which Wilde is so famous and yet for which he is seldom taken seriously, we can see that they enact at the level of style an inversion and displacement of some of the most powerful and covert social "truths." Relentlessly troping upon the multitude of clichés and platitudes which stud the social imaginary – and which perhaps we might conceive of in rhetorics of Lacan and Derrida as the *points de capiton* of social discourse – Wilde insistently demonstrates both that he knowingly abjures the "truths" which he speaks in inverted forms and that he *believes*, as he has Vivian tell Cyril in "The Decay of Lying": "Truth is entirely and absolutely a matter of style." To make this point, consider just one of the most famous and widely repeated examples of the Wildean wit: "It is only the shallow people who do not judge by appearances." Here Wilde plays with the most banal of truisms: "don't judge by appearances", or to supply the elided but philosophically critical terms, "don't attempt to ascertain essential truths from epiphenomenal representations." In bending the saying to fit his purposes,

Wilde here prefigures deconstruction's double gesture – albeit with a bit more panache: he simultaneously foregrounds the surface/depth metaphors which Derrida sees as underwriting the ground of Western metaphysics and suggests that it is precisely because such metaphors are embedded in everyday life that they operate philosophically *and* colloquially as "truth." However, since Wilde's is not solely a philosophical undertaking, he is also interested here in having some fun: his assertion that style or appearance tells us something "true" is purchased at the expense of those who are invested in the significance of the profound. Thus, he paradoxically deflects the force of his critique through a double displacement in which he initially mimes the conventional understanding of "shallowness" as antithetical to "truth" in order to sell a perception which challenges the conditions of possibility for producing such "true" attributions. It is this gesture continued at the level of personal style that I would argue constitutes the Wildean pose.

Certainly, the benefits afforded Wilde by such a strategic self-representation were personally significant: as a married father of two sons who relied on his income as a professional writer and cultural critic to support his family *and* his younger male lovers in a style to which he would have liked to become accustomed, the deferral embedded in his embrace of posing opened the space of possibility within which he could (temporarily, at least) embody the contradictions inscribed by his life. However, for Wilde the pose was more than just a personal expedient which enabled him covertly to live out one more, late-Victorian version of the "double life." Rather, Wilde was incessantly concerned to thematize this strategy – indeed, he quite obviously made it the crux for the comedies which were by far the most spectacular and financially successful of his writings – iterating its possibilities through numerous narrative and dramatic twists in order to disseminate both its aesthetic and social effects. Thus, it is not entirely surprising that, when the Marquis of Queensberry made it his goal to destroy Wilde in defense of both his youngest son specifically and the sanctity of English manhood more generally, the word "posing" should figure so prominently in his project. Yet, what *is* somewhat surprising is the deliberateness with which this word was chosen: for it now seems probable that the statement inscribed on the Marquis's card might not actually say "For Oscar Wilde posing as a somdomite" – the only distinct words being "For Oscar Wilde" and the misspelled "somdomite," with the crucial words linking them being entirely illegible – but rather that this was the phrasing explicitly chosen by Queensberry's attorney's who instructed him how to reply when he was asked at his committal hearing what it was that he had written. Thus, the introduction of the characterization "posing" into a legal contest that would – within the course of two months – precipitate the violent restriction of all Wilde's future movement, can be understood as a calculated legal tactic which obviated the defendant's need to prove that Wilde *was* a sodomite (which would have been nearly impossible) while simultaneously exposing the strategic indeterminacies that Wilde cultivated in order to live on and off the borders of normative masculinity.

In the journalistic coverage of the trial, then, the word "posing" came to occupy a position of unique significance. Metonymically elided with the signifier "sodomite," "posing" came to figure as a precursor which portended the horror bodied forth by the latter's subversion of unquestioned *and* unquestionable maleness. Indeed, the newspaper accounts were so obsessed with elucidating the particularities of Wilde's pose – in part because they were constrained by journalistic codes from actually specifying the sexual accusations made against him – that they made what was politically at stake quite explicit: i.e., the force that representation dis-plays in (re)producing the position of the "manly" *per se*. Consequently, the depiction of Wilde's attempts throughout the trial to dis-pose (of) the defense interpretations of both his life and his writings as "indecent" foregrounded intense imaginary work that was needed in order to sustain even the most common-sensical notions of gender. For as long as he was able to use his wit to interrupt the attempts to fix the meaning of his both his pose and his prose, he was able to resignify them and thereby (re)work the trap that he was in. Unfortunately, however, the limits of this resignifying practice were circumscribed by the power of the law, whose prerogative it is to pre-emptorily – if not violently – fix those meanings which function as truth. Hence when it became clear that there were witnesses who had deposed that Wilde's pose was in fact not a pose but a (sexual) position, and that in fact he had long since put his body on the line, Wilde's case was lost. In withdrawing his libel suit, then, Wilde was legally determined both to have "posed" and to have "posed as a sodomite." And while the former was a characterological determination which recognized the ambiguous "truth" of Wilde's gestures as a social actor, the latter conversely fixed the meaning of his pose in a univocal and unequivocal direction. Hence it became clear that the instabilities which Wilde's poses had engendered needed to be rigorously contained in order to fix the system of meanings that his strategic performances had problematized. Wilde's arrest and subsequent imprisonment, therefore, can be read both as a legal attempt to affix the significance of his pose to his incarcerated body and as a discursive effort to arrest the destabilizing play of gender that his freedom of movement might provoke. In other words, by legally disposing that Wilde was guilty of sexual crimes, the court effectively determined that Wilde could no longer pose the questions which he had tried for so long to embody.

NOTES

1   This very truncated account is expanded in my book, *Talk on the Wilde Side: Towards the Geneaology of a Discourse on Male Sexualities* (New York. Routledge, 1993).

2   Judith Butler, *Bodies That Matter: On the Discursive Limits of "Sex"* (New York: Routledge, 1993), pp. 12–13. All further references are to this edition.

3   Butler turns to this essay in the later chapter, "Phantismatic Identification," pp. 93–120.

4   Butler herself acknowledges the importance of this situated endeavor, though she does not undertake it herself: "[T]his imaginary morphology is not a pre-social or presymbolic operation, but is itself orchestrated through regulatory schemas that produce intelligible morphological possibilities. These regulatory schemas are not timeless structures, but historically revisible criteria of intelligibility which produce and vanquish bodies that matter." (14)

5   For example, one could consider Balibar's recent characterization of the "alchemy" which crystallizes the "citizen-subject."

6   Ed Cohen, "Writing Gone Wilde: Homoerotic Desire in the Closet of Representation," *PMLA*, 105. 5 (Oct. 1987).

4

DOING IT ANYWAY
Lesbian sado-masochism and performance
Lynda Hart

"Analogies depend upon maintaining the space between the lines, the categories of difference, the notions of consistency, the theoretical profile of singularity, purity, and detachment . . ."[1] These words are taken from Judith Roof's critique of analogical thinking in feminist literary criticism, *All Analogies are Faulty*. Roof's absolutism makes me a little uneasy, but it is perhaps better to err on the side of *all* when we encounter analogies, for I agree that "analogies abstract, separate, and distance terms from their original, perhaps fearsome, referents."[2] To Roof's observation that analogical thinking often signals a fear of intimacy, I would add that the "object" of this fear is sometimes one's own most intimate "others" – that is, those differences within that are easier to handle when they are reconfigured as differences between.

Analogical thinking is the staple of feminist arguments against sado-masochism. In two anthologies published over a decade apart, *Against Sadomasochism: A Radical Feminist Analysis* (1982)[3] and *Unleashing Feminism: Critiquing Lesbian Sadomasochism in the Gay Nineties* (1993) most of the contributors rely on drawing analogies at one point or another in their arguments. Basing their comparisons on sometimes the vaguest resemblances, they level all experiences and histories into the same, uncritically endorse and privilege empiricism, repeat and perpetuate the notion of an unmediated access to the truth of perception, and, once again, knowing collapses into seeing. Take your pick: sado-masochism looks like – and therefore is like – Slavery, the Holocaust, Heterosexist Patriarchy, the Jonestown Massacre. Sheila Jeffrey's classic attack on sado-masochism juxtaposes a description of SS men torturing a gay man to death with advice from a lesbian safer sex manual about how to trim your nails and and lube your hand for fisting.[4] Jamie Lee Evans tries to convince us that just as the Los Angeles police claimed that Rodney King could have stopped the beating whenever he chose, so lesbian sado-masochists tell us that the bottom is the one who is really in control.[5]

Whatever the choice of the first term in these analogies, the presumption remains that lesbian sado-masochism is a copy, an iconic reproduction of the

48

oppressive model. This presumption cuts two ways. For the Platonic spectator, lesbian s/m can be derided for *merely* approximating the original, as Leo Bersani argues that the straight macho man can look at a leather queen and deride him for his poor imitation.[6] Or, as feminists against s/m claim, the lesbian sado-masochist should be chastized *for* desiring to emulate the model. In either case, these spectators assume a resemblance between the model and the copy that presupposes an internal similarity. If one simply looks at the images of lesbian sado-masochism – the whips, chains, handcuffs, needles, razors, and other instruments; the bodies bound, gagged, tied, and suspended; the humiliating postures of the submissives; the military garb – it is easy to see how these representations are read as iconic. But the mechanism for seeing them as such is resemblance, which proceeds from a thing to an Idea.

Thinking outside this visual economy, where lesbians can only perform re-semblances, we could regard the value of dis-semblance to lesbian s/m, as impersonations that are not mimesis but mimicry. In her reading of the third section of Luce Irigaray's *Speculum of the Other Woman*, Elin Diamond gives us just such a way when she argues that Irigaray posits "two mimetic systems that exist simultaneously, one repressed by the other."[7] The first system she calls "patriarchal mimesis," in which the "model, the Form or Ideal, is distinguishable from and transcendently beyond shadows – images in the mirror – mere copies."[8] This is traditional mimesis, the system that is not repressed. But Diamond ferrets out another system in Irigaray's text, one that subverts the first one, which she calls "mimesis-mimicry, in which the production of objects, shadows, and voices is excessive to the truth/illusion structure of mimesis, spilling into mimicry, multiple 'fake offspring'."[9]

Homi Bhabha's theory of colonial mimicry as a "desire for a reformed, recognizable Other as a subject of difference that is almost the same, but not quite"[10] is also a useful way to articulate the dis-semblances of s/m. Bhabha's mimicry is a double articulation, a sign that retains the power of resemblance but menaces the authoritative discourse of colonialism by disclosing its ambivalence. Mimicry, as Bhabha describes it, is profoundly disturbing to a dominant discourse because it points out the necessity of producing prohibitions *within* in order to reproduce. Mimicry repeats rather than re-presents; it is a repetition that is non-reproductive. Mimesis operates in the order of the model/copy. Mimicry performs its operations in the realm of the simulacra.

Deleuze argues that the simulcrum is "an image without resemblance," but then, not quite. The simulacrum "still produces an *effect* of resemblance,"[11] but it is a looking like that takes place in the trick mirror where the spectator lacks mastery. The observer cannot dominate the simulacrum because it has already incorporated her point of view. Before the simulacrum, the spectator is mastered. If we think of the erotic interplay of lesbian s/m as resignifications that are no doubt enabled by certain heterosexual or homosexual models but at the same time dissonant displacements of them, we might move toward a better understanding of their erotic dynamics and better grasp the political and ethical controversies they have raised.

If some feminists insist that lesbian s/m is merely re-semblance, according to the psychoanalytic paradigm, lesbian s/m is only a semblance, at best. Radical feminism and psychoanalysis seem to have little in common. If the former sometimes takes the position that women *are* masochists who need to have their consciousness raised, the latter theorizes that lesbian sado-masochism is *impossible*.

The essayists in *Unleashing Feminism* continue to see many of the same problems that plagued the women's movement in the 1970s. In her book, *A Taste for Pain*, Maria Marcus remembers a women's studies conference in 1972 when Germaine Greer, the keynote speaker, was interrupted by a young woman from the audience who suddenly cried out: "But how can we start a women's movement when I bet three-quarters of us sitting in this room are masochists?" Greer replied: "Yes, we know women are masochists – that's what it's all about!"[12] Although twenty years later, I am more likely to hear the complaint that all women are masochists in the context of lesbians lamenting the scarcity of tops in the community, the mainstream, public image of feminism is still much closer to the attitudes expressed by anti-porn/s/m feminists.[13]

Ironically, while feminists continue to argue with each other about lesbian sexual practices, "masochism," the term that has become synonymous for some feminists with internalized oppression, has undergone a theoretical renaissance in which the erotics of submission have been reclaimed by a diverse group of scholars as an emancipatory sexuality for men. Leo Bersani's argument, which strikingly concludes that "sexuality – at least in the mode in which it is constituted – could be thought of as a tautology for masochism,"[14] leads the way in rendering arguments about the relationship between the fore-pleasures of the erotogenic zones (strongly associated with both femininity and the "perversions") and the end pleasures of discharge (the ejaculatory climax associated with masculinity) irrelevant. For as Bersani reads Freud, sexuality is the dialectic of seeking the end of pleasure through discharge and repeating the tension in order to increase it. Thus Bersani concludes that sexuality is masochistic and that "masochism serves life," for it is what allows the individual to "survive the gap between the period of shattering stimuli and the development of resistant or defensive ego structures."[15] Masochism, far from being a reversal of sadism or an internalization of oppressive patriarchal norms, is a survival mechanism.

The notion of a sexual ontology is clearly problematic. Nevertheless, Bersani's theory has the advantage of freeing sexuality from parental identifications where sexual difference seems to get unavoidably reproduced. Furthermore, Bersani's theory challenges the teleological narrative that ends with heterosexual genital sex. Thus, in his view: "sadomasochistic sexuality

50

would be a kind of melodramatic version of the constitution of sexuality itself, and the marginality of sadomasochism would consist of nothing less than its isolating, even its making visible, the ontological grounds of the sexual."[16]

For feminists who are struggling to articulate a sexual subjectivity that does not submit to the psychoanalytic imperative of an exclusively masculine libido, which ineluctably consigns femininity to a masculinized fetish, Bersani's theory might be welcomed, since it takes us out of the discourse of the symptom into a "nonreferential version of sexual thought."[17] Parental identifications, which inevitably reify Oedipus, are no longer constitutive; and the "lost object," which is relentlessly relegated to a feminized fetish, is diffused so that any object and any part of the body can become an erotogenic zone. This theory does not of course undo the historical/social attribution of masochism to women, but it does suggest a psychic model in which the sexual positions one takes up are not necessarily gendered. Nevertheless, Bersani implicitly assumes the now privileged masochistic position as a male prerogative, and hence claims sexuality itself for men. This presumption is clearer in his essay "Is the Rectum a Grave?" when he describes the dominant culture's revulsion at the sight of a man seductively and intolerably imaged with "legs high in the air, unable to refuse the suicidal ecstasy of being a woman."[18]

This is a graphic enactment of Freud's third form of masochism, "feminine masochism," which he also presumes to be occupied by a male subject in a feminine situation. The male subject in this space signifies "being castrated, or copulated with, or giving birth to a baby."[19] Since women presumably already experience one or more of the above, the notion of a feminine "feminine masochism" is redundant at best, if not impossible. According to this logic, women cannot *perform* the masochistic role becauses they are masochists. To borrow J. L. Austin's terms, masculine feminine masochism would be performative, while feminine feminine masochism would be *constative*.[20] Male masochism would not report or describe anything; it would be a doing rather than a describing; it would perform not after but *before* the referent. Feminine masochism, on the other hand, would merely report an adequation; it would correspond with the "facts" of femininity. If sadomasochism is a melodramatic version of sexuality itself, women have ironically been barred from playing on this stage that in all other contexts has seemed to most suit them.

Kaja Silverman acknowledges that psychoanalytic sexual difference relegates female masochism to a virtually ontological condition when she defends her focus on male subjectivity by explaining that the female subject's masochism is difficult to conceptualize as perverse because it represents "such a logical extension of those desires which are assumed to be 'natural' for the female subject."[21] She nonetheless unproblematically accepts and repeats the terms of a psychoanalytic symbolic in which there is only one libido and it is masculine. Women are denied sexual agency because they are incapable of mimesis. Their options are to take up the position of passive "normal femininity," or to reverse the position and appropriate masculine subjectivity and its desires, in which case they can "perform" sexuality, but only through their "masculinity complex." Bersani's desire is aimed at the pleasures gay men might experience from an alignment with femininity, as is Silverman's, though her project is to produce a revolutionary subject in a "feminine" yet heterosexual man. Both of these analyses add weight to feminist arguments against sado-masochism, for following their logic the lesbian masochist is either enacting the dominant culture's degradation of women or she is playing out the desire to be a man. In either case, the terms of sexual difference remain intact. These theories that posit male masochism as emancipatory thus continue to depend on the impossibility of desire between women. In this context, truth claims about lesbian sexuality such as this one made by Jan Brown:

> We practice the kind of sex in which cruelty has value, where mercy does not. What keeps those of us who refused to abandon our "unacceptable" fantasies sane is the knowledge that there are others like us who would not leave because we scream "Kill me," at the moment we orgasm. . . . We lied to you about controlling the fantasy. It is the lack of control that makes us come, that has the only power to move us . . .[22]

would easily fall prey to the argument that lesbian sado-masochists are merely reproducing heterosexist models, or at best, male homosocial ones.

The referent for Brown's "lies" can be located in earlier rhetoric by s/m practitioners who justified the acting out of their fantasies by claiming they were means of exorcising their real hold on the individual. Tacitly accepting the feminist contention that s/m lesbians had internalized cultural misogyny, these defenses asked for a tolerant reprieve, a period of playing through the fantasies in order to transcend them. S/m then, ironically, became therapeutic, like a homeopathic cure.

Theatrical metaphors were central to this defense. Susan Farr, for example, described s/m as "pure theater," "a drama [in which] two principals .. act at being master and slave, play at being fearsome and fearful." She cites the clues to the drama in the interchangeability of the roles and the repetitive, scripted dialogue. Even though, she acknowledges, much of the scene may be "pure improvisation," it is still "theater."[23] This dialectic between the scriptural and the spontaneous is prevalent in early pro-s/m accounts. On the one hand, there is the insistence that the scene is rigidly controlled, with a decided emphasis on the bottom's mastery of the limits. On the other hand, the eroticism depends on the anticipation that the limits will be pushed to the breaking point, that the "scene" will cross over into the "real."

To a certain extent, the controversy about whether s/m is "real" or performed is naive, since we are always already in representation even when we are enacting our seemingly most private fantasies. The extent to which we recognize the presence of the edge of the stage may determine what *kind* of performance we are enacting, but willing ourselves to forget the stage altogether is not to return to the real, as s/m opponents would have it; rather, this will to forget is classical mimesis, which, as Derrida points out, is "the most naive form of representation."[24] Nevertheless, it is precisely this most naive form of representation that would seem to be the most desirable of sexual performances. Bersani's objections to the frequent theorization of such things as "the gay-macho style, the butch-femme lesbian couple, and gay and lesbian sado-masochism" as .. "subversive parodies of the very formations and behaviours they appear to ape," rather than, "unqualified and uncontrollable" complicities with, correlatively, "a brutal and misogynous ideal of masculinity" [gay macho], ... "the heterosexual couple permanently locked into a power structure of male sexual and social mastery over female sexual and social passivity" [butch-femme], or "fascism" [s/m], are clearly based on his contention that these sexual practices are *not* performative. Parody, Bersani states emphatically, "is an erotic turn-off, and all gay men know this."[25] Although Bersani audaciously speaks for all gay men, I would have to agree with him and add that many lesbians know this too. Self-conscious mimicry of heterosexuality is a side show; when the main act comes to town, we all want the "real thing," or, more precisely, we all want the *Real* thing. That is, sexuality is always, I think, about our desire for the impossible-real, not the real of the illusion that passes for reality, but the Real that eludes symbolization. Whereas early radical lesbians spoke of a contest between "realesbians" and imposters, as psychoanalysis would have it, lesbians are the Real. If the "realesbian" of lesbian-feminism was a socially impossible identity, so in the psychoanalytic symbolic are lesbians only possible in/as the "Real," since they are foreclosed from the Symbolic order – they drop out of symbolization. If they can be signified at all it is only as an algebraic x. Given that the "Real" is, in part, the brute, inscrutable core of existence, the "Real" lesbian is in this sense coincident with the "realesbian." Hence as both real/Real, these figures make her "identical with [her] existence – self-identical – raw, sudden, and unfettered," but impossible to "see, speak or to hear, since in any case [she] is always already there." [26]

One sexual practice that has begun to figure much more prominently in lesbian erotica is the use of dildoes. Although it may be difficult to conceptualize strap-ons as s/m play, one rarely finds such representations outside the literature that is marked as s/m. Writers, visual artists, and practitioners have become increasingly assertive about claiming dildoes as the "real thing." Although strap-ons are advertised as "toys," *inside* the narratives and testimonials of lesbian s/m practitioners, references to an outside or a "model" are most often discarded in favor of descriptions that simply occupy the status of the real. So, for example, it has become common to speak of "watching her play with her dick," or "sucking her off," or "your dick find[ing] its way inside of me."[27] As one contributor to *Quim* puts it: "When I put on a strap on I feel male. I feel my dick as real otherwise I can't use it well."[28] Rarely if ever does one find lesbian erotica that refers to the dildo as a joke, an imitation, or a substitute, whether these narratives are explicitly in an s/m context or in the more prevalent accounts of butch/femme vanilla erotica. On the contrary, the erotic charge of these narratives depends on both tops and bottoms, butches and femmes exhibiting nothing less than respect for the "phallic" instrument.

Bersani's argument about gay macho depends on this notion of respect for masculinity as a model. But the slide from gay macho to lesbian butch-femme and s/m is too facilely made. Whereas gay macho's "mad identifications" are between gay and straight men, which he argues is a "direct line (not so heavily mediated) excitement to sexuality,"[29] the identifications made by b/f and s/m lesbians follow a more circuitous route in which the condensations and displacements are more complex. Most obviously, gay macho's relationship to straight masculinity remains a *hommo*-sexual affair; whereas lesbian b/f and s/m, as long as we are caught within the logic of this binary, would be *hetero*-sexual. In both cases, however, the erotic charge can only be articulated within the terms of a symbolic order that depends for its coherency on maintaining the distinction between homosexuality and heterosexuality. Nonetheless, even within the terms of this symbolic order, which I presume is what Bersani refers to when he speaks of sex "as we know it," there is already dissidence, rather than resemblance, in the image of a woman penetrating another woman with a dildo. Although both might be interpreted as a yearning toward "masculinity," in the gay man's case it is a masculinity that the dominant culture at least marginally assigns to him and that he thus might willingly surrender. In the lesbian top's case, it is a "masculinity" that she aggressively appropriates without any prior cultural ownership, only then to give it up. If we look at it from the bottom's perspective, there is quite a differerence between the gay man who cannot "refuse the suicidal ecstasy of being a woman," and the lesbian who is presumed by the dominant sexual order already to be a woman.

Over a decade ago, Monique Wittig implicitly enjoined us to write The Symbolic Order with a slash through the article, just as Lacan writes The Woman, when she made her then startling announcment that "Lesbians are not women."[30] The straight mind, she pointed out, "speaks of *the* difference between the sexes, *the* symbolic order, *the* Unconscious . . . giving an absolute meaning to these concepts when they are only categories founded upon heterosexuality . . ."[31] Returning to this article, it is interesting to remember that the example Wittig chooses to demonstrate the material oppression effected through discourses is pornography. Pornography, she argues, signifies simply that "women are dominated."[32] Thus Wittig might be aligned with Mackinnon when she argues that pornography "institutionalizes the sexuality of male supremacy, fusing the eroticization of dominance and

submission with the social construction of male and female."[33] It is this position that Bersani perversely asks us to reconsider when he temporarily allies
himself with Mackinnon and Dworkin only in order to argue for the necessity of proliferating pornography rather than banning it. However, if the
ultimate logic of the radical feminist argument for the realism of porn is
"the criminalization of sex itself until it has been reinvented,"[34] whether one
takes up a position for or against pornography on this basis are we not then
already acceding to the "straight mind" that can only think homosexuality
as "nothing but heterosexuality?"[35]

What has fallen out of these discussions is heterosexuality as a *social contract*,
one that as Wittig argues can not only be but already *is* broken by prac-
ticing lesbians. For when we hear of "sex as we know it" or the ultimate
logic of anti-porn feminists as the "criminalization of sex," this "sex" is always
already heterosexuality, and implicitly, a relationship of identity between the
phallus and the penis. Lacan seems to free us from this difficulty when he
argues that the phallus is a signifier (without a signified), not a body part,
nor a partial object, nor an imaginary construct.[36] However, in her reading
of Lacan's "The Meaning of the Phallus," *back through* "The Mirror Stage,"
Judith Butler shows that Lacan's denial of the phallus as an imaginary effect
is "constitutive of the Phallus as a privileged signifier."[37] At the risk of reduc-
tively summarizing her nuanced argument, what Butler's essay seems to
conclude is that the symbolic is always only *a* masculine imaginary that
produces the phallus as its privileged signifier by denying the mechanisms of
its own production.

Lacan's move to locate the phallus within the symbolic presumably breaks
its relation of identity with the penis, since symbolization "depletes that which
is symbolized of its ontological connection with the symbol itself."[38] Just as
Magritte's painting of a pipe is not a/the pipe, so the penis and phallus are
not equivalent.[39] But, as Butler points out, they do retain a privileged relationship to one another through "determinate negation."[40] If symbolization
is what effects ontological disconnection, we might ask what happens to those
"pipes" that are excessive to representation. Would not those things that
cannot take place within any given symbolic not end up accorded a radically negative ontological status? Would they not, in other words, become
that which is *real*, and *therefore* impossible?

When Wittig argues that rejecting heterosexuality and its institutions is,
from the straight mind's perspective, "simply an impossibility" since to do
so would mean rejecting the "symbolic order" and therefore the constitution
of meaning "without which no one can maintain an internal coherence,"[41]
she seems to suggest that the straight mind simply denies the possibility of
lesbianism. But phallocentrism/heterosexism does not merely secure its dominance through a simple negation. Rather, it *needs* lesbianism *as* a negative
ontology. It needs its status as both radically real *and* impossible.

That this is the case can be seen in Silverman's reconceptualization of the borders of male subjectivity in which her analysis at once ignores lesbian sexuality and persistently *depends* on it as yet another instance of a constitutive outside. Determined to undo the tenacious assumption that there are only two possible sexual subject positions, Silverman ends by positing three possible "same-sex" combinations: 1. two morphological men, 2. a gay man and a lesbian [both occupying psychically masculine positions], 3. a lesbian and a gay man [both occupying psychically feminine positions].[42] Given Silverman's sophisticated psychoanalytic rendering of the body's imaginary production, it might sound naive to suggest that the latter two positions are morphologically heterosexual, ie. one of each. Yet she retains the category of two morphological men, so there is obviously still some recourse to a materiality of the body outside its imaginary formations.

Silverman concludes her book by asserting that her third paradigm for male homosexuality has the "most resonance for feminism," which she claims to represent politically. But what is striking is that this is the only place in her analysis where lesbianism is represented. For it is in this most politically productive model of male homosexuality that the "authorial subjectivity" can be accessed "only through lesbianism."[43] What could this "lesbianism" be if not two morphologically female bodies, which oddly do not appear in her liberating models for "same-sex" desire? The feminism that Silverman speaks for politically is once again a heterosexual feminism; for her ability to make cases for imaginary gay sexualities is only intelligible *through* the assumption of a lesbian sexuality that remains stable and constitutively outside her recombinations of the relationships between psychic identifications and imaginary morphologies. Thus she depends on the orthodoxy of the impossibility of lesbian desire in order to challenge and break with the other orthodoxies that limit sexual choices for (heterosexual) women.

The model that proposes the impossiblity of lesbian desire, constructed as two morphological females with psychic feminine identities, is impossible within psychoanalytic terms precisely because there is no desire without a phallic signifier. In order for lesbianism to escape from its stabilizing function as the place-holder of a lack, Butler's fictive lesbian phallus would seem to be indispensable. Yet there is still in this formulation a submission to psychoanalytic orthodoxy; and lesbian sado-masochists have thought of much more interesting ways to practice dominance and submission.

Consider the following excerpt from *Bad Attitude*, which exemplifies the common s/m motif of the top's (literal) securing of the bottom, followed by a hiatus in which the bottom is left alone for an indeterminate amount of time to contemplate the acts that will follow:

> Will you please fuck me before I go mad? She smiled modestly, then said, "Not yet sweetie. I think you should learn a little patience. I'm going to have some breakfast now ..." Lying there helpless and horny, I could hear [her] making her meal. The refrigerator door opened and closed, dishes clinked, the microwave hummed and beeped ... I thrust my hips against the pillow.

I writhed, I moaned, I wiggled, I got hornier . . . Connie returned after 20 minutes . . . "Did you miss me?" she whispered in my ear.[44]

S/m's (form)ality depends on a stillness, a waiting that is acted out through both the suspense of deferred gratification as well as the re-enactment of suspense within the sexual scene itself. Hence the pleasure of binding, restraining, often literally suspending the bottom corporealizes the prolonged psychic negotiation. As opposed to the fluidity of conventional representations of sexual intercourse, the s/m scene is broken up, interrupted. This is a different model of continuance; for if suspense is understood as a desire to extend the scene for as long as possible, even when a "consummation" occurs it is not an endpoint, or goal, but rather a means to reproduce conditions that guarantee the necessity for endless returns.

If all desire is the perpetual pursuit of a lost object, s/m is the sexual practice that *formalizes* desire, repeating its movement with consciousness, deliberation, and ritualized control. And, quite self-consciously, s/m recognizes the body as the site of these transactions. Resisting the abstraction of the body as a signifier that refers only to itself, s/m practices are not about "speaking sex," but about *doing it*, and insisting upon the distinction. S/m acts out the word as bond – it effectuates the performativity of language.

Now suppose we agree with Bersani's argument that phallocentrism is "*above all* the denial of the value of powerlessness in both men and women,"[45] and consider what value women might find in powerlessness. I would agree with Tania Modleski that from a heterosexual woman's perspective there might not be much to value in powerlessness. But from a lesbian perspective things look different. Although Modleski acknowledges that lesbian sado-masochists' arguments must be taken seriously, and she points out the unresolvable contradiction between the acting out of power and the presumption of consensuality, I take exception to her assertion that the "defining feature of s/m [is] the infliction of pain and humiliation by one individual on another."[46] As Modleski's *own* discussion indicates, the s/m relationship resists that definition. What is important to point out here is that Modleski subtly posits the same distinction as Silverman between the "feminist" reader and the "lesbian." The former is a heterosexually gendered subject; the latter is something like the exception to the feminist "rule." Thus, once again, the lesbian becomes the constitutive outside – the necessary exterior – that facilitates the feminist argument.

Powerlessness, in Bersani's argument, seems to mean little more than submitting to penetration. When he takes anatomical considerations into account, he refers to the "real" of bodies which are constructed in such a way that "it's almost impossible not to associate mastery and subordination with intense pleasures".[47] If the value of powerlessness is equivalent to being penetrated, note that the "woman" in Bersani's imaginary must be either a heterosexual female or a gay man. Not only does Bersani then retain an equivalency between the phallus and the penis, but he also reinforces a morphological conflation of the vagina and the anus. At the same time, he insists upon a fantasmatic gender distinction that depends on these anatomical parts as referents. Bersani's argument then surely exceeds his intentions. For while he means to value the powerlessness of both men and women, it is paradoxically between these two penetrable orifices, which are at once the same and different, that on their front-to-back axis the illusion of an *impermeable* male body is sustained. As D. A. Miller puts it: "only between the woman and the homosexual *together* may the normal male subject imagine himself covered front and back" (my emphasis).[48]

If, as Butler argues, Lacan retains a relationship of identity between the phallus and the penis through "determinate negation," it is also possible to understand the valorization of a masochism that is explicitly male as further consolidation of this relation of equivalence. For male masochism, which presumably relinquishes the phallus by occupying the *being* of woman, would necessarily assume that she is the one who does not "have it." In other words, it is only by giving it up that one gets it. Hence the continuing postulation that female masochism is impossible depends on the assurance that she has nothing to give up. The female masochist would have to give up something that she does not have; and if she were represented as giving it up, then it would have to be admittted that the phallus is nothing more than an imaginary construct. According to Freud's narrative, women are presumed to have once "had" the penis. The phallus/penis as "lost object" always refers us to the past of a woman's body and the dreaded future of a man's body. Hence the cultural horror associated with "becoming a woman."

Lesbians who regard their strap-ons as the "real thing" instigate a representational crisis by producing an imaginary in which the fetishistic/hallucinatory "return" of the penis on to a woman's body goes beyond the "transferable or plastic property"[49] of the phallus to other body parts by depicting a phallus that has no reference to the "real" of the penis. The lesbian-dick *is* the phallus as floating signifier that has no ground on which to rest. It neither returns to the male body, originates from it, nor refers to it. Lesbian-dicks are the ultimate simulacra. They occupy the ontological status of the model, appropriate the privilege, and refuse to acknowledge an origin outside their own self-reflexivity. They make claims to the real without submitting to "truth." If the phallus was banned from feminist orthodoxy because it was presumed to signify the persistence of a masculine or heterosexual identification, and butch lesbians or s/m tops who wore strap-ons were thus represented, as Butler points out, as "vain and/or pathetic effort[s] to mime the real thing,"[50] this "real thing" was at least two real things, which were only each other's opposites. There was not much difference between the straight "real thing," and the lesbian "real thing," since the latter was only the *absence* of the former. Both these prohibitions converged on the assumption of an identity between the phallus and the penis.

Without that identification, the top who wears the strap-on is not the one who "has" the phallus; rather it is always already the bottom who "has it" by giving up what *no one* can have. In the lesbian imaginary, the phallus is not where it appears. That's why so many butches, as most lesbians know, are bottoms.

NOTES

This essay is an excerpt from my book, *Between the Body and the Flesh: Performing Lesbian Sado-Masochism*, which is forthcoming from Columbia University Press. An earlier version of the essay was published in *Postmodern Culture* (Sept. 1993).

1 Judith Roof, *The Lure of Knowledge: Lesbian Sexuality and Theory* (New York: Columbia University Press, 1991), p. 236.
2 Ibid., p. 224.
3 Robin Ruth Linden *et al., Against Sadomasochism: A Radical Feminist Analysis* (East Palo Alto, Calif.: Frog in the Well Press, 1982).
4 Sheila Jeffreys, *The Lesbian Heresy: A Feminist Perspective on the Lesbian Sexual Revolution* (North Melbourne, Australia: Spinifex Press, 1993), pp. 173–4.
5 Jamie Lee Evans, "Rodney King, Racism, and the SM culture of America," in *Unleashing Feminism*, ed. Irene Reti, (Santa Cruz: Herbooks, 1993), pp. 74–8.
6 Leo Bersani, "Is the Rectum a Grave?" in *AIDS: Cultural Analysis, Cultural Activism*, ed. Douglas Crimp (Cambridge, Mass.: MIT Press, 1988), pp. 207–8.
7 Elin Diamond, "Mimesis, Mimicry, and the 'True-Real'," *Modern Drama* 32. 1 (Mar. 1989): 64.
8 Ibid.
9 Diamond, "Mimesis, Mimicry, and the 'True-Real' ", p. 65.
10 Homi Bhabha, "Of Mimicry and Man: The Ambivalence of Colonial Discourse," in *October: The First Decade, 1976–1986*, ed. Annette Michelson *et al.* (Cambridge, Mass.: MIT Press, 1987), p. 318.
11 Giles Deleuze, "Plato and the Simulacrum," *October* 27 (Winter 1983): 49.
12 Maria Marcus, *A Taste for Pain: On Masochism and Female Sexuality*, trans. Joan Tate (New York: St. Martin's Press, 1981), p. 181.
13 For example, it is striking to notice that in a recent issue of *Ms.* magazine, the panelists brought together to discuss the issue of pornography tended to be dominated still by the Mackinnon/Dworkin theory that pornography causes violence against women. Although Marilyn French challenged the panel to stop "tiptoeing around" the issue of the censorship *within* feminist ranks, this panel hedged on the "problem" of porn created by and for women. When Andrea Dworkin was pushed, she said: "about the lesbian pornography . . . they are reifying the status quo. . . . And I think that lesbian pornography is extremely male-identified" *Ms.* 4. 4 (Jan./Feb. 1994): 39.
14 Leo Bersani, *The Freudian Body: Psychoanalysis and Art* (New York: Columbia University Press, 1986), p. 39.
15 Ibid.
16 Ibid., p. 47.
17 Ibid., p. 45.
18 Bersani, "Is the Rectum a Grave?," p. 212.
19 Sigmund Freud, "The Economic Problem in Masochism," *SE*, Vol. 19, trans. James Strachey (London: Hogarth Press, 1966), p. 162.

20 J. L. Austin, *How to Do Things With Words* (Cambridge, Mass.: Harvard University Press, 1962). Austin's most famous example is the "I do" in the Christian marriage vow, which effectuates the bond in its enunciation: "in saying these words we are *doing* something – namely, marrying, rather than *reporting* something, namely that we are marrying," pp. 12–13.

21 Kaja Silverman, "Masochism and Male Subjectivity," *Camera Obscura* 17 (1988): 52.

22 Jan Brown, "Sex, Lies, and Penetration: A Butch Finally 'Fesses Up," in *The Persistent Desire: A Femme-Butch Reader*, ed. Joan Nestle (Boston: Alyson Publications, 1992), p. 412.

23 Susan Farr, "The Art of Discipline: Creating Erotic Dramas of Play and Power," in *Coming to Power: Writings and Graphics on Lesbian S/M* (Boston: Alyson Publications, 1981), p. 185.

24 Jacques Derrida, "The Theater of Cruelty and the Closure of Representation," in *Writing and Difference*, trans. Alan Bass (Chcago: University of Chicago Press, 1978), p. 234.

25 Bersani, "Rectum," p. 208.

26 Catherine Clement, *The Lives and Legends of Jacques Lacan*, trans. Arthur Goldhammer (New York: Columbia University Press, 1983), pp. 168–9.

27 *Quim* 3 (Winter 1991): 10, 13. Similar language can be found in almost any issue of *On Our Backs* or *Bad Attitude*. And, in fact, in periodicals such as the now defunct *Outrageous Women* (which was published during the 1980s) one also finds such references to "lesbian dicks," sometimes without the qualifier. What is apparent is that s/m dykes have always considered their dildoes to be the "real thing."

28 Anonymous. *Quim* 3 (Winter 1991): 36.

29 Bersani, "Rectum," p. 208.

30 Monique Wittig, "The Straight Mind," *The Straight Mind and Other Essays* (Boston: Beacon Press, 1992), p. 32.

31 Ibid., pp. 27–8.

32 Ibid., p. 25.

33 Catherine A. Mackinnon, *Feminism Unmodified: Discourses on Life and Law* (Cambridge, Mass.: Harvard University Press, 1987), pp. 3, 172.

34 Bersani, "Rectum," p. 214.

35 Wittig, "Straight Mind," p. 28.

36 Jacques Lacan, "The Meaning of the Phallus," *Feminine Sexuality: Jacques Lacan and the ecole freudienne*, trans. Jacqueline Rose (New York: W. W. Norton, 1985), pp. 74–85.

37 Judith Butler, "The Lesbian Phallus and the Morphological Imaginary," *differences*, "The Phallus Issue," 4. 1 (Spring 1992): 156.

38 Ibid., p. 157.

39 Michel Foucault, *This is Not a Pipe*, trans. and ed. James Harkness (Berkeley and Los Angeles: University of California Press, 1982).

40 Butler, "Lesbian Phallus," p. 157.

41 Wittig, "Straight Mind," p. 26.

42 Kaja Silverman, *Male Subjectivity at the Margins* (New York: Routledge, 1992), p. 381.

43 Ibid., p. 387.

44 Liz Lasher, "Hot Buttered Bum," *Bad Attitude* 7. 4, p. 23.

45 Bersani, "Rectum," p. 217.

46 Tania Modleski, *Feminism Without Women: Culture and Criticism in a 'Postfeminist' Age* (New York: Routledge, 1991), p. 154.

47 Bersani, "Rectum," p. 216.

48 D. A. Miller, "Anal Rope," in *Inside/Out*, ed. Diana Fuss (New York: Routledge, 1991), p. 135.
49 Butler, "Lesbian Phallus," p. 138.
50 Ibid., p. 159.

Part II

GRAVE PERFORMANCES
The cultural politics of memory

5

PLAYING DEAD IN STONE, OR, WHEN IS A ROSE NOT A ROSE?[1]

Peggy Phelan

In 1989 one of the most dramatic plots in Renaissance theater unfolded in London. In a six-month dig in Southwark, archaeologists unearthed the startlingly well preserved remains of the Rose Theatre, the first home of Christopher Marlowe's dramatic plays. That the Rose, which had only an eighteen-year life span as a "living" building at all (1587-1605), could be unearthed some 400 years later was extraordinary. In addition to the Rose structural remains, coins, jewelry, shoes, and hazelnut shells ("Elizabethan popcorn") were found.[2] Over the course of the dig, it became clear that this was a very valuable site for historians, archaeologists, architectural historians, geologists, and other scholars. The many references in Renaissance plays to the theater space which have been notoriously difficult to decipher were tantalizingly close to being answered. (Or at least new conjectures could be based on "real" and "better" evidence.) As Andrew Gurr and John Orrell put it early on: "In the last three months theatre historians have been given more fresh and utterly reliable information about the design of the Shakespearean stage than they have managed to scrape together from written sources in the past three centuries. To lose it would be a new kind of Shakespearean tragedy" (Orrell and Gurr 1989: 429).

The idea that archaeology provides "utterly reliable information" is a curious one. For as Christopher Tilley points out, "All archaeology is an interpretive activity. This hermeneutic dimension to archaeological research is absolutely fundamental.[. . .] We can regard archaeology itself as the largely unconscious but nevertheless rule-governed production of statements about the past" (Tilley 1989: 277). These "largely unconscious" ideas controlled the reception of the Rose remains as much as they informed the archaeological framework of the excavation itself. Before examining the cultural unconscious at play in the hole in Southwark's streets, it is worth pausing over Gurr's and Orrell's characterization of what the Rose's excavation has "given" theater historians. "Utterly reliable information" is pretty rare and especially so when it is derived from rotting wood and old artifacts. The baldness of the claim, the lack of hedging or apology, can perhaps be attributed to the authors' awareness that the disposition of the Rose excavation would be determined by political and economic considerations. To hedge on the scholarly value of the site would perhaps make the case for continued excavations more difficult to justify. But more than the *realpolitick* at work in Gurr's and Orrell's characterization is a belief, a statement of faith, that the disinterred object will redeem us – or at least save those scholars toiling in the dark mysteries of the Shakespearean stage from tragedy. The belief in excavation as a transcendent source of utterly reliable information stems from the idea that by recovering the architectural design of the physical theater, one can recover the truth of Renaissance theater. For Gurr and Orrell, the physical object has an enormous truth value. "To lose it would be a new kind of Shakespearean tragedy."

Shakespeare's own tragedies were themselves far less sanguine about the truth value of physical objects. In *Othello*, for example, Desdemona's hand-kerchief is used by Iago to convince Othello of her infidelity. Enclosed within Iago's interpretative framework, the handkerchief, "the ocular proof" is profoundly deceiving. Orrell and Gurr are indeed correct to suggest that the disinterment of the Rose signals a new kind of Shakespearean tragedy, although not for the reasons they imply.

The discovery of the Rose, as Orrell and Gurr note here, was hedged in on all sides by the prospect of loss. In an effort to preserve the site, the Shakespeare connection was heightened and the Marlowe connection played down, in part because Shakespeare has a kind of cultural/tourist capital that Marlowe lacks. Only two of Shakespeare's plays, *Titus Andronicus* and *Henry VI Part I*, were performed at the Rose, and there is some evidence that they had originally opened at The Theatre.[3] But the Rose in 1989 certainly became, if not quite "Shakespeare's stage" a "Shakespearean stage." The reasons for this, I'd like to suggest, had something to do with factors other than scholarship and tourist capital – although assuredly these two factors played a prominent and decisive role in the debate about the Rose. For modern archaeology, like modern theater, is a hazard of politics, of money, and of ideology.[4] It participates in and is a product of the cultural unconscious's attitude toward history, an attitude which is in every way informed by contemporary anxieties, desires, and nationalist-economic politics.

Surprisingly thus far almost all of the scholarly work on the Rose excavation has concentrated on the "products" produced by the archaeological findings, and/or has analyzed the political conflicts of interests that were exposed by the public protests that arose when the Rose was feared to be "lost."[5] What I am interested in here is something closer to a psychoanalysis of excavation: I am interested in what it means to disinter a theater, what anxieties it creates and what fantasies it fosters. Our attitudes toward the return of buried bodies, including architectural ones, like our attitudes toward the return of the repressed, have much to tell us about how we organize our ideas and fantasies about living bodies. My analysis here is often associative and analogical, rather than strictly empirical, although there are many true facts here too. I am interested in the anal core of analogies and analysis: for, as we shall see, this mode of thinking informed the debate about the Rose.

The Rose is assuredly a special case – not any theater remains would incite the intense feelings created by the return of the Rose. The polygonal structure was built in 1587, only the third solid theater built in London. Philip Henslowe owned it and in 1592 he recruited Edward Alleyn and Strange's Men to act there. Shortly thereafter, the Rose mounted Christopher Marlowe's great plays – *Tamburlaine* I and II, *Doctor Faustus*, and *The Jew of Malta*, with Alleyn in the lead roles.[6] In 1594, the Lord Chamberlain set a new Privy Council policy permitting only two companies to play in London in designated playhouses. Alleyn became the lead actor in the newly formed acting company the Admiral's Men and the Rose became their permanent theater. (The other licensed theater was The Theatre, owned by James Burbage. When it was dismantled in 1598, the Globe was erected from The Theatre's old scaffolding. The Globe was of course the home of Shakespeare's company, the King's Men. Shortly after the 1989 excavation of the Rose, excavation began on the Globe, a very literal proof that political power, among other things, generates historical weight and continuity).[7]

To put the complicated story of the Rose excavation very briefly: In the 1950 *Survey of London* an 1875 Ordinance Survey Map was reprinted which clearly displayed the location of the Rose on Maiden Lane in Southwark (now called Park Street; it faces Southwark Bridge Road). In 1971, Richard Hughes, an archaeologist hired by developers interested in building on the site, advised them not to. He wrote, "Since the water table is relatively near the ground surface and since the area before the initial occupation was marshy, structural timbers are likely to be preserved, as are leather, wood, and fabric artefacts [. . .] [T]his should be considered one of those areas where public action could make excavation and preservation a national issue" (in Eccles 1990: 160).[8] In November of 1987 the site was purchased by the Heron Group and they applied to Southwark Council for planning permission to construct a nine-storey office building. After consulting with the Museum of London, the Southwark Council granted permission contingent upon the developers' funding excavation of the site before building. After the agreement was brokered, the Heron Group sold the site to Imry Merchant, another developing firm. They agreed to fund ten weeks of archaeological research before they began building. As the value of the excavations became clear, the ten weeks turned into six months (although during that time Imry Merchant did begin to build in the opposite corner of the lot), all of which was funded by the developers. The delay cost the developers over a million pounds (Wainwright 1989: 430).

Having concluded six months of excavation, the developers were legally scheduled to proceed with building beginning Monday morning, 15 May

1989. All archaeological research and the chance to preserve the Rose would end as soon as the developers' tractors moved in. During the weekend of 13-14 May, a series of protests led by Dame Peggy Ashcroft and Ian McKellen alerted Nicholas Ridley, then the Secretary of State for the Environment, that he would have a serious problem on his hands if the developers were allowed to continue building on Monday morning. The morning of 15 May, Ridley and Virginia Bottomley, the then Under Secretary of State for the Environment, met with representatives of Imry Merchant, English Heritage, and Simon Hughes, the MP from Southwark, in an effort to resolve the crisis. And it had by then become a crisis: Peggy Ashcroft had threatened to throw herself in front of a tractor and the group had suggested she be left behind as a hostage and the site vacated (Eccles 1990: 178). The protestors quickly organized themselves into an official group called The Rose Theatre Trust.

They quickly organized a petition to schedule the site; if successful, the site would be declared a national treasure and its preservation would be funded by the government. Ridley, often described as "the architect" of Margaret Thatcher's economic policy whose cornerstone was "privatize," eventually rejected the petition.[9] Had the site been scheduled the Government would have been obligated to compensate Imry Merchant because, by law, once permission to build has been granted it cannot be revoked without compensation.[10]

At the meeting on the morning of 15 May, Ridley was able to get Imry Merchant to delay building for a month by committing the government to pay a million pounds to compensate them for the delay. During the thirty days, Ridley hoped, a new architectural design that would preserve the remains, give the public access to them, and give the developers their office building, would materialize.

Later that afternoon, Ridley announced the thirty-day reprieve to Parliament. He was at pains to explain that the Government would not underwrite the cost of preserving and displaying the remains of the Rose, as many people not of his party had urged. He told the House, "The Government's financial commitment finishes with this statement."[11] To this, John Fraser, a Labour MP from Norwood replied, "I hope the Right Honourable Gentleman [Ridley] is not like Oscar Wilde, who believed where architecture starts, art ends." And Ridley retorted, "I claim dissimilarity with Oscar Wilde in more than one respect." In the transcript of the meeting published in *The Times* the next day, "(laughter)" punctuates the close of Ridley's statement. It's difficult to know who is laughing or why exactly, but it is not irrelevant to point out that Ridley was a vocal supporter of the infamous censorship law in England, Clause 28 of the Local Authorities bill, which banned representation "promoting homosexuality." The bill was passed in March 1988. We will return to this later.

In an effort to return Ridley to the question of government funding for the Rose, Eric Heffer (Liverpool, Labour) then took up the standard claim that English culture's claim to greatness rests with Renaissance theater. Heffer instructed Ridley that "the Government must now consider what financial help it could give to preserve the theatre, which was vital to the cultural development of the nation." Ridley deflected the comment by assuring Heffer that he would give him an opportunity to donate to any fund drives the public might take up to preserve the Rose. Whereupon Anthony Beaumont-Dark (Conservative, Birmingham) growing impatient with the whole drift of the conversation, yelled, "This is *not* a building!" He went on to say the Rose was not even a ruin; it was merely "footings." If the government tried to preserve "the footings every time some experts said that they were the remains of a theater or a brothel, London would still be composed of the ruins of Rome."[12] Drawing on one of the most historically sustained links between the similar "ruins" produced by theaters and brothels, Beaumont-Dark suggested that finally there really is no difference between a theater and a brothel at all. In this Philip Henslowe might agree, for in addition to owning the theater, he owned several properties which housed brothels.[13] Beaumont-Dark concluded that if the government had ten to twenty million pounds to spend, it should be spent on "living theatre" and not on something that looks like "a disused mine." In response to this outburst, Ridley once again returned to Wilde's distinction between art and architecture and contended that the excavation of the Rose was neither. He preferred the term "archaeology," to which Beaumont-Dark replied, "It's rubbish!"

Beaumont-Dark's point, for all its dark bluster, is actually very important. The remains of the Rose do not reveal "a building." They are literally the building's remains, the footings. To preserve such footings, Beaumont-Dark suggests, is to degrade the aspiration of architecture and, by implication, culture itself. It is to elevate old brothels or disused mines to the status of art objects. On an unconscious level also, associations between empty cavities, hollow caves, and open holes are consolidated as so much "rubbish" – and certainly not what the Government should be funding. Given the Tory Government's attitude toward coal mining, disused mines were particularly dense symbols in the country's economic-political imaginary throughout the mid- and late 1980s.[14]

Beaumont-Dark's argument rests on a distinction between the living and the dead: within his logic, "living theatre" is at the opposite end of the death space of brothels and "disused mines." Decisions about funding culture, then, must be based on the reproduction of a living theater and a living architecture: it must not support the mere *remains* of myth and memory.[15] (Thatcher's government had consistently cut funding for the "living" arts. Perhaps Beaumont-Dark is just covering the government's bases: no money for theater, living or dead.)

For Beaumont-Dark, it was unclear if the Rose could be a productive player in the construction and reconstruction of a national myth and memory.

The heritage industry, as Christine Eccles points out, is a huge business. In Stratford-upon-Avon alone, 50 million pounds a year is spent by 2.5 million tourists (Eccles 1990: 243). This kind of money has made it very tempting to play fast and loose with historical accuracy. As Eccles puts it, "If history could not confirm the fact that William Shakespeare was born in a thatched cottage in the market town of Stratford-upon-Avon, right in the geographical heart of England, then history would have to invent it" (1990: 243). But it is not some neutral, albeit economically driven "history" that invents geographical locations for cultural patron saints. The invention of history is the result of a dense nexus of competing and often contradictory moral, nationalistic, economic, and unconscious factors. These factors themselves change over time thus making historical production itself contingent upon the material, moral, nationalistic, and psychic needs of the present – as they are understood by those in power.[16] In the case of late-1980s England the heritage business was securely in the hands of the Right:

> [T]he culture of the New Right has actively fostered [the growth of the heritage industry]. The heritage is everywhere, all around "us," nothing less than a kind of collective memory of an entire people or nation. Such a notion of heritage does not involve a recognition of the *difference* of the past (thus enabling it to put the present into a comparative perspective) but an assertion of sameness and identity, the creation of the fictional unity of a national consciousness.
>
> (Tilley 1989: 279)

In the creation of such a consciousness, the cultural unconscious works double time. The invention of cultural history is generally not the product of a progressive, liberatory enterprise, in part because those powerful enough to impose that "invention" tend to be entrenched within the apparatus of the State. And in part because what Tilley refers to as the "largely unconscious but nevertheless rule-governed production of statements about the past" are, like all productions of the unconscious, subject to repression, disavowal, and phantasmatic structures that are usually far from "progressive" or "enlightened." The severe limits and rigid control over "historical invention" were exposed in the public and political discussion of the Rose remains.

These remains represent the "excess" that simply will not remain repressed, no matter how carefully mainstream culture works to solidify the normative. Oscar Wilde appeared in the House of Parliament on 15 May 1989 because he is the symptom which signals the (failed) repression of that other body, the "non-normative" homosexual.[17] As Ridley demonstrated, Wilde functions as a foil for political heterosexuals to declare themselves "dissimilar" to his "excessive" and flamboyantly theatrical life. Politicians such as Ridley and Beaumont-Dark use Wilde as a way to legitimate their own public performances as the proud owners of straight-forward, sexio-economical prudent, anti-theatrical bodies.

70

Moreover, it may be possible to discern an unconscious link between Wilde and Marlowe at play in the debates as well. The Rose was Marlowe's stage, not Shakespeare's. Marlowe wrote plays about a man who consorted with devils, about a homosexual King, about the persecution of a Jew; he also allegedly wrote "all they that love not tobacco and boys were fools."[18] Marlowe was murdered by a man in the courtyard of an inn. He was twenty-nine years old. Legend has it that he and his killer, Ingram Frazier, were fighting over the reckoning; then as now disagreements about footing the bill can be fatal. Thinking of the deaths of artistic young men at the hands of other men who spend nights together in hotels touches another contemporary cultural narrative: the deadly reckoning exacted by AIDS. Thus, Marlowe is a much more ambiguous contemporary cultural patron saint than the Bard of Avon. The ambiguity about Marlowe may well inform the attitude about the remains of the Rose as well.

In 1592, Henslowe expanded and renovated the Rose – enlarging audience capacity by about 400. The Rose remains discovered in 1989, then, are actually the remains of two theaters. One can discern how and where the second larger theater enveloped the first. What we have, then, is a series of mutating architectural bodies in which the boundaries of the previous body in every way inform the growth and development of the new body. Discovering the remains of the Rose, actually meant discovering the remains of a double architectural body: and the question posed to the architects who were hired to revise the plan for the original office building – "How can we make this new building allow us to see multiple distinct architectural bodies?" – was a question which was already ghosted by the query, How can one building display more than one body?

I am using the word "body" here quite deliberately; I'd like to suggest that the Rose Theatre is and was a mutating, mobile, and "theatrical" body. As the demands upon Henslowe's theater increased in 1592, he transformed and added to the building; as the archaeologists and politicians debated the remains of the Rose in 1989, new plans were drawn up to re-animate the footings that remained. In these mutations, the Rose of 1989 moved from an archaelogical site to an architectural one. In this movement, the Rose became less an "object" full of rocks, coins, and artifacts, and more a "subject," a living, difficult, even contradictory form that refused to stay dead.

The architectural question about the Rose remains can most properly be understood as a quintessentially theatrical challenge: how can one body display two (or more) distinct but coherent "selves"? And how is the articulation of that doubleness always already dependent upon a notion of a "proper" (singular) body? How do buildings themselves, in their solidity and singularity, contribute to the notion of "a proper body"?

These questions take on a particular force in relation to the excavation of the Rose. As the third solid theater built in London, the Rose re-presents the historical moment in which theaters *became* buildings. In *The Illusion of*

Power, Stephen Orgel indicates the impact of this architectural transformation on Renaissance England:

> Before this moment, the concept of theater had included no sense of *place*. A theatre was not a building, it was a group of actors and an audience; the theatre was any place they chose to perform. . . . [Once] embodied in architecture . . . theatre was an institution, a property, a corporation. For the first time in more than a thousand years it had the sort of reality that meant most to Renaissance society; it was *real* in the way that real estate is real; it was a location, a building, a possession – an established and visible part of society.
>
> (Orgel 1975: 2, emphasis in original)

Disintering the Rose rendered theater itself spatially and temporally mobile, fluid, a focus of passionate debate: it put into question "location, building, possession." If Renaissance theater architecture inaugurated an assured and certain place for theatrical activity (in the benign reading of theater history), or if it provided a spatial confinement and rigid border for theatrical activity (in the "hegemonic" reading of theater history), the return of the Rose made that theatrical place radically insecure. Who owned the Rose remains? How could the new building relate to the old building? Where was the theater actually located? The question of ownership raised ancillary questions about the relation between "public property" and commercial development, and about the relation between historical preservation and contemporary revitalization. Similarly, the question about "location" led to the complicated negotiations about where to place the pilings for the new building. The developers wanted to maximize the size of their building, and the historians wanted to maximize the protection of the Rose. What I am trying to suggest, in other words, is that the excavation of the Rose literally unearthed the epistemological claims about "the place of theater," claims that had been made possible by the construction of Renaissance theaters themselves. And these claims became particularly traumatic in relation to the male body.

The moment in which theaters became consolidated in and as buildings, the moment which returns in the discovery of the Rose, also signals a moment in which the male body joins an ongoing epistemological history of display. Having re-established a place for the male body to play, an enormous array of interpretive frames by which that body could be apprehended are made possible. Acting books, books of gesture, handbooks on expressing emotion, and all the other discursive "arts and sciences" that begin to emerge in the Renaissance are enabled by the fact that there is an architectural place in which the theater of the male body is displayed. In short, architecture informs and defines the espistemological possibilities of the male body once theater itself "takes (a) place."

Architecture has of course long been considered theatrical. Buildings are said to "stage" ideas about space and time, to dramatize a certain argument about form. Architecture also establishes a specific relation with its

72

inhabitants (think of Foucault's Benthamite prisons), and often insists on a mimetic relation to the human body. In this insistence, architecture is performative as well as theatrical, for it actively shapes and forms the bodies that inhabit it. Denis Hollier's brilliant reading of Bataille allows us to see the intensity of the anthropomorphism imbedded in architecture: "[E]ven though he seems to denounce the repression exercised over man by architecture, Bataille is really intervening against the catachresis requiring that man only take form with architecture, that the human form as such, the formation of man, be embedded in architecture. If the prison is the generic form of architecture, this is primarily because man's own form is his first prison" (1989: xi–xii). The mimetic relation between buildings and bodies insulates each from imagining revolutionary forms. Theater architecture, then, is doubly mimetic: it is constructed around an image of the bodies to be staged in its building. And these theatrical bodies display themselves in relation to architectural rules that govern their staging.

In the odd and complex dialogue between representational forms and "real" behavior, the possibilities of the body opened up by theater architecture are employed both to extend and enhance bodily practices (and thus are congenial to the strategies of progressive cultural workers), and also to mark the distinction between the "theatrical" body and the "normative" body (and thus are congenial to the strategies of prohibitive cultural workers). To wit, the male body is routinely made "normative" – singular and whole, the property of one person who has one gender, one proper name, one self – by virtue of becoming anti-theatrical. This schooling in "making the body" requires both a positive and a negative other.

Within the normative Symbolic of contemporary heterosexuality, the positive other is the singular self of the other gender with whom one will join in a monogamous union until "death do us part." The negative other is cast as the promiscuous homosexual who, in addition to seeking an other of the same gender, also eschews monogamy and long-term relations. Within this Symbolic, the heterosexual's quest for the "true" singular body it longs to (re)join, is set against the homosexual's wandering and false "body in disguise." Wandering actors, like wandering homosexuals, are dangerous because they threaten to expose the fiction of stable homes. These are emphatically not ontological claims: I am merely plotting how the Symbolic opposition between homosexuality and heterosexuality that so rankles the Right and the Left today, for very different reasons, employs ideas about the body derived from theater to carry out its oppositional thinking. Such thinking is not confined to the genre of theater as such: the homosexual "body in disguise" fuels the Right's paranoia about the gay male body far beyond the solid architectural confines of theater. From the phantasmal image of the homosexual predator about to be "unleashed" in the United States military, to the routine suspicion of homosexual men's relationships with children, to the terror-filled narratives of infected and infecting "AIDS-carrying homosexuals," the figure of the male homosexual as "the [dangerous] body in disguise" stalks the cultural imaginary and is fed by the paranoid fervor of the Right. This imaginary framed the discussion about the Rose remains in London. To put it perhaps too crudely and far too swiftly, I am suggesting that just as Renaissance theater helped focus the discursive and pragmatic possibilities of the arts and sciences and led to a new conception of man, so too does the contemporary "theater" of AIDS help focus discursive and psychoanalytic tensions around repression and death, leading to a new conception of the male body. This body is marked by the aggressiveness of its disavowal and is rendered as a form full of nothing but holes. The 1989 Rose, a hole, "a disused mine," so much "rubbish," is the iconic emblem of a body that carries death in its newly exposed holes and hollows.

I write this with a kind of breathless assertion rather than constructing it as a philosophical proof. My unconscious, my own repressions, and my own conscious allegiance to the conventions of the academic "subject" force me to abandon these associations in favor of "empirical" facts. So striking another note, let us return to the story of the Rose.

Instead of contracting to develop an office building in Southwark as Imry Merchant had proposed to do, the developers were suddenly in the business of designing a building which could stage the remains of a theater. In short, the building could no longer correspond to a normative body – singular and whole – but had to become a theaticalized, double body. The question of how to stage the remains of the Rose required a new architectural model. And, in the strange form of reproduction which prevails between buildings and bodies, several different proposals were conceived.

These plans are at once architectural and anatomical. For just as an anatomy makes visible the interior workings of a body, so too must the new Rose display, architecturally, the ground, the skeletal set, upon which the building takes its current form. Within the history of anatomy, a history enacted through public autopsies held in medical theaters, the accuracy of the drawing was dependent upon securing a corpse: a dead body was required for anatomical representation to be born. In the case of the Rose the dead architectural body was, if anything, all too present: the new architectural building had to, as it were, compete with its own corpse.

Hollier points out that the invention of architecture was motivated by a desire to forestall and forget death. This desire functions according to the rule of psychoanalytic desire, which is to say the desire is displaced on to an object which perpetuates, rather than satisfies, that desire. In order to forestall or forget death, architecture invents the tombstone which both distracts us from the specificity of the dead body and underlines the stone cold fact of death itself. As Hollier puts it:

74

The monument and the pyramid are where they are to cover up a place, to fill in a void: the one left by death. Death must not appear: it must not take place: let tombs cover it up and take its place. [...] One plays dead so that death will not come. So nothing will happen and time will not take place.

(Hollier 1989: 36)

In other words, architecture robs death of its personal interiority: it publicly displays death as smooth surface – as an external solid slab.[19] The smooth stone is appealing precisely because it is static and still, unlike the decomposing body it covers.[20] If death were guaranteed stillness perhaps it would be less dreadful. As it plots the grids of the cemetery in horizontal and vertical squares, architecture offers us this monumental stillness. Architecture participates in the reassuring fantasy that one can outlast temporal decomposition by displacing the terror of a porous, leaking, expiring, and decomposing body, on to a solid monument, a building.[21] (To put it slightly differently: architecture transforms dying into death.)[22] When Hollier claims, "One plays dead so that death will not come," he implicitly links architecture to theater, to the art of disguise.[23] Theater itself is the space in which death is made to play, to be a play. (Marlowe's *Faustus* is still perhaps the best example of the dramatic conjunction between plotting a death and plotting a play.) The continual restaging of theatrical performances' appearance and disappearance records the history of Western culture's attempt to play *fort/da* with dying itself. The Rose remains threatened to make the "here-ness" of death in the contemporary city too visible.

The disinterment of the architecture of the Rose Theatre raised a question about the place of play that contemporary culture accords to death itself. The architectural challenge inaugurated by the Rose necessitated a shift in the axis of architecture itself, a shift whose causes and implications are much larger than the local challenge of the Rose. The story of the Rose's remains is a significant one because it dramatizes an art form – architecture – inverting its ontological paradigms in response to a past that continually erupts into the present. The Rose forced architecture to abandon its customary assumption of itself as a spatial art, and to reinvent itself as a temporal one.[24] This reinvention parallels the reimagining of the erotic body as it confronts the grave of AIDS.

D. A. Miller has argued that we now live in what he calls "morbidity culture," in which social life, public discourse, and art are preoccupied with questions of health, and of death and dying (Miller 1990: 70–4).[25] The advent of gym addiction on the one hand, and of intricate disease vocabularies sprinkled through everyday discourse – metastasize, T-cell count, stem-cell removal – on the other, are symptoms of morbidity culture. While there are many reasons for our new consciousness of morbidity, from the structure of health care to the exorbitant increase in cancer, AIDS is surely the most explosive catalyst for the formation of this new culture.

As I have argued elsewhere, AIDS is and will remain indelibly linked to "promiscuous gay men" in the cultural unconscious, despite statistics which reveal that the level of HIV infection in that group decreasing (Phelan 1991). As Leo Bersani has astutely demonstrated, the cultural anxiety generated in relation to gay men's sexual practices, especially "passive" anal sex, are tied to particular psychic anxieties about male submission itself (Bersani 1987). This leads him to the central question of his essay, "Is the Rectum A Grave?," a question he was prompted to ask after reading Simon Watney's study, *Policing Desire*. Watney contends that AIDS "offers a new sign for the symbolic machinery of repression, making the rectum a grave" (Watney 189: 126). Watney's thesis that the mainstream media is displaying a kind of paranoid reading of gay male sexuality is re-posed by Bersani in order to suggest that male submission, and male masochism itself, is deeply subversive in a culture which insists on male dominance. While Watney bemoans the logic which reads the rectum as a grave, Bersani hopes that it may portend the welcome death of the belief that male sexuality is completely expressed in acts of penetration. This belief, Bersani insists, is undone by a consideration of male submissiveness, a consideration accented by the architectonics of gay male "passive" anal sex.

Let's compare an anatomical diagram of the male rectum and an aerial photograph of the Rose remains [see Figures 5.1 and 5.2]. I am aware that on one level this comparison is comical, and I hope to recall the laughter in the House of Commons when Ridley claimed his dissimilarity from Wilde. When Ridley suggested that the Rose excavation was neither art nor archi-tecture, but rather was archaeology, he evoked Freud's favorite analogy for psychoanalysis: "The analyst's 'work of construction' or, if it is preferred, of reconstruction, resembles to a great extent an archaeologist's excavation of some ancient edifice that has been destroyed and buried" (Freud 1937: 259). For the psychoanalyst, like the theater historian, the project of ex-cav-ation always involves mapping the hollow which is not there and the hollow that is.

In the ground of the Rose there is plenty present to help recall what is missing, and plenty to create an uncanny new presence. I cannot be alone in thinking there is something in this archaeology. The Rose remains retained its drain: the single best preserved finding in the dig was the original timber *drain pipe* made of Baltic pine and measuring eighteen feet. Similarly, the biggest revelation for Renaissance theater scholars unearthed in the remains is the size of the Rose. It is much smaller than any one anticipated. The stage seems to have been only about five to six meters from front to back. The "pit" also appears to have been raked, not flat as previously assumed, thus giving a whole new conception of the experience of being a "groundling." The capacity of the 1587 theater was between 1400 and 1800 people, depending on how packed one assumes people were willing/forced to be; and roughly 1800–2200 after the 1592 expansion (Orrell and Gurr 1989).

76

All of these calculations are based on the assumption that the average Elizabethan was 5'5¾" inches. This number is in turn based on one firm fact: the size of the burial plots for plague victims (Eccles 1990: 133).

The deadly reckoning of measurement also led to the contestation over the placement of the pilings for the office building. The developers wanted to place them directly beneath their building so that the structural support would be in smooth verticals. They wanted to have the legs of the building (the pilings), as it were, placed directly beneath the building itself. English Heritage wanted to spread the legs of the building, place the pilings far apart, and have them lead to a central beam well above the remains which would then support the office building. This plan was (inaptly) dubbed "the office on stilts." Since the whole site had not been excavated, guesswork was involved about the actual dimension of the remains. If the pilings were placed too close to the site, there was a risk of damaging the Rose. The placement of the piling positions was rendered in the same way crude drawings render the rectum – as a circular bold line covering a hole.

To turn the interpretive screw one more time it is helpful to expand our lens just a little bit. Ian McKellen, Dame Peggy Ashcroft, and Lord Laurence Olivier were the three most prominent members of the Rose Theatre Trust. When Olivier died in July 1989, the members of the Trust wanted to mark his death by placing a wreath at the Rose construction site. Imry Merchant viewed this gesture as "deeply provocative and [in] extraordinarily bad taste" (in Souster 1989). Eccles notes that this was the first time during the long campaign that Imry Merchant "got into a direct confrontation" with those who sought to preserve the Rose (1990: 221). She attributes the developers' "tetchiness" to the impending takeover of the company by Marketchief, a large conglomerate. Perhaps she is correct, but I think the developers' heated rhetoric may well spring from the implication that by placing a wreath, a hollow hole, at the site, the campaigners would directly convert Imry Merchant's building into a grave site. Nourishing the idea that the developers were going to erect a building against the wishes and "over the dead bodies" of actors, the protestors' desire to place a wreath on the construction site was a calculated gesture that sought to portray Imry Merchant as uncaring capitalists. The developers' aggressive response implied that the protestors were using Olivier's death to make a political point, an exploitative and unseemly use of a dead man.

But the desire to place a wreath commemorating the death of an accomplished actor on the site of a "dead theater" is also a desire to create a tradition, to establish a connection between Renaissance actors and contemporary ones. More profoundly though, the gesture expresses a desire to transform the (economic, architectural, future-directed) aspiration implied by a "construction site" into a place of retrospection, memory, and history. "Nothing defines the specific rootedness of a location – the transformation of a place into a site – more than its being founded on a grave" (Pellizzi

Figure 5.1 Rose Theatre, aerial view (Andrew Fulgoni Photography)

1990: 84). The failure to secure the boundaries of the Rose site led to a desire to insist on mapping the past by turning the location into a grave site – a tomb, a place meriting deeper "grave-r" contemplation.

For those in the homosexual community who have had to replot the "usefulness" of death, finding new ways to memorialize the dying has become a common preoccupation. McKellen had, in the course of campaigning against

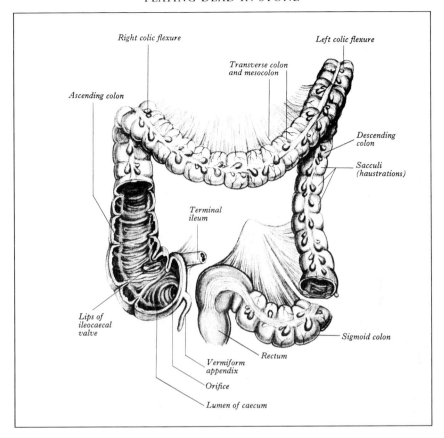

Figure 5.2 Anatomical drawing of the male rectum. From Frank Netter's *Atlas of Human Anatomy*, 1989, Ciba-Geigy Corporation: Schmit, NJ.

Clause 28 in 1988, at the age of 50 come out as a gay man. As we think about the male homosocial environment of the Rose Theatre, all the men playing all the parts under the protection of Queen Elizabeth and then under a reputedly homosexual King James I, in relation to the male homosocial environment of the 1989 Parliament, the invocation of Oscar Wilde begins to make more sense. These sites harbor more than a passing interest in the politics of the display of the male body. Just as the architectural solidity of the Renaissance theater served as an epistemological consolidation of the "art and science" of the actor's body, the prohibitions and possibilities of displaying contemporary bodies were given new anatomies after Clause 28 was added to the Local Authorities Bill and approved by the House of Commons on 28 March 1988, a few months before the first digging for the Rose began. Clause 28 reads:

A local authority shall not:

a) intentionally promote homosexuality or publish material with the intention of promoting homosexuality;

b) promote the teaching in any maintained school of the acceptability of homosexuality as a pretended family relationship.

Addendum: Nothing in subsection one shall be taken to prohibit the doing of anything for the purpose of treating or preventing the spread of disease.

(*Index on Censorship*, September 1988: 39)

In short, representations of homosexuality are acceptable if they yoke it with disease: all "positive" representations are prohibited. At the Olivier Awards in 1988 McKellen came out again and outlined the danger Clause 28 would do to theater in particular.[26] Under the rules of Clause 28, Marlowe's *Edward II*, an uncannily frequently cited example in the press coverage of the bill's passage, could not be taught or performed in schools.[27] By the time McKellen began campaigning to save the Rose he was a well-known political fighter for gay rights. And by the time Ridley publicly claimed his dissimilarity from Oscar Wilde he was a well-known opponent of such rights. In short, the opposition between McKellen and Ridley had a history before the Rose was unearthed.

At the end of 1990 McKellen was awarded a knighthood, which he accepted. On 4 January 1991 Derek Jarman, a self-identified "queer artist with HIV" whose film of Marlowe's *Edward II* makes the parallels between contemporary gay society and Marlowe's world very clear, wrote a letter to the *Guardian* criticizing McKellen for accepting a knighthood from a government "which has stigmatized homosexuality through [Clause 28] . . . and is poised [. . .] to take important steps toward recriminalizing homosexuality." Jarman continues, "I think it's a co-option and allows anyone to say: 'The Tory party isn't so bad: it's not really anti-gay. After all, it gave Ian McKellen a knighthood.'" Jarman's letter set off a round of defenses, in which more theater professionals came out as lesbians or gays.[28] Many of the letters noted McKellen's public attacks on the homophobia of the Tory party. He was also loudly praised for his efforts to raise funds for AIDS research with his one-man Shakespeare performances.

At the heart of the debate about the Rose there is another debate about access to vital and fatal male bodies, a debate which is informed at every turn by the AIDS crisis. That this debate would touch a political discussion about the remains of a theater, Marlowe's theater, is not a coincidence. Acting has long been associated with male homosexuality, in part because mainstream modern Western acting is about the creation of a *double* body. The actor is trained to reproduce the gestures, bearing, and "being" of some other body, the "character." In this culture, the visible display of a double body is naturalized by the body of the pregnant woman – which is not to say that this image creates no psychic anxiety.[29] In Adrian Spigelius' *De formato foetu*, a plate prepared by Casserius, but first published in Padua in Spigelius' 1626

Figure 5.3   De Formato Foetu, Adrian Spigelius, 1626

text, shows the fetus nestled on top of a woman's body in a flower (see Figure 5.3).[30] Before the history of anatomy secured the corpse, the pregnant woman was rendered as a fecund human flower – a doubly flowering Rose.

When men attempt to display two bodies at once they are labeled effeminate. This is part of the long-held suspicion that male actors are homosexuals. (And the hope that maybe homosexuals are only acting out, going through a phase.[31] This homophobia is also part of the long-held suspicion of theater as a "high" cultural form in the United States.)

The architectural challenge raised by the excavation of the Rose asked that an office building become a double body. In the proposed plans, there is an implicit feminization of the building, and a marked theatricality to the designs. The architectural proposal of John Burrell imagines the building as a tall column abutted by a swollen base (see Figure 5.4). This double body was rejected because at twenty-six storeys it was seen as "too tall" (Eccles 1990: 227). The so-called "office on stilts" was the preferred plan. The office on stilts, in name, if not in design, may remind us of the "intolerable image of a man, legs high in the air, unable to refuse the suicidal ecstasy of being a woman" (Bersani 1987: 212). Legs akimbo, the office building squats on the Southwark bridge. Beneath it, the Rose remains remain covered in sand.

It comes as only a dull surprise to note that the magical "office on stilts" which would preserve *and* display the remains "intact for all to see" (the phrase is Ridley's) *and* allow "office business" to be performed, has not yet materialized. Imry Merchant was purchased by Marketchief in July 1989. A year later, Ridley resigned his post after an interview in which he spoke skeptically about Germany's role in the new European community caused outrage. Displaying his "private" opinion "intact for all to see," Ridley exposed his own vulnerability. Drawing on the Tory version of national myth and memory, Ridley said it was up to England to hold the balance in the new Europe against the "uppity" Germans (Ridley 1990). While this was an idea that Thatcher was acting on without announcing, Ridley's public exposure of this belief let out a dark secret, and thus Ridley himself was le(f)t out of Thatcher's Cabinet.

After the new building was complete, the Government did schedule the Rose, thus avoiding the cost of compensating the developers and leaving the problem of finding the funds to display the Rose in the hands of John Major. The minimum estimate for display is 1.65 million pounds (see Tait 1991). As of this writing (September 1993), the Rose remains are in a deep hole, covered in sand and invisible to the public. Above them the new office building, aptly called Rose Court, sits completely empty. Opened now for twenty months, Rose Court has been unable to find a single tenant. Thus, what has been produced is the *preservation* of the Rose remains; there is no public display and no office business. An ironic monument to monuments, the new building's tombstone-grey facade faces the austere black and gold of the *Financial Times* building directly across the street.

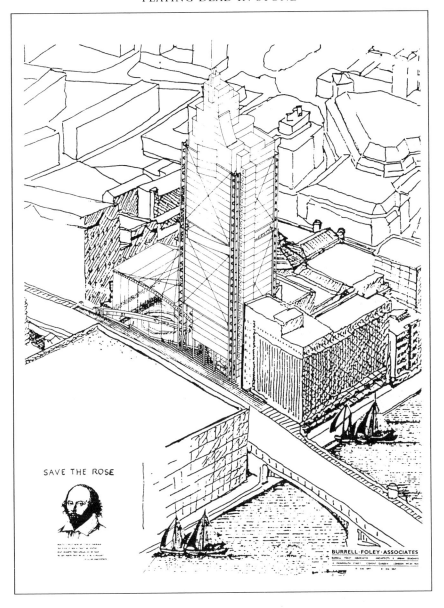

Figure 5.4 Drawing of the Rose Theatre site (Burrell Foley Fischer)

In psychoanalytic terms, the desire to preserve the object is associated with the anal drive. This drive is the foundation for the ability to hide and to keep secrets. Part of the uneasy humor provoked by Ridley's attempt to distance himself from Wilde is that Wilde himself was forced to live a life in which he was left with nothing to hide. As a "convicted sodomite" Wilde's holes were publicly exposed. Contemporary politicians, of course, have turned hiding into a fine art. The political similarities between Marlowe's world of deathly reckonings and high-flying rhetoric and Ridley's own were accented both by the debates about footing the bill and by Ridley's stated antipathy toward the "uppity" Germans. Like a secret held too long, Ridley's remarks escaped his usually well-disciplined, tightly puckered lips. And for this momentary looseness, he lost his job.

The body exposed by the excavation and evacuation of the Rose site was a body with nothing to hide. (Evacuated of its drain pipe, its coins, popcorn, and odd shoes, the Rose remains were "removed.") It was flagrantly non-reproductive, a "disused mine." The burden of the story demonstrates that national myth and memory cannot tolerate (never mind "promote") unreproductive remains, any more than it can tolerate (or "promote") un-reproductive homosexual sex.[32] Both must be buried, repressed, and/or converted into (tourist) capital and reproductive knowledge.

NOTES

1 This paper has benefitted from the opportunity I had to read it in various forums: the American Society for Theater Research meetings in November 1992; the University of Exeter, Department of Theatre, March 1993; the University of Bristol, Department of Theatre, Film, and Television, March 1993; and Cornell University, February 1994. Remarks made in the ensuing conversations have influenced the current version and I would like to thank my interlocutors. I am also grateful to Christina Duffy, Carolyn Shapiro, Robert Sember, Lynda Hart, Timothy Murray, and Elin Diamond for helpful suggestions on previous drafts.

2 The popular press took up the idea that the nutshells found in the site were vestiges of Elizabethan audiences' food. But see Orrell 1992 for a full explanation of how the shells came to be there. They actually comprise part of the soap yard used to make the mortar for the theater. (They were also found at the Globe site.)

3 See Gurr 1991 for a full discussion of the production history of these plays.

4 For an extremely interesting analysis of the relationship between theater and archaeology see Tilley 1989.

5 See Eccles 1990, Biddle 1989, Orrell and Gurr 1989, Wainwright 1989, Foakes 1991, Kohler 1989, and Tait 1989 and 1991.

6 One of the most famous stories about Marlowe's *Faustus* is relevant here. Apparently during Act V when Faustus is carried off to Hell, the curtain at the Rose cracked and the audience became convinced they saw a real ghost, a real devil, and rushed out of the theater screaming. The remains of the Rose that appeared in the cracked ground of contemporary Southwark can be said to have promoted a similar panic about ghostly bodies.

7   For a comparison of the two excavations and their value for theater historians see Gurr 1991.

8   One section of this quote is taken from Tait 1989.

9   It is only fair to note that both Thatcher and Ridley were in favor of preserving the Rose; they simply were trying to avoid paying for it. Ridley's decision not to schedule the Rose was made after the thirty-day "breathing space" had been granted. He said he believed the site would be preserved "voluntarily" and that it was not necessary for the Government to prohibit the developers from having their building. He did say that it might be necessary to schedule the Rose at a later date. See *Antiquity*, September 1989, "Editorial." On 11 May 1989 Thatcher said, "everything must be done to preserve those remains so that one day they may be on public display" (in Eccles 1990: 170). This statement probably inspired Ridley's million-pound thirty-day "breathing space" four days later.

10 The legal obligations are summarized straightforwardly in the *Antiquity* "Editorial." Estimated costs of this compensation were over 60 million pounds.

11 See Transcript from House of Commons 16 May 1989. All quotes from the politicians are taken from this piece and supplemented by Parris 1989.

12 Beaumont-Dark's impatience with urban archaeology may have been due to the fact that the Rose was the third archaeological crisis to reach Parliament that year. The Huggin Hill site in London and the Queen's Hotel site in York had also created public outcries. See *Antiquity* "Editorial."

13 For a more detailed discussion of the historical links between theaters and illicit sex, see Sinfield 1991.

14 Regarding the 1985 coal-mine strikes see, for example, Getler 1985; and for the 1992 legacy see Robinson 1992.

15 As we shall see, it is my contention that the Rose itself could not be smoothly reproduced within the heterosexual reproductive economy upon which the construction of national myth and memory depend.

16 For a fascinating post-Foucauldian discussion of the "invention" of history see Davis and Starn 1989.

17 Lynda Hart has argued that much of the "drama" around homosexuality involves a challenge about seeing homosexuals at all. For an extended argument about this in relation to lesbians see Hart 1994; for a briefer treatment see Hart 1993. For a discussion of visibility, theater, and gay men see Sinfield 1991.

18 This is what is stated in the Thomas Baines note, the note supplied to the authorities after Marlowe's death.

19 These remarks are confined to modern Western burial practices. In no way are these remarks intended as an "anthropology" of burial practices.

20 One of the most intriguing motivating aspects of the political uncertainty and about-facing done by the Tory Government in relation to the Rose derived from the fact that the theatrical "body" of the Rose had not fully decomposed, disappeared, died, as most people would expect a building built in 1587 to do. The very fact that it could be recovered and seen at all was an enormous shock – despite the fact that Hughes (and others) had predicted it would be well preserved. Not above exploiting the psychic consequences of this shock, George Dennis, from the Museum of London, "brandished the bone, now known to have come from a European Brown Bear, as evidence that the spoil produced by piling was not being recorded by English Heritage" (Eccles 1990: 230). The bear bone functioned as the indexical image of the always shocking and uncanny force of the historical/corpo/Real.

21 On the other side of the terror of decomposition, there is a rigid demarcation and policing of who can decompose and where. For example, part of the reason

Roman Catholic doctrine does not allow people who commit suicide to be buried in Catholic cemeteries is because the leaking body of the sinner who sins against God, must not sully the bodies of those sinners who (merely) sin against men. A murderer is less damnable than one who commits suicide because, theologically, God "intended" the one who was murdered to die that way. The victim's death was in the hands of God. But the person who commits suicide inscribes his or her own death and that is the deepest violation of the Law of the Father. Not surprisingly, the Catholic Lacan thought suicide was the only successful act: see Zizek 1992.

22 I am adapting Leo Bersani's argument about literature, especially Proust, in the opening chapter of his *The Culture of Redemption*. It may well be that "inscription" as such – from tattooing to stamp designing – functions to appease the terror of decay beating away in time itself.

23 For different contemporary meditations on the ontological relationship between theater and architecture see *Perspecta* 1990.

24 Rachel Moore argues: "we look across boundaries of space at the living rather than across time at the dead" (Moore 1992: 23). It may well be that spatial art forms are fundamentally philosophies of vital bodies and temporal art forms are philosophies of dying bodies. It may be that the work of mourning requires movement and motion – the transformation of space into time.

25 For a discussion of contemporary art as the art of dying see Phelan Winter 1993.

26 For a very inspiring and helpful conversation about McKellen's coming out I am grateful to John McGrath.

27 For a representative article see Billen 1988. Note the word "even": "Since most regional theaters are in part funded by local authorities, the Bill, if it becomes law, could preclude [teaching/presenting] such plays as *The Normal Heart, Bent* and even Christopher Marlowe's *Edward II.*"

28 In a Group letter from "gay and lesbian artists" defending McKellen, twelve men and two women sign. In debates such as these women usually take up about one/sixth of the visual field.

29 For a fuller discussion of the psychic anxieties raised by pregnancy for men see Phelan 1993.

30 I am grateful to Jane Malmo for calling this image to my attention. Her own fascinating work on Renaissance anatomy is forthcoming.

31 For a thorough critique of this notion see Sinfield 1991.

32 Anxiety about "promoting" unreproductive sex also motivates the theater of abortion protests in the United States. In other words, the opposition I am trying to highlight here is not exclusively a hetero/homo divide – it is more of a reproductive/nonreproductive divide.

REFERENCES

Antiquity 63. 240 (Sept. 1989): "Editorial," 411–13.

Appleyard, Bryan (26 Sept. 1984) "The Globe Cast as Political Football," *The Times.*

Bersani, Leo (Winter 1987) "Is the Rectum a Grave?" *October* 43: 197–222.

—— (1990) *The Culture of Redemption*, Cambridge, Mass. and London: Harvard University Press.

Biddle, Martin (Dec. 1989) "The Rose Reviewed: A Comedy (?) of Errors," *Antiquity* 63. 241: 753–60.

Billen, Andrew (23 Jan. 1988): "Arts Council Criticizes 'Gay' Clause," *The Times.*

Billington, Michael (9 July 1987) "An American in London Plans a Restored Globe Theater," *New York Times*: C17.

Cerassano, S. P. (Winter 1989) "Raising a Playhouse from the Dust," *Shakespeare Quarterly* 40. 4: 483–90.

Davis, Natalie Zemon and Starn, Randolph (Spring 1989) "Memory and Counter-Memory," a special issue of *Representations*, 26.

Drakakis, John (1988) "Theatre, Ideology, and Institution: Shakespeare and the Roadsweepers," in *The Shakespeare Myth*, ed. Graham Holderness, Manchester: Manchester University Press, pp. 24–41.

Eccles, Christine (1990) *The Rose Theatre*, London and New York: Nick Hern, Routledge.

Foakes, R. A. (1991) "The Discovery of the Rose: Some Implications," *Shakespeare Survey* 43: 141–8.

Freud, Sigmund (1937) "Constructions in Analysis," *Standard Edition* vol. 23: 259.

Getler, Michael (6 Mar. 1985) "Year-old British Coal Strike Ends in Confusion," *Washington Post*: A1.

Group letter (9 Jan. 1991) [defending McKellen] the *Guardian*.

Gurr, Andrew (18 Oct. 1991) "The Glory of the Globe," *Times Literary Supplement*: 5–6.

Hart, Lynda (1993) "Identity and Seduction: Lesbians In the Mainstream," in *Acting Out: Feminist Performances*, ed. by Lynda Hart and Peggy Phelan, Michigan: University of Michigan Press: 119–40.

—— (1994) *Fatal Women: Lesbian Sexuality and the Mark of Aggression*, Princeton: University of Princeton Press.

Hollier, Denis (1989) *Against Architecture: The Writings of Georges Bataille*, trans. Betsy Wing, Cambridge, Mass. and London: MIT Press.

Index on Censorship Sept. 1988, London: Writers and Scholars International.

Kohler, Richard (Winter 1989) "Excavating Henslowe's Rose," *Shakespeare Quarterly* 40. 4: 475–82.

Miller, D. A. (Summer 1990) "The Late Jane Austen," *Raritan*: 55–79.

Moore, Rachel (Fall 1992) "Marketing Alterity," *Visual Anthropology Review*: 8. 2: 16–6.

Orgel, Stephen (1975) *The Illusion of Power: Political Theater in the English Renaissance*, Berkeley and Los Angeles: University of California Press.

Orrell, John (Spring 1992) "Nutshells at the Rose," *Theatre Research International*, 17. 1: 8–15.

—— and Gurr, Andrew (June 1989) "What the Rose Can Tell Us," *Antiquity* 63. 239: 421–89.

Parris, Matthew (16 May 1989) "Art of Stealing the Limelight," *The Times*: 17.

Pellizzi, Fancesco (Spring 1990) "Tombstone: Four Pieces and a Coda on the Idea of Burial," *Terrazzo* 4: 77–92.

Perspecta (1990) *The Yale Architecture Journal*, 26, a special issue on "Theater, Theatricality, and Architecture."

Phelan, Peggy (Fall 1991) "Money Talks, Again," *Tulane Drama Review: a journal of performance studies*: 131–42.

—— (1993) "White Men and Pregnancy: Discovering the Body to be Rescued," in *Unmarked: the Politics of Performance*, New York and London, Routledge: 130–45.

—— (Winter 1993) "Radical Democracy and the Woman Question," *American Literary History*: 750-64.

Ridley, Nicholas (14 July 1990) "Interview" [on Germany], the *Spectator*.

Robinson, Eugene (22 Dec. 1992) "British Court Rebuffs Move by Government to Shut Mines," *Washington Post: A17*.

Sinfield, Alan (Fall 1991) "Private Lives/Public Theater: Noel Coward and the Politics of Homosexual Representation," *Representations* 36: 43–61.

Souster, Mark (14 July 1989) "Clash over Wreath for Lord Olivier at the Rose," *The Times*: 1.

Tait, Simon (17 May 1989) "Value of the Rose Theatre Site Highlighted in 1971," *The Times*: 1.

—— (5 June 1991) "Rose Theatre 'could attract 150,000 visitors a year,'" *The Times*.

Tilley, Christopher (June 1989) "Excavation as Theatre," *Antiquity*, 63. 239: 275–80.

Transcript from House of Parliament (16 May 1989) "Rose Theatre Site Wins a Breathing Space," *The Times*: 12–13.

Wainwright, G. J. (Sept. 1989) "Saving the Rose," *Antiquity* 63. 240: 430–35.

Watney, Simon (1989) *Policing Desire*, Minneapolis: University of Minnesota Press (2nd edn).

Zizek, Slavoj (1992) "Why Is *Woman* a Symptom of Man?" in *Enjoy Your Symptom!*, New York and London: Routledge, 1992: 31–67.

6

SPECTACLES OF SUFFERING

Performing presence, absence, and historical memory at U.S. Holocaust museums

Vivian M. Patraka

No term is fixed forever in its meaning (unless it has become invisible through disuse); rather it constitutes a set of practices and cultural negotiations in the present. Thus the narrative of making meaning out of the term "Holocaust" continues. The public performance of the term among Jews is multiple, varying in different cultural sites and being used for differing political agendas and pedagogical purposes. The search for the best term to designate the Jewish genocide outlines an attempt to mark both its historical specificity and its uniqueness. This uniqueness has been linked to the extent of the perpetrator's intentionality, the degree to which the state apparatus legalized the devastation, the measure of its use of "technological weapons of destruction" (Stannard 151), and the number of people killed. But every genocide, in the particularities of its specific history, is unique. And while each genocide is known by this distinct history, it also is understood in the context of other genocides even though these relationships are not ones of simple analogy or equivalence.

While both the terms "Holocaust" and "genocide" were originally conceived to respond to the events in Europe against the Jews, genocide quickly took on the status of a generic, both describing the persecutions of other groups during this period and providing a means for defining actions against groups that would constitute genocidal destruction. Moreover, however proprietary the claims on the use of the term Holocaust have been in some quarters, the evocative power of the term has begun to extend its use tropologically to contemporary considerations of the destruction of groups other than Jews. Perhaps this is precisely because the term genocide functions as a delimiting generic, while Holocaust brings with it all the protocols of the unspeakable, the incommensurate, and a sense of unlimited scope to the pain and injustice. Or perhaps Holocaust connotes not just the violent moment of elimination of a whole people, but all that goes into it: the beginning of terror and circulating discourses of oppression and exclusion, the constructing of a state apparatus of oppression and the disinformation it produces,

89

the incarcerations, the annihilation, and then the revolting denials and cleanups. The entire array of cultural, social, and political forces amassed to effect genocide may be historically embedded in the term Holocaust.

No historical referent is either stable, transparent in its meaning, agreed upon in its usage, or even engaged with in the same way by any large group of people. One way of contextualizing the current movement of the term Holocaust is by invoking Michel de Certeau's distinction between a place and a space in his application of spatial terms to narrative. For de Certeau, the opposition between "place" and "space" refers to "two sorts of stories" or narratives about how meaning is made. Place refers to those operations that make its object ultimately reducible to a fixed location, "to the *being there* of something dead, [and to] the law of a place" where the stable and "the law of the 'proper'" rules. Place "excludes the possibility of two things being in the same location." "Space occurs as the effect produced by the operations that orient it, situate it, temporalize it, and make it function in a polyvalent way." Thus space is created "by the actions of historical *subjects*." These actions multiply spaces and what can be positioned within them. Finally, the relationship between place and space is a process whereby "stories thus carry out a labor that constantly transforms places into spaces or spaces into places" (117–18). De Certeau's distinction between a place and a space is crucial to my argument in the way it clarifies the differing strategies of attempting to move people through a landscape whose meanings are uniquely determined, in contrast to providing an opportunity for contestation and multiplicity of association.

Though the domain of the Holocaust is mass death, the narrative(s) created about it need not make it an immobile, tomblike place nor create an inert body of knowledge intended only to conserve and preserve. Producers of public discourse on the Holocaust can actively engage in redefining this space so that, as I'll presently show, even the seemingly standard definition of the Holocaust as relating solely to Jews comes under interrogation at sites as formal as Holocaust museums and their fundraising materials. And while I do not mean to be facile about the terrible stakes involved in memorializing these events, a narrative space for producing knowledge of the Holocaust – one that would construct its consumers as actively engaged in producing meanings – might be a powerful means to prolonging remembrance. Even if some contemporary groups do deliberately use the term Holocaust in a way designed to compete with or even erase the original referent, if we assert an exclusive, proprietary claim over the term in response, we run the risk of magnifying one current perception: that the discourse of Jewish Holocaust functions as a kind of controlling or hegemonic discourse of suffering that operates at the expense of the sufferings of other groups. Instead, the notion of space, rather than mutually exclusive places, could signify a discourse on the Holocaust in which genocide stories of different groups could occupy the same locale without necessarily ejecting or evacuating the original referent of Jewish history and suffering. Even so, I wonder whether so much of the history of the Jewish genocide, the meanings attached to it, even the ethical, cultural and linguistic protocols of where to look for meaning about such events, is so deeply embedded in the word Holocaust as to make the Jewish genocide a paradigmatic frame for other genocides located with the term.

Given all of these risks, it is worth considering how the referent of the Holocaust is configured by contemporary American Jews. Despite the very palpable differences among us, both culturally and politically, it is still the case that many of our responses to the images, objects, and words connected to the Holocaust are "hard wired," provoking automatic emotional meanings and an attitude of reverence. This makes it hard to get beyond a consensus on the agony, the loss, and the mindful viciousness that produced them so we can discern the actual discourse generated about the Holocaust and how it functions. Some of the strategies of this discourse are manipulative; they solicit our anguish, horror, and fear as the grounds for asserting larger meanings to which we may not wish to assent. But neither avoidance of the places in which these "fixed" narratives reside nor simple dismissal is, I think, useful. For this would risk separating us from our own emotions about the Holocaust, entombing them in these monumental stories so that they are no longer available for either examination or change. Instead, we have to create spaces for critique within and among those seemingly inevitable emotional hard-wirings and the places to which they get connected.

I offer the discussion below as a step in that direction. I explore how the referent of the Holocaust is currently being configured at sites in the United States where a cultural performance of Holocaust history is being staged for public consumption – the U.S. Holocaust Memorial Museum in Washington D.C., and the Beit Hashoah Museum of Tolerance in Los Angeles. My purpose in doing so is to honor this history, but also to renegotiate its effects by rethinking the set of practices set up by these two important museums for the sake of both the present and the future. I also want to view each of the museums against the background of their mass-mailed fundraising letters to explore some of their ideological underpinnings. In doing so, I want to mark both the ideological underpinnings that are fulfilled by each museum and those that are dislodged, whether deliberately by the designers or by museum-goers themselves.

THE U.S. HOLOCAUST MEMORIAL MUSEUM AND ITS FUNDRAISING MATERIALS

In order to elicit donations, the fundraising materials for the United States Holocaust Memorial Museum in Washington, D.C. indicate what the museum promises to accomplish – a self-presentation that represents the main thrust of this institution (Bal 558), prefiguring many of the strategies designed for the museum itself. I believe the target audience for these fundraising

91

letters is, primarily, the American Jewish community, while the letters identify the target spectatorship for the museum as the public at large. A captioned photograph locates the museum by its proximity to the Washington Monument as a means of validating it spatially as a national project. Quotations by Presidents Carter, Reagan, and Bush about the Holocaust further authenticate this undertaking, along with a 1945 statement by Eisenhower – not as President, but as General and liberator – asserting that he could give "firsthand evidence" of the horrors he saw "if ever there develops a tendency to charge these allegations merely to 'propaganda'." Also included on the flyer is an official-looking image of the 1980 Public Law to create an independent federal establishment that will house "a permanent living memorial museum to the victims of the Holocaust" ("a short walk from our great national memorials" and hence, implicitly, connected to them). The effect of this is deliberately to blur the boundaries between the privately sponsored and the governmentally mandated.

Of course, any Holocaust museum must enter into a dialogue with the country in which it is located and the positioning of that country in these events, but the D.C. museum's emphasis on its geographies of announcement is insistent. A clear anxiety about denials of both the events of the Holocaust and its moral significance for Americans is embedded in these recurrent claims for legitimacy, even if some of the hyperbolic language can be chalked up to the discourse of fundraising, which in itself constitutes a kind of melodrama of persuasion. Inevitably, an American Holocaust museum is caught on the cusp of happened here/happened there, a conundrum, as James Young formulated it (Young 1992), over whether American history means events happening here or the histories Americans carry with them.

Presumably, then, learning about the events of the Holocaust, *precisely* because they didn't happen here, creates what one newsletter calls a "meaningful testament" to the values and ideals of democracy, thereby inscribing it within the history of American democracy, if not American history *per se*. It could be argued, then, that in this museum the Constitution is to be viewed through the prism of Jewish history as much as Jewish history is to be viewed through the prism of the Constitution. Thus one of the central strategies of the museum is to assert the way in which American mechanisms of liberal democratic government would prevent such a genocidal action from occurring in the United States, as well as partially to overlap, for the U.S. viewer, the perspective of the victims of genocide with that of the victors in World War II. This latter aspect would enhance what Philip Gourevitch describes as the museum's project to reinforce "the ethical ideals of American political culture by presenting the negation of those ideals" as well as our historical response to them (55). In fact, images of American troops liberating the concentration camps constitute part of the final exhibit of the museum as well as the opening tactic of the Holocaust exhibit proper, where all that is seen and heard is presented through the eyes and ears of the liberating soldiers. Even the survivor testimony played for us in an amphi-theater at the end of the exhibit prominently includes one narrative by a Holocaust survivor who eventually married the soldier who liberated her. Indeed, this marriage emplotment seems to embody a crucial strategy of the whole museum, with Jews and Jewish history (the feminized victim) married to American democracy (the masculinized liberator). Recalling that the American liberator in this survivor testimony is Jewish as well, I must note another, more implicit enactment in the museum, that of consolidating an American Jewish identity by marrying the positions of liberator and victim.

If what is critical for the museum's project is to extend our fictions of nationhood by the premise that a democratic state comes to the aid of those peoples outside its borders subjected to genocide, then the conferring of liber-ation becomes the story of American democracy. To assert this story entails backgrounding the masses of people who died before liberation (as opposed to the pitiful remnant left). It entails foregrounding the assumption that waging war can actually accomplish something and, more precisely, that saving Jews, Gypsies, Leftists, Catholic Dissenters, Homosexuals, and Polish forced labor from the Nazis was one of the goals of World War II, rather than a by-product of winning the war by invading the enemies' territory. I could dismiss the museum's overall strategy as a simplistic appeal to hegemonic structures of governance. But to do so would be to deny that the museum *must engage* United States viewers with an ethical narrative of national iden-tity in direct relation to the Holocaust. The alternative is to risk becoming a site for viewing the travails of the exoticized Other from elsewhere ("once upon a time"), or, even worse, "a museum of natural history for an endan-gered species" (Bal 560).

Moreover, the museum itself does not produce this idea of liberation from genocide as a completely unproblematic and unquestioned historical reality. Within the physical and conceptual envelope of its democratic discourse, the museum offers viewers a display of documents, including actual telegrams, that communicate how, as late as February of 1943, with the Final Solution fully operational in European death camps, the State Department tried to shut down the channels for receiving information about what was happening to European Jews (Berenbaum 1993 161–2). This policy of suppression of information about and denial of aid to European Jews was challenged only by the intense labor of several men in the Treasury Department whose efforts finally culminated in Randolph Paul's January 1944 "Report to the Secretary [of the Treasury] on the Acquiescence of This Government in the Murder of the Jews." To make a long, painful story short, in January 1944, Secretary of the Treasury Morgenthau took this informa-tion to Franklin D. Roosevelt, persuading him to establish the War Refugee Board by threatening (in a presidential election year) to release documents pertaining to the government's suppression of information and assistance (Berenbaum 1993 163–4).

93

Despite the references to its proximity to national memorials in the fundraising materials, the museum is actually closest physically to four mundane-looking government buildings, including the Treasury Building diagonally across the street. Much has been made of the way the museum copies the blocky functionality of these buildings in its initial entranceway, because this entrance is a false one, without a roof, while the actual doors to the museum are located several feet behind it. Thus the facade of the building recreates the solemn, neoclassical, and universalizing style of the government buildings around it, but marks its relationship to them as architecturally false. However, the documents issuing from the Treasury Building during the 1940s manifest another relationship, one based in precise historical detail, previously suppressed. This creates a chronotopic connection, i.e., a scene of interaction produced simultaneously out of temporal and spatial relationships, between the two buildings and the histories they contain. In offering this information, the museum constructs a localized historical contradiction to its own ideological claims about how democracies respond to genocides, thereby complicating the narrative of our national identity and, in so doing, turning an ostensible narrative place into a space for negotiating meanings.

However, while my reading of the actual museum emphasizes sites for constructing multiple meanings and relationships, the fundraising materials recall the larger ways in which the exhibits are to function. One flyer promises the museum will orchestrate our emotions in the mode of a spectacle designed to command attention, transfix spectators, and narrativize in advance the experience of those who approach it: "You will watch, horrified" and "you will weep" over this "heroic and tragic story." There is also an overpowering sense of desire in all these descriptions, a need to create an utterly convincing spectacle that will say it all, stop time and space, prevent denial and make the suffering known. Of course, no representation can do that, even if we hear the "actual voices of death camp survivors tell of unspeakable horror and pain." How could the unspeakable of genocide be spoken? How could the interiority of individual suffering on a massive scale be turned into an exterior, if respectful, spectacle? Perhaps the consuming desire for the real in representation, for the convincing spectacular, is inversely proportionate to the process of genocide itself, which is not spectacularized, but silent, dispersed, concealed, and denied. But the personal artifacts that the letters claim will be collected in one of the museum's rooms – the suitcases, hair brushes, razors, photographs, diaries, dolls, toys, shoes, eyeglasses, and wedding rings – despite their vivid materiality, are finally only the small detritus of annihilation that point to the inevitable absence of complete representation.

And yet, in practice, even the sites of artifacts whose meaning is intended to be self-evident can become spaces, instead of places, changed by the paths visitors themselves create as historical subjects. The museum went to great pains, including revising its architectural plans, to exhibit a fifteen-ton freight car used to deport Jews. Walking through it offers us a physical trace of the frightening darkness and claustrophobic agony of the 100 people crushed into this and other such cars. But as I moved toward this traincar on the second day of my visit to the museum, I was approached by a married couple, Mrs. Sonya Zissman and Mr. Harold Zissman, who noticed I was speaking into a tape recorder and came to talk to me. Both had been involved in resistance in rural Poland. They criticized the museum for overemphasizing victimization in its portrayal of the Holocaust, while not including enough material on Jewish acts of resistance in its exhibit. Pointing to the freight car, Mrs. Zissman told me they had been part of a group that had managed to blow up several trainloads of German soldiers. She grinned at me and said, "We gave them hell." They also both wept; this isn't a happy story. The live performance of survivor testimony by the Zissmans, "unmanaged" as it was by the museum proper, powerfully produced me as an engaged witness to their history, forcing me to negotiate their "unofficial" story with the "official" one surrounding it. What this conversation especially marked for me was how the museum's larger project of locating itself within a narrative of democracy displaced representations of acts of resistance by Jews in order to embed its narrative in the frame of American liberation. In other words, ideologically speaking, liberation requires a victim; there don't have to be resisters.

THE BEIT HASHOAH MUSEUM OF TOLERANCE AND ITS FUNDRAISING MATERIALS

In the process of evaluating aspects of the U.S. Memorial Holocaust Museum, I've asked myself "Just what would *you* have such a museum do? Position spectators as complicitous bystanders? As potential perpetrators of genocide? Who would come to such a museum?" The answers to these questions are not self-evident. Locale and funding sources play a part in shaping what a Holocaust museum shows and who sees it. That the United States Holocaust Memorial Museum identifies itself as a national project, imbricates the Holocaust into our national narratives, and keeps a tight focus on the history of the Holocaust, suits its Washington, D.C. locale and its federal grant of extremely scarce land. Although privately funded, its quasi governmental status helps produce what is and is not displayed within its walls.

The Beit Hashoah Museum of Tolerance is located in Los Angeles, adjacent to the Simon Wiesenthal Center (to which it is organizationally connected). It was built on private land, but received considerable funding from the State of California. As a result, this museum has a more insistent emphasis on pedagogy and is more explicitly targeted for school children and adolescents, although adjacent claims for extremely current technologies of representation are clearly intended to lure the public at large and attract funding from private donors. Under the rubric of teaching tolerance by providing examples of intolerance, it can display injustice in the United States and include a multiracial awareness of past and current American events. It also responds to its more immediate locale, L.A., as a site of racial and ethnic tensions and includes those tensions in its exhibits (witness its speedy creation of an exhibit on the L.A. Uprising). While responding to the local, the museum also locates itself as an international project that globally documents past and present violations of human rights.

In accordance with these projects, the fundraising letters sent to private donors prior to the museum's opening employed a primary strategy opposite to that of the U.S. Holocaust Memorial Museum: The Beit Hashoah Museum of Tolerance would represent the United States as a site of "bigotry and intolerance," that is, as a potential place of genocide, with the Holocaust as the most horrific illustration of where intolerance could lead. While the D.C. museum quoted U.S. presidents to authenticate its project, the Beit Hashoah's Charter Member fundraising flyer quotes Martin Luther King, Jr.: "Like life, racial understanding is not something that we find, but something that we must create." Thus the Beit Hashoah articulates the history of the Holocaust to an American landscape of prejudice and racism, a more liberal narrative that, to some degree, troubles our sense of national identity if not, as will be noted later, our fictions of nationhood. Moreover, given its claim to respond to and represent the international, the national, and the local, the focus of the museum is as diffuse (despite the presence of Holocaust exhibits that take up a fair share, but by no means most, of the museum's space and much, but not all, of the fundraising descriptions) as the U.S. Memorial Holocaust Museum's focus is specific. This diverse range of arenas configured under the rubric of intolerance is represented in the fundraising materials which describe the path of this museum as follows: First, visitors are confronted by ethnic and minority stereotypes as a means to challenge their current attitudes and perceptions. Second, they enter a Tolerance Workshop where they are given an "authentic social dilemma" and asked to choose and motivate others to moral action. Third, visitors view "stereotypical ethnic and racial depictions from early movies," hear demagogues vilifying minorities, and "meet" via video "individuals who have made a difference." Fourth, "in a series of illuminated, computer-synchronized tableaux," visitors "go back in time" to experience "the events of the Holocaust" and Nazism. Fifth, and finally, visitors stand before a replica of the Gates of Auschwitz and hear the voices of Holocaust victims speak of "suffering and heroism."

While I can appreciate the goals of a Holocaust museum that seeks to serve not only as a place to memorialize victims of persecution, but as a laboratory for combating hate, violence, and prejudice in the present, I note several problems in the strategies proposed to achieve this. The continued insistence that the museum presents "real life" obscures the way it is adjusting the parameters of a discourse. Moreover, while "persecution and devastation" have been the results of both anti-Semitism and racism, the museum risks creating an abstract equivalence between the two by configuring both as "an internalized matter of prejudice" (Bourne 14). When tolerance becomes a personal matter, it cannot, for example, take into account the way racism functions as "a structural and institutional issue" within a system of power "hierarchically structured to get the maximum benefit from differentiation" (14). Showing this system of exploitative differentiation is especially critical for a museum about genocide, since it is just this system that would profit most from the construction of competing narratives about the suffering of various groups, creating the divisiveness of what Berenbaum called "a calculus of calamity" (1990 34). I recognize this is exactly what the Beit Hashoah Museum of Tolerance is trying to avoid, but I don't think it takes its goals far enough. And missing from the museum's landscape of intolerance are the violent outbreaks of homophobia now occurring in the United States, as well as much mention of sexism: in practice the museum privileges racism as the site of intolerance, which is not surprising if its purpose is to forge links with other genocidal situations using the more traditional notions of "group" that govern definitions of genocide. Finally, the threat of genocide and even actions deemed potentially genocidal may not be the best measure for evaluating the everyday oppressions to which people and groups are subject, and such a treatment may even serve to minimize the importance of daily oppressions, especially when they are not in line with a teleological narrative of escalating violence.

And, despite its emphasis on the interactive, by ending with the gates of Auschwitz the museum takes the space it tries to open up for a consideration of the interconnections among oppressions and recontains it into a (computer-synchronized) place. Auschwitz becomes a monumental metonymy for the Holocaust, for all anti-Semitism(s), and for the consequences of intolerance. Using Auschwitz as an emblem of all anti-Semitism(s) may actually obscure the current mechanisms by which they function. Using Auschwitz as a metonymy for the consequences of intolerance facilitates the museum's Eurocentric gesture of locating its history of genocide only in the twentieth century. In so doing, the museum erases the historical reality that not only could genocide happen here, it *has* happened here, if not with the same obsessive deliberateness associated with the Final Solution. A museum with the goals of this one must take into account the massive genocidal annihilations in the Americas, and in particular, the United States, committed against indigenous peoples and against Africans during slavery.

Why doesn't it? Is showing genocide within our borders "going too far" for such a museum? More generally, should we assume that if the Jewish genocide in Europe were backgrounded in a site dedicated to showing intolerance, other genocides, indigenous to the United States, would inevitably become foregrounded, historically more visible? There are African American and Native American museums slated for the Smithsonian Mall, but, as Philip Gourevitch has noted (62), no Museum of Slavery or Trail of Tears museum. Perhaps recognizing the contributions of specific ethnicities, emphasizing what their continuing presence and vitality offers us as a nation, constitutes a celebratory means of covering over what was done to them and who and what has been permanently lost. Our democratic discourse must repress highly visible representations of any genocide that occurred within our own national borders. In order to sustain its fictions of nationhood and its imagined community, it must produce yet another set of highly visible representations of what it marks as a genocide occurring "elsewhere." From this perspective, it is the very performance of hegemonic democratic discourse, more pertinently our own "hard wired" fictions of nationhood, that we would need to interrogate and revise in order to make genocide "at home" visible.

But that still doesn't fully account for what is shown at the Beit Hashoah as the last big exhibit before the Holocaust wing and how it is situated: the multiscreen feature on the civil rights struggle, "Ain't You Gotta Right?", directed by Orlando Bagwell, who also directed the series "Eyes on the Prize." Between the civil rights film viewing area and the Holocaust wing, there's a peculiar little film displaying the lives of the rich in the 1920s. It's like a sorbet, a palette cleanser between two gourmet courses. Why this rupture? Perhaps because historically, the directional signals are different: the call for African American civil rights is the call for removing the last vestiges of genocidal slavery (when is massive slavery not genocidal?); the elimination of civil rights for Jews in Germany is the beginning of the escalation toward genocide, a teleological narrative that would not suit the African American example. The introduction to *Nationalisms and Sexualities* notes a convergence between the "persistence of nationalism explained as a passionate 'need,'" " and "the rights of sexual minorities legitimated through a discourse of civil liberties" (Parker *et al.* 2), suggesting our deep ideological and political investment in the arguments of legal personhood. Moreover, the call for extending democracy to everyone fits with our "imagined communities of nationalism" even if this assimilative model, drawing as it does on the experience of white ethnic immigrants to the U.S., fails to describe the circumstances of those brought here forcibly *to* genocidal conditions or those here before us submitted to them. The historical reality of slavery existing legally within democracy does not fit our national ideological fictions and is therefore always already in danger of being suppressed.

To some degree, then, the model of civil rights and tolerance used by the museum, though certainly useful, glosses over very different histories and obscures the ideological interconnections of genocidal events that "happened here" and "happened there." In other words it is problematic to assume that because of the history of the Holocaust, Jews can function as the best guides to the larger landscape of intolerance in this country; such an assumption imparts an overarching symbolic significance to the events of the Holocaust. And yet, to the degree that this museum and this ethnicity assume the responsibilities of representing oppressions beyond their own, they make a gesture more unparalleled in the U.S. than dismissals of this museum as a Disneyesque themepark would acknowledge. This museum, though flawed, is at least an ambitious first step toward putting the mechanisms of oppression (and not simply diversity) into public discourse.

PERFORMING PRESENCE, ABSENCE, AND TRAUMATIC HISTORY AT U.S. HOLOCAUST MUSEUMS

It is the museum-goers (along with the guards) who constitute the live, performing bodies in museums. They are the focus of a variety of performance strategies deployed by museums for the sake of "the production of knowledge taken in and taken home" (Bal 56). Some of these strategies produce the passivity and fascination of "gawking," some induce a confirming sense of "seeing" by covering over what cannot be "seen," and some position us to struggle *to see* at the same time we are conscious of our own difficult engagement in "seeing."

If this applies generally to museums, it has special significance for museums that represent the Holocaust. In a museum of the dead, the critical actors are gone, and it is up to us to perform acts of reinterpretation to make meaning and memory. To some degree, then, the usual museum situation (us looking at objects) is deployed/exploited to underscore the "goneness" of which they are only the remains. That is, a Holocaust museum can constitute a particular metonymic situation: inanimate material objects document and mark the "goneness" and the loss instead of simply substituting for them through representation. In this case, the enormity of the absent referent is neither contained nor scaled down through a representation that claims its presence over the terrible absence produced by genocide.

Holocaust Museum as Performance Site

Along with the notion of a moving spectatorship, the museum is a performance site in the sense that the architect, the designers, and the management of the museum produce representations through objects and so produce a space and a subjectivity for the spectator. The museum is a complicated, crowded stage, always soliciting a certain spectatorial gaze through very skilled presentations. Everything one sees in a museum is a production by somebody. A Holocaust museum, in particular, can be a performance environment where we are asked to change from spectator/bystander to witness, where we are asked to make our specific memory into historical memory. In a Holocaust museum, when we are really solicited to change, we are asked to become performers in the event of understanding and remembering the

Holocaust. If the self-depiction of the D.C. museum as "living memorial" is to be accurate, it is precisely because of this spectatorial performance.

Performance Place and Space

How is the concept of De Certeauian place versus space related to these museum sites? For my purposes, place refers to a pre-scripted performance of interpretation, while space produces sites for multiple performances of interpretation which situate/produce the spectator as historical subject. Performance place, then, is narrativized in advance, soliciting us to perform the script that is organized for and given to us. A clear example of such a performance place is the entrance to the tolerance section of the Beit Hashoah. We are faced with two sets of doors by which to enter – one set, outlined in bright red light, is marked "Prejudiced" and one set, outlined in green light, is marked "Unprejudiced." In actuality, the museum makes the decision for us: the "unprejudiced" doors are just a prop, unusable, and everyone is herded through the "prejudiced" doors when the computer-synchronized exhibit mechanism opens them. Although linked to a single narrative, place is more than that: it is a single performance of interpretation elicited by that narrative, in this case a forced acknowledgment of our own inevitable status as prejudiced. Moreover, our bodies are implicated in the task by performing the required movement.

De Certeau maintains that we all live in places but should think of them as spaces. The liberating move that allows us to understand the experience of everyday life is a move from place to space. When linked to performance, the de Certeauian model would suggest the difference between a pre-scripted performance and a site that invites multiple acts of interpretation. Indeed in de Certeauian space, interpretation itself becomes a kind of complex performance, a way of experiencing subjectivity. The environment of the museum is also performative: not only does it permit multiple acts of interpretation, museum design also provides multiple scenarios for these performances – scenarios whose relationship to each other is not narrativized in advance.

In one sense we can understand representation as a place concept, while performance is about space. But in another sense, both place and space construct the subject as a performer. If both are performances, the place of performance is more likely to be rigid, more about the spectacular or the quest for the Real, whereas performance space suggests multiple crisscrossing performances, the possibility of interpretations that foreground the historicity of the individual subject.

Throughout the D.C. museum, architectural detail creates a performance environment for multiple, overlapping spaces of interpretation. This especially pertains to the Hall of Witness, a huge, skewed, multi-storied, glass-topped courtyard at the center of the museum to which museum goers have free access (and which contains the museum information desk, some

spaces to rest, and so on). In this hall, repeating architectural detail reverberates associatively: the curved archways of brick and metal suggest a train
station for deportation; windowlike structures with geometric plates of metal
covering them suggest the small spaces of restricted visibility to the outside
world left after the ghettos were closed up; metal barred windows and
protruding single bulb lights suggest the outside of a concentration camp
(and structures resembling guard towers surround the glass-topped courtyard
ceiling); metal doors shaped like ovens (repeated in the doors to the archive
downstairs) along with metal slatted niches, whose slats open inward, suggest
the crematorium itself. These associative details resonate with the literal images
documenting these historical events, but rather than seeming pre-scripted,
they provide a sense of surprise and discovery, however ominous, for the
spectator.

Indeed, walking through the D.C. museum is performative in just this
sense of discovery. There has to be a cognitive moment when the spectator
realizes she is doing it (spectating), when she realizes she is *in* a doing. One
such cognitive moment at the D.C. museum hinges on how its designers
located the video monitors showing archival film footage. The monitors at
floor level are positioned in such a way that spectator crowding is required
even to see what is on the screen. On the middle floor, which includes the
most elaborate depictions of atrocity, some of the monitors are placed in a
kind of raised well, so that spectators already clustered tightly around the
well are jostled by those who come later who crowd in fairly aggressively to
see what the monitors depict. Once there, we view videos of grotesque medical
experiments forced by Nazi doctors upon concentration-camp inmates.
Physical agony and humiliation witnessed on screen combine with our awareness of pushing, or having been pushed, to see. What this performance
environment does is allow us to experience our subjectivity in unusual ways:
when we crowd around the monitors, we become voyeurs (and not a community of witness). Our curiosity *to see* is itself thrown back at us and we are
challenged, I think, to create a more self-conscious relationship to viewing
materials about atrocity, to take more responsibility for what we've seen.

Close by this video well, in a glass enclosed space with benches where we
hear Auschwitz survivor testimony (no visuals), the museum exploits spatial
possibilities differently. Here, in order to make out the words, we must share
looseleafs containing xeroxed testimony with other museum-goers. The only
other thing to look at in this space is the responses of other spectators to
this painful material on atrocity. The potential for physical intimacy in the
design of this exhibit space creates a site for community of witness; as strangers
we are confronted with the presence of others, other bodies with whom we
must cooperate. We experience multiple perspectives, the sense that no single
perspective can absorb this information.

In the Beit Hashoah, on the other hand, due to its more explicit pedagogical
purpose, the spectator's experience is more akin to the delimiting place of

representational theater. The materials in the first half of this exhibit are enclosed in raised dioramas, suggesting information that can be contained by a single representational frame. Each diorama includes the same three figures – an historian, a researcher, and an exhibit designer – cast out of plaster, ¾ sized (scale as a way of manipulating performance space), and unmoving. They could function in a self-referential way to make viewers aware of the constructedness of the narrative being presented, but they actually constitute another fixed frame for making meaning. Although the three "characters" can't "perform" physically on stage, media technologies such as voice-overs represent them, and films and videos that relate Holocaust history do the performing. Moreover, each diorama exhibit is computer-synchronized; each lights up and, after the timed presentation is finished, blacks out, just like a little theater. Groups of spectators led by a volunteer walk from the now-darkened site to the next one lighting up (against the darkness of the larger space for spectator movement) in the prescribed path. This mode of framed display means spectators have more equal access to the Holocaust information, but the guarantee of an equal place to each viewer comes at the price of restricted movement, passivity in response to "the show," and a place everyone engages in and moves through in a standardized way.

Holocaust History and "Manageability"

The exhibition was designed, in a number of places, to make you feel confused, disoriented, closed in. The same way that the people who lived during the Holocaust felt. It's narrow in more than one place during the exhibition. You think everything is going all right, you've come into a lot of space, and then all of a sudden it gets narrow again. It creates a mood. The whole exhibition.

> Museum guard at the United States Memorial
> Holocaust Museum, speaking to the author

You have to personalize the story. We are using technology to that end.
> Rabbi Marvin Hier, founder and Dean of the
> Simon Wiesenthal Center, about the Beit Hashoah[1]

In answer to the question of "How can we know the Holocaust?" both museums try to impart knowledge, not only about the history of these events, but about how to remember them. Ostensibly, the project of both museums is to make the unmanageable history of the Holocaust manageable.

Much of the U.S. Memorial Holocaust Museum presents the history of the Holocaust as an accretion of detail – shoes, documents, photographs, artifacts. The irony is that in an effort to make the unmanageable manageable, to give a sense of presence, of place, the D.C. museum conveys the incommensurability of loss by making the density of detail unmanageable for the spectator. We are forced to enact this unmanageability at what I refer to as the tower of pictures. During the exhibit, we must cross via walkways through a tower of pictures that is taller than the exhibit's three stories. The enlarged photographs, taken between 1890 and 1941, convey the quality of Jewish life and culture that was extinguished in the Polish town of Ejszyszki where no one Jewish survived. One virtue of these pictures is that they represent how these people wanted to be seen, rather than how the Nazis made them look or how they looked when the liberators found them. But while the photographs' arrangement in the structure of a tower keeps directing us to look up, the top photos are so high they recede into invisibility. So we rehearse with our bodies not only the immeasurability of the loss, but the imperfect structure of memory itself.

The museum's choice to include a roomful of nothing but piles of shoes produces another experience of unmanageable detail. The pile of shoes, a fraction of the masses of shoes collected by the Nazis, metonymically represent the murdered people who wore them and thus the unmanageability of the history to which they point. Because they are malleable enough to retain the shape of their owners with, here and there, a frivolous bow or tassel, each shoe provides an intimate remnant of an individual, which multiplied by thousands, coveys the magnitude of human loss without becoming abstracted or aestheticized. Moreover, in their very materiality the shoes mark presence as much as absence. Despite constantly blowing fans, the shoes smell from their own disintegration, and thus involve our bodies in making memory. The smell of the shoes is organic, like a live body, and in this way they become performers, standing in for the live bodies that are absent. To borrow Peggy Phelan's words in *Unmarked*, the shoes, as objects made to perform, do "not reproduce" what is lost, but "rather help us to restage and restate the effort to remember what is lost." The performativity of the shoes "rehearses and repeats the disappearance of the subject who longs always to be remembered" (Phelan 147).

In fact, the D.C. museum seems to acknowledge in its very architecture that such a modernist project of accretion is only a rearguard effort to produce manageability. The sense of this history as absence and as loss echoes through the great empty halls that alternate with the densely detailed exhibits. These large spaces of absence become part of the performance space: the horrific notion of absence, which is all one can really experience of the slaughter, is built into the museum architecture itself. Edifice produces edification. Inviting us into emptiness allows us an awareness of the unseeable of genocide. And, by its creation of subtle links among objects, repeating structures, and movement elicited from spectators, the D.C. museum provides resonances that are not limited to one narrative performance but positions spectators to perform in spaces that are, ultimately, unmanageable.

Even the seeming obviousness of the ideological envelope of democracy and liberation that encases the museum is overlaid with a subtler, less manageable narrative. There are metal gates throughout the inside and surrounding the outside of the museum (including the loading dock). They look, at first glance, like prison doors and so seem to fit in with the resonating architectural details I mentioned earlier. But within the Holocaust exhibit, unobtrusively located among other exhibits, is the artifact that inspired this repeated design: the double gates of a Jewish cemetery. We move in the topography of the desecrated dead of Jewish genocide whenever we enter this museum. The gates of the cemetery and the gates of the museum make it clear that the whole museum is a graveyard. Even the presidential inscriptions on the outside of the museum that confirm the "Americanness" of this project also look like inscriptions on giant tombstones, so that not even the most obvious ideological narrative is wholly manageable or usable. These gates in relation to this cemetery lend the museum a sense of unreality; it bursts out of the boxes, the containment, of the usual museum exhibit.

Moreover, this repeating graveyard structure relates to what I believe to be an unstated mission of this museum, the consolidation of a Jewish American identity that can include the Jewish genocide in Europe within the frame of Jewish identity in the United States. Whatever else can be said about its ideological implications and motives, this performance of "Americanization" is about living in the United States (in the wake of the Holocaust) *and* bringing our dead with us. Although this construction of Jewish collectivity is one to which we may have no right, at our American distance from these events, the designers of this museum appear to assert just such a claim.

While the D.C. museum acknowledges that it can never manage, the Beit Hashoah in L.A. primarily asserts the manageability of Holocaust history and of its relation to our experience and world view, however reverently it seeks to do this. In this it foregrounds its use of postmodern technologies, its applications of what Constance Penley and Andrew Ross term "technoculture," with its "postmodernist celebrations of the technological" and its employment of "new information and media technologies" (Penley and Ross xii). Much more of its design relies on computer-synchronized and computer-created exhibits. This, in a way, reduces history to information – information that then can be simulated and re-simulated through various performance technologies. That these media technologies are performance technologies is made especially clear when they are used to simulate and invoke live presence. The "Agent Provocator," as the museum calls him in its publicity – the white male middle-class guide to the tolerance exhibit who is designed to express "polite" or unthinking intolerance – repeatedly turns up. He appears as/on a pile-up of video monitors, each one a screen for a different part of his body. Since he only simulates tolerance in the first place, simulating him on multiple screens (like a creature with multiple media parts threatening to impinge on our frames of reference) is an effective visual deconstruction, as well as a comment on his cultural ubiquity.

The techniques of simulation (combined with the 1960s-type exhibit tech-nologies of the ¾ sized plaster-cast figures in the dioramas) employed to perform live presence are more problematic as used in the Holocaust section. If, generally at the Beit Hashoah, what is heard by visitors is privileged over what is read, this is especially true here. Music is used to narrativize our emotions in advance throughout the exhibit. Actor voice-overs, most often performing survivor testimony, are heard throughout as well. We are offered a kind of "you are there" melodrama of plaster figures seated at tables in a cafe (not in a diorama, but at our level) with voices of actors representing the figures' conversations about whether they should flee 1930s' Germany. We then are given a narrative of what happened to each of them, so it turns out these were "real" people whose situations are being simulated to create a theater of identification for us.

Finally, one diorama contains a holographic image of the table at Wannsee at which the Final Solution was planned. The table is littered with glasses, filled ashtrays, and so on, while voice-overs convey the Nazi presence. I know this "scene" ought to induce horror, but when I saw it, I was fascinated by the simulation itself and by how they made it and faintly embarrassed that I was peering at it as I would into a department-store window. Yet this is not surprising. Because in simulation there is no longer a link to the referent the copy passes itself off as the real, thereby covering over the historical trauma of the incommensurable absence of the genocidal referent.

More successful is another section of the museum called the Other America. It includes a large wooden colored map of the U.S. that charts the locations, state by state, of 250 hate groups. By touching a computer screen, visitors can choose to learn more about each group, but the entire body of infor-mation becomes unmanageable for a viewer. The map, itself frighteningly effective, is made more so by the use of computers, thereby constituting a combination of low and high tech that creates an unmanageable space.

In general, the Beit Hashoah has a postmodern project of presenting history as a flow of information. Sometimes it is a "one-way flow" of information (places for single performances of interpretation); sometimes there is a "multi-directional distribution of cultural and data flows" (spaces for multiple performances of interpretation) (Penley and Ross x–xi). Interestingly, one of the most extensive sites for multiple performances at the Beit Hashoah occurs in hyperspace. When visitors come in, they are directed to the top floor of the museum first. This floor contains an archival collection room, with the rest of it devoted to computer stations. Volunteer greeters of various ages and genders welcome us to these computers, urging us to play with them and giving us any information we might need to operate them. We need very little. At the D.C. museum, the computers only seem to path users to well-presented films of survivor testimony or to sounds of Jewish music; the effect is a de Certeauian "place" in hyperspace. But at the Beit Hashoah, we need only touch the screen with one finger to enter a space of multiple interconnections in which visitors can create multiple paths for information and multiple relationships among the Holocaust information offered.

If the D.C. museum alternates between intensity of detail and spaces of absence, neither of which is manageable, the Beit Hashoah creates manageability through simulation and a scaled-down narrative of Holocaust history. Moreover, in its focus on tolerance, the Beit Hashoah simulates social problems and prejudices in a way that asserts their manageability (i.e., places masquerading as interactive spaces) even if they're on sixteen different television screens at the same time. Located in a structure like a video arcade, multiple "tolerance" games can be played in any order. It is frenetic and noisy there. But the games are all abstracted encounters with difference that ultimately lead to the same one narrative about tolerance. In general, however, the way the L.A. museum's presentations are configured under the rubric of information makes them more available for contemporary linkages amongst differing cultural concepts and historical events related to the theme of intolerance. None the less, because of its urgent desire for *narrative* connections to the present, it is less available than the D.C. museum for the project of making memory and witness in response to the historical events of the Holocaust. One exception to this is a space of absence called the Hall of Testimony. It is a big, cold, windowless room, suggestive of a bunker or a crematorium. Located at the end of the Holocaust section, it is made of concrete, with concrete benches and raised video monitors, also encased in concrete. Holocaust survivor testimony and the words of those who did not survive play on the monitors. Between showings of individual narratives, cantorial voices sing. The voices are full of the weight of a history that cannot be absorbed, full of sorrow that cannot be managed, full of absences that never can be filled, full of contradictions that never can be resolved.

NOTES

I would like to thank the following people for their editorial advice and encouragement: Elin Diamond, Peg Lourie, Jill Dolan, and Vida Penezic. I thank Kate Davy, Hilary Harris, and Peggy Phelan for accompanying me on my trip to the Beit Hashoah. I especially acknowledge my researchers, Mary Callahan Boone and Annette Wannamaker, whose work was funded by Graduate Research Assistance Awards from Bowling Green State University.

1   As quoted in James Anderson's "A high-tech tour through hate," *Orange County Register*, 31 Jan. 1993.

REFERENCES

Bal, Mieke (1992). "Telling, Showing, Showing Off," *Critical Inquiry* 18 (Spring 1992): 556–94.

Beit Hashoah Museum of Tolerance. Fundraising letters, especially between 1991 and 1992.

Berenbaum, Michael (1990) "The Uniqueness and Universality of the Holocaust," in *A Mosaic of Victims: Non-Jews Persecuted and Murdered by the Nazis*, New York: New York University Press.

—— (1993) *The World Must Know: The History of the Holocaust as told in the United States Holocaust Memorial Museum*, Boston: Little, Brown.

Bourne, Jenny (1987) "Homelands of the Mind: Jewish Feminism and Identity Politics," *Race and Class*. 29.1 (Summer 1987): 1-24.

Certeau, Michel de (1984) *The Practice of Everyday Life*, trans. Steven Rendall, Berkeley and Los Angeles: University of California Press, 1984.

Gourevitch, Philip (1993) "Behold Now Behemoth: The Holocaust Memorial Museum: One More American Theme Park," *Harpers* 287. 1718 (July 1993): 55–62.

Parker, Andrew, Russo, Mary, Sommer, Doris, and Yaeger, Patricia (1992) *Nationalisms and Sexualities*, New York: Routledge.

Penley, Constance and Ross, Andrew, eds (1991) *Technoculture*, Cultural Politics Series, Vol. 3, Minneapolis: University of Minnesota Press.

Phelan, Peggy (1993) *Unmarked: The Politics of Performance*, New York: Routledge, 1993.

Stannard, David E. (1992) *American Holocaust: Columbus and the Conquest of the New World*, New York: Oxford University Press.

United States Holocaust Memorial Museum. Fundraising letters, especially from 1991 through 1992, including its "Charter Supporter Acceptance Form."

Young, James (1988) *Writing and Rewriting the Holocaust: Narrative and the Consequences of Interpretation*, Bloomington: Indiana University Press.

—— (1992) "America's Holocaust: Memory and the Politics of Identity," presented at the panel, "The Holocaust and the American Jewish Imagination: Memory, Text, and Myth," Modern Language Association Conference, Dec. 1992.

—— (1993) *The Texture of Memory: Holocaust Memorials and Meaning*, New Haven: Yale University Press.

7

FESTIVITIES AND JUBILATIONS ON THE GRAVES OF THE DEAD

Sanctifying sullied space

Glenda Dicker/sun

Goin' down the road, Lawd / Goin' down the road.
Goin' down the road, Lawd / Way down the road.
Got to find somebody / To help me carry this load.

Road's in front o' me / Nothin' to do but walk.
Road's in front o' me / Walk . . . an' walk . . . an' walk.
I'd like to meet a good friend / To come along an' talk.

Road, road, road, O! / Road, road . . . road . . . road, road!
Road, road, road, O! / On the no'thern road.
These Mississippi towns ain't / Fit fer a hoppin' toad.

Langston Hughes[1]

Thirty pounds heavier and a hundred cypress swamps deeper in thought, I emerge out of a labyrinth of rooms to drag my foot into the twenty-first century. I'm staring fifty down with a loaded gun and a string of invectives. If you want trouble, I can offer you a wide variety. I step out of a caul of invisibility to pick up my load, to get on down the road.

White men sail the world planting flags, gathering slaves and spreading syphilis; then they retire to walk golf courses, comfortable in the belief that it is their sacred prerogative to order the world. White men feel entitled to space. Sitting with their legs wide open. Putting on airs as they open doors and pull out chairs. Saying no with laughing ease. Pretenders to the throne of rejection.

Black women see the world from their own Black reality, but the world we inhabit doesn't recognize that reality. Black women are invisible, but we feel like we take up too much space, like we are robbing the people around us, eating their air. Today, Black women are walking down the sidewalks, sick of getting out of the way; ruminating over rituals of preparation for battle. Cosmic collisions will soon occur.

Road's in front o' me / nothin' to do but walk.
Road's in front o' me / walk and walk and walk.

The road is dusty. It winds uphill. At its end freedomspace stands like Golgotha. "Golgotha is a mountain, a purple mound out of sight."[2] Along the way I stop to make performance events like stations of the cross. In creating these performance events I strive to liberate the uppity Black woman from the shroud of invisibility, take her off the auction block; make for her a Blackreality space, a space to talk out her life, a sassy space to witness the act. I am pushed from the rear and tickled under my feet by ghosts hovering about graves over which america plays at festivities and jubilations.

I'd like to meet a good friend to come along an' talk.

My traveling companions for this stretch of the road are a painter named Ana Bel, an eel catcher named Rachel, and the ghosts of Ibo Landing. The trees, the water, the burying ground. I make drama from these. I'm aiming for a nexus, I'm longing for a matrix, I want to touch that old omphalos. I'm bound for the freedom, freedom bound. And oh susannah, don't you cry for me.

ANA BEL'S BRUSH

A Live Oak Drama

It was many and many a year ago
In a kingdom by the sea . . .

Edgar Allen Poe

"Heahd bout duh Ibo's Landing? Das duh place weah dey bring duh Ibos obuh in a slabe ship and wen dey git yuh, dey ain lak it an so dey all staht singin and dey march right down in duh ribbuh tuh march back tuh Africa, but dey ain able tuh git deah. Dey gits drown."[3]

On Feb. 12, 1733, General James Oglethorpe's expedition landed at Yamacraw Bluff and proceeded to establish the planned city of Savannah on the first high bluff of the river of the same name, as the focal point of the new Georgia colony. . . . In June 1735, the Trustees of the Georgia colony consented to Oglethorpe's request for two fortified towns in the Altamaha River region of old Guale. Scottish Highlanders were to establish a town and garrison near the site of old Fort King George, while Englishmen and Salzburgers were to settle a town and garrison a fort on Saint Simons Island.[4]

St. Simons Island is one of the so-called Golden Isles, sea barrier islands just across a high sloping causeway from Brunswick, a sleepy little town in

McIntosh County, Georgia. You can see Ibo Landing from the causeway, but you can't step on it because the land is now owned by Georgia "crackers." I went plunging in there one day directed by a Black man who works for the water company. The owners came barreling up in a truck with a shotgun and confirmed this was indeed the place and it was strictly off limits.

A plaque on the St. Simons golf course reads:

> Just across St. Simons Sound lies Jekyll Island. Called by the Indians, Ospo, Jekyll Island was the site of the Mission of Buenventura built by the Spaniards during the latter part of the 16th century and maintained until 1686. Oglethorpe changed the name to Jekyll Island in honor of Sir Joseph Jekyll, who contributed liberally towards the founding of the Colony of Georgia. For almost a century the island was owned by the duBignon family whose negro slaves cultivated extensive fields of Sea Island cotton. In 1858 the Wanderer, last slave ship to bring negro slaves to this country, landed its cargo on Jekyll Island. In 1886 Jekyll Island was bought by the Jekyll Island Club.

St. Simons is costumed in huge live oaks which drip with resurrection moss. The oaks are so old that some of them have plaques, acknowledging that they were there to meet Oglethorpe. At least one is 900 years old. There are also pine trees, which sprinkle their cones all over the island. The oaks and the pines, creeping out on to the roadways, forming lush blankets of shade in idyllic spots, turn the island into a magical, mythic place. When I touch the trees, history rushes out into my hand, sending chills up and down my spine. O-o-oh! if trees could talk.

And then you come to the ocean. You seem to be standing on the edge of the world, just you and the sky and the water. Schools of dolphins appear from time to time. I pay my respects to Yemaya, Mother of the Ocean, who some folks say is the same woman as Aunt Jemima.

> But then the sky – if no human chisel ever yet cut breath, neither did any human pen ever write light; if it did, mine should spread out before you these unspeakable glories of these Southern heavens, the saffron brightness of morning, the blue intense brilliancy of noon, the golden splendor and the rosy softness of sunset ... Heaven itself does not seem brighter or more beautiful to the imagination than these surpassing pageants of fiery rays, and piled up beds of orange, golden clouds, with edges too bright to look on, scattered wreaths of faintest rosy bloom, amber streaks and pale green lakes between, and amid sky all mingled blue and rose tints, a spectacle to make one fall over the side of the boat, with one's head broken off with looking adoringly upward.
>
> (Sullivan, *Early Days*, p. 193)

St. Simons Island is always magical, and especially so at sunset. While the sun is going down, the salt marshes turn colors, dappled by the sun, looking like Bogalofini Bamana – woman resist-dyed cloth from West Africa. Big white herons swoop down and light in the water or in the scraggly trees.

The sand crawls along the beach, swirling in little puffs, as though driven by l'armatemp, Senegal's unpredictable desert wind. Also reminiscent of Senegal is St. Simons' miraculous illusion. At low tide you can walk out for miles on the big sand bars that twice a day emerge out of the water like dragons. Standing on the beach, between wind and water, tiny bodies seem to be walking right on the water silhouetted against the setting sun. Perhaps this is what Jesus of Nazareth was up to.

Walking the beach at night, I can hear the poles of the furled sailboats talking to each other in delicate musical tones. The zephyr's nudge turns them into giant wind chimes. Late one Thanksgiving night I walk the beach. Summoned by the full harvest moon, the water comes on up and soaks the pier, splashing my feet, tickling up memories.

Walking the sand bars in the morning, I create a curious sensation among the few scattered white residents. But they are invisible to me. This is my beach, land of my ancestors.

Walking on the water at St. Simons Island is a necessary experience to mount a piece called "Ana Bel's Brush," creating a space for a sassy woman painter to talk out her life.

My brother, the explorer – like a latter-day Oglethorpe – discovered both St. Simons Island and Ana Bel Lee during his frequent-flyer business travel. When he suggested we take our family vacation there in the summer of 1992, he told me about a woman painter whose work I would love. On that first trip, we visited a local gallery to see some of her paintings. The work was brightly colored in the primitive tradition, images of the island, populated with Black faces. At the gallery, they told us to come back on Tuesday evening when she would be there. We arrived in the nick of time. They thought she was already gone. My brother went around back and found Ana Bel Lee (Washington). He brought her to meet his wife, my daughter, his children and me. The moment seemed serendipitous. She was a short, cameo colored woman with a halo of white afro. She was sportily dressed in shorts and a tailored shirt. She wore sandals and puffed on a Salem cigarette. She reminded me of an old-time blues singer, but she had a '90s sensibility. I said your work speaks to me and I want to see more. She said come to my studio. I said I'm moving to Georgia to teach at Spelman. She said I'm having a show there in the fall. You could have knocked me down with a swath of resurrection moss.

The next day we went to her studio and entered a world magical like the island, gutsy like the blues singers, and dangerous like Bocio, personal secrets too dangerous to express verbally. The spot, where she also lived, was jammed and crammed with canvases everywhere like bouquets of flowers. She displayed her paintings with a shy ferocity, puffing relentlessly on Salems as she spoke. She paints on her sun porch, screened against the vicious mosquitoes. The people in the paintings made the place seem like a space for forgotten rituals to occur. They seemed ready to jump out and beat the drum for dancing or for death. "Doze days dey ain only beat duh drum fuh dancin; dey beat it on duh way tuh duh grabe yahd" (*Drums and Shadows*, p. 184).

I bent my knee repeatedly before paintings big and small and listened to the story of each one.

> And then with mine I make up stories as I'm painting . . . you know . . . I told you the one about the woman I had running and she really wasn't running to nothing or whatnot . . . I took her out three times . . . and each time she would come back the same way . . . so I stuck a little baby in front of her and I said, "Now chase that."[5]

I heard of the Retreat Plantation hospital and its slave burial ground. Of the old tabby slave cabins, one now a gift shop.

> The first one (of Retreat Plantation) is my interpretation of what it must have looked like . . . that one was the first one that I did and I called it Ghostly Night . . . I tried to make the people transparent.

Many paintings were of the Black churches on St. Simons and surrounding sea islands like Sapelo.

> I started painting the church . . . the red church . . . was the first one that I painted. Churches . . . and the tabby houses . . . slave houses fascinated me and I use to call it my work that was after the civil war . . . not during slavery . . . and a lot of pictures gave me ideas and they show old and ragged folks . . . you know . . . patched up and what not . . . I couldn't paint them that way . . . I made them . . . you know . . . made them pretty . . . because there were some that were pretty . . . everybody wasn't poor and ragged . . . you know . . . so that's why I started doing them and then I realized sometimes after a while that I was hooked on churches . . . but only Black . . . old churches.
>
> I haven't done the cemetery . . . it's kind of in the back of my mind . . . after I saw it . . . when we went it was fall . . . and leaves covered up so much . . . over there I was really disappointed because I thought they were not taking care of it . . . and whatnot . . . you know . . . But you see when the tourists start coming . . . and the rich folks start coming . . . then you go back there and look! . . . they've got it fixed up nice!

The painting that I finally settled on was not for sale. It was called "Ibo Landing." I hadn't seen *Daughters of the Dust* yet and didn't know the myth of Ibo Landing. In her painting of Ibo Landing, the people emerge from the bushes and walk down into the water, holding hands. They are going home. The pattern of their bodies forms a V like a flight of birds swooping over the ocean. She put bright circles of cloth on their heads so you could see them against the water. The people have no faces. Three live oak trees in the background solemnly watch the ceremony. I asked her how much she wanted for the painting – prepared, if necessary, to lie in ambush for yesterday to own it. She said . . .

> When I did Ibo Landing . . . I had mixed feelings . . . when I did it . . . I felt . . . Are you supposed to be glad that these people didn't want to be slaves

and they drowned . . . or are you supposed to be sad because these people drowned . . . so I had those kind of feelings while I was trying to paint it . . . and that's why I said I would never do it again . . . But there was an emotional feeling . . . you know . . . when I did it . . . and somebody today, asked me about it . . . and I said, "It's priceless."

The stories from her mouth and from her paintings made me hunger to see these places with my own eyes. She said she could take us, but like me she didn't drive. The next day we all piled into my brother's car and went around the island. First we went to the Sea Island Golf Club/Retreat Plantation. The ruins of Retreat Hospital blare a warning: "Tabby ruins are fragile. Please stay clear."

A plaque in front of the ruins reads:

> This building, more than a century old, was the hospital for the slaves of Retreat Plantation. It was two and one half stories and contained 10 rooms. Two women lived here as nurses and when necessary a doctor came from Darian to minister to the sick slaves. An average of 1,000 dollars a year was spent for medicine for the Retreat negroes.

The Retreat Burying Ground is across the golf course from the hospital. It too has a plaque. "Since 1800 slaves on Retreat Plantation belonging to the Page and King families have been buried beneath these live oaks."

> Mr. King did try to order the lives and environment of the slaves, but he was constantly frustrated by the irregularities in the behavior of the slaves . . . King forced Judy, flogged her severely for having resisted him, and then sent her off, as a further punishment, to Five Pound – a horrible swamp in a remote corner of the estate to which the slaves are sometimes banished for such offenses as are not sufficiently atoned for by the lash.
>
> (Sullivan, *Early Days*, pp. 196–7)

A little pond, live oak trees, brash wildflowers, pine cones and ancient ancient tombstones sanctify the burying ground in old man King's kingdom by the sea. Names like Neptune Small 1831-1907 and Sadie Life 1897-1965 conjure a time when burial was no simple thing.

> The desire of every Ibo man and woman is to die in their own town, or, at least, to be buried within its precincts. It was very difficult to persuade a man to travel any distance from his native place. In case of death occurring at a distance, if it can be done at all, the brethren will bring the body home for burial.[6] All Ibo place great faith in the due and proper observance of the funeral ceremony, for they are of the opinion that it enables the soul to go to the Creator and to find its final destination, and that without this sacred rite the soul is prevented by the other spirits from eating, or in any way associating with them . . . it becomes an outcast and a wanderer on the face of the earth, haunting houses and frequently burial grounds . . . [7]

Members of the exclusive Sea Island Golf Club have so much room to play their games. They spread out over the rolling green and under the trees.

Figure 7.1 Ibo Landing, Ana Bel Lee, 1987 (the original oil painting is in the collection of the artist)

They stand in marked contrast to the tiny crowded cemetery. The wandering Ibo spirits hover about protesting as golf balls whizz over the old bones in the burial ground. Graves and golf. I said to myself, "Well, I better tell this tale."

We continued around the island seeing the sights, hearing the tales. After the long day was over I said let us take you to dinner. She said we have to go to Alphonso's, the Black-owned cajun restaurant and see the Black part of the island. I'll make the reservations.

Alphonso's is a big old Louisiana-looking place sitting up in the sand and trees. Alphonso himself is a big old jet-black man who looks like High John de Conquer. I imagine him to be a direct descendant of Gasamin San Foix who was "John Couper's cook on St. Simons Island in 1835. He was not a slave, but a freed man and was highly regarded for his culinary skills" (Sullivan, *Early Days*, p. 78). Alphonso's Cajun Restaurant sits between South Harrington and North Harrington. These streets border the "Black part of the island," where the Frederica People, descendants of the enslaved people, still live.

By the time we picked up Ana Bel to take her to dinner, I had already decided and told my brother that I wanted to make a live oak drama about

114

Ana Bel to be performed at Spelman during the opening reception of her exhibit. Oak both living and dead is more durable than iron.

With Ana Bel's permission, the project became a collaboration between the Spelman Departments of Drama and Art (Lev Mills, Chair and Arturo Lindsay, Ana Bel's exhibit curator). I hired a professional actor named Marguerite Hannah to portray Ana Bel and we went back down to the island to tape about four hours of interviews with the painter and to give Marguerite a chance to observe her. We listened to the sailboat windchimes and watched the moon rise. Ana Bel's talkstory, as revealed by the oral history tapes, is an incredible tale of a singular woman who worked in the welfare system in Detroit and then retired to walk the island of the sun.

At Spelman College on 13 September 1992, the audience was seated on the stage, with the artist front and center. We created a performance environment from her own artifacts – paintbrushes, canvases, photographs, newspaper articles, her first painting, books she was reading. We blew up pictures of Ana Bel and they formed the backdrop for the playing area. We hauled back pine cones, sand, and resurrection moss from the live oak trees of St. Simons for the environment. Some of the magic of the island clung to the moss and sand as Marguerite, who looked uncannily like young pictures of the artist, brought her words to life.

In the art gallery outside the theater, Ana Bel's own paintings were hung. In an adjacent space in the Drama Department a beautiful display of her personal artifacts and a constantly running videotape were available to the browsing audience as well as blown up transcripts from the oral history tapes.

What is your full name?
Annabelle Washington.
What is your age?
67. I'm not ashamed of it. I was born in 1924.
What date in 1924?
October 15, 1924. A woman's age and weight is always so intriguing to men more so than any other vital statistic.
Where were you born?
Detroit, Michigan.
What was your occupation while you were there?
I worked for the state of Michigan and I went from a clerk up to Social Worker. I was there 38 years.
What brought you to St. Simons Island?
My brother's wife grew up here on the island. Then she left and went to Detroit and they met in Detroit. So when he retired, she wanted to come back. And he had been down a lot to visit, and liked it and so he came on back and I followed them down here. I had no reason to stay in Detroit. If my mother had still been living I probably still

would have stayed because of that but I had neither chick nor child so I had no reason. And after I came down here to visit then I liked it. I came twice in '83. March of '84 I was moving in.

So two visits sold you.

Yes. The peace and the quiet. Because even in Detroit, well in my younger days, you know, you run. But after things in the '70s, you know, in Detroit things began to get bad. So it wasn't any good catching buses and going wherever you wanted to go because it might be that something might happen on the bus. Anything. Cabs weren't that safe. So I would have been stuck in an apartment, coming out only when someone came to pick me up and I'd run to the car and get in. *On this island I can walk anywhere I want to* (my italics).

How did you start painting?

In '84 I volunteered at the Arts Center. I would stand there and watch the women paint . . . and I decided I wanted to see if I could paint. I joined the beginners' class that September . . . and when the woman said paint . . . I just took the paint brush to see what I could do. I think I stayed with her for almost a year . . . and then I asked Hendricks if I could come into his class . . . Could I bring some of my paintings and see if he thought I could go into his class . . . He said "I've already seen your paintings. Come on." So I did . . . and he's the one that said one day "Why don't you put people in it . . . and of course I said that I couldn't draw and he took the paint brush and put a head in there and showed me how to do it. I've been putting them in ever since . . . And it was funny I used to laugh . . . I would giggle . . . when I would be putting the little people in and somebody would say "Oh Lord, she's putting in people again."

Tell us how you chose the name Ana Bel Lee . . . the name you use on your paintings

Well the first teacher I had . . . she said the first thing you should do is pick out a name . . . and my full name is so long . . . I dropped . . . I always liked the poem Ana Bel Lee for one thing . . . and I had decided that I was going to be Ana Bel . . . and you see that wouldn't take up much room . . . and then I said, "How about Lee?" . . . and someone said, "That sounds so southern" . . . and I said, "Well since I am in Georgia I will be Ana Bel Lee."

When the audience heard about her life in her own words, they fell in love all over again with the woman whose paintings had moved them so profoundly. A painter named Ana Bel who used to say, "I try to paint. And I don't remember when it happened but I began to say 'I'm an artist'." An artist who can walk anywhere she wants to.

EEL CATCHING IN SETAUKET

A Living Portrait of the Christian Avenue Community

"Alexanduh, the old root doctor, wuz stil libin when I wuz a boy. Dey say duh boat leab fuh Savannah and Alexanduh he yuh. He say goodbye frum yuh and tell em tuh go on widout im but he say he see em deah and wen duh boat git tuh Savannah, Alexanduh he in Savannah on duh dock tuh ketch duh line."

(Drums and Shadows, p. 184)

Alexander, the root doctor, is a folk son of John Henry and Aunt Hagar. He lives eternally in Georgia Sea Island lore. He has a blood brother living in the village of Setauket on Long Island, who can perform the same miraculous feats.

When Pete Tucker felt like dancing, he walked all the way from his home in Setauket to the county seat in Riverhead. He walked slow and easy, not in a hurry. Carriages filled with lustrous ebony, sepia, butterscotch, and tea-rose party-goers passed him on the way; but when they arrived, he was always there ahead of them lounging insolently against a gnarled post in the barn which served as their dancing space. The villagers of Setauket speculated, but they did not know how he accomplished this feat. Most of them thought he was "nothin' but the devil." Ted Green told me that he could make the hoes work by themselves or lay down in the field, according to his mood.

One thing they knew for sure, Pete Tucker was a "bad nigger" who fought white men, but could not be kept in jail. Pete Tucker lives in the collective memories of the Christian Avenue folk.

Setauket's Christian Avenue community is one of the oldest African American communities on Long Island. Pete Tucker revolves in their minds along with visions of pipe-smoking great-grandmothers and babies stolen by gypsies. His tale symbolizes for us the magic power of oral history. The folk whisper and glance around when they say his name. They drop their eyes, reluctant to tell his story. They remember his icy, grey eyes and they make of that memory an incantatory protection, a repository of fear, taking a sly pride in his arrogance.

One day not too long ago, I was looking out the window of my lonesome house in Setauket. I was trying to think of something to do since New York City was farther than the posted sixty miles, Africa was across the water, and Heaven only comes to those who wait. The toothless trees outside my window soughed and sighed and prepared to blabber their delicious secret. My hair stood on end as they whispered invitingly, "Want to have some oldtime fun? When you take your sunset walk today, keep on going till you come to the Mill Pond. Seek out the spot where the Setalcott Indians first camped and called it 'land on the mouth of the creek.' You'll know when you come to it because you'll be standing on holy ground. From there it's an easy step to Christian Avenue."

Well, that's exactly what I did. When I got to Christian Avenue and walked past the cemetery, past Bethel African Methodist Episcopal Church, past the houses, sitting there warm and solid like my grandmother's fresh-baked monkey bread, I tell you Shango danced on my spine. It was a moment of whirring wings and glad awakening.

I ran home willy-nilly, pummelled by purpose, and did not forget to thank the blabbering trees. I had heard how old this community was (some say it predates the revolutionary war) and that its important history was in danger of being lost. The folk have been there as long as the Village, but the university folk weren't aware they existed. They were invisible. That very day, I took as my goal the task of documenting and preserving the history of the people who lived in those houses, along with the histories of their ancestors and descendants, by collecting their stories in their own words.

Collecting the stories and devising the means to tell them took two years. A performance and exhibit was presented 22-25 June 1988 in a huge black box in the Theater Arts Department at the State University of New York at Stony Brook where I was on the faculty. The event was called "a living library" and included a walking tour, an exhibit of artifacts produced by the community – arranged to felicitous impact by Tyrone Mitchell, a visual artist imported from New York to create the environment – and dramatic vignettes woven from the collected stories which were performed amidst the artifacts.

The title of the project is taken from a painting by William Sidney Mount, an american painter born in Setauket in 1807. His 1845 painting, "Eel Spearing at Setauket," depicts Rachel Holland Hart spearing for eels in a canoe navigated by a young caucasian. Rachel Holland Hart is the foremother of the Hart/Sells clan. Her descendants are the premier families of Christian Avenue.

The Harts and Sells live where their ancestors were born. They are surrounded by historic sites and landmarks. The ancestors sleep at either end of the community, enclosing the residents in a magic circle, with Bethel A.M.E. Church at its center. Near one end of Christian Avenue, a haphazard array of tombstones rambles over Laurel Hill. Wildflowers cozy up to the tombstones. At the other end, enclosed by an old picket fence, Bethel Cemetery sits upon her dignity. The burying ground is dotted with jaunty little american flags, placed by veteran Theodore Green, memorializing veterans of the world wars.

Mr. Green, descended from both the Harts and Sells, was my guide on the two-year journey deep into the community.

> "Now those families in the old cemetery, other people don't know about like we do. Those stones is, ah, almost 167 years old, those stones up there . . . if they ever move the stone, I wrote it down myself . . . because if I ever go

there and the monument is gone I can put another one there . . . I can put another monument up there."[8]

For two years "Eel Catching" was centered at Bethel African Methodist Episcopal Church. The Black church, born in slavery, was the sole source of personal identity and sense of community for a people peremptorily stripped of the comforts of home. It became the home base for revolution. For these reasons, I wanted to make Bethel the home base for "Eel Catching."

For two years I, along with consultant Fai Walker and student interns, visited in the homes of the community, looking at old photographs and other artifacts, marking them down, wooing them away from the folks for the coming exhibit at Stony Brook. When completed, the exhibit would include photographs, paintings, family Bibles, cooking utensils, clothing, hair ornaments, sports equipment, furniture, pot-bellied stoves, and many other artifacts. The photographs and artifacts told their own stories, themselves as eloquent as the stories we heard from women and men who have walked this ground for nearly 100 years.

The stories are sepia-toned. They are ebony, butterscotch, and tea-rose like those long-ago party-goers. They are delicate like the white lace handkerchiefs the church ladies wear on missionary Sunday. They are strong, like the hands of community resident Alfred Hobbs, New York State's only Black farmer. They are vital, like Harry Hart's shovel, which hollows out the community graves. They are legendary, like Pete Tuckers's mandolin which made the hoes fall down in the field. "I sho heahd em talk bout grat doins an Ise headh Onkle Israel say duh hoe could wuk by itsef ef yuh know wut tuh say tuh it" (the speaker is Ben Sullivan, St. Simons Island. *Drums and Shadows*, p. 182).

For two years, I sho heard 'em talk their lives and listened closely, spinning a drama in my head all the while.

Lucy Agnes (Hart) Keyes, Mother of Bethel Church, was born in 1900. She was one of twelve children of Jacob and Hannah Hart. She is a great-great-great grandmother. Many evenings as the sun went down, I sat in Mrs. Keyes's front room or garden and listened enraptured to her talkstory.

> I'm known as Lucy . . . I love that name . . . Lucy. And my mind is so clear bout as clear about back then as it is about now. What happened a month ago I have to stop and think, but it is clear as a crystal all the way back when I was 4 or 5 years old.

Mrs. Keyes told me the story, told to her by her mother, of a minister finding her grandmother.

> I wish I could remember the name of that minister. He came to Setauket to preach and mama was telling him . . . she never knew after her mother (she was) sold from her. This minister got in touch with different people and he found mama's mother and mama was married then, had several children. Papa got enough money together and she went down to Richmond to her mother. She stayed down with her, I guess, a whole month.

119

I heard 'em talk of a neighborhood changed forever.

> "The water is bad." This is what they said. That was the reason why they decided to move the people out . . . They tried to use the whole area for development . . . no homes at all, just stores, office buildings. After they decided that! . . . they had to get out and go find homes all over. That was a big human saying for awhile, "We don't know where to go! Where are we going to go?" . . . .A whole street full of people out – could be put out with no place for them to go.
>
> (Ethel Lewis, community resident)

I sho heahd 'em talk about ties with the Shinnecock Nation which have woven patterns through the Hart/Sells lineages. On Labor Day, I rode with them on a rented bus up to the Shinnecock Pow Wow. It was wonderful to see the faces of women who looked like my daughter, dressed in traditional garb, celebrating their native heritage. I heard 'em talk their heritage.

> There were a lot of nationalities. I think we were the only Indians in there . . . One time, one time in our class we were the only Americans in the class . . . the rest of the kids were Irish, Polish, Lithuanians, all from Europe and the Blacks were the only true citizens.
>
> (Nellie Edwards, community resident)

Student interns, under the tutelage of Fai Walker, oral historian, assisted in the recording of existing history and in the interviewing process. In May 1987, the students presented oral reports at Bethel Church. These reports drew sketches of community dwellers the students had interviewed, such as Hazel Lewis and Nellie Edwards, and served as a prelude to the living library event which would follow the next year. I heard 'em talk.

> I can see now why they say 50 is the golden age. Before conducting my interview, I'm ashamed to say that I had preconceived notions of what it would be like to be 50. Nellie Edwards changed my mind.
>
> (Karen Thomas, student)

The year leading up to the Eel Catching living library was one of shifting, reading, researching, arranging, plotting, planning, checking, cross-checking, and re-checking. The volume of collected material was tremendous and the list of donated artifacts long. The effort it took to weave them into a unified whole was a challenge the blabbering trees had not warned me of.

Beverly C. Tyler, president of the Three Village Historic Society, provided invaluable aid and assistance in my research. He provided me with space, in an upstairs room of the historic house which served as the society's headquarters, to house the volumes of tapes, notes, and paper artifacts I was collecting and contributed tidbits of local history. Bev devoted the entire May 1988 issue of the Journal of the Three Village Historical Society to "Eel Catching," a beautiful souvenir journal containing photographs and quotes to document my project. The middle section of the journal served as the program for the actual event. Together, we stewed and typed and argued over the layout.

In May 1988, the professional actors came to town. Lynda Gravatt, Lee Dobson, Kenshaka Ali, and Gwendolen Hardwick, together with Stony Brook student performers Jo-Ann Jones, Gerald Latham, Rhonda Lewis, and Michael Manel, and stage manager Anitra Dickerson, spent weeks steeping themselves in the community lore, witnessing the tone and mannerisms of the people we would portray and rehearsing deep into the night, often crashing at my rented house.

Saturday night, before we were all to go to Bethel for Father's Day services Sunday morning, we visited Mrs. Regina Morrison, widow of the former pastor. She told us how God had delivered her from a vast illness. She served us cake and lemonade, lent us a stylish hat (which she modeled) and would not let us escape until we fell to our knees so she could pray over us. We formed a circle, joined hands and went back to Sunday School as she sang

> Spirit of the Living God
> Fall afresh on me.

Jo-Ann Johnson and Gerald Latham, two angelic-voiced students, sang this old spiritual during the performance as other actors read aloud the names from each stained-glass window and pew in Bethel, along with the year of dedication by the family which had purchased it. Mrs. Morrison saw herself portrayed to a saucy turn by Lynda Gravatt, but died soon after I left Stony Brook. My daughter represented me at her funeral, a magnificent homegoing put on by the congregation of Bethel A.M.E. Church.

From all the Sisters of Bethel who were to be represented in the drama, I had the actors coax church hats and missionary white lace handkerchiefs to wear from scene to scene.

Finally 22 June 1988 arrived and all was ready. Before being bussed to the black box to witness the drama, the audience took a guided stroll through the community with Bev Tyler and me. At the beginning of the tour, I read from the souvenir journal inviting them to become "eel catchers":

> An Eel Catcher is a person who loves people and old pictures and history and characters and folklore and drama and textures and art and fun and laughter and doesn't mind experiencing them all at one time.

Each evening during the walking tour, I picked flowers from Lucy Keyes's garden. When we returned to the black box to see the performance, I presented the flowers to Linda Gravatt who stood in a canoe holding a real eel spear – borrowed from Bev Tyler's brother-in-law – frozen in a tableau which conjured up Mount's painting. At that moment the painting came to life and addressed the audience. At that moment, the Christian Avenue community dwellers, past and present, sprang into visibility.

121

Now step this way and I will learn you how to see and catch eels. Steady there at the stern and move the boat according to the direction of my spear. Slow now, we are coming on the ground. On sandy and gravelly bottoms are found the best fish![9]

And we were off! From there the audience, who never sat down, followed a swirling travel of vignettes spoken out in the midst of community artifacts which documented that particular story. Both actors and audience rested for only moments on their journey through time. Periodically the actors would freeze in tableaux of other William Sidney Mount paintings on display such as "The Banjo Player" and "Farmer's Nooning." Great huge slides hung in the air in an ever-changing tapestry.

We enacted the history of the African Methodist Episcopal Church from Richard Allen down through all the pastors of Bethel, ending with Reverend Raynor's Fathers' Day sermon which he had just preached the previous Sunday. Lee Dobson portrayed each of the pastors in turn. Reverend Raynor was just dumbfounded and the audience could not believe their eyes when Lee Dobson put on a pair of shades and mimicked exactly the rakish pose revealed in the big slide of Reverend Raynor which hung over his head. One former pastor, Reverend McKenzie, who had left Bethel under a cloud and required much persuading to attend the event, buried his face in a big white handkerchief when he heard his words (I had salvaged them from an old souvenir program), and wept aloud for the duration of the speech.

> This is a crowning experience for a beautiful dream come true. It is a moment of great joy and pride, yet filled with deep humility.
>
> (Reverend Albert McKenzie)

Lee Dobson's eyes rolled in his head and big beads of sweat stood on his forehead as the old preacher wept, but he did not break character. Mysterious chills and shivers ran through the crowd. The old people intoned in an undercurrent, "just hold to his hand, to God's unchanging hand" and murmered – in benediction – "amen."

Lucy Keyes, with the other elders, sat on church pews in the middle of the performance space. When time came for her story to be told, Kenshaka Ali, in the persona of Levi Phillips the Root Doctor, escorted her to an arrangement of her own Queen Anne dining-room table and crystal inherited from her grandmother. Gwendolen Hardwick sat at one end of the table and Mrs. Keyes at the other. When Gwendolen quoted Mrs. Keyes, punctuating her lines with Lucy's famous refrain – and I'm 88 – she would turn to Mrs. Keyes and Lucy would smile and say "that's right," blessing and sanctifying the story. By the second night, Lucy Keyes didn't wait for her escort. She walked to her space by herself, to relish again the Richmond reunion (see p. 119 above) she had only heard of before. As Lynda and Gwendolen, the actors portraying her mother and grandmother, embraced, our eyes filled with tears. We were all returned to

GUIDE TO EXPERIENCING THE EXHIBIT

This is an invitation to become an Eel Catcher. An Eel Catcher is a person who loves people and old pictures and history and characters and folklore and drama and textures and art and fun and laughter and doesn't mind experiencing them all at one time.

From June 22–25, 1988, Eel Catchers will be able to enter into the magic circle of Christian Avenue.

6:00–6:30   Eel Catchers will gather at SUNY/Stony Brook and be driven by bus to Christian Avenue for an introduction to and brief history of the community.

6:30–8:00   Eel Catchers will walk along Christian Avenue to see the major sites such as Bethel A.M.E. Church (which has worshiped on the same site for 114 years) and say a prayer with Rev. Melvin Rayner; the Irving Hart Legion Post to sample a traditional dish and meet Post commander, Theodore Green and other Christian Avenuers like 88-year-old Lucy Keyes; and Bethel and Laurel cemeteries where the ancestors of Harts and Sells and other early family names are buried.

8:00   Bus back to Theatre Arts Department.

8:30–10:00   Eel catchers will visit the living exhibition which illuminates and dramatizes the Christian Avenue community. The living exhibit will feature community artifacts such as hairdressing utensils, church hats, old crystal, sepia-toned photographs, and church pews; here also Eel Catchers will hear the stories of Christian Avenuers they just met as well as the stories of Rachel Holland Hart, the foremother of Christian Avenue, "bad nigger" Pete Tucker and root doctor Levi Phillips.

WON'T YOU COME AND BE AN EEL CATCHER TOO?

Figure 7.2   "Eel Catching in Setauket," from the souvenir issue of the *Journal of the Three Village Historical Society* (May 1988)

our mothers' bosoms. We were children again. The frozen tableau took on biblical dimensions.

In the magical space created by concrete birdbaths, crystal, sepia photographs, church hats and lace handkerchiefs, old furniture, baseball gloves, and grave-digging shovels, Lucy Agnes Hart Keyes sat in a place of honor, witness to the grandeur of her life.

In my vision, today's residents of Christian Avenue are one with the eelers and other workers who first came to Setauket, not voluntarily, and stayed to make history. In my vision, the autumnal elders will live in eternal Indian summer, safe in the magic circle. In my vision, Rachel Hart rests easy as she spears her eels and tosses them into my basket.

WISHES

The poem the song the picture
Are only water taken from the well of the people
And should be given back to them in a cup of beauty
That they may drink and in drinking come to understand themselves.
Frederico Garcia Lorca

I worked for a time in Newark, New Jersey, called by Mayor Sharpe James the Renaissance City. I worked for a time on an ambitious project, "Wellwater: Wishes and Words," an oral history project which would create a living portrait of Newark and her people. The portrait was to be drawn from stories told by Newark community dwellers and focus on their dreams, wishes, and aspirations.

Part of the community outreach program of the Department of Theater Arts and Speech at Rutgers University Campus at Newark, where I was chair, the project began in 1989, collecting videotaped oral histories at such sites as North Ward Center, the Northern State Prison and the Straight and Narrow Drug Rehabilitation Center for Kids. My wish was to illuminate Newark's rich history and culture, exploring her diversity and discovering how she fell so low from her rich beginnings.

I began researching the old steamboats, the old trains. I read about the fiery frustration that torched the city. About the invisible people who tried to burn her at the stake. But she refused to die. Now she lies about like a slattern, sleeping until noon, trying to regrow her singed hair and graft new skin to cover her scars. Like Marla Hanson, she hawks self-protection devices for a living. And the Renaissance City is stubborn as Sapphire. My prying fingers could not force her mouth open. She holds her secrets close and is close-mouthed about her checkered past. She would not yield her talkstory to me.

I wound up with a work-in-progress at the Newark Public Library on Monday, 28 October 1991. The excerpt was performed by a combination of student and professional actors, two of whom had spent their youth in Newark. The evening's program began with a documentary made from the videotaped interviews at the above-named sites. The play scrap, augmented by slides of familiar Newark sites, including epitaphs from the stones and markers in the Mount Pleasant Cemetery, featured dramatized stories from three sources: memories of the two actors who grew up in Newark; a book edited by Rutgers professor Wendell Holbrook, entitled *When I Was Comin' Up, An Oral History of Aged Blacks*; and oral histories gathered through the New Jersey Historical Society, donated by Dr. Giles Wright, curator.

With the excerpt from "Wellwater," we wellwishers helped the Renaissance City celebrate her 325th Anniversary. Then I walked away from Newark forever.

> I've traveled a lot, so I've roamed all over. Ain't many places that I haven't been. I've traveled there – down in the Islands – the West Indies Islands and I've been to the Hawaiian Islands . . . like I can't stop.
>
> (Lucy Keyes)

> Road, road, road, O!
> On that no'thern road.

I walked away from my Renaissance Sister to train women warriors at Spelman College to dance with swords in their hands. To a city where Native Americans protest a development complex being built on their burial ground:

> The commission was asked to curtail plans for a 372 home subdivision on 187 acres in Dacula because on the parcel are some 200 ancient Indian burial mounds. The rest of the land could be used for housing but each mound must be protected by a six foot chain link fence, before building permits would be issued.

> This is our cemetery. If this was Arlington Cemetery . . . They're not going to put a fence around Jackie Kennedy's grave now and start building sub-divisions . . . It's like allowing a soccer game in a cemetery.[10]

I imagine the red ghosts of the First People, hovering about the chain-link fence, wondering among themselves if the grave-robbing contractor, who protests (in Wiechard's article) that he always does things by the rules, follows the letter of the law, ever heard of the interior tribes of the West Coast of Africa who say that however great a thief a man may be, he will not steal from a grave. "The coveted mirror will lie there and waste in the rain, and the valuable garment will flap itself to rags in the wind, but human hands will not touch them."[11]

To a city where Mammy stands glowering in regal splendor next to Scarlett O'Hara, ready to march through america like Sherman through Georgia.

To the city where the marta (moving Africans rapidly through Atlanta) is my transportation of choice. On a train going to Lenox Mall, a huge crowd of beer-soaked white guys coming from a game at the Georgia Dome, loaded into my car. I am the only Black person in the car. A picked pocket is discovered. I feel right. I cannot wait for the suspicious eye to turn my way so I can launch into a sermon about the space race in america.

BLUE MOON OVER IBO LANDING

"Alexanduh say he could fly. He say all his family in Africa could fly."

(Floyd White, *Drums and Shadows*, p. 177)

It is October and November on Ibo Landing. The blue moon hangs in anticipation as the shadow of the earth approaches shyly, hungrily, to nibble her into darkness. The great wide pointed belly of Gaia rises in a taut mound out of her primeval lap. She is etched in bas-relief against the crystal night sky. Her thighs fall open in ecstasy. Her arms stretch back beyond the horizon, calling her soul to come see. And on her navel sits a Black woman, firmly held in place by her umbilicus, looking everywhere, seeing everything, gobbling greedy gulps of out/her space.

The stories of the painter, the eel catcher, and the wellwishers are haphazardly documented. Some with audio, some with video, some with handwritten note cards. I am the documentation. Within my body I hold the voices, sights, sounds, songs, that constitute the lives of these invisible people as they were told to me. Like Christian Avenue's Theodore Green I can remember if they move the monument.

Some Black women I know, such as Anabelle (Lee) Washington, Rachel Holland Hart, Lucy Hart Keyes, never have to get out of the way again. They can walk anywhere they want to. They have a space for their own Blackreality. The sassy, sacred space created when I put their talkstories up for the world to see and for they themselves to witness. It is like the moment in a *vodun* ceremony when the Mambo raises her skirt above her head and hollers, "If you would look upon life, it is here to see!" In creating drama from oral history, I pay homage to my ancestors while praising my living kin.

"The reception of the soul of the deceased in spiritland and his final prestige are altogether dependent on the grandeur and liberality of the human entertainment" (Leonard, *Lower Niger*, pp. 157–8). Gravesites of all the wandering ghosts, wherever they may be, call to me to honor their dead, to remind and to re/member. To celebrate their lives and the lives of their descendants with grandeur and liberality. And to sanctify the space so sullied by the obscene festivities enacted over their heads. So, like the griots of old, I dress up in my finery, silk, and spun gold, and prepare myself with meditation and prayer for Toh-fo (one lost),[12] a ceremony held when a person has met with death, for instance by drowning, and the body cannot be recovered. I dance with my sword in my hand as the sanctified spirits gather from all the places of invisibility, staring at each other with deep drinks of recognition. I fight to sing their praises, to keep alive their voices, to make them visible. I jubilate as I pour libation on the sacred graves of the dead.

I continue on the northbound road.

NOTES

1　From "Bound No'th Blues," in *Selected Poems* by Langston Hughes, copyright 1927 by Alfred A. Knopf and renewed 1955 by Langston Hughes. Reprinted by permission of the publisher.

2　The quote is from a poem, "Golgotha Is a Mountain" by Arna Bontemps, in *The Poetry of the Negro, 1746–1949*, ed. Langston Hughes and Arna Bontemps (Garden City, New York: Doubleday & Co., 1949).

3　The speaker is Floyd White, a resident of St. Simons Island *c.* 1940. His story and others cited here are found in *Drums and Shadows, Survival Studies Among the Georgia Coastal Negroes*, a project of the Savannah Unit, Georgia Writers' Project, Work Projects Administration (Athens, GA: The University of Georgia Press, 1940), p. 185.

4　See Buddy Sullivan, *Early Days on the Georgia Tidewater* (McIntosh County, GA,: Board of Commissioners, 1990), p. 16.

5　The words of the painter quoted in this section are from tape-recorded interviews with Annabelle (Lee) Washington on separate occasions over a four-day period in August 1992 on St. Simons Island.

6　See George Basden Thomas, *Among the Ibos of Nigeria* (Philadelphia: J. B. Lippincott Co.; London: Seeley, Service & Co., Ltd., 1931), pp. 115–16.

7　See Arthyr Glyn Leonard, *The Lower Niger and Its Tribes* (New York: The Macmillan Co., 1906), p. 142.

8　Ted Green and other Christian Avenue community dwellers whose words are quoted throughout this section gave generously of their time for tape-recorded interviews conducted over a two-year period by Glenda Dickerson, Fai Walker, Bev Tyler and SUNY/Stony Brook student assistants. The oral histories gathered by the "Eel Catching" Project are housed in the archives of the Three Village Historical Society.

9　This quote is from the "Eel Catching" script. It is pieced together from various historical sources.

10　See "Burial Rights" by Kelly Wiechard in the 26 May 1994 edition of *Creative Loafing*, a local Atlanta newspaper. Metro Beats section, p. 7.

11　See Robert Hamill Nassau, *Fetichism in West Africa* (New York: Charles Scribner's Sons, 1904), p. 232.

12　See A. B. Ellis, *The Tshi-Speaking Peoples of the Gold Coast of West Africa* (London: Chapman & Hall., 1887), p. 223.

Part III

MOVING/SEEING
Bodies and technologies

8

PYGMALION'S NO-BODY AND THE BODY OF DANCE

Susan Leigh Foster

As the story goes, sculptor Pygmalion loved his work of art so much, he wanted it to come to life. He yearned to turn his sculpted female no-body into a living, breathing some-body, perhaps even a dancing body. In her enlivenment she could put into action all the aesthetic values he had put into her making. In her dancing body might be found the perfect realization of his artful ideals. Venus, goddess of love, took pity on Pygmalion and brought his ideal to realness. Yet whatever dancing the sculpture then performed, we have no record of it. The first melting of stone into motion, the shifting postures and developing gestures of that somebody's embodiment are all lost. The duet that artmaker and work of art choreographed for themselves has left no trace.

The dance historian, staring at the blank space in history created by the sculpture's vanished dancing, aspires, like Pygmalion, to imagine it into performance. But just as the sculptor's story has been told many times with many different emphases, many different outcomes, so the historian's project can revivify the past in a variety of ways. Historical dancing bodies may be brought to life in partnered ensemble with the historian or as precious puppets that must denote events without ever showing a motivation of their own, or as perpetual evanescence whose very vanishing captures the historian's focus. Whether as partner or puppeteer, the historian moves on the stage of historical inquiry, her own gestures foregrounded by the very absence of the dancing body she seeks to animate and then describe.

This essay focuses on three different choreographic realizations of Pygmalion's story – by Marie Sallé in 1734, by Louis Milon in 1799, and by Arthur St. Léon in 1847 – as allegories for the dance historian's project. At the same time, the essay casts these successive versions of Pygmalion as a chronicle of the narrativization of theatrical dance. When Marie Sallé choreographed her Pygmalion, theatrical dance nested within grand operatic structure as an elaboration on the narrative that lyrics provided. Sallé's was one of the first dances to tell a story using movement and gesture alone. Milon's production testified to the vitality and autonomy of this new form of spectacle whose relationships among danced characters spawned logical motivations, credible responses, and resolute actions, and whose interactions, over the course of the performance, orchestrated the sense of a beginning, middle, and end. By the time of St. Léon's ballet, theatrical dance had established itself as an autonomous art form that presented danced stories as a genre of spectacle entirely independent from opera. In the intervening years, the consequences of dancing a story inscribed themselves on the dancing body, altering radically its expressivity. As emblematized in the roles constructed for Pygmalion's sculpture, the projecting of narrative through dance eventually prohibited the dancing body from becoming a somebody. Even as the sculpture came to life, her dancing gestured a vacant physicality and a stereotypic interiority.

The effects of dance's narrativization continue to reverberate throughout the contemporary world of dance where the opposition between "abstract" and "representational" movement vocabularies embroils choreographers and critics in endless dilemmas concerning dance's significance. Contemporary modern and balletic theatrical dance traditions toss and turn between the needs to convey didactic meaning and to explore physical possibilities. In an effort to corporealize new dancing and storying bodies that are not no-bodies, this essay undertakes the double-bodied project of staging critically a past for dance while also watching the choreography of the historian at work.

In 1734 a letter published in the Mercure de France described for the edification of
In its role as a dancing historian's body, my body shifts uncomfortably as
her adoring Parisian audience the latest accomplishments of renowned dancer and
it apprehends the distance between the letter's spirited account of Sallé's
choreographer Marie Sallé.[1] Performing in the pantomime-rich London theater world,
performance and a fuller resurrection of its choreographic impact – the
Sallé had introduced a radical new interpretation of Ovid's story about the sculptor
significance it held and holds for audiences eager to participate in the
Pygmalion. As detailed in the letter, Sallé had chosen to appear uncorseted, without wig or
pleasures and responsibilities of dance viewing. My body must stretch
mask, and to adapt movement from the vocabulary of pantomime in order to depict a
across this gap between factual residue and choreographic meaning,
faithful likeness of a Greek sculpture. These scandalously realistic choreographic choices
between then and now, between danced step and written word. My body
achieved instant acclaim, prompting re-publications of the letter in newspapers across
begins its dance across the gap in this way:
Europe and inspiring numerous plagiarized productions.[2]

The whole ballet, lasting perhaps twenty minutes, commenced with Pygmalion in his atelier surrounded by six assistants, mallets and chisels in hand, whose spirited frolic played one *tour de force* against another. At Pygmalion's request they opened the back of the workshop where they found a statue of uncommon perfection. Pygmalion regarded it tenderly, touching its feet and waist, adding bracelets to its arms and a necklace, and kissing its hands. His passionate transports gave way to anxious frustration and finally a dream-like stupor. Finally, arousing himself, he prayed to the goddess Venus to bring his beloved statue to life. A new and charming musical air accompanied by three sudden shafts of light signaled Venus' acquiescence to his plea. Galatea, much to the astonishment of Pygmalion and his assistants, slowly stirred to life. As the sculptor offered her his hand so that she might descend from her platform and touch the ground, she began to dance, forming simple steps with an elegant ease. Pygmalion then demonstrated more complicated sequences of steps, each of which Galatea elaborated upon with graceful aplomb. This dancing lesson culminated in mutual expressions of love, celebrated in a final dance performed by assistants, sculptor, and living work of art.

Two aspects of Sallé's *Pygmalion* struck Parisian audiences as especially arresting. The first derived from her status as *premiere danseuse* at the Paris Opéra, the most elite institutionalization of the arts of music and dance in all Europe. As an employee of the Opéra and hence an emissary of the King, it seemed remarkable that Sallé would abandon the decorous trappings that signalled both her identity as an artist and the accomplishments of her art form – all in order to implement a new choreographic concept. And second, her ballet used pantomime to portray faithfully the sincere feelings of danced characters. Pantomime had become a familiar staple at fair and street performances in Paris where it played the subversive role of satirizing or circumventing narrative, but it had seldom been invoked as the principal medium for sustaining a coherent exchange of thoughts and feelings among all those onstage.[3] Thus Sallé's production simultaneously transgressed boundaries in the hierarchical systems of status and genre.

But Sallé's audacious initiative reverberated with an import that extended far beyond the innovative and fashionable trends of the moment. Her dance did not simply evidence a new generation's tastes and sensibilities coming to embodiment. Rather, it gestured towards an aesthetic and political rupture of enormous proportions. It demonstrated an unprecedented kind of individual initiative in its control and direction of artistic creation. It likewise intimated a new conception of individual identity in its prefigurement of the Enlightenment value of *sensibilité*, with its focus on emotion, motivation, and empathy, and the body's authentic participation in hosting and communicating these feelings.[4] This new notion of the individual, contained within and supported by the physical body, provided the foundation for the political ideals of citizenship and the supporting definitions of public and private space and masculine and feminine behavior upon which the Revolution would be based.

133

Fifty five years later, at the very end of that Revolution, the aspiring choreographer

In its effort to fathom the physicality of such by-gone dancing,

Louis Milon selected the Pygmalion myth as subject for his first full-length ballet.[5] Its

my body seizes upon a simple, comparative strategy:

premiere at the Théâtre Ambigu-Comique enjoyed such success that it was produced at the

analyze two, or even three distinctive ballets that utilize

Paris Opéra the following year. Divided into two substantial acts, each probably the length

the same storyline in order to find embedded in their

of Sallé's entire ballet, Milon constructed his version within the larger frame of an

disparate choreographic emplotments the systems of

anacreontic pastorale. The whole first act expanded on the differences between Constant

representation that guide each choreographic decision.

and Inconstant Love, personified by two cherub-like figures, one with arrows of gold, the

My body can move more fully into the physical framework

other with arrows of paper, who vied to determine the fate of Pygmalion's love for the

of each ballet by contrasting their choreographic

shepherdess Delphide. Inconstant Love triumphed with a series of manoeuvres that

renditions of the same scene, character, or gesture.

embroiled Delphide in other amorous liaisons. Pygmalion's repeated attempts to attract her

Tacking back and forth among them, my body

ended in dejected despair. As Act I drew to a close a cloud covering the stage lifted to reveal

builds fluency in each of their approaches

a sculptor's studio with several apprentices busily at work on a group of statues. Inconstant

to dance composition.

Love handed Pygmalion a chisel and mallet and then exited.

The second act seems to have been heavily influenced by Jean Jacques Rousseau's *Lyric Scene* of the Pygmalion story published in 1762 and first performed at the Paris Opéra in 1772.[6] Like Rousseau's mimed monologue, Milon's choreography consisted almost entirely of a long solo for the sculptor in his atelier. As the curtain parted, Pygmalion could be seen holding open a corner of the drape surrounding a large pedestal. After gazing once more with charmed approbation at the statue beneath the drape, he proceeded to commence work on one of the several partially formed stones in the room. The results of his gestures failed to meet his approval and he moved on to the next stone. Here again, he became disillusioned with his own gestures, so much so that he threw his tools on the table and slumped to the floor. Soon, however, he was back on his feet, dismissing each stone in turn as inadequate to his task. He approached the draped pedestal and slowly opened the curtain to reveal the perfectly executed Galathea, an exact replication of his unloving Delphide. Captivated by her grace and proportions, Pygmalion moved closer, then further away, examining the statue from all angles. He perceived a possible flaw and retrieved his chisel to amend it, but then reconsidered, fearing that he could do irreparable damage. He cast his tools across the room and started to close the drape, but could not. Again his passionate devotion to the statue inspired him to alter her form slightly, this time by adding a garland of flowers around her neck. He stepped back to admire his work, but immediately determined that she was more beautiful without ornament and rushed to remove the necklace. He stood still, absorbed in tender regard. Eventually aware of his reverie, he became embarrassed and then full of resolve. He toured the studio, gathering up his tools, which he hung on the wall before leaving for the night. Still, he could not resist one last glance at the statue, and the sight of her impelled him to her. He fell on his knees and expressed his love. Suddenly the studio and sculptures vanished, and Galathea and Pygmalion found themselves transported into the gardens of Cythera where Venus brings the statue to life. Graces, Amours, and Pleasures joined in the festive ballet that ended the act.

Milon's version of the Pygmalion story presented a striking contrast between the pastoral idyls of shepherds, shepherdesses, and Amours in Act I and Pygmalion's long, introspective soliloquy in Act II. The revolving flirtations of young men and women in the first act conformed to many of the eighteenth-century conventions for ballets representing rural life. The hunting and chasing, hiding and seeking, and chance amorous encounters among all characters created the kind of pleasing, perpetual change that had delighted audiences for a century. Act II, however, required viewers to focus exclusively on a single individual's conflict-ridden actions. Here they saw the inner life of the character portrayed more fully than ever before. Pygmalion's extended deliberations, full of doubts and new resolve, focused on an immobile image who was incapable of returning his gaze. Repeatedly, he gestured towards her, demonstrating his attachment to her, but the statue, in its unresponsiveness, pointed him back towards his new role as artist. The statue thus functioned as a manifestation of ideal form, a source of inspiration but also of distraction from his ongoing work as sculptor. Charged with these two contradictory roles, and utterly impassive, the statue created the narrative conditions under which Pygmalion's mental and emotional life could unfold.

Salle's immobile statue had sustained the erotic encounter between sculptor and work of art during moments when he touched her feet and waist or decorated her with jewelry. But she had not served as the stationary measure of his feelings, the mute and stony partner in his internal dialogue. In Salle's ballet, the artwork, once created, was attributed a life of its own. Not only did the major portion of the action center on the interplay between Pygmalion and Galathea, but both artist and artwork coordinated their actions so as to enable a series of discoveries, shot through with eros, about their own identities. Galathea systematically assimilated society through her instruction in that most consummate of all civilized pursuits – dancing. Pygmalion likewise discovered how to translate his artistic sensibilities into mobile form, responding to each of her exquisitely interpreted phrases with an elegant proposal for the next dance. The cadre of assistants,

a social frame around their evolving relationship, underscored the insepara-
bility of self from society.

Milon, in contrast, used the statue's immobility to focus the action on
the artist's appraisal of himself and his work. His Pygmalion, entirely alone,
danced out an interiorized subjectivity and also a new conception of art as
the sublimation of desire. In the same way that he divided Amour into
constant and inconstant types, Milon fashioned Galathea as a real person in
Act I and as Pygmalion's projected desire in Act II. For the first time viewers
were given an explanatory origin for the identities of both artwork and artist:
Delphide's fickle abuse of Pygmalion's devotion caused his conversion to
sculptor. The fidelity and intensity of his love for her, sublimated into art,
produced a masterpiece. The magnificence of his artistic creation, like the
depth of his character, could be traced to her inconstancy. Thus Pygmalion's
ability to transform life into art and his striking revelations of doubt and
desire ultimately depended upon a series of non-negotiable distinctions.
Life and art, constancy and inconstancy, creator and created became essentialized opposites embodied in the characters of the two Amours, Delphide,
and Galathea.

This technique of configuring dichotomous oppositions, so evident in
Rousseau's theorization of the social contract, resonated throughout the political and artistic production of the late eighteenth century. It enabled a new
conception of human agency by stipulating an actor and an acted-upon that
rationalized the political re-formations undertaken throughout the Revolution.
In place of the mutually defining identities of monarch and subject, participants in the Revolution argued that autonomous, individually active agents
might collectively determine their own destiny. Yet this liberatory agenda, as
Foucault has clearly shown, included new strategies of control and new
subjects of domination that served only to redistribute rather than abolish
oppressive structurings of power. Galathea, for example, icon for the feminine and the bodily, had in Sallé's ballet been able to descend from her
pedestal and dance, whereas Milon's statue remained excruciatingly fixed in
her place. Sallé had staged her ballet at the intersection of categories such as
life and art, elaborating an exchange between artist and sculpture whose spontaneity heightened the eros of their communication. Milon's Pygmalion, in
his encounters with the real and then the ideal, could gesture his sentimental
longing for an ideal love, but never dance out the consequences of a love
come to life.

In 1847 Arthur St. Léon choreographed yet another version of Pygmalion and
As my body moves around and through these versions of Pygmalion, it begins
Galathea, *La Fille du Marbre* which he organized into two acts, preceded by a lengthy series
to register the relations between one body and another, between body and subject,
of virtuoso dances that showed off all the dancers in their Spanish dress.[7] A lavish
and between subject and surround that are embedded in each choreographer's choices.

production that moved from the palace of the Genie of Fire to the crowded streets of 15th-

Each choreographer's every decision articulates some aspect of corporeal,

century Seville, the ballet none the less received substantial criticism from journalists, who

individual, gendered, and social identity. These choreographic choices

found the plot unnecessarily complicated, the extravagant scenic changes dutifully

constitute a theorization of embodiment – how bodies express and interact in a

presented, and the dancing redolent with effort.[8] St. Léon had varied the plot by imbuing

given cultural moment. But in order to comprehend the impact of the dancing body

the woman-statue with a power, unknown to her, to come to life but also to determine her

as it performed these choices in its historical time, I need to situate it

ultimate destiny. Where both Sallé and Milon structured their ballets along a trajectory that

alongside other contemporaneous bodies engaged in related cultural endeavors. Only then

culminated in the union of sculptor and statue, St. Léon fashioned characters whose

can I begin to detect what story these three stories of Pygmalion, taken together, may tell.

entanglement with one another could only end tragically.

When the curtain opened the sculptor had just concluded negotiations with Satan to exchange his own soul for the enlivenment of his beloved statue, provided that the Genie of Fire would agree to inspire her with the breath of life. The Genie placed his own further stipulation on the deal: this woman-statue could never fall in love or she would suffer the return to inanimate stone. The sculptor, relegated to the role of fatherly chaperone, then watched in wonderment as the unattainable object of his desire slowly came to life as the gypsy girl Fatma. Satan followed his new property who, in turn, followed his beloved creation up from the bowels of the earth and into the center of Seville. Bewitching passersby, guards, religious penitents, and even the city's mayor, the beautiful gypsy could not herself resist the impassioned overtures of a young Moorish prince, imprisoned in the palace where she was to dance for the King of Spain. Yet a revolt had already been planned, and at a pre-ordained signal the prince led his subjects into fierce battle, eventually reclaiming the city and his crown. He returned triumphant to his gypsy-queen, but as he drew her up the stairs to the throne she suddenly turned to stone. The sculptor, ever vigilant but increasingly powerless, swooned with grief and died. The ballet's final image presented Satan resting his foot on the body whose soul he had just received.

Satan, and not Venus, presided over the fates of characters in St. Léon's ballet, his dark will triumphing over love in the end. Rather than a classical Greek sculpture whose purity of form could easily assimilate to societal norms, the female character Fatma displayed all the elements of the classic Orientalist fantasy: she descended from an exotic community whose mysterious way of life aroused fascination and terror;[9] her unabashed interest in fleshly desires enhanced the appetites as well as the status of all those who could contain her exuberant body. Sensuous, joyous, and certainly not immobile as in Milon's ballet, Fatma was none the less pinned among the controlling gazes of five male characters: the adoring creator who determined her appearance; Satan and the Genie who constructed her fate; the lecherous mayor who authorized her public life; and the amorous Prince who defined her love. Like Milon's Galathea who fulfilled contradictory functions of inspiration and distraction, Fatma's identity revolved around the prohibition and desire to love. Unlike Milon's heroine, whose power resided solely in her ability to attract her creator's attention, Fatma was given one "act of free will" – the suicidal acknowledgement of love on which narrative closure depended.

In Milon's *Pygmalion* the statue constituted the masculine projection of the feminine through which the male sculptor could manifest interiority. Here the statue functioned as a feminized commodity whose exchange among men ensured their potency. Milon's sculptor, full of emotion yet utterly ineffectual, became integrated in St. Léon's ballet into a range of male character types whose interactions mutually enhanced their power and influence. In a period of intense political disillusionment and on the eve of another revolution, St. Léon's ballet referenced the masculine domain of public governance struggling to assert itself in the face of a powerful, burgeoning capitalist market and a massive, obfuscatory bureaucracy. Implicit within the ballet's homosocial world of rulers and reformists was a new conception of human agency, one in which actor and acted-upon no longer maintained a clear, causal connection. The economic momentum of capitalism with its abstraction of product from labor, on the one hand, and the civil bureaucracy's tortuous routinization of governance, on the other, intervened so as to render seemingly ineffectual any attempts at shaping a social destiny.

Serving as a cipher for the disrupted connection between actor and action, the gypsy girl Fatma shimmered with the same attractiveness as merchandise issuing from the new capitalist machinery of production. Alienated from the labor that produced them, commodities arranged in stores invited consumers to acquire them as accoutrements to their social identity, as prophylactics patching over the discrepancy between concrete labor and symbolic capital. Similarly, the gypsy girl supplemented male political and sexual agency, giving it an illusory sense of efficacy. As in Milon's ballet she never attained any personhood. The sculpture's identity in both ballets resulted exclusively from behavior, prescribed by male characters, that fulfilled their amorous and sexual desires. In Milon's *Pygmalion* these desires were cast as auto-erotic, whereas in St. Léon's they appeared as homo-erotic.[10] In both ballets Galathea's behavior was essential to the story's getting told: her *inaction* created narrative suspense, and her actions, coming to life or falling in love, permitted narrative closure.

Only in Sallé's ballet did the primitive and protean structure of the narrative enable the woman-statue to participate in the construction of her own identity. She and her creator, through their seemingly spontaneous danced dialogues, mutually defined their relationship as well as their individual contributions to it. Their ongoing reciprocity similarly signaled the self-generating, polysemic properties of art itself. Once created, the art object's meanings could expand and change as one continued to interact with it. Unlike Milon's ballet, where art endured as the fixed product of sublimated desire, or St. Léon's production, where art, entirely commodified, carried a different purchase price for each potential buyer, Sallé's depiction of art celebrated its renewability: erotic, passionate, and intelligent, in turn.

Following Sallé's lead, this essay seeks to dance with the historical dances it
Theorizations of embodiment – body's relation to subjectivity,
analyzes. Not a pictograph, or a verbal portrait, or a sentimental paean to the unsayable, it
expressivity, community – found in dance and in related cultural practices
looks for bodies in the texts that describe the danced action and tries to partner
can mutually inform one another. Excavating conceptualizations of the
them. It is a dance of excess. In an effort to resurrect bodies from the past, the
historical body in medicine or etiquette or sports
choreography of this essay projects the Pygmalion ballets as maps of their political and
renders the meaning of the dancing body more precise,
cultural surround, and, at the same time, infuses the ballets with an overabundance of
just as an analysis of choreographic choices that construct
meaning culled from related cultural practices within that surround. It claims far
the dancing body elucidates the role of body
more about the significance of those dances than their historical records warrant. It situates
in those other pursuits. The interdisciplinary project of yoking
them at points of crucial transition in the history of danced narratives. It finds in their
choreography to other forms of theorization about the body
vocabularies of movement, the ornamentation and variation they introduce, their
is what permits our contemporary bodies to understand the cultural labor
characteristic disposition of bodies in space, their integration of dance with staged
of dance. This interdisciplinary gathering of bodies together is what
spectacle theoretical moves with analogues in other cultural practices, that, through their
shows dance as one instance of culture making itself.
unison movement, create noticeable historical change.

Marie Sallé, daughter of fair theater performers and niece of a famous harlequin, grew up as member of that international and itinerant class of professional artists who joined aristocrats at their houses for evenings of private entertainment after having performed at the fair theaters before an audience composed predominantly of the working classes and the *petit bourgeoisie*.[11] In her contact with the fair theaters and her many London engagements, she had ample opportunities to witness the innovative use of pantomime, gesture, and physical theater that were the featured mediums of expression in their productions. It was her unique contribution to the concert dance tradition, however, to find in pantomimed satire a vocabulary and syntax for a new genre of dancing.

Remarkably, her *Pygmalion* was never presented at the Opéra, perhaps because its short length and narrative integrity contravened the grand aesthetic objectives of the five-act opera ballets. Her extraordinary artistry as a dancer, however, not only won her the top-ranking title at the Opéra, but also the opportunity to choreograph several ballets as acts within larger operas throughout the 1730s and 1740s. In these she began to work out the intercalation of mimed gesture and danced step.[12] A subsequent generation of influential choreographers – Hesse, Hilverding, and probably Noverre – saw her choreography there. Their work from the 1750s, along with performances by English pantomimists and actors such as David Garrick, gave critical momentum to the new genre of the story ballet and also helped to consolidate the Encyclopédists' conception of gesture and its role in theatrical reform.[13] Sallé's choice of costume and movement met their criteria for reform even as it signaled the demise of Baroque aesthetic values.

Sallé's experiments at the Opéra took place against the backdrop of an altogether different kind of dancing. Typical productions there alternated characters who sang the story with dancers who displayed the pomp, gaiety, or somberness of the situation. Following the static staging of singers in dialogue, dancers would suddenly sweep on to the stage, their majestic symmetry, intricate floor patterns, the just and regulated exchange of their bodies in space, all celebrating, even as they interrupted, the circumstances of the singing characters. These sumptuous danced interludes augmented in splendour with each act until the climactic spectacle, which usually featured a solo by one or more of the *premiers danseurs* at the Opéra.

Casanova remarked upon one such performance, that of Louis Dupré in *Les Fêtes Vénétiennes* from 1745. Accustomed to the Italian pantomime, he was baffled by his glimpse of this superb but ephemeral and seemingly irrelevant dancer:

Suddenly the whole of the pit burst into loud applause at the appearance of a tall, well-made dancer, wearing a mask and an enormous black wig, the hair of which went half-way down his back, and dressed in a robe open in front and reaching to his heels ... I saw that fine figure coming forward with measured steps, and when the dancer had arrived in front of the stage, he raised slowly his rounded arms, stretched them gracefully backward and forward, moved his feet with precision and lightness, took a few small steps, made some battements and pirouettes and disappeared like a butterfly. The whole had not lasted half a minute. The applause burst from every part of the house; I was astonished, and asked my friend the cause of all these bravos.

"We applaud the grace of Dupré and the divine harmony of his movements.

He is now sixty years of age, and those who saw him forty years ago say that he is always the same."

"What! Has he never danced in a different style?"

"He could not have danced in a better one, for his style is perfect, and what can you want above perfection?"[14]

Like many other French dancers of his background and training, Dupré had perfected a kind of dancing which itself derived from perfected noble comportment. His carriage, the easy articulation of his arms and legs, the refined measure of his gestures, his alacrity – all demonstrated an ideal way of moving in the social world. Quick darting motions of the legs, the coordinated rise and fall of arms, and a responsive torso conducted hands, feet, and head along desired pathways in ways that resembled the prescribed manners for performing proper social intercourse.[15]

Whether walking or standing, greeting or acknowledging one another, courtiers necessarily learned a style and manner for the performance of every task. These protocols of behavior, well-documented since the Renaissance, had been substantially enriched and refined by Louis XIV in the early years of his reign as a way, literally, to control the bodies of those around him. The adherence of each body to its specifically assigned tasks and of all bodies to a generalized manner of interaction was mandated by the king as a primary means of consolidating and protecting monarchic authority. One important feature of this style, identified by William Hogarth in his *Analysis of Beauty*, was the gracefulness of its trace made by the body part as it moved through space. In presenting one's hand, for example, the curve traced must neither exaggerate nor under-inflect the ideal "S" shape. In walking, the waving trace created by the head must alternate smoothly between low and high. The minuet, the most perfect of all dances, amplified on this trace by exploring a range of heights for the erect body. As Hogarth observed:

> The ordinary undulating motion of the body in common walking (as may be plainly seen by the waving line, which the shadow of a man's head makes against a wall as he is walking between it and the afternoon sun) is augmented in dancing into a larger quantity of *waving* by means of the minuet-step, which is so contrived as to raise the body by gentle degrees somewhat higher than ordinary, and sink it again in the same manner lower in the going on of the dance. The figure of the minuet-path on the floor is also composed of serpentine lines, . . . when the parties by means of this step rise and fall most smoothly in time, and free from sudden starting and dropping, they come nearest to . . . the beauty of dancing . . ."[16]

Courtiers performed their requisite duties leaving in their wake a graceful tracerie, and they also embodied that mandated grace as they devoted themselves to dancing at general *bals* held after the ballets and during evenings of mixed *divertissements*. One's social status could be enhanced or jeopardized at such gatherings as a result of one's composure and facility while moving. Accomplishment at dancing provided a base for the competent execution of all other activities.[17] Its mastery assured the aristocrat of the ability to achieve a calm, moderated easefulness – neither too erect nor too floppy, always agile, always cool – in fencing, tennis, and all the martial arts. Dupré's dancing thus celebrated the stylistic values inherent in the execution of quotidien aristocratic responsibilities as well as the social dancing in which all aristocrats participated.

Sallé's character Pygmalion would have reflected the graceful orderliness requisite of all gestures in his attempts to sculpt, his adjustments of the statue, and his conversations with his assistants. The dancing lesson with his live sculpture recapitulated the meta-disciplinary status of dancing. Because skill at dancing insured a defectless body, an easeful execution of all actions, it was the first accomplishment the statue should achieve. Their duet also demonstrated the central role of dancing in purveying sociability. Through the slight change in focus, the inclination of the head, the rounding of a shoulder, adumbrations of feelings in all their delicacy and complexity were articulated discreetly in public.

Through her choice of the Pygmalion story, Sallé registered these familiar grammars of aristocratic bodily comportment, its capacity to purvey a physicalized sociability. Yet what viewers found most arresting, what Casanova knew intimately from attending the Italian opera, were the self-propelling sequences of passions which the sculptor faithfully portrayed: despair resolving into determination dissolving into doubt returning to greater despair; or quizzical uncertainty transforming into wonderment and then into overwhelming joy. Courtly behavior never permitted these extremes of sentiment, much less an exact and faithful representation of them. In celebrating this courtly aesthetic, Dupré's dancing, moderated and constant in its motion, avoided expression of precise passions in favor of intensities of various affects. His characters had embodied wistfulness, amusement, or melancholy but never outright joy, chagrin, or hatred.[18]

Yet the affective magnetism of Dupré's display had, by the 1730s, already begun to dissipate, and Sallé's ability to integrate representations of the passions into the danced actions presaged a new approach to choreography as an art capable of depicting realistic, moving images of human nature. These danced dramas began to appear all over Europe in the 1750s and 1760s, finally making their way into the Opéra's seasons in the 1770s. Rather than the majestic pomp evoked by orderly rows of dancers encrusted with feathers, ribbons, and jewels, embroidering the space with a never-ending series of configurations, they engaged realistically costumed characters in tensile, asymmetrical configurations whose push and pull depicted their passion-filled responses to one another. Instead of the pristine, rational perspective defined by a stage highly charged by the various kinds of spatial inscription – traceries of feet on the floor, arms and hands in the air, the collocations of bodies distributed across the stage – they presented the viewer with tableaux vivantes – frozen moments of angst, joy, intrigue, or anger in which each character registered a unique and vivid participation. The face engaged in these stereotypic depictions as both a part of the total bodily response and also as the final arbiter of the movement's meaning. No longer masked, it presented the most condensed version of the passion, whether pain, anger, shock, adoration, interest, confusion, flirtation, amazement, being represented in the drama.

Dupré's dancing, always signaling the precise location of the body within spatial and social grids, always moving with soft poignancy or brilliant vivacity, never vivified feeling so didactically. From within his dance's world of aestheticized affect, characters elaborated a refined, but nonetheless compelling, orchestration of desire. Their elusive restraint invited a thousand different fantasies. When masked, the dancers' immobile faces failed to clarify their inclinations, allowing viewers instead to find multiple attachments for their longing in the abstract articulations of the body's joints. Even without masks, the dancers' faces, charismatically calm, rebuffed any definitive emotional connection to one another, even as they drew eros-filled eyes to them.

The emerging pantomime ballets never seduced in this way. No barriers, such as the mask, the costume, or the interlocked patterns of the choreography, stimulated the viewer's desiring imagination. Instead, coquetry of all sorts was faithfully depicted, plainly evident. What evoked attachment to the characters was their winsomeness or courage, their woeful plight or their audacious valiance. The desirable thus became wrapped within a personality, a character one could get to know over the course of the story and whose nature could easily be summoned up in the imagination via review of the narrative for a re-eroticized encounter after the performance had long past.

This kind of attachment to story and character came to replace the connection to the bodily that Dupré's dancing offered. In Dupré's tradition, dancers' bodies displayed with daring and whimsical accuracy, the proper comportment in greeting, touching, and gazing, while also maintaining the proper proximities to one another. These displays of bodily inscription – the symmetrical to and fro, the calculated clusters of individuals, the graceful resolve from one configuration to the next – showed bodies suspended within and reticulated by the linear patterns of both desire and the social. Individual identity, established as much by how one moved as what one said, never existed apart from the patterns of all bodies in regulated motion together.

The pantomime ballets embodied a new conception of individuality as contained within and supported by individual bodies. Each body could undergo, just as it could faithfully depict, self-generating sequences of passion. Each body could be compelled into reactive responses to other bodies according to the causal logic of emotional syntax. No longer suspended within the web of gestures hierarchized by the perfect perspective of the stage as universe and the single, most favorable viewing location of the monarch, these mimetic bodies opened up the spectacle to a wider range of viewing positions from which their discursive messagings could be apprehended. They disentangled the aristocratic subject from the requisite protocols of bodily comportment, and they extended to all human beings regardless of class or profession the same capacities to feel and to empathize with another's feelings.

Salle's dancers, in transit between these two representational strategies, maintained dual types of identity: they each coalesced as self-propelling, autonomous entities, but they also required one another in order to establish that identity. One moment the ballet depicted a body enmeshed in a sequence of causally linked emotions and another body literally animating itself into life. The next it showed both bodies dependent upon each other for the impetus that would flesh out the formal protocol of danced repartee. In that duet the dancers simulated and probably even actualized an improvised dialogue in which one's response derived from the phrase, never known in advance, just executed by the other. Salle, poised between these two varieties of identity, may well have chosen the myth of the sculptor whose sculpture is brought to life as the version of metamorphosis most expressive of the choreographic changes she envisioned.

Like Salle, Louis Milon came up through the ranks of Opera, making his debut in 1790 and assuming the position of assistant Maître de Ballet in 1815. Where her career spanned a period of relative political stability, his witnessed two major reorganizations of political power with concomitant redefinitions of the function of art and the institution of the Opera. Studying at the Opera in the 1780s, Milon would have attended the highly popular story ballets that were produced as a regular part of the season there and also transported to Versailles for special viewings by members of the court. As a member of the Opera staff in the 1790s, he would have participated in the patriotic pantomimes held there and also in the outdoor festivals that incorporated pantomime into their choreography of and for the People. He saw the overthrow of monarchic jurisdiction over theatrical production and the consequent burgeoning of small independent theaters, as well as the vilification of the Opera as an instrument of the King and its eventual reinstantiation as monument to the state of France. And he saw the repeated, seemingly spontaneous seizure of bodies by the Carmagnole, the street dance that embodied patriotic ideals most fervently.

His *Pygmalion* joined the conservative repertoire of productions at century's end that achieved stability for the Opera through their advocacy of grace, beauty, and visual opulence in the marked absence of any obvious or even

144

muted allegorical political references. Ironically, in Rousseau's version of the story, the self-interrogation that Pygmalion underwent was envisioned as the formative process through which he could assume a role as responsible participant in the governance of the nation.[19] In Milon's rendition, however, the sculptor lived through all the angst, doubt, and frustration of artistic production as a way of diverting audiences from any active participation in politics. Venus, now an absurdly vacant symbol of aristocratic life, after all Pygmalion's anguish, simply granted his wish.

In the absence of any political message, Milon's production nonetheless instructed viewers in docile citizenship. His Pygmalion exemplified both the causal logic of emotion and also the self-regulating control over those emotions required of all members of the new nation state. As shepherd he had learned to sublimate his thwarted desire into artistic creation. As sculptor he vented his frustration only on the air around him. And these self-disciplining actions were reiterated in the actual style of performance required for the production. Milon, performer of his own choreography, demonstrated a magnificent command over bodily representation. He showed a person capable of motivating his own body into highly credible renditions of feelings that may or may not have been sincere. This mastery over bodily display signaled an entirely new relationship between body and self, one that dismissed the body as intersubjective discursive field in favor of a responsive and responsible instrument for individual expression, one that identified the individual citizen.

The development of a responsive, objectified dancing body resulted from the increasing scrutiny given to the body in general scientific and medical research and from the intensive study of bodily expressivity conducted by anatomists dedicated to understanding the skeletal and muscular basis of expression.[20] It likewise grew out of increasingly scientific and regimented dance training procedures designed to meet the demand for more virtuoso physical accomplishments in performance. Just as viewers applauded the new achievements of danced narratives in the second half of the eighteenth century, so they pressed for dazzling skill in the intricate vocabulary of classical steps and their variations.[21] Training programs in Sallé's time had consisted of the repetition of rudimentary exercises such as *pliés* and *tendus* followed by the practice of dances. Fundamental bodily defects such as knock-knees or bow-legs would be addressed through special exercises that strengthened and stretched the legs. The execution of dances themselves progressing from the simple to more complex was seen as capable of imparting all the perquisites necessary for dancing. By the late eighteenth century, however, dancers necessarily engaged in numerous repetitions of a lengthy series of exercises designed to establish clear spatial paths for the body and to extend it further along those paths. Rather than study individually with Dancing Masters, they attended classes where groups of dancers worked simultaneously on the same series of exercises.[22]

The emerging discipline of anatomy enhanced this project by providing a detailed vocabulary for and analysis of body parts in relation to one another. Anatomical discourse was taken up by choreographers and also by teachers of correct posture as an objective framework for evaluating bodily deficiencies. The new exercises for dancers – *ronds des jambes*, leg circles, *developés* – were seen to give the body an internalized strength through which the musculature could correctly support the skeleton. In the new science of physical education teachers likewise abandoned the corset as a corrective device that would prop the body up and focused instead on a regimen of exercises that would allow it to erect itself.[23]

This kind of exercising of the body not only consolidated it as an object but also gave it an enduring volume – one that was conceptualized as having an interior, an exterior, and a relation between these two. Sallé's dancers had traced out volumes as they moved through space, yet the body itself evidenced little interior depth. Early-eighteenth-century prescriptions for proper alignment treated the body in silhouette as a set of block-like sections that should be pushed or twisted so as to abut one another. By the early nineteenth century, however, the body, simply by standing in place, indicated a volume. Programs to develop its erectness referenced an ideal line located inside the body towards which all parts of the body should be drawn. The dance vocabulary used in the early eighteenth century to indicate volumes by tracing their contours through space now became the medium in which the body's limbs could literally embody a linear ideal. Hidden at the very core of each mobile unit, in fact, establishing such a core, this geometric ideal provided an absolute and objective framework for learning dancing and for evaluating each dancer's performance.[24]

Pygmalion's soliloquy depended upon, even as it metaphorized, this interiority. Physically his body swelled and then ex-pressed in expanding cycles of agitated desire, each returning him to a moment of repose before instigating a new syntax of feeling. The welling up of feeling, the conflicting impulses and internalized debates could only take place inside a volumetric body. Metaphorically the abstract ideal defining the core of each expressive movement reappeared as the moments of repose out of which the next need to move would spring. The plot cleverly provided the pretext for this alternation between movement and stasis by rationalizing new forms of desire that propelled his body around the atelier, towards and away from Galathea, or his tools, or the other half-formed sculptures.

None of Pygmalion's motions, however, would have been conceivable without the fixed point of the statue. Galathea, the ultimate extension of the abstract ideal that defined bodily interiority, presided over Pygmalion's agitated subjectivity, making his peregrinations plausible. Her static monumentality, her steady source-ness enabled the measure of the sculptor's emotional progression. Unlike Sallé's ballet where the couple, perpetually redefining their own identities, could not accumulate interiority, much less dramatic tension,

146

Milon's *Pygmalion* built and built and built before finally opening out into the extravaganza of Venus' pleasure-filled gardens.

Both the volumetric body, by containing the emotions, and the fixed object of desire by fomenting them, permitted this progression. The fact of the abstract ideal within the dancing body confirmed the body's autonomy just as its regulation of the body of the story created narrative closure. Porous bodies, such as those danced out by Sallé's couple, could only mutually regulate within an overarching system of authority such as the prescriptions for bodily comportment and conduct at court provided. But that entire system of social regulation had lost all valence long before Louis XVI lost his claim on the body politic. Even with an emperor in the making, the citizens who had danced the Carmagnole through the streets of France could no longer resume places within the hierarchized spaces of absolutist government. Their newly bounded bodies, like those in Milon's *Pygmalion*, submitted themselves instead to the disciplining of narrative itself.[25]

St. Léon, accomplished violinist and originator of a new kind of dance notation, travelled throughout Europe staging ballets in which he, like Sallé and Milon before him, often danced one of the principal roles. By the time he began to choreograph, the relative proportion of male and female dancers on stage had drastically altered. Up through the 1820s at the Opéra, men and women participated in equal numbers as principles and also in the *corps de ballet*. By the early 1830s, however, ballets often featured large numbers of female *corps* dancers with only a few male dancers appearing in principal and supporting roles. And by the time of *La Fille du Marbre*'s premiere, diatribes condemning the ungainly and unsuitable appearance of male dancers commonly found their way into reviews of ballets.[26] Men, although they still undertook most of the prestigious jobs as teachers, choreographers, and producers of dance, enjoyed little respect as performers.[27] Given the small number of male principals and the exceptionally large number of male roles in *La Fille du Marbre*, St. Léon's presence, round-shouldered and none too adept, may well have been a prerequisite to the realization of his choreographic vision.

Not only was the male dancer seen as a grotesque apparition, necessary only for the faithful execution of the storyline, but ballet itself had become feminized. Increasingly, dancing was thought to convey only the lighter emotions of joy and delight and to serve as a medium for the elaboration of sexual desire. A kind of diversionary entertainment, ballet promoted the decorous and spectacular display of a body that carried little social import. In contrast to painting, music, or poetry, all of which left permanent records, dancing seemed incapable of documentation.[28] The dance's ephemeral nature, its emphasis on feeling over thought, and its cultivation of the body – all pointed away from the abstract, rational, and permanent social monuments that male society worked to achieve.

In a society that strictly separated male and female responsibilities and marked that separation through the division of social space into public and private domains, the ballet endured as one of the only public venues where feminine values could be seen. Yet as a representation of the feminine within a masculine-controlled public domain, the ballet's aesthetic increasingly derived from a masculine version of femininity. Female dancers, notorious in the press for their sexual escapades after the performance, projected while onstage the cornucopia of sensual charms stipulated as alluring to the male viewer. Male dancers, repugnant for their clumsy largeness, were equally despised for their potential effeminacy. Where a hundred years earlier, male and female dancers had danced similar vocabularies of steps alongside each other enjoying equal respect, they now entwined their separate vocabularies to form sculptural wholes in which the female partner consistently performed in front of the man. On *pointe*, the woman depended upon her partner's support to accomplish attenuated leg extensions, balances, and turns. His admiring gaze consistently directed the viewer's attention through his eyes to her body. Her exquisite lightness and irrepressible flirtatiousness embodied the ideal masculine image of the desirable yet unattainable female.

This choreographic division of labor found its perfect vehicle in the Romantic ballet plots of the 1830s and early 1840s that featured either an exotic foreigner or a supernatural creature as the female leading character. Sylphs, naiads, and wilis offered an enigmatic ephemerality, dream-like, vaporous, incomparably light. Gypsies, Creoles, and other Orientalist characters constituted the sylph's pagan counterpart. Rapturously sensual, unabashedly suggestive, these heroines after innumerable obstacles eventually consummated their romantic attachments, whereas the sylph's unequivocal Otherness always led to tragic conclusions. In either case, the male lead indulged his longing attachment to her, seeking her out, adoring her, and partnering her with solicitous mastery.

The tragic ballets depicting the impossible love between man and sylph used the separate vocabularies and stereotypic character types to greatest advantage. Their heroines symbolized not only love lost, but also dreams unrealized and unrealizable. The spectacle created by low-level gas lighting and elaborate flying machinery for tulle-skirted dancers offered both optical indefiniteness and opulence. Viewers witnessed mirage-like forms dissolving, vanishing, escaping the mortal with such softness. The sprites' world exuded a ravishing melancholy that transcended diversion and referenced truly lost hopes. The sylphide's death after her mortal lover has removed her wings carried a moral and aesthetic significance comparable to the great literature of the Romantic period.[29]

But the number of variations on this haunting tale could never supply scenarists with consistently compelling storylines. Both plots and characters became increasingly predictable in the decades following St. Léon's production. His version of Galathea, a gypsy girl conforming to the exotic

148

model for the female lead, offered nothing innovative. The formulae for choreographic production – flirtation and angst combined with lavish spectacle and *tour de force* dancing – took on the inevitability of mass-manufactured goods.

Performances were not only stereotypic, they were socially and politically insignificant. Capitalist marketing strategies initiated by producers in the early 1830s pitted one ballerina against another in intensive, objectifying advertising campaigns and opened up backstage areas where wealthy patrons might enjoy the company of dancers before, during, and after the performance. Poorly paid dancers and insubstantial government support left the institution of dance vulnerable to exploitation, both sexual and specular. Having remained in a public venue, ballerinas eventually became *femmes publiques*, and dance, no longer an art, combined, spectacularly, physical daring and thinly disguised sexual intercourse.[30]

This erosion of dancing's dignity would not have been possible without supporting changes in the conception of the body. The demise of any symbolic system of physicalized sociability, the rise of physical education as a regimen of exercises designed to provide a healthy constitution, and the intensive anatomical scrutiny received by the body had effectively morselized it. The responsive body object was no longer thought to portray candidly or convincingly the range of human feeling. Dancers either demonstrated proficiency at mime or they did not. What mattered was how their physical attributes added up to a kind of character or enabled a certain look onstage. Their individual body parts were compared in leering tones by critics. While the men were despised for their ungainliness, the women, repeatedly likened to fillies, that a man might mount, re-mount, or exchange for a new mount, or small rats, grateful for the crumbs that might fall from the master's hand, took on the lustre of a fetishized object of desire. Thus it is no surprise that St. Léon's Fatma would gasp for breath amidst the male figures who determined her every move or that she would necessarily die from having loved.

The only uncanny feature of St. Léon's productions was the fact that men and not women played all the male roles. By the mid-1840s female dancers *en travesti* frequently performed the parts of male lead and supporting characters. A commonplace in lower-class theaters since the 1820s, this titillating display of the female form in revealing masculine garb and of the female bodies together further eroded the power of dancer and dance. The female lead's charismatic allure dissipated alongside the ironizing moves of her burlesque partner. The potential of dance to evoke haunting places and unspeakable feelings devolved into teaseful amusement. But St. Léon's ballet aspired to tragedy, to ballet's Romantic past rather than its formulaic future, and male performers provided the weight necessary for such a serious statement even if their own reputation had been compromised by latent aversion to the nascent category of the homosexual and a rampant commodification of female physicality.

149

The story suggested by Sallé's, Milon's, and St. Léon's consecutive versions of the Pygmalion myth also aspires to the tragic. As theatrical dance, having entered into a *pas de deux* with narrative, learned to tell stories, the dancing body transformed from a medium of expression into its instrument. Once a locus of mobile signifying forms, it became the dumb thing through which messages necessarily passed. Like the sculptor Pygmalion, narrative constructed dance in its image, imparting its structure and syntax to the spectacle and utilizing the dancing body to convey its concerns. In order to attain a classical coherence, narrative dialecticized the body in two directions: into an interiorized expressive force and an exterior physical messenger; and into either masculine or feminine bodies gendered as opposing, complementary, and mutually dependent.

Yet the "sculptor's" work, the labor of narrative itself, cannot be separated from the crucial changes in political and economic structures and in gender roles that occurred in France from the mid-eighteenth to the mid-nineteenth centuries. The particular trajectory of narrative's effects suggested by the Pygmalion ballets both incorporated and enjoyed support from the successive attempts at a populist government, from the rise of capitalist manufacturing and marketing procedures, and from the solidification of a separate-sphere division of labor for men and women.[31] These sweeping changes affected attitudes towards the body and art and determined new pathways along which desire might move. Before dance told stories, the free play of eros across the dancing body/subject was permitted by the rigidly fixed social hierarchies of an absolutist regime. Once narrative took hold, the body, disciplined by an interiorized subject, aroused the sympathy and love of all good citizens. Only with the proliferation of capitalist and nationalist initiatives, did dancing come to reiterate the fetishistic repetition of desire and conquest that turned the female body into a commodity and the dancing body into a no-body.

But Sallé's ballets endure as reflections on and of dancing bodies that are not no-bodies. Balanced at the brink of narrative's development, they inspire a choreographic approach to the analysis of historical dance, one in which both the subject of history and the historian remain in motion. Transposing Sallé's scenario on to the process of writing dance history, the historical dancing body would descend from the pedestal of objectified knowledge and improvise a duet with the historian in which body/body-subjects mutually discover and identify themselves. Such a dance might take many forms. Yet in its ability to allow past and present bodies to affiliate, it could provide a moral, if mobile, grounding

My privileging of Sallé's choreography, motivated by feminist concerns for a woman artist and for a treatment of female characters in art that does not deny them personhood, attempts to redress the trend in twentieth-century dance history that noted her contribution as dancer but not as dance-maker. But how to accomplish such a revision without fixing a body of facts like Milon's immovable Galathea? Sallé's version of Pygmalion's story performs one possible strategy

of dance reconstruction: projecting my body into those of artist
for research. Constantly in pursuit of strategies of representation that do not speak *for* the
and artwork, I try to copy their movements as faithfully as I can, all the while knowing
historical body,[32] such a "dance" would articulate inter-discursive spaces where writing
that my dance with those historical dancing bodies is a freshly choreographed event.
and dancing can roam together, and where the historical *no*-body might revivify as a body.

NOTES

1 M***. *Mercure de France* April 1734, pp. 770–2.

2 One such production took place at the Comédie Italienne in Paris two months later. Renée Viollier's book on the composer Mouret, *Mouret, Le Musicien des Graces, 1682–1738* (repr. Geneva: Minkoff, 1976, p. 145) provides a detailed account of the Paris performance whose scenario by Panard and l'Affichart was danced by Mlle. Roland and Sr. Riccoboni to music by Mouret, who, according to Viollier, may also have composed the music for Sallé's *Pygmalion*.

3 This was not the case in London, where boundaries between "high" art and popular entertainment were not so stable and where pantomime played a more prominent role in many kinds of productions. For an indication of pantomime's success in England, see Richard Ralph's biography of the early-eighteenth-century choreographer John Weaver, who used pantomime frequently in his ballets: *The Life and Works of John Weaver* (New York: Dance Horizons, 1985). Pantomime was also highly developed in Italy. for some sense of its prominence there, see Marion Hannah Winter's *The Pre-Romantic Ballet* (London: Pitman, 1974).

4 See especially Denis Diderot's *Discours sur la Poésie dramatique* (Paris: Larousse, 1970); "Lettre sur les sourds et muets," ed. P. Meyer, in *Diderot Studies VII*, ed. O. Fellows (Geneva: Librarie Droz, 1965); and *Lettres à Sophie Volland*, ed. A. Babelon (Paris, 1938). See also *Diderot's Writings on the Theatre*, ed. F. C. Green (Cambridge: Cambridge University Press, 1936).

5 L. J. Milon, *Pygmalion, ballet-pantomime, en deux actes* (Paris: l'Imprimerie à Prix-Fixe), VII.

6 Jean-Jacques, Rousseau, *Quevres Complètes* Vol. II (Paris: Bibliothèque de la Pléiade, 1961), pp. 1926–40.

7 Arthur St. Léon, *La Fille du Marbre, ballet-pantomime en deux actes et trois tableaux* (Paris: Michel Levy Frères, 1847).

8 See Charles Maurice's review "La Fille du Marbre" in *Courrier des Spectacles*, 21 Oct. 1847, pp. 1–2.

9 For more background on gypsy life in bohemian France, see Marilyn Brown's *Gypsies and Other Bohemians: the myth of the artist in nineteenth-century France* (Ann Arbor: University of Michigan Press, 1985).

10 This analysis alludes to Eve Sedgwick's proposal in *Between Men: English Literature and Male Homosocial Desire* (New York: Columbia University Press, 1985) that nineteenth-century narratives most often revolved around the homo-erotic desire felt by two male protagonists camouflaged as the devoted attachment that each expressed for the same female character.

11 For more information on Sallé, see her biography by Émile Dacier *Une Danseuse de l'Opéra sous Louis XV: Mlle. Sallé (1707–1756)* (Paris: Plon-Nourrit et Cie, 1909) and also Pierre Aubry and Émile Dacier, *"Les Caractères de la Danse." Histoire d'un Divertissement pendant la première moitié du XVIIIe siècle* (Paris: Honoré Champion, 1905). For an excellent summary of the function of entertainment at the fair theaters, see Thomas Crow, *Painters and Public Life in*

Eighteenth Century Paris (New Haven: Yale University Press, 1985).

12 Her experiments included the pantomime ballets that occurred as single acts with the five-act opera ballets *Les Indes Galantes* (1735), *L'Europe Galante* (1736), and *Les Fêtes d'Hébé* (1739).

13 See entries to the *Encyclopedie* for gesture, sensibility, pantomime, and dance. For an insightful discussion of the role of gesture in Diderot's thinking see Herbert Josephs, *Diderot's Dialogue of Language and Gesture: "Le Neveu de Rameau"* (Columbus: Ohio State University Press, 1969).

14 Quoted in Giovanni Giacomo Casanova de Seingalt's *Histoire de ma vie* (Wiesbaden: F. A. Brockhaus, 1960), vol. 3, ch. 8, pp. 140–1.

15 For summaries of the literature on comportment and lengthy bibliographies, see Joan Wildeblood and Peter Brinson's *The Polite World: A Guide to Manners and Deportment from the Thirteenth to the Nineteenth Century* (Oxford: Oxford University Press, 1965) and Esther Aresty's *The Best Behavior: The Course of Good Manners – From Antiquity to the Present – As Seen through Courtesy and Etiquette Books* (New York: Simon and Schuster, 1970).

16 William Hogarth, *Analysis of Beauty* (1753). Repr. ed. Joseph Burke (Oxford: Oxford University Press, 1955), p. 147.

17 In giving his rationale for the establishment of an Academy of Dance, Louis XIV cited dance's role in the preparation for war as well as entertainment and edification during peace. See *Lettres patentes du roi pour l'établissment de l'Académie Royale de Danse en la ville de Paris*, Mar. 1661, p. 1; reprinted in *Danseurs et Ballet de l'Opéra de Paris depuis 1671* (Paris: Archives Nationales et Bibliotèque Nationale, 1988), p. 27.

18 Here and in the following discussion of the masked or unmasked face, I am paralleling an argument made by Norman Bryson concerning the figural charisma of Watteau's subjects. See *Word and Image: Franch Painting of the Ancien Regime* (Cambridge: Cambridge University Press, 1981), p. 74.

19 Victor Gourevitch informs me that Rousseau's *Pygmalion* was tied to the working out of the difference between "amour-propre" and "amour-de-soi," categories of attachment whose theorization was necessary for determining the nature of each individual's participation in government. Personal communication.

20 This line of argument parallels and takes inspiration from Joseph Roach's analysis of medical practices, theories of representation and theories of acting in the eighteenth century. See *The Player's Passion: Studies in the Science of Acting* (Newark: University of Delaware Press, 1985).

21 A remarkable number of reviews in the *Mercure de France* comment on the audience's desire for more *tour de force* dancing.

22 A good summary of these changes is recorded in Carlo Blasis' first publication on dance pedagogy, *Traité Elémentaire, Théorique et Pratique de l'Art de la Danse* (Milan, 1820. Repr. Bologna: Forni, 1969).

23 George Vigarello's remarkable book on changing conceptions of bodily posture and physical education makes this argument. See *Le corps redressé* (Paris: J. P. Delarge, 1978).

24 Blasis' book (*Traité Elémentaire*) contains numerous illustrations of dancers in basic positions. Frequently the illustrations show a dotted line running through the center of the leg or arm or torso, indicating the abstract ideal to which the bodily shape should conform.

25 By casting narrative in this active role, I am trying to elucidate correspondences that I perceive between a number of cultural practices which all seem to undergo an analogous process of narrativization during the eighteenth century. Henry Abelov, for example, has argued that sexual practices increasingly orchestrated a beginning, middle and end for the heterosexual couple. See "Some Speculations

on the History of Sexual Intercourse during the Long Eighteenth Century in England," *Genders* 6 (Nov. 1989): 125–30. And Edwin Lowinsky makes a similar kind of argument for the decline of polyphony and the rise of melody. See his "Taste, Style, and Ideology in Eighteenth-Century Music," in *Aspects of the Eighteenth Century*, ed. by Earl R. Wasserman (Baltimore: Johns Hopkins University Press, 1965), pp. 163–205.

26 See, for example, Jules Janin's much quoted diatribe, presented here in translation by Ivor Guest from his *The Romantic Ballet in Paris* (Middletown, Ct.: Wesleyan University Press, 1966), p. 21: "The *grand danseur* appears to us so sad and so heavy! He is so unhappy and so self-satisfied! He responds to nothing, he represents nothing, he is nothing. Speak to us of a pretty dancing girl who displays the grace of her features and the elegance of her figure, who reveals so fleetingly all the treasures of her beauty. Thank God, I understand that perfectly, I know what this lovely creature wishes us, and I would willingly follow her wherever she wishes in the sweet land of love. But a man, a frightful man, as ugly as you and I, a wretched fellow who leaps about without knowing why, a creature specially made to carry a musket and a sword and to wear a uniform. That this fellow should dance as a woman does – impossible! That this bewhiskered individual who is a pillar of the community, an elector, a municipal councillor, a man whose business it is to make and above all unmake laws, should come before us in a tunic of sky-blue satin, his head covered with a hat with a waving plume amorously caressing his cheek, a frightful *danseuse* of the male sex, come to pirouette in the best place while the pretty ballet girls stand respectfully at a distance – this was surely impossible and intolerable, and we have done well to remove such great artists from our pleasures. Today, thanks to this revolution which we have effected, woman is queen of ballet. She breathes and dances there at her ease. She is no longer forced to cut off half her silk petticoat to dress her partner with it. Today the dancing man is no longer tolerated except as a useful accessory."

27 According to Kristina Straub the situation was apparently quite different in England and in the medium of drama where female travesty performers became a threat by the early nineteenth century. See Kristina Straub's essay, "The Guilty Pleasures of Female Theatrical Cross-Dressing and the Autobiography of Charlotte Charke," in *Body Guards: The Cultural Politics of Gender Ambiguity* ed. by Julia Epstein and Kristina Straub (New York and London: Routledge, 1991), pp.142–66.

28 St. Léon himself attempted to revitalize dance notation, but his system, of enormous interest for what it tells us about the conception of the dancing body prevalent in his time, gained little support.

29 One of the most famous and enduring ballets of the Romantic period is Filippo Taglioni's *La Sylphide* (1832) with a scenario by Adolphe Nourrit, which ends in the sylph's death at the hands of her mortal lover.

30 Much of the discussion that follows has already been expeditiously presented by Abigail Solomon-Godeau in her excellent analysis of the body's significance in mid nineteenth-century photos of the Countess Castiglione, and also by Lynn Garafoloa's strategic intervention into Ivor Guest's histories of the Romantic ballet. See "The Legs of the Countess," *October* 39 (Winter 1986): 65-108, and "The Travesty Dancer in Nineteenth-Century Ballet," *Dance Research Journal* 17.2 and 18.1 (1985–6): 35–40. I am trying to complicate their analysis by considering the surround of body-related practices that helped to construct an objectified body and also by resisting an immediate connection between the erosion of the male dancer's status and the demise of an absolutist political system.

31 This separation of male and female roles into functionally distinct yet entirely separate domains included a whole theory of procreation, as Tom Laqueur's wonderful history of sexuality demonstrates. See *Making Sex: Body and Gender from the Greeks to Freud* (Cambridge, Mass. and London, Harvard University Press, 1990).

32 See Donna Haraway's powerful critique of the position that claims to speak for someone or something incapable of speech: "The Promises of Monsters: A Regenerative Politics for Inappropriate/d Others," in *Cultural Studies*, eds Lawrence Grossberg, Cary Nelson, Paula Treichler (New York, London: Routledge, 1992), pp. 295–337.

9

AFTER US THE SAVAGE GODDESS

Feminist performance art of the explicit body staged, uneasily, across modernist dreamscapes

Rebecca Schneider

> After Stephane Mallarmé, Chavannes, after my own verse, after all our subtle colour and nervous rhythm, after the faint mixed tints of Conder, what more is possible? After us the Savage God.
>
> W. B. Yeats on seeing Jarry's 1896 production of *Ubu Roi*

An invocation of ghosts may seem an odd place to begin an essay on contemporary explicit body performance art. Ghosts, after all, are explicitly disembodied signifiers. They are also particularly postmodern entities. Within the ruins of the modernist myth of originality, every act, public and private, is ghosted by precedence. Form is ruin, ghosted by content, and content is ghosted by the historical trajectory of its forms. A swastika is not a content-less form and neither is a human body in any imaginable stretch of technological or surgical transmogrification. Modernist tropes double back upon themselves, becoming "post" in an after-modernism in which anything recognized as "new" is recognized, in being "new," as old. Here, the old paradoxically erupts on the scene as the true new even as it ricochets back into temporal position again as outmoded. Postmodern artworks garner their post-modernity in their ghost dancing, their playful mimicry of precedence, positioning themselves relative to an extant, continually eruptive field of precursory modernist imagery and modernist obsession. In artworks with a conscious political agenda – such as feminist works – this playful, ping-pong mimesis is also political strategy. [1]

Modern construction and inscription of the female body, and more insidiously the "reality effects" occasioned by those inscriptions, ghost contemporary feminist counter-constructions. [2] Even in combat boots feminine form is hounded by the historical legacy of sex discrimination in everyday social

155

practice, by the history and control of woman's "appropriate" imaging, and by the effects which that appropriation (the Modern Woman, the Cult of True Womanhood, the House Wife) has had upon women's lives. The raging '90s impulse to herald identity as performative rather than fixed, natural, essential, or foundational is an impulse that must at all times acknowledge the historical backdrop of its own project.[3] That backdrop is simply the fact that performable insignia of identity – mimetics – are inevitably relative to the extant exigencies of identity-fixing, identity-forcing, and the politics of identity naturalizing that has fueled the long-burning furnace of western cultural "reality effects" – the social ramifications of alterity. If that backdrop is ignored or dismissed, theories of gender performativity risk tumbling into an "anything goes," *laissez faire* of mix-n-match gender codes without political drive. After all, to discover gender performativity does not in and of itself alter the show. To be "just acting" doesn't necessarily mean anything to Desdemona if the climax continues to result in her death.[4]

As postmodern thought and critical inquiry head ever more deeply into complex interrogations of the boundaries between the so-called performative and the so-called real, so-called culture and so-called nature, the impetus to rapidly disintegrate culturally constricting binarisms risks the very thing such binarisms are famous for: the privileging of a single term. The impulse to wrest gender away from the constrictions of "nature," to see it as completely constructed and performative, may shine a light on the mythic stature of debilitating heterosexist categories of masculinity and femininity, but it also risks obscuring the still operative reality effects of those same constructed categories. The degree to which the "real" is a ruse of performance does not alter the mechanism by which such ruses bring everyday realities into their effects. Put yet another way: while the "real" may always be performative, or constructed, that construction and its reconstruction and its re-reconstruction exist in a battlefield ghosted by that construction's historical effectivity – its reality.

So, how can we approach these ghostings? It is by now an established conundrum in cultural studies: to treat any subject matter or object of study "objectively" is to shroud that object in an armature of disinterest that veils the viewer, thinker, writer and her/his vested interest or subjective implication in the scene of viewing, studying, representing. And yet, the unveiling of a viewer's subjective investments can equally serve to obscure an object of study, wrapping it only in the potentially endless displacements of the viewer's attempts to locate herself. In the dialectical pull between objective and subjective approach, it can be a complicity, a mutuality, that is ignored or disguised. The notion of "performance" bears better than "construction" the complexities of complicity, in that it implies always an audience/performer or ritual participant relationship – a reciprocity, a practice – and as such the notion has become integral to a cultural critical perspective which wants to explore the dynamic two-way street, the "space between" self and others, subjects and objects, masters and slaves, or any system of social signification. Foucauldian examinations of power and knowledge as discursive formations and examinations of discursive formations as *events* have implicated the body, or social embodiment, in any scene or site of knowledge. Thus, sitting before an "object" of study, the question becomes one of how to apprehend – with the double connotation that word bears of both "know" and "fear" – such an embodied space a second time, after/in/aware of the history of objectification?

Particularly because the disprivileging of woman has been so closely aligned with her general cultural representation as sex, her status as object given-to-be-seen, this question of how to apprehend the space between masculin-ized subject (given to know) and feminized object (given to be known) has prompted feminist inquiry into the dynamics of western cultural ways of knowing traditionally wrapped up with visuality, with vision set forth as proprietary, transcendent of tactility, omnisciently disinterested, and essen-tially separate from the object which it apprehends.[5] The question becomes: how can we see otherwise, without replicating the dynamics of indifferent visuality as if for the first time, in a kind of Nietzschean Eternal Return of the Same? How do we see for a second time? Interestingly, Webster's definition for "second sight" is reminiscent of the general irrational, anti-foundational attributes ascribed to the second sex: "The power of seeing beyond the visible; intuitive, visionary, or prophetic power." Like "woman's intuition," second sight is a feminized domain. Seeing beyond the visible is, of course, oxymoronic, as is the materialist impulse to see sight, to show the show. And yet this impulse toward the oxymoronic might fit the scene of "woman" with some precision, for women are culturally positioned as inher-ently oxymoronic in the sense that, after Theresa deLauretis, woman is unrepresentable except as representation.[6] And, as has been amply pointed out in feminist texts as academically endowed as Peggy Phelan's *Unmarked* or as popularly broadcast as Deborah Tannen's "Marked" in the *New York Times Magazine*, there is no way a woman can escape the historical ramifi-cations of that representation unless she passes from visibility as woman, passing as a man.[7] As "woman," she is a preceded by her own markings, standing in relation to her body in history as if beside herself.

MODERN WHORES AND POSTMODERN PERFORMANCE ARTISTS

In many ways, contemporary feminist performance artists present their bodies as dialectical images. Key to Walter Benjamin's materialist theory-cosmology, a dialectical image is an object or constellation of objects which reveal or expose the traces of their service to the dreamscape of commodity capitalism. They are objects which give themselves away, showing signs of the "two-way street," indicating that they are not entirely that which they have been given

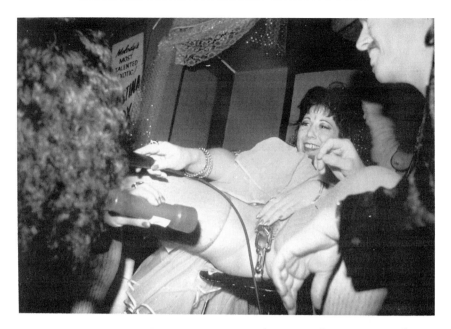

Figure 9.1 Annie Sprinkle during a 1989 performance of *Post Porn Modernism* (Copyright Annie Sprinkle)

to represent (the way cracks in face-paint or runs in mascara might show the material in tension with the constructed ideal). For Benjamin, the prostitute presented a prime dialectical image in her inherent split as both "commodity and seller" in one. The whore has certainly been an obsession for modernists in general and, as Baudelaire illustrated and as Christine Buci-Glucksman has explicated, she can be read as an allegory for modernity itself.[8] In Susan Buck-Morss's words, carved through Benjamin out of Marx's *Capital*:

> The prostitute is the ur-form of the wage laborer, selling herself in order to survive. Prostitution is indeed an objective emblem of capitalism, a hieroglyph of the true nature of social reality in the sense that the Egyptian hieroglyphs were viewed by the Renaissance – and in Marx's sense as well: "Value transforms . . . every product of labor into a social hieroglyph. People then try to decode the meaning of the hieroglyph in order to get behind the secret of their own social product [. . .]." The image of the whore reveals this secret like a rebus. Whereas every trace of the wage laborer who produced the commodity is extinguished when it is torn out of context by its exhibition on display, in the prostitute, both moments remain visible.[9]

Prostitutes are inherently ambivalent. By showing the show of their commodification and by not completely passing as that which they purport to be, dialectical images such as prostitutes or used "outmoded" commodities, can talk or gesture back to the entire social enterprise which secret(e)s them. For Benjamin, such images provide a history of objects accumulating in the cracks of capitalism's "progress" which can be read back against the pervasive myths of nature, value, and social order.

It is somehow in the flickering undecideability between the subject's reading and the object's cracks that dialectical images threaten to work. The challenge in engaging dialectical images seems to lie somewhere in between – a space at once exceedingly private, full of personal particulars, and radically public, full of social inscriptions – a fraught space – a space feminist performance artists, and cultural critical theorists "writing performances," have been approaching as deeply imbricated in the social dynamics of the marked body. Into this fraught space I found myself repeatedly placing a specific performance artist, prostitute Annie Sprinkle, as one places a question mark. In my mind, Sprinkle also sat at the threshold of the impasse between essentialist and constructivist critiques of gender.[10] Sprinkle's work became, for me, problematically emblematic of the tense stand-off between the literal, material body and the symbolic body of "woman."

I had been running the Sprinkle performance of *Post Porn Modernism* I had seen at the The Kitchen in Manhattan across my memory in a kind of eternal return. I kept replaying the image of Sprinkle's spectators standing in the line that bridged the magic gulf between the stage and the house, waiting to accept Sprinkle's invitation to shine flashlights through the speculum she had inserted into her vagina. As spectators, we were in line for the show within the show: the theatrical "moment" when one by one we would peek at the performer's cervix as the name of art slapped against the name of porn across the stage within the stage, the proscenium of the prostitute's body. Unfolding the scene again and again across my memory, I found myself encountering Sprinkle's cervix as theoretical third eye, like a gaze from the blind spot, meeting the spectator's – my – gaze and instantly doubling back over a field of modernist obsessions. I thought about Bataille's horror and fascination with the envaginated eyeball in his *Story of the Eye*, about Freud's inscription of the female genitals as "blinding" in "The Uncanny," and about Walter Benjamin's efforts to "invest" an object or the objectified with its own gaze, as if it might not already possess such capabilities of its own. Passing such remarkable modernists across the path of my inquiry I tried, in my mind's eye, to hold on to the tactile and viscous pinkness of Annie's cervical eyeball, peering out, effulgent, from the socket of her vagina. I also thought about my own eye meeting this cervical gaze as well as my own eye seen seeing by Annie's other eyes, the ones in her head, watching me watch her and perhaps even catching the glint of her own cervix reflected in my retina.

Literally speaking, it was a storm – a hurricane – that interrupted my repetitive rethinking of this encounter. I was far from The Kitchen, off the coast of Massachusetts, but still entranced, caught, by the lingering after-image of Sprinkle's performance and the theoretical questions that followed in its wake, when I found myself in the midst of a "natural disaster." The storm disrupted my inquiry and dispersed the Sprinkle spectators lined up in my mind's eye. I had come, in any case, to an impasse. The notion of a "returned" gaze or an object's eye seemed always to be reacting to an initializing challenge, always servicing a scene marked by the self-perpetuating and ultimately boring tango-hold of patriarchal objectification, always complicit in a drama of submission. The impulse to find an "object's eye," like a "female gaze," seemed fraught with the impulse to create yet another de-objectified subject, caught in the binaried dance between subject and object that had set the stage for the shadow play of gender in the first place. The tempest offered more than a good reason to break.

Break

I stepped outside the house on to the porch. Taking the enormous push of the wind as some kind of invitation and sensing the rush of first fear, I misrecognized myself as vital, witty enough to survive, ready. Never mind that the windows had been creaking as though possessed by spirits of the shipwrecked drowned. Never mind that there was something close to my own flesh color in the spiky tentacles of tree interiors twisted into sudden exposure. I stepped off the porch and on to the wide field of the yard. I was alive and infinitely capable – whipped by the rush, defying the elements, balancing on the edge of destruction.

I found my body flat on its face in an instant. Hit by a blast that must have jumped round the corner of the house, I was thrown well off the spot I'd been bravely, or naively, romancing. I crawled back to the porch, then into the house. Shaken by the infinitude of my own naivety, I watched the rest of the unrest from the inside, through windows preoccupied with the whispered potential of instant explosion, sudden death. I watched trees twist off of their own trunks, almost gracefully, and come dramatically down as if in a bow of submission, as if in respect for the quick visibility of invisibility, the sudden fact of a fall, the instant blast of devastation.

Then came the eye – like a hole in the real. The eye of a storm is a hollow, sunny place in the middle of devastation where a force that hit one way inverts itself and hits in reverse. Past and future at once, the eye is vacated of the present. A horrible stasis where an impulse that threw itself outward waits for ricochet, as a gaze, reflecting against glass, is thrown back upon itself in a moment of recognition. Or perhaps the uncanny calm in the eye of a storm resembles the force of a gaze which, meeting its object in a literal eye, stands for moment uncertain of the force of the countergaze by which it may be expelled against itself, abjected.

In that unsettling space of silence when force circles back as its own counterforce, I began to rethink the notion of the object's eye and came,

160

eventually, to reframe the question in terms of an uncanny counterpart, shrouded, or secreted, in the raging rush of invisibility. What is the danger in the uncanny calm? What is the danger in unseen eye, or the eye of the unseen, suddenly seen? Perhaps attempts to rescue a female gaze or discover an object's eye – to bring, we might say, the seeming blinded to seeming sight – displaces or shrouds another, more complex issue. Can the drive to invest the objectified with a countergaze be considered relative to another notion: the unsettling eye of a secret? The eye of that which has been secreted? The eye, hidden and denied, which still sees? And what does the secreted see?

The storm passed

I went back to thinking about Sprinkle, a make-up bedecked, teddy-bearing disaster in the natural.

In theory, "real" "live" Prostitute Annie Sprinkle in her *Post Porn Moderism* lay at the threshold of the impasse between true and false, visible and invisible, nature and culture as if in the eye of a storm. As any "whore" is given to be in this culture, she is a mistake, an aberration, a hoax: a show and a sham made of lipstick, mascara, fake beauty marks, and black lace. But she is also somehow woman untamed, woman unsocialized, woman unclassed, woman uncultured, woman, that is, "natural." When she lays, literally, at the edge of the stage and inserts a speculum into her vagina so that art-world spectators and porn fans alike can line up to catch a glimpse of her cervix, she one-ups Duchamp, appearing as a living toilet seat in the art gallery. Here we have Living Whore, icon of modernism, historic toilet seat of humanity, the oldest (illegal) profession, revealed in the frame of flesh and declaring herself, adamantly, "Post."

As porn and art collide in The Kitchen – which nevertheless in a tangle of class issues remains a trendy "art" space versus an arty "porn" theater – this scene might read as a postmodern parody of a modernist aesthetic – a doubling back over modernist canonical obsession with the explicit female body, and explicitly the prostitute's body, as a primary foundation for the erection of high modern identity. Perhaps Sprinkle's porn/art could be read as a "take" on high art such as *Origin of the World*, Gustave Courbet's 1866 painting of a woman's belly, thighs, and genitals so "realist" that its one-time owner, Jacques Lacan, kept it veiled behind an abstract "hiding device" constructed by surrealist painter Andre Masson. Or perhaps Sprinkle's *Post Porn Modernism* can be read as a performative "take" on Manet's *Olympia*, taken a few steps further than *Site*, the 1964 Judson Church remake of *Olympia* by Carolee Schneemann and Robert Morris, in which Schneemann posed nude as Olympia while Morris built a wooden frame around her. Sprinkle's version might be dubbed *Sight*. Sprinkle spectators line up to get a peek at the scene of her cervix embedded in her exposed pussy, which is

Figure 9.2 Etant donnés: la chute d'eau; le gaz d'eclairage, Marcel Duchamp, 1946–66 (Philadelphia Museum of Art; gift of the Cassandra Foundation)

in turn embedded in her specific body: a kinkily clothed, porn-queen's body. The body, on a bed raked for visibility, is embedded on the stage of The Kitchen, which is an art space embedded in the tradition of the avant-garde, embedded in the larger frame of the "Art" establishment, embedded in ideals of Western History, a history of a Patriarchy which, broadly speaking, can be said to be embedded in the effort to manipulate and control . . . the scene of the cervix.

If we can dub Sprinkle's show "Sight," we can also see her piece as a doubling back, a performative riff on another modernist classic: Duchamp's *Etant donnés*, ("Given that . . ."). In this 1946 assemblage, Duchamp makes an overt depiction of western habits of specularity: perspectival vision, with woman as vanishing-point as well as origin – she is infinite recession, infinite reproduction. Rosalind Kraus, after Jean-François Lyotard, suggests that Duchamp's piece is based on the system of classical perspective but is simultaneously "maliciously at work to lay bare that system's hidden assumptions." In *Etant donnés*, Kraus writes, "all the elements of perspective are in place, but in a strangely literal way."

> The role of the picture surface that slices through the visual pyramid of classical perspective is played, for example, by a brick wall, with the possiblity of seeing-through that is normally a function of pictoral illusion now a matter of literally breaking down the barrier to produce a ragged opening. And the viewing and vanishing point, or goal of vision, is manifested by the dark interior of a bodily orifice, the optically impenetrable cavity of the spead-eagled "bride," a physical rather than a geometrical limit to the reach of vision. And the viewing-point is likewise a hole: thick, inelegant, material.[11]

Unpacking Duchamp's assemblage even further, Kraus, again through Lyotard, makes evident a veiled secret written into the geometrical underpinnings of perspectivalism. If perspective is orchestrated around the theoretical identity between viewing-point and vanishing-point, and if the vanishing-point is inscribed as inscrutable lack, as always already vulvic, then "He who sees is a cunt." Here we glimpse an underpinning of patriarchal terror, written into the very mechanism of visual perspective: when the peeping eyes "think they're seeing the vulva, they see themselves."

Sprinkle can be read as taking Duchamp's literality, "maliciously at work," a step further. Sprinkle places her *particular* body as terrain, as view. The bride is, here, not general woman, but particular woman – particular whore – with a particular life story. Sprinkle's body, unlike Duchamp's bride and Courbet's *Origin*, bears a head and a gaze which complicates the exchange between view-point and vanishing-point. Might we consider Sprinkle's performativity as perspectivalism on the flip? A rupture produced by the occluded perspective of the blind spot suddenly given to see?

EYE/BODY

In 1963 Carolee Schneemann reclined nude in her own art installation. *Eye/Body* was criticized in its day as self-indulgent exhibitionism, but historians such as Lucy Lippard have since recognized the work as prescient – one of the first American installations to incorporate the artist's own body as object-terrain.[12] Schneemann's "kinetic environment" consisted of 4×9 foot panels, broken glass and shards of mirrors, photographs, lights, motorized umbrellas, and her own nude body. In what she called a "kind of shamanic ritual," she incorporated her naked body into her construction by painting, greasing, and chalking herself. With *Eye/Body* Schneemann was keenly aware of the paradox that her physical body was eagerly seen (she had appeared nude in numerous Happenings and had been dubbed "body beautiful") while the body of her art work was hardly or skeptically seen. In fact, much of her impulse to include her body, explicitly, in her work came from the fact that when Schneemann began constructing the installation in 1962, the painter was fed up with feeling that her gender inhibited her consideration as a serious contributor to the art world. Beyond the dance-identified circles of Judson Church, she felt she had partial status, and was personally troubled by the suspicion that she was included only as a "cunt mascot" in the heavily male cliques of Fluxus and Happenings.[13] Her response to this feeling – covering her naked body in paint, grease, chalk, ropes, and plastic, and incorporating it into her work – was to address her mascot-dom directly. *Eye/Body* established her artist's body as "visual territory," as if to declare: if I am a token, then I'll be a token to reckon with. But the work also suggested a complex theoretical terrain of perspectivalism on the flip. *Eye/Body* suggested embodied vision, a bodily eye – sighted eyes – artist's eyes – not only in the seer, but in the body of the seen.

Female Fluxus artists, Happeners, and early cultural feminists began to use their bodies explicitly in their work, exploring, among other things, the paradox of being artist and object at once. Very often these women's works were, in Yoko Ono's words, "rejected as animalistic" by male colleagues and the male-dominated art establishment.[14] When Kubota performed her *Vagina Painting* at the Perpetual Fluxfest in New York City in 1965 she squatted on the floor and painted on a paper with a brush that extended from her vagina. Her male colleagues hated the piece, despite the fact that Yves Klein's 1960 use of nude women as "living brushes" in 1959 had been widely celebrated. Woman as artist's brush, woman fetishized as phallus – acceptable, even posh. But woman *with* brush was in some way woman *with* phallus and thus unnatural, monstrous, threatening, primitive – not artistic. Women artists making actions when "the actors were all men"[15] demanded a certain transvestism that not all were prepared to employ. Some, like Kubota, Ono, and Schneemann, wanted to remain "woman" *and* wield the brush, that is be both female and artist. Such works were, as David James wrote of

Schneemann's film *Fuses*, "hardly able to be seen" and were most often dismissed with mockery.[16]

The demonstrative medium of live performance meant that the fact of an artist's gender, among other things, could not be easily dismissed. Of course, performance and the artist's actions (if not *explicitly* his marked body) were increasingly the mode of the art world in general, most notably since Jackson Pollock's mid-1950s emphasis on the "action" of his brush and the flight of his paint through air, but traceable in avant-garde lineage back through Duchamp, dada, and the futurists. In contradistinction to the general emphasis on purely "concrete" actions, however, the bodily works of women could not be approached as if embodied actions transcended social prejudices of gender, race, and class – as if the base and elemental body with which artists, with rapid increase after 1945, had become particularly enthralled were not riddled in its materiality with non-concrete socio-political significances.

Works by men which did employ the political overtones of the explicit body – such as Paik's 1962 *Young Penis Symphony*, in which ten young men, hidden from the audience behind a large sheet of paper, stuck their penises through the paper one at the time – were subject to very different responses than explicit body works created by women. Paik's piece might have "poked" fun at the spectacle of phallic size and power, but his display remained, under his authorizing signature, in good humor. In contrast, Martha Edleheit has said of her early 1970s paintings of male nudes with penises which "droop" that even her "neutral" eye bothered men "who are not used to being treated so indifferently, or only literally . . . a straightforwardly presented penis much disturbs them too: mere viewing is a kind of judgment."[17] While it might be possible to argue that Paik's piece *was* in good humor and works like Edleheit's neutral "droop" or Louis Bourgeois's *Fillete*, a two-foot long penis done in moist-looking malleable latex and hung from a meat hook, were not, it is also possible to argue that "good humor" was extended to male artists and their utilizations of the body far more generously than to female. Another example, also concerning Paik, better illustrates the situation: Charlotte Moorman was arrested for, tried, and found guilty of indecent exposure during her 1967 performance of Paik's 1966 *Opera Sextronique* in which she exposed her breasts. Paik, however, was not found not guilty as the judge deemed it impossible to create "pornographic music." As Kristine Stiles writes, "Paik and Moorman's actions are extraordinary demonstrations of the role the body plays in structuring not only the meaning and presence of objects, but the juridical and institutional practices that control, manage, and litigate that body."[18]

For the woman artist authoring work, the problem was immense. The explicit body itself was not the problem – there has been "exposure" in art for centuries – but the lines by which the explicit body is explicated, by which it is framed, displayed and, even more importantly, "authored," have been very well policed, by juridical and avant-garde establishments alike.

In the 1960s embodied works by women could not be easily digested into the territorial "bad boy" oeuvre of the avant-garde. Their authorizing signatures were suspect. And very often these works bore autobiographical or at the very least "personal" overtones which challenged the formalism at the base of so much avant-garde practice, pointing to socially and politically contexted experience of form versus abstracted formal principals, a fact which had enormous influence on the broader 1970s generation of feminist performance art.

The 1970s was a decade art critic and historian Moira Roth has called "The Amazing Decade" of women's art. Feminist performance art burgeoned on the West Coast around Judy Chicago and Womanhouse and in New York among women who had been either excommunicated, like Schneemann, from the Art Studs Club, or who were entering the scene with their "consciousnesses" already raised.[19] In the 1980s, artists falling under the rubric "female" commanded greater recognition. Interestingly, this recognition grew in direct proportion to the demise of the stronghold of formalism in the arts, a demise forwarded by the innovations of feminist painters, photographers, filmmakers, and performers such as Sherrie Levine, Cindy Sherman, Laurie Anderson, Yvonne Rainer, Linda Montano, Nancy Spero, Jenny Holzer, Barbara Kruger, and Louise Lawler, and promoted by editors such as Ingrid Sischy of *Artforum* and curators such as Marcia Tucker of the New Museum and Martha Wilson of Franklin Furnace in New York City. As women artists became more difficult to ignore, feminist theory and practice gained in complexity, and as theory and practice gained in complexity, women artists became more difficult to ignore. If the 1970s feminists had, in an effort to establish a feminist voice and a feminist stronghold, largely been seeking a "true" or positive image of Woman, by the early 1980s artists were able to declare that the Woman they sought was a cultural construct, a strategic moment, and could move to the more materialist notion that identity is produced through the machinations of representation. Intersecting with poststructuralist theories in a powerfully burgeoning amalgam of French and Anglo-American feminisms, by the mid-1980s artists could aim beyond the "essential" woman to analyze how and why meaning and its engenderment is produced. This shifting of emphasis away from essentialized female nature toward a radical interrogation of both engenderment and nature motivated and gained motivation from the general politicization of aesthetics at the backbone of critical postmodernist inquiry.

Critiques of essentialism can thus be said to have grown out of essentialist critiques, as one generation grows out of another.[20] With obvious inheritance from their cultural feminist predecessors, the body remained a performative site for a generation of materialist explicit body performers, but the terms of the drama had shifted from, broadly speaking, invocation of positive female imagery to parodies played out across bodily parts in which identity became a manipulable *mise-en-scène* of physical accouterment and "self" became something as shifty as costuming or plastic surgery. One of the dramas played out across the explicit body became, increasingly in the later 1980s and early 1990s, a drama at the juridical and institutional intersection of porn and art. The issue of the "appropriate" venue for the explicit body became most clearly an issue not only of who bears the right to wield the pornographic detail *as art* (Manet or Olympia?), but also and perhaps more insidiously who bears the right to explicate the social, historical significances of those details.

LEGACIES OF SAVAGERY

> Thus I learned to battle the canvas, to come to know it as a being resisting my wish (dream), and to bend it forcibly to this wish. At first it sounds there like a pure chaste virgin . . . and then comes the willful brush which first here, then there, gradually conquers it with all the energy peculiar to it, like a European colonist . . .
>
> Wassily Kandinsky[21]

Though Kandinsky was doing battle with the canvas and not, like many avant-gardes, the institution of high art, the characters in his battle were clearly marked: women and colonials. With Picasso's 1905 "D'Amoisselle's dauvignon" most often marked as origin,[22] mimetic incorporation of the spoils of colonialism into the halls of western art simply extended the general appropriation and incorporation into the body of European culture of, as Kenneth Coutts-Smith succinctly put it, "the diverse cultures of the whole world and of all history."[23] A massive consumption of others into the scope of the western self was underway. Mimesis through high art, or reproduction with aesthetic distance, assured that the assimilation took place on western terms. And yet the terms of the incorporation of the colonial other (the primitivized) was, at least between the years of 1880 and World War II, a site for debate. That is, the primitive was represented both as a site of nostalgia and desire (the noble savage) and as a site to provoke fear, repudiation, and horror (the savage savage). Mimetic allusion to the savage savage in arts of confrontation, such as dada and later the dissident surrealists of the Collège d'Sociologie, bear a ghostly relevance to contemporary feminist performers of the explicit body. In making their bodies their canvases – Schneemann smearing her body with paint or Karen Finley smearing her body with viscous substances or Sprinkle explicating her make-up as whore – feminist artists of the explicit body might be read as literalizing Kandinsky's metaphor, talking back to their historical inscriptions.

As we struggle to understand ourselves as postcolonials, the iconography of the colonial and "savage" body – the black body, the female body of explicit physical markings and implicit, hidden questions and dangers – still circulates as that which potentially threatens civil identity.[24] The scandalizing potential of primitivity and the concomitant aestheticization of artifacts of the "primitive" inscribe a veritable history of modern art. In the early confrontative avant-garde, before Picasso's mimetic initiative in style effected the long migration of African fetish objects out of the Trocadero and into art museums, primitivism as confrontation was almost a *modus operandi*. In the history of performance, Alfred Jarry's staging of his *Ubu Roi* at Théâtre de l'Oeuvre in 1896 is a famous case in point. The show caused a riot on each of the three nights of its run. Jarry's "Ubu" spoofed the general symbolist attempt to accentuate a transcendental or dreamlike reality. In *Ubu Roi*, Jarry chose as his ultimate symbol something so profane, literal, and explicit that it could not be transcendent, could not evoke for his audience any higher ideal. Jarry chose loudly and repeatedly to exclaim "shitr!" ("merdre!") in the hallowed halls of the theater. Importantly, his excremental affront was coupled by an important parallel confrontation: the fat and whiny King Ubu (a name with an obvious Africanism) who uttered the expletive. The King Primitive, obsessed with bodily functions, disallowed transcendent or distanced aestheticization. Ubu has been historicized as the birth of the confrontative avant-garde – a confrontation that caused the symbolist Yeats to write sadly after one riotous performance: "After us the Savage God."[25]

Reminiscent of Jarry's "savage god" affront to Symbolism, a number of Surrealist artists and writers, notably Georges Bataille, Michel Leiris, André Masson, Desnos, Queneau, and Artaud (whose theater was named Théâtre Alfred Jarry), set off a crisis within Breton-identified Surrealism and found themselves excommunicated from Surrealist ranks. An undercurrent issue of their affront concerned, again, the place of "primitive" artifact and ethnological account, especially regarding transgressive social practice relative to aesthetic or formal properties of "art."[26] Sitting squarely in the realm of the material, bodily detail was base. In its alignment with matter, the body then shared a common space with all things "primitive." Acceptable Surrealist primitivism (that is, Surrealism passed by Breton) employed what Rosalind Kraus has called soft primitivism, "a primitivism gone formal and therefore gutless," part of the general "art for art's sake" aestheticizing discourse on the primitive. To this Kraus contrasts the dissident group's "hard primitivism," which sought in the primitive a kind of "primal vandalism."[27] For dissidents surrounding Bataille, mimesis of primitive expression was a means of triggering a critique of positivist, "civil" identity. Hard primitivism was not a means of expanding the marvelous domain of western aesthetic sensibilities but of transgressing that domain and thus exposing its veiled but ever-present "sadistic" underbelly.

Bataille's treatment of the issue of literality reverberates with some of the work of contemporary explicit body performance artists. Bataille situated his dissident primitivism relative to his general theory of the ambivalent split in all signification, an ambivalence of the interdependency of binary terms that stoked the obsessive fire heating up the Collège de Sociologie: the violence at the heart of all sacred acts, the sacred moment at the center of sadism. Mimesis of (hard) primitivity was inexorably linked with sadism in that it was seen as inherently confrontative to the humanism and idealism of western civilization. Thus practice of primitivity, like practice of transgressive sexuality, could function as a "crack in the system," disrupting humanist and idealist unities and aspirations.[28] For Bataille, the savage body functioned like a pothole in a sidewalk wreaking violent slippage in upright, or upward reaching, secularizing systems of meaning.[29]

Like his Surrealist pseudo-siblings, Bataille was intent upon prying open the eyelids to get at that which exceeded appropriate (civil) vision. While for Breton that which exceeded normative, quotidian vision was linked to the "marvelous" symbolism of the unconscious, for Bataille that which exceeded appropriate vision was linked to the fearful potential of base matter to implode upon any and all symbolic structuring. "To the extent that knowledge takes itself for an end, it founders on the blind spot." Bataille saw "Hegel's immense fatigue" as "linked to the horror of the blind spot." In Bataillian formulation the blind spot is that which exceeds the symbol, exceeds the foundational or rationalizable. He found this excess in laughter, ecstasy, violence, death, and combinations of the above of which the erotic was the most accessible for the modern. The blind spot is where duality overflows, exceeding its own distinctions – for instance, where something is both *heimlich* and *unheimlich*, familiar and strange – not without contradiction, but inexorably *in* contradiction, or "alteration." Yet, very importantly, this was not a high-flying site of transcendence or an "Icarian adventure" such as he accused the Surrealists of seeking. Bataille articulated this site, this blind spot, as where "laughter no longer laughs and tears no longer cry, where the divine and the horrible, the poetic and the repugnant, the erotic and the funereal coincide," saying, this is *"not a point of the spirit."* The irony and the horror in Bataille is that this blind spot is an insistently base and material instant in which symbolic constructs encounter their own inversion in concrete particular, in *literal*, often bodily detail. This (blinding) point of excess coagulates in matter and becomes not a site of spirit, but rather a site at which dream or symbol defecates, is literalized. Looking back at the viewer, the blind spot made literal disallows perspectival remove and "castrates the eye." Thus imagined, the blind spot is a fearful space of collapse in the distance needed to maintain a distinction between the symbolic and the literal. The matter of the literal detail, as a flipside of the symbolic, points up the blind spot – that which a symbolic system can not allow to be seen. In this sense, the *view of* the explicitly marked body and the view from the marked body come into disturbing, even horrifying, contact as the prerogatives of disinterested perspectival vision get turned belly up by the literal detail which sees back.

LOOKING AT THE PAST, SEEING THROUGH
THE BODY

Now I stood up and, with Simone on her side, I drew her thighs apart, and found myself facing something I imagine I had been waiting for in the same way that a guillotine waits for a neck to slice. I even felt as if my eyes were bulging from my head, erectile with horror; in *Simone*'s hairy vagina, I saw the wan blue eye of *Marcelle*, gazing at me through tears of urine. Streaks of come in the steaming hair helped give that dreamy vision a disastrous sadness. I held the thighs open while Simone was convulsed by the urinary spasm, and the burning urine streamed out from under the eye down to the thighs below ...

Georges Bataille[30]

To ask a woman to read [see] as a woman is in fact a double or divided request. It appeals to the condition of being a woman as if it were a given and simultaneously urges that this condition be created or achieved.

Jonathan Culler[31]

As suggested above, Bataille was a modernist writer extraordinarily attentive to the paradoxical condition of detached vision and enthralled with the experience, often the horror, of its demise. His inverted anthropologies repeatedly returned to a thinking through the body and its organs. If distanced, *flâneur*-like vision was the primary modern sense for knowing, then the eye as a visceral and material organ, the literal mechanism of sight, became particularly provocative when thinking through the body. In its materiality as a literal thing, an enucleated eyeball garnered a special kind of horror in that it could signify the split, implicating both body and mind at once.[32] Bataille provides, in a sense, a careful and provocative biopsy of the modernist obsession with the separation of the visual from the visceral – an obsession he simultaneously exemplifies through his endlessly self-reconstituting horror at the very blind spot he attempts to make literal.

In a close reading of the quintessential scene from Bataille's notorious *Story of the Eye*, we can remark how the narrator's "horror" depends upon a literal site that is not simply the en-visioned vagina, but is coupled by the unacknowledged (blindspotted) gaze of Simone.[33] A reader is given to identify with, or certainly to see through the "erectile" eyes of the male narrator as he views Simone's sideways body and sees the eyeball of another woman, Marcelle, peering out of her vagina. A reader thus finds herself as male narrator spectating a classic female split: the acephalic body of one woman (the sexually liberated Simone) and the envaginated eye of another woman (the sexually repressed and victimized Marcelle). If a reader imagines the vaginal eye looking back at her, as the eye peers at the narrator with whom she is identified, then the reader would find herself (mis)recognized through

170

the vaginal eye as male, or at least as (perhaps unconvincingly) cross-dressed. On the other hand, when a reader shifts her perspective to identify with Marcelle rather than the narrator, to *see through* the envaginated eye of Marcelle entirely, then she stands outside the narrator's identity and witnesses the gaze of the modernist as he peers at Simone's vagina (with which the female reader's eye is intimately associated), his own eye's bulging from his sockets, "erectile with horror."

It is significant here that the envaginated eye and the narrator's gaze are the only eyes admitted to the scopic field of the erectile vision. There are the eyes in the head of the sexually active woman, Simone herself, but they are not admitted, remaining unseen in the scene. When a reader shifts again to see through Simone's unacknowledged eyes, she finds herself beyond modernist peripheries, authoring an unwritten perspective. Though "laying on her side," Simone's eyes might not be averted. Unwritten, they might nevertheless look over her shoulder, witnessing the frenzied author in his culminating scene. From this "space off,"[34] the reader would watch the author's predictable shock as he sees, or thinks he sees, the eye of another woman between her legs. In this reading, Simone witnesses the narrator's authorial horror at encountering what he has conceived – his terror at what he has written as an explicitly female (envaginated) gaze.

Why horror? Why not pleasure? Why not glee? As Bataille's horror illustrates, the institution of a "female" gaze necessitates, within modern imagination, the reembodiment of detached or disinterested vision. If detached vision is disturbing, the notion of reembodiment is even more horrifying, as reembodiment is necessarily figured by the particularity, the literality of the marked body. Reembodied vision bears the horror of the marked body, a horror linked inexorably to woman. Reembodied vision bears the savagery of feminization, here literally framed by the female genitalia. Thus reembodiment of the detached gaze is rife with the horror of feminization, destroying the veil of disinterestedness shrouding supposedly "distanced" vision. A reembodied gaze threatens the prerogatives of disembodied perspectivalism, the prerogatives of the veil, and doubles as a terror of female sexuality. This reembodied female gaze is authored by and relative to patriarchal horror. Again, it is important to remember that the female gaze given to see from Simone's vagina is not Simone's own but the victimized and virginal Marcelle, herself radically disembodied – the female gaze as the gaze of the disembodied reembodied, always relative to a female body she herself does not possess. The eyes of the woman with sexual agency are relegated to the space-off where Simone is not admitted to witness how an explicitly female gaze is authored as always already dissimulating, or duplicitous, as never of a woman, but always already that of an *other* woman, infinitely recessing , split off from her own agency.

The project of looking back at the modernist in thrall, amid the admittedly self-splintering notion of reading "as a woman," here exemplified in a reading through Bataille, becomes not only a looking back in time, but even more provocatively a looking back *in space*, which is to say, across the "savaged" bodies which demarcated modernist perspective. The contemporary feminist project to turn the eye of the visceralized, marked object back on to the detached eye of the modern attempts not simply to re-annunciate modernist horror, but to examine the terms of that horror, to survey the *entire* field of her visceralization from the (space-off) perspective of the visceralized. What is uncovered rather than reconstituted in this project is a plethora of patriarchal fears.

Earlier in this essay I posed the question of whether we might imagine feminist works such as Schneemann's *Eye/Body* and Sprinkle's explicit perform-ativity as perspectivalism on the flip, a view from the vanishing-point of the terms of that vanishing. Linked to Bataillian fascination with the literal, savage body and the blind spot as sites of subversive potential within western symbolic systems, how might such a performativity nevertheless avoid the endless self-reconstitution Bataille's horror exemplified? Porn-queen Sprinkle smiles, chuckles, and exchanges quips with her peeping spectators, watching the scene unfold across her own body in the frame of "art." The display of the cervix becomes a kind of ludicrous moment in which voyeurism is taken to a certain extreme where the viewer encounters not an infinitely recessing negative space, a vanishing-point of "Origin," but explicitly, and somewhat clinically, a cervix. If the cervix can be imagined as an eye, catching the viewer at the keyhole as it were, any horror that scene might occasion would be noted by the author, Annie Sprinkle, and remarked. Unlike Simone's, Annie's eyes are not secreted. Rather, they seem to be brimming with an unexpected load of irony. Here the interrupting third eye – the eye that catches the peeper at the keyhole in Sartre's imagination – is Annie's own eyes upon the scene of her prostituted body. Here, then, the interrupting eye is acknowledged within the scene, implicated upon the body of the seen itself rather than in an intrusive third, implicitly paternal party.[35] The "seen" takes on an agency of her own (like the dialectical image of the whore) and wields the unnerving potential of a subversive reciprocity of vision, an explicit complicity, or mutual recognition between seer and seen, subject and subject, in the scene of viewing. Such reciprocity threatens in that it suggests a disavowal of the terror that veils distantiation and demarcates subject from object in western cultural habits of knowing. In the wake of such reciprocity, in the avowal of Simone's eyes, horror at reembodiment has the potential to be replaced by acknowledgment – acknowledgement of the historical terms and tangled terrain of horror, "savagery," and the marked body.

NOTES

1   See Elin Diamond, "Mimesis, Mimicry, and the 'True-Real'," *Modern Drama* 32.1 (1989): 58–72 and "Realism and Hysteria: Toward a Feminist Mimesis," *Discourse* 31.1 (1990–1): 59–92.

2   "Reality effects" is taken from Roland Barthes's "The Reality Effect" in *The Rustle of Language*, trans. by R. Howard, New York: Hill and Wang, 1986. I use the term, however, in a way that inverts Barthes's usage. Barthes was explicating textual effects of the detail, utilized in naturalist texts to speak of the real. I use the term to indicate the way in which the perception of the real is indeed effected through the historical accumulation of cultural texting . I also use the term to refer to the way text and image bear effect on persons in a cultural complex of mimesis and alterity. Writing on gender, Klaus Theweleit has used the phrase "reality production," culled from Deleuze and Guattari (*Male Fantasies*, trans. Stephen Conway, Minneapolis: University of Minnesota Press). I prefer the term "effect" to "product" for, while it loses some allusion to capitalist machinations, it nonetheless retains a sense of impact and concrete, visceral immediacy – in a sense, the effect of the production of the real.

3   See Judith Butler, *Gender Trouble*, New York: Routledge, 1991.

4   See Vivian M. Patraka, 1992, "Binary Terror and Feminist Performance: Reading Both Ways," *Discourse* 14.2 (Spring):163-85.

5   The long-standing modern privilege afforded vision and visual perspective – or better, the instituting of a one-way modality for visuality – has propped the supremacy of objectification as the prime western cultural mode of knowledge, contributing to the dynamics maintaining "others" and "selves." Though there are many debates on when and whether Cartesian perspectival occularcentrism has been outmoded or whether it persists, albeit reconfigured to meet the pressures of modernization, the fact remains that the trope of perspective and the disinterest it promotes is extremely important ingredient of Western cutlure. See Martin Jay's *Downcast Eyes*, (Berkeley and Los Angeles: University of California Press, 1993) for an argument on the demise or perspectivalism and Jonathan Cary's *Techniques of the Observer* (Bloomington: Indiana University Press, 1987), for an argument on its reconfiguration. There is a very large body of work on perspective historically, including Panovsky's *Perspective as Symbolic Form* (New York: Zone Books, 1991). For some contemporary treatments generally, see Hal Foster, ed., *Vision and Visuality* (Seattle: Bay Press, 1988); Evelyn Fox Keller and Christine Grontkowski, "The Mind's Eye" in *Discovering Reality: Feminist Perspectives on Epistemology, Metaphysics, Methodology, and Philosophy of Science* (Dordrecht: D. Reidel, 1983). As a result of critiques of perspectivalism across the twentieth century, a host of alternatives have been suggested. Anthropology, for example, has seen emphases placed on sensual perception other than vision explicitly to offset the "antipersonalist orientation of visualism" (Fabian in Emily Martin, "Science and Women's Bodies: Forms of Anthropological Knowledge" in *Body/Politics*, edited by Mary Jacobus *et al.*, New York: Routledge, 1990: 69), such as Ong's emphasis on the aural, Clifford's later emphasis on "discursive " or vocal and gestic expression, and Taussig's exploration of tactility, including tactility in vision (see Taussig, "Physiognomic Aspects of Visual Worlds" in *Visualizing Theory*, edited by Lucien Taylor, New York: Routledge, 1994). However, the legacy of perspectivalism can be traced even into alternative modes, such as visual tactility, and we have to repeatedly caution against our ready desire to jettison ourselves beyond our histories, as if those histories could not continue to ghost and inform our "new" ways of viewing, inscribing, knowing bodies in social, cultural, and political space.

6   de Lauretis, *Technologies of Gender: Essays on Theory, Film, and Fiction.* Bloomington: University of Indiana Press, 1987, p. 20.

7   See "Markers: Wears Jump Suit, Sensible Shoes, Uses Husband's Last Name" in *The New York Times Magazine*, 20 June 1993. In *Unmarked*, Phelan is so sensitive to the problematic of passing from visibility that she argues against the grain of the effort to "see" at all, advocating an active vanishing and suggesting a feminist anti-perspective born of blindness.

8   Christine Buci-Glucksman, 1987, "Catastrophic Utopia: The Feminine as Allegory of the Modern," in *The Making of the Modern Body:Sexuality and Society in the Nineteenth Century*, ed. by Catherine Gallagher and Thomas Laqueur, Berkeley and Los Angeles: University of California Press, pp. 220–9.

9   Susan Bucks-Morss, 1989, *The Dialectics of Seeing: Walter Benjamin and the Arcades Project.* Cambridge, Mass.: MIT Press, p. 184.

10 See Sue-Ellen Case on the "feminist stall" in her introduction to *Performing Feminisms*, Baltimore: Johns Hopkins University Press, 1990. See also Tania Modleski's first chapter in *Feminism Without Women*, New York: Routledge: 1991.

11 Rosalind Kraus, *The Optical Unconscious*, Cambridge, Mass.: MIT Press, 1993, p.113.

12 See Lippard's "European and American Women's Body Art," in *From the Center: Feminist Essays on Women's Art*, New York: E. P. Dutton, 1976, p. 122 n.1.

13 Fluxus, a neo-dada movement dating between 1962 and 1970, was actually more inclusive of women than avant-garde movements preceding it, yet demarcations of appropriate and inappropriate expression often corresponded to explicit gender coding.

14 Ono in Kristine Stiles, "Between Water and Stone," in *In the Spirit of Fluxus*, exhibition publication edited by Elizabeth Armstrong and Joan Rothfuss. Minneapolis: Walker Art Center, p. 77.

15 On paint-brush-as-phallus see Carol Duncan, "The Aesthetics of Power in Modern Erotic Art," in *Feminist Art Criticism*, ed. Arlene Raven *et al.*, New York: Icon Editions, p. 62. "The actors were all men," comes from Norman O. Brown, prime wielder of the "pen as phallus" metaphor, who cites Levi-Strauss on the primacy of the male as active agent in his 1966 *Love's Body*, New York: Random House, p. 23.

16 David E. James, *Allegories of Cinema: American Film in the Sixties.* Princeton, NJ: Princeton Universtiy Press, 1989. pp. 317–21.

17 See Maryse Holder, "Another Cuntree: At Last, a Mainstram Female Art Movement," *Off Our Backs* (Sept. 1973). Reprinted in *Feminist Art Criticism*, ed. by Arlene Raven, Cassandra Langer, Joanna Frueh, 1–20, New York: Icon Editions, 1988, p. 14.

18 See Kristine Stiles, "Between Water and Stone," in *In the Spirit of Fluxus*.

19 See Moira Roth, *The Amazing Decade: Women Artists in the 1970s*, Los Angeles: Astro Artz, 1983.

20 See Diana Fuss, *Essentially Speaking: Feminism, Nature, and Difference*, New York: Routledge, 1989.

21 Quoted in Carol Duncan, "The Aesthetics of Power in Modern Erotic Art," in *Feminist Art Criticism*, ed. Arlene Raven, Cassandra Langer, and Joanna Freuh, New York; Icon Editions, 1988, p. 63.

22 See Michel Leiris and Jacqueline Delange, *African Art*, London: Thames and Hudson, 1968, p. 8. Robert Goldwater's 1938 *Primitivism in Modern Art*, revised in 1967 (New York: Vintage), is not only the earliest, but for many scholars still remains the classic work on primitivism. See Susan Hiller, ed., *The Myth of Primitivism* (London: Routledge, 1991). It is possible to cite earlier origins,

though they are generally confrontative of the high ideals of art, such as Jarry's Africanisms in his 1896 *Ubu Roi*, discussed in this essay.

23 See Kenneth Coutts-Smith, "Some General Observations of the Problem of Cultural Colonialism," in *The Myth of Primitivism*, ed. Hiller, pp. 14–31.

24 The Helmsian anxiety prompted by Mapplethorpe's "Man in a Polyester Suit" which pictured a large black penis sticking out of the unzipped fly of a polyester suit and the NEA funding scandal around Karen Finley's explicit body performance stand now as near canonical examples. See Peggy Phelan "Money Talks," *TDR: The Drama Review* (Spring 1990): 4-15 and "Money Talks, Again," *TDR: The Drama Review* (Fall 1991): pp. 131–42.

25 See Yeats, *Autobiographies*, New York: The Macmillan Company, 1927.

26 The intellectual center for this group was the journal *Documents* and ethnography was a core issue. See James Clifford, "On Ethnographic Surrealism," in *Comparative Studies in Society and History*, 23. 4, October 1981, for a discussion of the way Bataille's thought was shaped by ethnography, particularly Marcel Mauss. By 1931 Leiris had become an ethnologist. Carl Einstein, one of the original Zurich dadaists, had published a study of primitive sculpture and was also influential in the group.

27 See Rosalind Kraus, "No More Play," in *The Originality of the Avant-Garde and Other Modernist Myths*, Cambridge, Mass.: MIT Press, 1988, pp. 51, 52, 54.

28 See George Bataille, "Sexual Plethora and Death," in *Erotism*, San Francisco: City Lights Books, p. 105, for his use of "crack in the system."

29 Bataille, "The Big Toe," in *Visions of Excess*, pp. 20–3.

30 Georges Bataille, *Story of the Eye*, trans. by Joachim Neugroschel, San Francisco: City Light Books, 1967 (1928), p. 84.

31 Jonathan Culler, *On Deconstruction: Theory and Criticism after Structuralism*, Ithaca, NY: Cornell University Press, 1982, p. 49.

32 See Barthes, "La metaphore de l'oeil," *Critique*, no. 195–6 (1963). Barthes's reading of Bataille would have it that the explicit detail continually services metaphor and, slipping into and out of other details in the way that the eye, in *The Story of the Eye*, becomes the sun, an egg, testicles and other globular objects, trips up the fixity of any meaning (such as gender) so that "any term is never anything but the signifier of a neighboring term." I think this reading, in bleeding meaning away from its effects, misses the point. I would argue that the crux of Bataille's use of corresponding details lies not in the result that any term is "never anything but" its neighbor, but much more in the terror that what goes around comes around through a nervous system of sensuous correspondences in which acts, words, ideas impact, imprint, and have literal effect upon an entire neighborhood of corresponding details. Rosalind Kraus upholds Barthes's reading in "No More Play," but for two important feminist readings which take issue with Barthes's reading of the detail, see Naomi Schor, *Reading in Detail* (New York: Methuen, 1987) and Jane Gallop's "The Bodily Enigma," in *Thinking Through the Body* (New York: Columbia University Press, 1988), pp. 11–20.

33 See Hal Foster, ed., *Vision and Visuality*, Dia Art Foundation Discussions in Contemporary Culture, No. 2. Seattle: Bay Press, 1988; Fredrick Jameson, *The Political Unconscious*, Ithaca, NY: Cornell University Press, 1981, 63; Walter Benjamin, *Charles Baudelaire: A Lyric Poet in the Era of High Capitalism*, trans. Harry Zohn, London: New Left Books, 1973. Michel Leiris's *Manhood*, closely linked to Bataille's work and written in the same year as Duchamp's *Etant donnés*, provides as a further example of the horror/thrall of the envaginated eyeball:

You blindfold the one who is "it" and tell him you're going go make him "put someone's eye out." You lead him, index finger extended, toward the supposed victim, who is holding in front of his eye an egg cup filled with moistened bread crumbs. At the moment the forefinger penetrates the sticky mess, the supposed victim screams.

I was "it" and my sister the victim. My horror was indescribable.

The significance of "eye put out" is very deep for me. Today I often tend to regard the female organ as something dirty, or as a wound, no less attractive for that, but dangerous in itself, like everything bloody, mucous, and contaminated.

Michel Leiris, *Manhood*, transl. Richard Howard,
San Francisco: North Point Press, 1984 (1946), p. 46.

34 See Teresa de Lauretis on "space-off" in *Technologies of Gender*, Bloomington: Indiana University Press, 1987.
35 See Jean Paul Sartre "The Look", in *Being and Nothingness*, trans. Hazel E. Barnes, New York: Pocket Books, 1966.

10

FLAT-OUT VISION

Herbert Blau

She closed her eyes, and Felix, who had been looking into them intently because of their mysterious and shocking blue, found himself seeing them still faintly clear and harmless behind the lids – the long unqualified range in the iris of wild beasts who have not tamed the focus down to meet the human eye.

Djuna Barnes, Nightwood

Tokay grapes are like photographs, Mr. Ekdal, they need sunshine. Isn't that so?

Henrik Ibsen, The Wild Duck

We don't see what we look at.

Alexander Rodchenko,
"The Paths of Modern Photography"

My own first reflexes, when thinking of photography, are somehow not a remembrance of pictures but, in the unqualified range of the iris, a regres-|sive association through the tactility of the form: fingers on a glossy surface, grained, a stringent odor at the eyes. That phototropic sensation might have come from some old forgotten experience of a darkroom, but I suspect it was, like the daguerreotype itself, nurtured in the theater, where I've spent much of my life as a director, sitting in the dark, I mean really in the dark, struck by the wild and furtive odor, when the sunshine hits the grapes, of the thing forbiddingly seen, in a landscape of specularity that is, all told, a field of dispersed speech. This has been extended through the camera obscura into that rhetoric of the image which is, according to Barthes, a message without a code, or like the mutely alluring syntax of the stains upon the ground (tar like blood? behind that man, a shadow?) in Rodchenko's picture with the somewhat duplicitous name: *Assembling for a Demonstration* (Szarkowski 210; see Figure 10.1) – a flat-out vision in an estranging frame. If we don't *see* what we look at there, it's not only because of the unpurged persistence of "old points of view," as Rodchenko thought, what he called " 'shooting from the belly button' – with the camera hanging on one's stomach" (Phillips 246);

rather, it's because the thing to be seen is in its copious imagining, like the theater's god itself, or its ghosts, essentially *imageless*, invisible, though the stomach is a decisive factor, as we shall momently see.

Meanwhile, the synesthesia in these thoughts corresponds to what Lacan describes – in answering the question, "what is the gaze?" – as "the function of *seeingness*," from which the I emerges as eye in the radiant "flesh of the world, the original point of vision" (82), as it does with the smell of defile-ment, the hunt, the feast, in the most ancient drama we know. If this is myth and not history, it is of some historical significance that Ibsen preserved it, late in the nineteenth century, in the subliminal wilderness of *The Wild Duck*, the recessive hunting ground of his devastating realism, where there is the compulsion "to find that imperceptible point at which, in the immediacy of the long past moment, the future so persuasively inserts itself that, looking back, we may rediscover it." That is actually what Benjamin says, in his "Short History of Photography," about the optical unconscious, "a different nature that speaks to the camera from the one which addresses the eye" (7). The double exposures of Ibsen's play, and its time-lapse dramaturgy, occur with photography in the foreground, already commodified, as the emblematic image of the illusions of history, whether in the retouched portrait of the family romance or the culinary theater of the bourgeois parlor, where the Fat Guest says, savoring his Tokay, "it's an excellent thing for the digestion to sit and look at pictures" (225).

This is a virtual setup, of course, for the later critique by Brecht, of theater, of photography, which has subsequently grounded further critique, including the question raised by Benjamin about "the aesthetics of *photography as an art*" ("Short History" 22). But before we return to that it may be chastening to remember, or particularly difficult for some of us to digest, that the realism of Ibsen – driven, like Marx, toward a "ruthless criticism of everything in existence" – is about nothing more devastating than the vanities of critique, as if the future of illusion were the illusions of demystification. I take that liability as the anxious datum of any pretense of deconstruction, as well as the limiting prospect of any "oppositional practice," inhabited by the structures it would oppose, as photography still seems to be inhabited by painting (an avatar of theater) despite the mechanical reproduction that, repetitively punctures the auratic and brings an end to art; or the beginning of the end which has been our history, repeating that beginning, almost from the time that photography began. That is, I suppose, what we mean by modernism.

As for the looking at pictures, I won't review the history that brings us to the indigestion, which may be, in our fast-food version of the "gastronomy of the eye," the symptomatic condition of the postmodern scene, where the *flâneur* memorialized by Benjamin is caught up in the visual orgy deplored by Baudrillard. This tactile vertigo of the image can be exhausting and was so, apparently, long before Baudrillard, as in *The Waves* of Virginia Woolf, where in the receding voices of an undertow of consciousness, there is longing

Figure 10.1 Assembling for a Demonstration, Alexander Rodchenko, 1928
(The Museum of Modern Art: gift of the Cassandra Foundation)

179

for release from a surfeit of pictures, image upon image producing a torpor, and the desire to find something *unvisual* beneath. But in the lugubrious perspective of Baudrillard, release from the vertigo can hardly be imagined, for the superfetation of image is a function of the obscene, which "is no longer the hidden, filthy mien of that which can be seen," but its paralyzed frenzy, "the abjection of the visible" (42), a sinkhole of fascination in which – with America controlling the fantasy machine, the viral contamination of image satellized through the world – the real is nullified and there is nothing to see.

Whether things are all that null in the void we'll put in abeyance, but at the still-breeding end of the real, the question before us, perhaps, is whether seeing – the most impatient activity of the senses, ever avid for more to see – has been irreparably damaged in our visual economy, the proliferous spectacle in which, to say the least, there is now without respite too much to see. If seeing was once the most dangerous of the senses, punished in myth for overweening desire, looking at the forbidden, the subject of taboo, it has now become a sort of endangered species. "We must revolutionize our visual reasoning," said Rodchenko (Phillips 262), after he reduced painting to its primary colors, said it's all over, and turned to photography and photomontage. But in the atmosphere of recent discourse, the other side of seeing too much, or having too much to see, is that one is almost induced by the critique of the specular – the hegemony of surveillance, its secret archives – to conduct one's life with lowered eyes. (Or in the now obsessive rhetorics of the body, to reverse the hierarchy of the senses, as if the essential truths were certified by touch or, without the taint of logocentrism, metaphysics came in through the pores.) For we think of sight as a categorical faculty, analytic, obstrusive, discriminative, even exclusive, encroaching on otherness with an appropriative gaze, as if the scopophilic drive itself were engendered in the unconscious as an ideological fault and the dialectic of enlightenment spawned in Plato as a mere bourgeois hoax.

Neurobiologists tell us, however, that the dominion of vision actually began with a single, light-detecting spot like the aperture of a camera in the body of an animal three million years ago. That spot may be, with a certain "protoplasmic irritation" (in a speculation by Freud, the reluctant source of life) the site of the incipience of *time* as well, drawn into history by the sun. That was – in its huge imagining of the unremembered, hinged on the granting of sight, with fire, to subhuman creatures underground – the heliotropic substance of the Promethean myth, the still-flaming divinity of which haunts our visual technologies, and which, despite all deconstruction, is still sovereign on the mediascape. That is why we can still argue whether or not the photograph is "an emanation of the referent" that was indubitably there, as Barthes insists in *Camera Lucida*, invoking the phenomenology of Sartre and the memory of his mother (in the photograph he withholds: "just an image, but a just image" [70]) against his semiological past. This emanation comes not from a mere historical construction but, he says, "a real body," whose radiations "will touch me like the delayed rays of a star. A sort of umbilical cord links the body of the photographed thing to my gaze: light, the impalpable, is here a carnal medium, a skin I share with anyone who was photographed" (81).

One may not want to go so far as to revive the "layers of ghostlike images" or "leaflike skins" that, in the paranoid theory of Balzac reported by Nadar, would be "removed from the body and transferred to the photograph" each time someone had his or her picture taken, every successive exposure entailing "the unavoidable loss of subsequent ghostly layers, that is, the very essence of life" (9). Yet in the concept of the photographic trace there linger variants of this notion, a photochemical transfer of the real resembling fingerprints or palmprints, the tracks of birds on beaches, or, with intimations of spirit photography, "death masks, cast shadows, the Shroud of Turin" (Krauss and Livingston 31), or the stains upon the stancher, the handkerchief or Veronica, which, in the camera obscura of Beckett's *Endgame*, with its attrition of ghostly layers, inscribes the face of the blinded Hamm. And if in this memorial plenum of imprints there is still anxiety about what is being left *out*, and *why*, what also remains at issue, unresolved, is whether photography's essence is to ratify what it represents, if not claiming it as recoverable – that imperceptible point at which, in the immediacy of the long-past moment, the future seemed persuasive – then attesting that it *was*. Whatever it was, it came to us in a dazzle of light, and it is this "solar phenomenon," eventually acceded to by Alphonse de Lamartine, who had called photography "a plagiarism of nature" (qtd. in Newhall 69), that still shadows our finest photographs in something like a foundation myth. It may strike us now, however, as the shadow of a shadow and there are some memorable photographs that seem to attest to that, if not, as in the lamentations of *Endgame*, to the waning of the light.

There is a picture by Brassaï, in the *Paris de nuit* series – there are others of spectacular light at the opera or splayed in a brilliant haze over the Place de la Concorde – of the railroad tracks at Saint-Lazare taken from the Pont de l'Europe. The tracks curve dimly from the foreground, with several trains at the *quais*, a monitoring trestle overhead, and a wash of light on the tracks from the banded glare in the concourse and the headlights of the trains. It is a picture which seems to require scanning, for there is nothing conspicuous to compel attention, except perhaps for the leaning ray from an indeterminate source. But then, in back of this angled ray, recessed in the frame, there is a row of nubby bulbs leading to another glare, and high above, as if it were the enlarged memory of that spot on the brain, looking for a moment like the moon, a clock, its handles barely perceptible, but an immanence in the scene, presiding not over the movement of traffic, half forgotten here, but over the spectral fact, the negative itself, which is to say the dark obscure. There is, as a variation on this theme, a photograph by Minor White that seems, in its most startling element, the inverse of Brassaï's. Over a frozen field, with the spikes of a gathered crop, the granaries behind, there is way up in the frame, about the size of Brassaï's clock, not the image of an eclipse but an adventitious black sun. It was caused, according to White, by a temperature so cold that when the picture was taken the camera's shutter froze, and in the severe overexposure certain tones were reversed. "I accept the symbolism with joy," White wrote. And then with the vanity of imagination whose power yields nothing but its complicity to the operations of chance: "the sun is not fiery after all, but a dead planet. We on earth give it its light" (*Great Photographers* 217). Every now and then we may see a photograph whose startling contingency is such that it seems justified in getting its science – in this case, astronomy – wrong. I am reminded of William Butler Yeats who, when informed that the sun doesn't rise, simply said that it should.

Rising or setting, it is in terms of the solar phenomenon, its economy of exchange, that we may think of the history of photography as an analogue of our cultural history. Or – not only because the camera disrupts the envisaged tissue of our cultural codes – as the fate of representation which is the representation of our fate. I was very conscious of this recently in Japan, land of the rising sun, at the Tokyo Metropolitan Museum of Photography, which had just bought up an astonishing collection of the earliest work, much of which was hard to see in the vigilantly low kilowatts of the exhibition: daguerreotypes, including Chavaut's *Portrait d'un mort*, death in the photograph doubled over, that vision, light unto light protected from the light in the miniature of a coffin, its velvet reliquary box; salted paper prints, including the famous autoportrait of Hippolyte Bayard, the photographer who, because unrecognized like Daguerre and Niepce for his pioneering effort, performed (for the extended period of the exposure) his own death; calotypes and calotype negatives, suggesting the double hauntedness of photography in the hauntedness of its object. It was, in the remembered suspension of light, a spectacle of disappearance.

Which is why Barthes, speaking of entering, with the photograph, into "*flat Death*," associates photography with the theater, the economy of death whose substance is disappearance: now you see it now you don't, the photograph raising the question in its apparent permanence of whether you see *it* at all, "it all, it all" as the figure says in Beckett's *Footfalls*, for "it is a denatured theater where death cannot 'be contemplated,' reflected and interiorized" (Barthes 90). However lifelike, then, the photograph may be, however activated its surface, it is the energetics of its flatness that makes it a kind of primitive theater or *tableau vivant*, "a figuration of the motionless and make-up face beneath which we see the dead" (32). This is a theater, however, in which there remains the abyss between actors and audience, like that between the living and the dead, which was, in Benjamin's imagining of an epic theater, filled in with the orchestra pit, and its indelible traces of a sacred origin. The earlier Barthes was Brechtian too, remaining so through much of his career, and the ontology of photograph in *Camera Lucida* is quite specifically conscious of the illusory status of a sacred origin, which required us to seek in the modern world a new image of "an asymbolic Death, outside of religion, outside of ritual" (92). Yet if he claims that putting aside the social and economic context permits us, provisionally, to think of photography *more* discretely, not less, that is because the click of a camera literalizes, for him, the division between this life and a "total, undialectical Death" (92) – the representation of which is, as the first and last vanity of the dispensation of light, the fate of representation.

We may have ideological sentiments in the matter, but on the difference between Benjamin's vision of a tribunal rising from the abyss and Barthes's vision of a severed space, an edge, shutter closed, between the living and the dead – these two forms of theater, and what they imply for action and demand of actors – history itself has thrown a variable light, from culture to culture, and particularly recent history. As for the course of our cultural history seen in terms of the history of photography, there the darkness drops again, as in the nightmare vision of Yeats's poem, where images came out of the *Spiritus Mundi* with all the wonder of their appearance on a photographic plate. The question, of course, was how to keep them there, and, as Ibsen saw in the constructed wilderness behind the photographic studio, where the miracle was to occur, as in the darkroom itself, there was the reality of the image that won't take.

Thus, even before Fox Talbot's calotypes – the photogenic but unstable botanical specimens and light-gathered lace – there were Thomas Wedgewood's frustrating experiments, around 1800, with the imprinting of leaves, the wings of insects, and images of paintings on glass. The problem with these early "sun prints" or photograms was how to preserve them before they turned black. Wedgewood had to keep them in the dark, virtually unseeable, snatching a peek in tremulous candle-light, because the unexposed silver salts were insoluble in water, and without discovering how to dissolve them, it was impossible to fix the fugitive image. This task, to *fix the image*, marks the laborious history of early photography, as of early modernism, sometimes to the point of fanaticism, the crux of the problem being, as with the history of culture, *how to ward off the action of light before it goes too far*. The distressing thing is that it seems to have gone too far even after the quick fix, as if the hypo released hysteria, a cataract of the eye.

"History is hysterical," writes Barthes, of the history inseparable from the photographic image: "it is constituted only if we consider it, only if we look at it – and in order to look at it, we must be excluded from it. As a living soul," he declares, working up thus a little hysteria of his own, "I am the very contrary of History, I am what belies it, destroys it for the sake of my own history (impossible for me to believe in 'witnesses' . . .)" (65). But as he examines the rip, the tear, the wound, the breach, the *punctum* in the personal array of photographs, in what might be regarded as the self-mesmerized domain of a capricious eye, ahistorical, arbitrary, purely affective, the hysteria seems contagious. (Barthes, we know, was perfectly capable of reading the photo-graph as a cultural production or a specimen of mythology.) And even when we return to what he calls the *studium*, the reading that passes through knowledge and culture, none of us is excluded, for there seems to be a *punctum* or puncture in reality as well, between private and public, the two kinds of history, and there are times when, fixed and fascinating as they are, monocular, quicker, chemically occulted, the hallucinatory profusion of photographs around us seems to be an immense defense mechanism of culture itself, a last-ditch defense, trying to drain the light before another sort of breach, when the ozone layer widens and, after an imprint of the "intense inane," it all turns black, a photogram of apocalypse – the one master narra-tive of the modern that we can hardly do without.

Which is why mourning, or the repression of mourning, has been, when we think it over – as a photographically oriented art history has started to do – the constitutional emotion behind the politics of the postmodern, with Benjamin's panoramic vision of the baroque as its material setting: a place of ruins and corpses, funerary, bereaved, the seeds of history spilled upon the ground (*Origin* 92). I am reminded of the stains of Rodchenko's picture, assembled for a demonstration, like the Soviet youths in formation at the top of the street, demonstrating nothing after all but the making of a picture. Without eschatology, as Benjamin said, only allegory in sight, but as in the photomontage of John Baldessari today, a "blasted allegory," where even the captions are collapsed into the combinatory sets, with meaning as a prospect, but always impeccably severed from any semblance of truth. These are not at all, however, the Brechtian captions whose antecedents were, in the ruined landscape of the baroque, the emblematic inscriptions around the tombs. Nor is the mood of Baldessari's work, the wit and irony of its teasing opacity, anything like what suffuses Benjamin's study of the *Trauerspiel*, no less the emotion which rises from the surface of Rodchenko's photograph if, the revo-lution already failing him then, we happen to look at it now.

Could we really contain that within a caption? And what kind of caption would it be? The problem of the caption posed by Brecht was brought up by Benjamin in the "Short History," that of attaching an instructive reading to a photograph of the Krupp works, since without a construction put upon it, the indifferent camera "yields almost nothing about these institutions" (24), where, with reality slipping into the merely functional, reification takes over. It is at this point, Benjamin writes, that "the caption must step in, thereby creating a photography which literalizes the relationships of life," directing attention to the scene of action like, presumably, the photographs of Atget (25). That the photographs of Atget seem to lead, as Benjamin implies, to the scene of a crime doesn't seem to me invariably true, but even when they do (impossible for me to believe in witnesses), what crime are we supposed to see? "Is it not the task of the photographer – descendant of the augurs and haruspices – to uncover guilt and name the guilty in his pictures?" (25). This is the mystical side of Benjamin mixed with his social conscience. We can also see in his feeling for prophecy and divination that, while he rejected the mystical-scientist nexus in photography, he was always fascinated by the prospect of the aura, its rematerialization, even when as in Atget the object seemed to be liberated from it.

As a practitioner of the art of light, Atget is surely in the tradition of the augurs and haruspices, like Fox Talbot himself speaking of photography as the pencil of nature. But if he was not quite in the tradition of the spirit photography described by Huysmans in *Against the Grain*, or that of Buguet, who was called upon after the Franco-Prussian War to photograph the first ghosts, which he did – by overexposures superimposed upon images of the living dead who would thus return – he did photograph himself as mirrored in the entrance of a café, and among the ten thousand pictures in the archive there are numerous multiple exposures and superimpositions that suggest either playing with visual identities or experiments in spatial geometries or the resources of light itself or the self-reflexivity of the photograph rehearsing how it was made. However we read all this, and the enormous body of Atget's work – whether as mostly utilitarian, documentation for artists, or, with various ventures into the mysteries of form, the slow emergence of a master with the most scrupulous certitude of craft, or, as Rosalind Krauss does, the visual accumulation which is, to begin with, in the service of the archive itself, "*subjects*, . . . functions of the catalogue, to which Atget himself is *subject*" (149) – one certitude we do not have, because of his reticence, is how he stood on any questions that bear upon politics, aesthetics, the relation between them, or photography as a discursive space.

It is hard to believe that a man so observant was totally unaffected by the innovative artists – Braque, Utrillo – he also served. But so far as his own technique is any testimony, and the processing of his prints, they suggest that he was very much of the nineteenth century, and there is reason for Beaumont Newhall saying, in his history, of Atget, that "it is often hard to believe that he did most of his work after 1900" (195). Even if one distrusts Newhall's contribution to the ideology of the aesthetic in photography, and the canonical in his history, there is more than sufficient evidence that Atget shared those nineteenth-century habits of mind that, as with other photographers, still moved between science and its other, whatever that was; and it could be more or less spiritistic. Thus, a photograph might have both the qualities of an effigy or fetish, while the registration of an object, the activity of the trace, might still convey its material status in an actual world. The trace itself might be understood, as in countless photographs of Atget, as a

185

manifestation of meaning, though I'd hesitate to say with any confidence that I knew what that meaning is. There is the possibility that, at the scene of the crime, he may have, in a precipitation of consciousness, uncovered guilt, as in the store window on the Avenue des Gobelins (Atget 4:136), with its grinning mannequins (male) in stiff collars, all of them with a price, so caught up, however, in reflections of buildings, trees, and the window's fabric that the photograph was thought to be a mistake; or the pictures of brothel life commissioned by the artist André Dignimont, one outdoor scene so astutely composed that the sloping cobbles and angled walls lead to the self-possessed woman, oddly perched on the porch (she seems not exactly to be sitting or standing) with a shadow flowing from her black skirt into the rectangular blackness of the corridor (4:107). The minimalist geometry of that black plane may be telling a story, as of something blocked or off-limits, but it is still hard for me to imagine Atget *naming* the guilty in his pictures.

Or, if he should approach something like that, not anymore, surely, than two pictures actually taken at the Krupp Cast-Steel Factory, by anonymous photographers, one in 1900, the other in 1911, and shown at an exhibition at the Museum of Modern Art in 1989 (Szarkowski 143, 161). It may be that being shown at MOMA is, any way you look at it, the wrong construction to put upon a photograph, even the most demystifying by Atget, about whom Benjamin conjectures that, as a former actor "repelled by his profession, [he] tore off his mask and then sought to strip reality of its camouflage" ("Short History" 20). There is nothing so melodramatic in either of the anonymous photographs, which seem part of the history of utilitarian reports on factories, machinery, industrial processes; and while they lack the "pristine intensity" of the imaged materiality in Atget's pictures – the quality attributed by Benjamin to the photographs in Breton's *Nadja* – it seems to me that they more specifically uncover guilt, if you're looking for it, than the more impassive revelations you'll find in Atget; and, though maybe intended as nothing but documentation, without any captions.

The first picture is of a worker rolling the steel tire of a locomotive wheel. The man, wearing a cap, is stripped to the waist, with what looks like the waistband of his trousers flipped down, slouched below the belly's flesh. The leading edge of the tire and the man's back foot are cut off at the frame, like (if you'll forgive the conjecture) the projected logic of advancing capitalism, though the muteness of effortless muscle might bring it down on either side of the unstable equation, *then*, of exploitation/productivity in an irreversibly industrial world. The second photograph is, in a retrospective look, potentially more ominous. There is another man in a cap, his somewhat grimy jacket buttoned, and a grimly mustached face, at the lower end of the frame dominated by a turbine tube. He is holding a ruler vertically to measure the diameter of the tube, of which he is – disconsolate? embarrassed? indifferent? bored? – less than half the size. Possibly because the photographer told him to, he is turned half away from the camera, looking somewhere beyond the frame, perhaps at a supervisor also giving instructions. Already diminished by the massive tube, it is as if he were belittled additionally by the photographic occasion, a "technique of diminution" (Benjamin), and so far as I can read his expression, his sense of inconsequence is not at all disguised. But then, of course, he doesn't speak.

Could this muteness be a preface to action, calling for a caption? And, given the guesswork in my readings, any readings, what might a caption do? That would depend, of course, on where the photographs might be shown again, when, and for whom. That would have been true at least since the Brechtian distrust of the unaided camera and the unarmed eye, but we are especially vigilant now about the social formations in which photography occurs, having become aware of the emergence of an economy in which it functions everywhere as the instrumental means of a system of surveillance and documentation. And within this dispensation of thought, the measure of photography as practice, artwork perhaps, but always suspiciously art, would be the degree to which the work itself contained an analysis, along the lines of Martha Rosler or Hans Haacke, of the institutional frame: gallery, museum, systems of distribution, the curatorial elite, and the long investment, paying off in the rising prices for photography, of the idea of photography as art. We are quite a long way now from what Nadar could say about photography in 1856, putting aside what was required for a portrait, no less the portrait of his mother (or wife), which Barthes – comparing it to the Winter Garden photograph of his mother – called one of the loveliest ever made: psychological acuity, a combination of directness and empathy, communion with the subject, the sitter, all of which we might consider humanistic garbage now. "Photography is a marvellous discovery," said Nadar, "a science that has attracted the greatest intellects, an art that excites the most astute minds – and one that can be practiced by any imbecile. ... Photographic theory can be taught in an hour, the basic technique in a day. But what cannot be taught is the feeling for light" (Newhall 66).

It was light that once gave meaning to photography, and I want to return to that; but if it is true, as current theory would have it, that photography has no meaning outside of the specific relations of production in its historical context, one thing is clear about our present context: any caption that I might imagine for the Krupp factory photograph would contribute no more, nor less, to the class struggle, the ostensible motive of a caption, than the critical discourse and photographic practice, some of it in museums, that is presumably aligned with it. Abigail Solomon-Godeau has written of "critical practices not specifically calibrated to resist recuperation as aesthetic commodities," that they "almost immediately succumb to this process" (72). One can hardly think of a practice of any consequence, Rosler's, Haacke's, Brecht's itself, that does not succumb anyhow, just as eliminating the hard-and-fast distinction between art and activism does not prevent, even for some activists, the "apparent collapse of any hard-and-fast distinction between art and advertising" (73). In this collapse of art, advertising, activism, the enigma, I suppose, is Andy Warhol, who also collapses the distinction between art, photography, and performance.

Since I have reflected on photography as a form of theater, in the drift of theory determined by Brecht, what follows is not exactly an aside, though I am conscious of a certain wariness about theorizing from experience: having directed some of the earliest productions of Brecht's plays in the United States, including the American premiere of *Mother Courage* – attentive to the class struggle (San Francisco, at the time, was a rabid labor town, with a Communist newspaper besides), scrupulous about historicization, estrangement, the emblematic coding of events, the caption, I am still not at all convinced that the double articulation of a narrative has any more ideological potency than the autonomous image in the indirections of thought, depending on the intelligence that went into the image and who, in the activity of perception, is doing the thinking. (It is very likely to be, as with Brecht's own productions at the Berliner Ensemble in East Berlin, an audience of bourgeois intelligentsia, to puzzle with him over why all the captions in the world or other alienating devices couldn't keep Mother Courage from eliciting sympathy, misleading emotion, and undoing what he wanted us to understand.) The fact of the matter is that the most efficacious political production of that period in San Francisco – a matter of timing and attunement to the exigencies of the time, yet almost a matter of chance – was the rather bewildering action, then, or want of it, in Beckett's *Waiting for Godot*, which corresponded, in the plaintive image of its negative capability, the waiting, the passivity, the sitdowns, to the early stages of the civil rights movement, as well as to the waiting, the slave/master consciousness at San Quentin Prison, where it became legendary, and a model for alternative forms of theater, in prisons, factories, Indian reservations, the ghettos, the streets, wherever. Beckett, by the way, told me shortly after our production that he had always thought of political solutions as going from one insane asylum to another; this didn't prevent him from working, during the occupation by the Nazis, in the French resistance.

"[One] feels the need," says Hal Foster, "all the more urgently for a historically redemptive, socially resistant cultural practice" (25). One may feel the need but practice quite differently than anticipated by those who share it, and some who do not share it, the need, may turn out to be more redemptive, socially resistant – over a period of time, historically – than those who might articulate their resistance, some of them eloquently, movingly, but rarely so, as always in art, most of them predictable, outguessable, always already heard. At the same time, the argument for a self-conscious, intentional oppositional practice has again been put in question by chance, in the political uproar around the works of Andreas Serrano and Robert Mapplethorpe.

Serrano, by his own testimony, is a somewhat reclusive artist whose earliest pieces reworked Christian iconography in stylized tableaux, the images growing more rather than less abstract as he approached various social and religious taboos, using a variety of body fluids: breast milk, menstrual blood, semen, and the piss which caused a scandal when he immersed a crucifix in it. He remains fascinated with religious iconography, though transplanted now to a more specifically political terrain: his photographs of the Klan and the homeless. The style was never quite political before, and there is nothing inarguably oppositional in his practice now. The Klan pictures – and the rapport he had to establish with the Klansmen to get them – are equivocal; and who is not sympathetic to the homeless, whom he similarly ennobled *as images*, after paying them to pose, though we are surely more conflicted when we encounter the Klansman in full regalia and the same style. Actually, Serrano's current style – which I saw at the Galerie Templon in Paris, something like being shown by Leo Castelli in New York – is not radically different from the indirection and ambiguity of his earlier work, the technique cool, conceptual, symbols outside the mainstream (like symbolism itself), charged with his own emotions as a former Catholic who does not mind, even today, being called a Christian (Fusco 43).

What made Serrano's *Piss Christ* oppositional, then, was the award from a government agency that occasioned the controversy; not anything designed as oppositional practice, but an unexpected attack by the fundamentalist Right, whom he is trying to understand better now in the formal if not formalist portraits of the Klansmen. As for Mapplethorpe, here we have various ironies, given the ideological animus of the critique of modernism. I am hardly the only one to think his photographs were not in any way oppositional, whatever his sexual practices. They were adept, rather, in drawing upon the formal resources of modernist photography, but as if filling in the prescription with a more powerful medicine, S&M, B&D, without any criticism whatever in the photographic space of the artistic regimen or its institutional structures that he was more or less ripping off. In this regard, one may want to contrast the photographs of Mapplethorpe with certain pictures by the fashion photographers Richard Avedon or Irving Penn, both of whom extend the resources at their disposal or, critically, even severely, narrow them down, as Penn did quite literally in the portraits where celebrities (Noel Coward, the young Joe Louis) are wedged into a corner, as if the imperiousness of the modernist artist were being literalized in the visual text (Coward playing it to the hilt; in the case of Joe Louis, a standoff, since he was there, ready to go, a menace in the corner). All of this is to say, again, as Brecht did to Lukács, that formal innovation may be dissident content in the mind as content alone is unlikely to be, at least for very long. As for the controversy over Mapplethorpe's most repellent content, the hard stuff itself, need I comment on the hypocrisy that eventuates when, in the necessities of a legal defense, those who have bought all the platitudes about modernism and formalism assure us that content, as such, has no existence in a work of art except as form. How, indeed, are you going to caption that?

Which is not to say that captioning can't be honest and complex, with a suggestiveness in its own right, as it is in Rosler or Baldessari, although it's a toss-up as far as I'm concerned as to which of the two is more effective politically. With both of them, of course, we are dealing for the most part with either deliberately banal or appropriated photography, as on the billboards of Barbara Kruger, which for all her intelligence, and a commendable politics, are obviously not in the same ballpark with the photomontages of John Heartfield – impact muted in any event by the dispersions of our history and, however specifically calibrated her resistance, the counter-appropriation of the institutions that commission her. I moved into this discussion of the caption through Benjamin's designation of Atget, the actor who tore off his disguise, as a figure of oppositional practice, but it should be obvious that whatever politics we have in the photographic work of the postmodern, little of it has the quality of feeling, the tonality, the texture, that confronts us in Atget, who almost reverses the loss of aura by drawing the banality from a boot, a doorknob, a lampshade, a leaf, making them iridescent, not unlike Pound's petals on a wet black bough; or when the reflections deepen and glisten, warmed in the browning of overexposures, the datum of that image, not the crowd, which is "the social basis for the decay of the aura" (Benjamin, *Illuminations* 225), but "the apparition of these faces in the crowd," as Pound wrote: direct treatment of the object, even when mirrored, reduced to essentials; in short, that concentrate of an image, fixed, an intellectual and emotional complex in an instant of time.

If that should make the photographs of Atget in any way a model of revolutionary practice – as Allan Sekula suggests at the end of a finely researched essay on the juridical use of archives of images of the body – it is not merely because of the detective work or spying in the telling detail, but because of the *precise ambiguity* of the detail, its *profane illumination* – like the materiality of light, to which we give light – "a materialistic, anthropological inspiration," which was precisely the quality discerned in Atget by the surrealists, about whom Benjamin, in his remarkable essay on surrealism (entitled "The Last Snapshot of the European Intellectuals") used that term with that definition (*Reflections* 179).[1] The surrealists also responded, no doubt, to intimations of "convulsive beauty" in the capacious reflections surrounding the details, as in another store window on the Avenue des Gobelins (4:137–8), with the curled (beckoning?) fingers of the mannequins (this time female, also with a price); or leading up to the details, the classical statues like dolls in the distance, in the lonely curvature of the pond at St. Cloud (3:122–31), trees, clouds, topiary lyrically mirrored, a chrysalis of time, as if mourning the passing of the formal existence of that culture whose barbarities paid for it – which hardly seems to me, overcast as it may be, an incrimination of the exploitative indulgence of civic beauty by institutionalized state power, represented perhaps by the exquisite presence, in some of the many views, of the Petit Trianon (3:39, 59).

Such beauty is also liable, of course, as it reflects itself in art – and while there are many boring prints of Atget, I insist that this is art – liable to what has become the much theorized crime or vice of representation: "stylistic transcendence." This is, we know, the incessant charge brought against modernist art and its desire in a world divested of the sacred for what might also be described as profane illumination, epiphanic in its materialism or "shot through with chips of Messianic time," as in Benjamin's "Theses on the Philosophy of History," the shock, the blast, the arrest, crystallized into a *monad*, "the sign of a Messianic cessation of happening, or, put differently, a revolutionary chance in the fight for the oppressed past" (*Illuminations* 264–5). This chance would seem to come from that "secret heliotropism" of which "a historical materialist must be aware" (257), the past seized only as image, flashing up in an instant, more or less intoxicating in its accomplishment of form. Thus it is, it seems to me (without the Messianism perhaps, although what are we to make of the obsessional patience in the archive?) in the prints of Atget, with their early morning light, made through long exposure, on aristotype paper toned with gold chloride, as if to affirm the photograph's autonomy, whether the image was a historic monument, a ragpicker with his cart, the inside of a palace, or a bourgeois home. Or like his predecessors who struggled with preserving the image, the encrypted trace of natural things, spectral twigs or fallen leaves, the seeds of history scattered on the ground, as on the elegiac landscape of the baroque.

As for those with a heavy investment today in mechanical reproduction as the instrumental means, indeed, the basic principle for undoing formalism and its vice of transcendence, with photography as the ground of an oppositional aesthetic, they have not always been able to absorb from Benjamin's study of the *Trauerspiel,* along with the ethos of montage, its tone of lamentations. Nor have they picked up from its modernist inclination to disjuncture and obscurity that it may be closer to the T. S. Eliot of *The Waste Land,* and its heap of broken images, than to the plays of Brecht, unless it be the early Brecht, creator of Baal, that imageless image of the Canaanite god. Born of the great sky above, Baal exists in his successive deteriorations, like the light first trapped on a sensitized plate. The intractable referent of the photograph, what it can't get rid of, suffuses our sense of both, the referent and the photograph, as Barthes says, with an "amorous or funereal immobility, at the very heart of the moving world," which is like a description of Baal, who is also "glued together, limb by limb, like the condemned man and the corpse in certain tortures, or even like those fish . . . which navigate in convoy, as though united by an eternal coitus." Yet, in aspiring to be a sign, this fatality of the photograph gets in the way: "photographs are signs which don't *take*, which *turn*, as milk does" (Barthes 6). Baal is a sign that does not take, which turns, and in turning smells to high heaven, abode of his mother and mother's milk. We may be reminded of the wild and furtive odor in the beginning, in the theater's landscape of dispersed speech, and the conflation of theater and the diorama and painting and photography (and ideology as well) through the camera obscura, so that "whatever it grants to vision and whatever its manner, a photograph is always invisible, it is not it that we see" (Barthes 6). The scenes of *Baal* occur with the rapidity of photographic exposures, each of them with a caption that he escapes, while his swelling and stinking body – that pale lump of fat that makes a man think, like the fat in the fetishes of Joseph Beuys – seems in its mortifications like an imprinted residue of the radiant flesh of the world, original point of vision, flat-out vision, susceptible at every moment not to the logocentrism but to the maternal womb, vast and hugely marvelous, in the vicissitudes of light.

This dubious imprint was foreshadowed in the "ungainly luminous deteriorations" of the early photograph – a phrase I take from the "shuttered" night of Barnes *Nightwood* (34) – and the issues focused in those deteriorations have become today, as with Brecht's turn to a more rationalizable drama, profoundly ideological. That the solar phenomenon remains confounding we can also see in the negative theology of poststructuralist thought, but post particularly in Derrida's essay on Levinas, which tries to make distinctions about violence and metaphysics within the orders of light, its commandment, conceding at the outset that "it is difficult to maintain a philosophical discourse against light." So, too, "the nudity of the face of the other – the epiphany of a certain non-light before which all violence is to be quieted and disarmed – will still have to be exposed to a certain enlightenment" (85). If this "certain" seems a little uncertain, or begrudging, that may be attributed, by those who have been critical of poststructuralist thought, to an incorrigible ahistoricism.

Yet, as we historicize the matter in a visual culture whose history moves before us in the blink of an eye, we find ourselves faulting vision, the mandate of light in the spot on the brain, the ethic in the optic, the specular drive, precisely when it finds itself baffled by overdrive: eyesight fading from too much sight, and with it the difficult-to-attain, costly powers of discrimination; that is, the capacity in seeing to distinguish this from that, which remains the basis of any moral measure we have, and without which a politics is only a question of power. I say this with full knowledge of the possibility of vision's excess, the voracity of the eye which is, in the critique of modernism, the ubiquitous issue I've described. I also realize that I have conflated in passing various meanings of the word *vision*, eliding the difference at times between what's in here and what's out there, although I have wanted to project in all this not only the ideological but the discretionary basis of simple sight, its capacity for *distinction*, which may sometimes occur – as it does, I think, in the greatest art – *by eliding the difference*, and in the process bringing to simple sight the resources of the imaginary. As for the ability to sort things out in the microphysics of power, that remains without vision a mere vanity of thought, or – not that *this* not this *that*, click, click, like a parody of distinction – the metonymic longing of semiotic desire.

I alluded before to the new rhetorics of the body, and a reversal of the order of things in the hierarchy of the senses, all of which are in their way, as Marx called them, "direct theoreticians" – none of them getting their way, theoretically, without incursions of the other senses, which are intersected at every moment, as Marx also said, by the entire history of the world. It may be that the theory of the eye – the evil eye, the envenomed eye, the eye whose erection constitutes the gaze – has been caught up from time to time in the wrong part of that history. But there is also the eye of conscience, the eye that parses, cuts, gets to the heart of the matter, and the eye that keeps an eye, as Shakespeare knew, on the liabilities of the other senses. We may hear around corners without knowing who's there, and if touch has been sentimentally restored as the privileged sense of intimacy, it is also the tactile measure of an unnegotiable distance of which, in the microphysics of affections, the intimacy is the index of what we'll never cross.

As we reach, then, an impasse in the quest of eyes – amid the media into which all our senses have passed, and now seem prosthetically to surpass our senses – it is the photograph that still retains the pathos of this distance, as if its surface were a screen, the flat truth of the dimension between seeing and not-seeing, where the thing to be seen remains the still compelling shadow of what we've seen before. In my view, or viewfinder, there are those who can see and those who can't. And while I am prepared to believe that what they see or choose to see may occur within a system of representation that tends to reproduce its power, there are also those who see so profoundly deep or so thick and fast – with such flat-out vision, in short – that it seems at times that the codes are merely catching up, while the signifying practices are in their self-conscious transgressions suffering in comparison a semiotic arrest. Not that this, not this that, another version, *this*, like the tireless facet-planes of Cézanne, studied by the artists of the Photo-Secession after the scandal of the Armory Show.

"We have to learn how to see," said Steiglitz, who stayed in the shadows but masterminded the show. And then maybe with a sense that this *Flatiron Building*, photographed ten years before, was a little too misty for flat-out vision, repeated as if referring to himself, "We all have to learn to use our eyes. . . ."[2] I know Steiglitz's reputation, that he could be imperious, that he also masterminded the perhaps dubious terms for photography as an art, but I suspect he also understood, like the superlative modernist he was, that in urging us to see, there was no guarantee that – even in his *Equivalents*, of inner and outer, the (in)capacities of all the senses – we would ever see at all.

NOTES

1   It was in that essay, too, that he issued a premonitory caveat to our cultural critique and, as in Peter Bürger, its view of the avant-garde, the new "obligatory misunderstanding of *l'art pour l'art*." "For art's sake," Benjamin adds, "was scarcely ever to be taken literally; it was always a flag under which sailed a cargo that could not be declared because it still lacked a name" (*Reflections* 183–4). If this suggests certain contradictions in the apparent politics of Benjamin, what he had in mind is a project that would illuminate what, in the year of our stock market crash, he considered the crisis of the arts. This project, "written as it demands to be written," would arise not from critique itself but from "the deeply grounded composition of an individual who, from inner compulsion, portrays less a historical evolution than a constantly renewed, primal upsurge of esoteric poetry – written in such a way that it would be one of those scholarly confessions that can be counted in every century. The last page would have to show an x-ray picture of surrealism" (184), like a rayograph of Man Ray, its precise mystifications, a deposit through light of reality itself, inscribed.

2   Qtd by Guido Bruno, "The Passing of '291,' " *Pearson's Magazine* 38.9 (1918): 402–3; my source for this is Dijkstra 12.

REFERENCES

Atget, Eugène, *The Work of Atget*, ed. John Szarkowski and Maria Morris Hambourg. 4 vols. New York: Museum of Modern Art, 1985 (Vol. 3: *The Ancien Regime*; Vol. 4: *Modern Times*).

Barnes, Djuna, *Nightwood*, New York: New Directions, 1937.

Barthes Roland, *Camera Lucida: Reflections on Photography*, trans. Richard Howard, New York: Hill. 1981.

Baudrillard, Jean, "What Are You Doing after the Orgy?" *Artforum* 22.2 (1983): 42–6.

Benjamin, Walter, *Illuminations*, ed. Hannah Arendt, trans. Harry Zohn, New York: Schocken, 1977.

—— *The Origin of German Tragic Drama*, trans. John Osborne, London: NLB, 1977.

—— *Reflections: Essays, Aphorisms, Autobiographical Writings*, ed. Peter Demetz, trans. Edmund Jephcott, New York: Harcourt, 1978.

—— "A Short History of Photography," trans. Stanley Mitchell, *Screen* 13 (1972): 5–27.

Brassaï, *Paris de nuit/Nächtliches Paris*, texts by Paul Morand, Lawrence Durrell, Henry Miller, Munich: Schirmer/Mosel, 1979.

Derrida, Jacques, "Violence and Metaphysics: An Essay on the Thought of Emmanuel Levinas," *Writing and Difference*, trans. Alan Bass, Chicago: University of Chicago Press, 1978, pp. 79–153.

Dijkstra, Bram, *Cubism, Steiglitz, and the Early Poetry of Williams Carlos Williams: The Hieroglyphics of a New Speech*, Princeton: Princeton University Press, 1969.

Foster, Hal, *Recordings: Art, Spectacle, Cultural Politics*, Port Townsend, WA: Bay, 1985.

Fusco, Coco, 'Andreas Serrano Shoots the Klan: An Interview," *High Performance* 14.3 (1991): 40–5.

Great Photographers, New York: Time-Life Books, 1971.

Ibsen, Henrik, *The Wild Duck. Four Great Plays*, trans R. Farquharson Sharp, New York: Bantam, 1958, pp. 217–305.

Krauss, Rosalind, "Photography's Discursive Spaces," *The Originality of the Avant-Garde and Other Modernist Myths*, Cambridge, Mass.: MIT Press, 1985, pp. 131–50.

Krauss, Rosalind, and Jane Livingston, *L'Amour fou: Photography and Surrealism*, Washington, DC: Corcoran Gallery of Art; New York: Abbeville, 1985.

Lacan, Jacques, *The Four Fundamental Concepts of Psychoanalysis*, ed. Jacques-Alain Miller, trans. Alan Sheridan, New York: Norton, 1978.

Nadar (Gaspard-Felix Tournachon), "My Life as a Photographer," *October* 5 (1978): 7–28.

Newhall, Beaumont, *The History of Photography: From 1839 to the Present*, New York: Museum of Modern Art/New York Graphic Society; Boston: Little, 1988.

Phillips, Christopher, ed. *Photography in the Modern Era: European Documents and Critical Writings, 1913–40*, New York: Metropolitan Museum of Art/Aperture, 1989.

Sekula, Allan, "The Body and the Archives," *October* 39 (1986): 3–64.

Solomon-Godeau, Abigail, "Living with Contradictions: Critical Practices in the Age of Supply-Side Aesthetics," *The Critical Image: Essays on Contemporary Photography*, ed. Carol Squiers, Seattle: Bay, 1990, pp. 59–79.

Szarkowski, John, *Photography until Now*, New York: Museum of Modern Art, 1989.

11

LIVENESS

Performance and the anxiety of simulation[1]

Philip Auslander

In its 1979 study known as the Williams Report, the Committee on Obscenity and Film Censorship established by the British government to review and make recommendations concerning obscenity law and its enforcement notes that "little of the controversy surrounding our subject and only a small part of the evidence we received has touched on the field of live entertainment." The Committee explained the apparently greater public concern over alleged obscenity in films than in live performances by saying: "The reason for the low level of public concern about live entertainment no doubt has to do with its not being a mass medium. [. . .] Live entertainment . . . affects few people" (Williams 137). The Williams Report thus points to a cultural fact with implications that extend well beyond the specific issue of pornography: in our current, mediatized culture,[2] live performance is largely a marginal enterprise. Even such relatively large-scale attractions as sporting events and pop concerts cannot command audiences on the scale of the mass media. (In their current forms, events of this kind are in any case mediatized, even in the concert hall or stadium, as I shall discuss.) Performance theorists often make a virtue of live performance's marginality by arguing that the value of live performance genres such as theater and (especially) performance art resides precisely in the fact of their *not* being mass media, in their ability to engage audiences in ways not available to mediatized representations, in their possibly serving as alternatives to – even critiques of – those representations.

One of the most articulate versions of this position is Peggy Phelan's account of what she calls "the ontology of performance." For Phelan, the basic ontological fact of performance is that its "only life is in the present. . . . Performance occurs over a time which will not be repeated. It can be performed again, but this repetition marks it as 'different' " (146). "Performance honors the idea that a limited number of people in a specific time/space frame can have an experience of value which leaves no visible trace afterward" (149). For Phelan, performance's devotion to the "now" and the fact that its only continued existence is in the spectator's memory are what enable it to sidestep the economy of reproduction. "Performance's independence from mass reproduction, technologically, economically, and linguistically, is its greatest strength" (149).[3]

Phelan realizes that few, if any, performances produced within the context of a mediatized culture like the late-twentieth-century United States can realize this promise. The sentence that immediately follows the one I just quoted is: "But buffeted by the encroaching ideologies of capital and repro- duction, it [performance] frequently devalues this strength," (149) presumably by succumbing to the lure of what Phelan describes in a note as "the poli- tics of ambition" (191 n.3). Much as I admire Phelan's commitment to a rigorous conception of an ontology of liveness, I doubt very strongly that any cultural discourse can actually stand outside the ideologies of capital and reproduction or should be expected to do so.[4] It interests me that although Phelan discusses performance artist Angelika Festa's *Untitled Dance (with fish and others)* (1987) in the context of her argument on the ontology of perform- ance, she does not specifically address the encroachment of technologies of reproduction on this piece, in which Festa made extensive use of video tech- nology to construct the images Phelan analyzes.

It is ironic that the video camera, perhaps the *sine qua non* of the pressures that Phelan sees as compromising the ontological integrity of performance, is itself integral to the performance in question.[5] This is symptomatic of the "technological and aesthetic contamination" of live performance that Patrice Pavis sees as inevitable in our current cultural formation: " 'the work of art in the era of technical reproduction' cannot escape the socioeconomic- technological domination which determines its aesthetic dimension" (134). Herbert Blau describes the situation as it pertains to the theater in particular:

> [The theater's] status has been continually threatened by what Adorno named the culture industry and . . . the escalating dominance of the media. "Do you go to the theater often?" That many have never gone, and that those who have, even in countries with established theater traditions, are going elsewhere or, with cable and VCRs, staying home, is also a theatrical fact, a datum of practice. (76)

As Pavis and Blau recognize, we cannot realistically propose that live perform- ance can remain ontologically pristine or that it operates in a cultural economy separate from that of the mass media. Live performance now often incorporates mediatization such that the live event itself is a product of reproductive technologies. This is true across a very wide range of performance genres and cultural contexts, from the instant replay screens at ball parks to the video apparatus in Festa's and other performance art. It is also the case, as Blau observes, that live performance is now often in direct competition with media- tized forms that are much more advantageously positioned in the marketplace.

In his book on the political economy of music, Jacques Attali offers a useful description of the cultural economy in which performance currently takes place. He distinguishes an economy based on representation from one based on repetition:

> Stated very simply, representation in the system of commerce is that which arises from a singular act; repetition is that which is mass-produced. Thus, a concert is a representation, but also a meal a la carte in a restaurant; a phonograph record or a can of food is repetition. (41)[6]

In his historical analysis, Attali points out that although "representation emerged with capitalism" when the sponsorship of concerts became a profitable enterprise and not merely the prerogative of a feudal lord, capitalism ultimately "los[t] interest in the economy of representation." Repetition, the mass-production of cultural objects, held greater promise for capital because whereas "In representation, a work is generally heard only once – it is a unique moment; in repetition, potential hearings are stockpiled" (41). By being recorded and mediatized, performance becomes an accumulable value, a commodity. Blau's calling the pressure of live performance's competition with mediatized forms within the economy of repetition "a datum of practice" suggests that this pressure is inevitably reflected in performance practice, in the material conditions under which performance takes place, in the composition of the audience and the formation of its expectations, and in the forms and contents of performance itself.

Before engaging these issues, I want to problematize the binary logic on which the positions I have quoted are based, for all place the live and the mediatized in a relation of opposition, an antagonistic relation reflected in Phelan's vocabulary of *encroachment*, Pavis's of *domination* and *contamination*, and Blau's of *threat*.[7] In the melodrama implied by these analyses, virtuous live performance is menaced by evil mediatization. Liveness is depicted as engaged in a life-and-death struggle with its insidious Other – from this point of view, once live performance succumbs to mediatization, it loses its ontological integrity, as Phelan suggests. This agon of liveness and mediatization is the ideologically charged binary opposition that authorizes the privileging of the live in these theorizations.

I would argue that the live and the mediatized exist in a relation of mutual dependence and imbrication, not one of opposition. The live is, in a sense, only a secondary effect of mediating technologies. Prior to the advent of those technologies (e.g., photography, telegraphy, phonography) there was no such thing as the "live," for that category has meaning only in relation to an opposing possibility. Ancient Greek theater, for example, was not live because there was no possibility of recording it. (I would suppose that the concept of "liveness" as we understand it was *unthinkable* by the Greeks for this reason.) In a special case of Jean Baudrillard's well-known dictum that "the very definition of the real has become *that of which it is possible to give an equivalent reproduction*" (146), the "live" has always been defined as that which can be recorded.[8]

198

That the mediated is engrained in the live is apparent in the structure of the word *immediate*. The root form is the word *mediate* of which *immediate* is, of course, the negation. Mediation is thus embedded within the immediate; the relation of mediation and the im-mediate is one of mutual dependence, not precession. Far from being encroached upon, contaminated, or threatened by mediation, live performance is always already inscribed with traces of the possibility of technical mediation (i.e., mediatization) that defines it as live. Although the anxiety of critics who champion live performance is understandable given the way the economy of repetition privileges the mediatized and marginalizes the live, theorizations that privilege liveness as a pristine state uncontaminated by mediatization misconstrue the relation between the two terms.

Steven Connor summarizes the relation between the live and the mediated in somewhat different terms:

> In the case of the "live" performance, the desire for orginality is a secondary effect of various forms of reproduction. The intense "reality" of the performance is not something that lies behind the particulars of the setting, the technology and the audience; its reality consists in all of that apparatus of representation. (153)

Connor's frame of reference is the performance of popular music.[9] A good example of the inscription of the apparatus of representation within live performance in that realm is the status of the microphone in popular music performance: consider its central role in Elvis Presley's performance style, the microphonic acrobatics of James Brown, or the way the Temptations' choreography is centered around the positioning of their microphones. As Connor implies, the very presence of the microphone and the performers' manipulation of it are paradoxical markers of their performances' status as live and im-mediate. Far from suppressing the apparatus of reproduction (as a performer such as Madonna may be said to be attempting when she uses a headset mike that is not clearly visible from much of the auditorium), these performers emphasize that the apparatus of reproduction is a constitutive element of their liveness. In short, they *perform* the inscription of mediation within the im-mediate.

Recent developments have problematized the traditional assumption that the live precedes the mediatized[10] by making it obvious that the apparatus of reproduction and its attendant phenomenology are inscribed within our experience of the live. Straightforward examples abound in the use of video screens at sporting events and rock concerts. The spectator sitting in the back rows of a Rolling Stones or Bruce Springsteen concert or even a Bill Cosby stand-up comedy performance is present at a live performance, but hardly participates in it as such since her main experience of the performance is to read it off of a video monitor. The same is true for the spectators at major league baseball games and other sporting events, who now watch significant portions of the games they are attending on giant video screens. The rhetoric of mediatization, such as the instant replay, the "simulcast," and the close-up, at one time understood to be secondary elaborations of an originary live event, are now constitutive of the live event itself. The games – their scheduling, the distribution of time within them, their rules, and so forth – have themselves been molded by their entry into the economy of repetition, which demands that the form of the games as live events be determined by the requirements of mediatization.

Just as mediatization as "a datum of [performance] practice" is reflected in the presence of the apparatus of reproduction in the live setting, so too is it reflected in the forms and cultural positions of both performance and performing. I first became aware of the imbrication of theater in the economy of repetition in the early 1980s when I noticed that a number of Broadway productions I was seeing had been underwritten in part by cable television money with the understanding that taped versions of the productions would appear later on cable networks. Whether by conscious intention or not the productions themselves, particularly their sets but also their staging, were clearly "camera-ready" – pre-adjusted to the aspect ratio, intimate scale, and lack of detail of the television image – a suspicion borne out when I later saw the televised version of one of them. It is true that throughout its history, television has drawn on the theater for programming material, whether by broadcasting adaptations of popular stage offerings or calling on playwrights to write directly for the small screen. (In the United States, this kind of activity was most prevalent during the so-called "Golden Age" of television which began after World War II and lasted through the 1950s.) What distinguishes the productions I am discussing from earlier versions of televised theater is the relationship of the theatrical event to the televisual one. In his book *The Post-Modern Aura*, Charles Newman declares that "the adaptation ... has become the primary literary convention of the age ..." (129). As compared with those of the Golden Age, the productions to which I refer here did not *need* to be adapted to make the journey from stage to television because the live versions had been constructed to be seen *as television* – they were pre-adapted (so to say) to the demands of their new medium. Contrary to Newman's suggestion that the adaptation is the essential postmodern form, I would argue that the fact that these productions required *no* adaptation in making the transition from representation to repetition is what defines them as postmodern. While I would not say that the live event I saw while sitting in the theater was no different from its television counterpart, its identity as *theater* rather than television and its specificity as a *live* rather than mediatized event had been called into question long before it actually showed up on television.

The incursion of mediatization into the live setting has taken place in avant-garde performance as well as Broadway theater and is manifest not only in the presence of the reproductive apparatus in performances like

Festa's but also in the kind of performing characteristic of the avant-garde. Over twenty years ago, Michael Kirby characterized the kind of performance taking place in much experimental theater and performance art as "nonmatrixed representation" in which the performer does not embody a fictional character but "merely carries out certain actions" that nevertheless can have a referential or representational significance (100). As Kirby observes, the decade from the early 1960s through the early 1970s saw a trend away from conventional acting and toward nonmatrixed performance in American avant-garde theater (110). Although "character" did make something of a comeback in the performance art of the later 1970s and 1980s, the concept of non-matrixed representation remains a useful (and underemployed) one for describing the kinds of performing evident in much performance art from the 1960s to the present. It also serves as a conceptual bridge from the experimental theater of the 1960s, which was frequently ideologically opposed to the mass media, to the mediatized performance of today.

The sense in which nonmatrixed representation provided a beachhead for mediatization within artistic practices that resisted mediatization is evident in Kirby's statement, "In nonmatrixed representation the referential elements are applied *to* the performer and are not acted *by* him" (100). In other words, the performance requires some form of mediation of the performer's actions in order to attain meaning. Although that mediation was not usually technological in the performances Kirby discusses, film acting seems to be a good example of nonmatrixed representation. There are, after all, many times when a film actor, like the avant-garde performers Kirby mentions, is called upon merely to carry out certain actions which acquire representational and characterological significance only in the editing room.[11] Clint Eastwood's squint, for example, becomes meaningful only through the mediation of the camera in close-up and the editing. Prior to this mediation, it is just Clint squinting.

Willem Dafoe suggested the parallel between avant-garde performing and film acting when I interviewed him in 1985. He told me that from his point of view as a performer, the phenomenology of what he does when performing in a Wooster Group piece is virtually identical with that of acting in films – to him, both are primarily nonmatrixed, task-based performing (Auslander, "Task" 97). Dafoe is one of a growing group of cross-over performance artists whose experiences in the avant-garde have enabled them to make a smooth transition into acting on film or television; the careers of Spalding Gray, Ron Vawter, Ann Magnuson, Eric Bogosian, and many others are noteworthy in this regard. More importantly, their more experimental work itself has found its way into mass-cultural contexts in many cases: Gray's and Bogosian's monologues as movies, Magnuson's pop performance extravaganzas as cable television specials, and so forth.[12] Ironically, one of the factors that contributed to the performance avant-garde's becoming ready for prime-time was its adoption of nonmatrixed performance, an approach originally meant to differentiate "performing" from conventional acting but that ultimately served as a training ground for the kinds of performance skills demanded by the mass media because, like film acting, it depends on mediation for its significance. In effect, the performance avant-garde had absorbed the phenomenology of mediatized performance even before it embraced the economy of repetition.

The net effect of these developments is that live performance now serves to naturalize mediatized representations. Roger Copeland has pointed out, for example, that "on Broadway these days even nonmusical plays are routinely miked, in part because the results sound more 'natural' to an audience whose ears have been conditioned by stereo television, high fidelity LP's, and compact disks" (29). (The use of the headset mike to generate an amplified voice invisibly would be another example of this phenomenon.) As the personnel involved in staging Madonna's tours freely admit, the goal of their productions and of many rock and pop concerts today is to reproduce the artist's music videos as nearly as possible in a live setting on the assumption that the audience comes to the live show expecting to see what it has already seen on television.

The pop concert as reenactment of the music video is, in effect, a new performance subgenre. This and another subgenre, the high-tech musical play, offer particularly clear examples of the effect I am describing. Both the illusionistic special effects in such musicals as *Cats* and *Miss Saigon* and the recreation of music video imagery on the concert stage show that such images can be produced live and thus serve to naturalize their mediatized sources. The celebrated helicopter effect in *Miss Saigon*, for example, represents a direct importation of cinematic or televisual realism into the theater. (This development lends credence to Pavis's claim that "the formation (or rather *deformation*) of audience taste by television necessarily rebounds on the future audience for theater, particularly in the demand for realism . . ." [121].) The case of the Madonna concert is trickier. One could say that because the music video sets the standard for what is "real" in this realm, only a recreation of its imagery can count as "realistic." Reciprocally, the fact that images from Madonna's videos can be recreated in a live setting enhances the realism of the original videos. Live performance thus has become the means by which mediatized representations are naturalized, according to a simple logic that appeals to our nostalgia for what we assumed was the im-mediate: if the mediatized image can be recreated in a live setting, it must have been "real" to begin with. "What irony: people originally intended to use the record to preserve the performance, and today the performance is only successful as a simulacrum of the record" (Attali 85). This schema resolves (or fails to resolve) into an impossible oscillation between the two poles of what had seemed to be a clear opposition: whereas mediatized performance derives its authority from its reference to the live or the real, the live now derives its authority from its reference to the mediatized, which derives its authority from its reference to the live, etc.

All of these instances exemplify the way mediatization is now explicitly and implicitly conjoined to live experience. The paradigm that best describes the current relationship between the live and the mediatized is the Baudrillardian paradigm of *simulation*: "nothing separates one pole from the other, the initial from the terminal: there is just a sort of contraction into each other, a fantastic telescoping, a collapsing of the two traditional poles into one another: an IMPLOSION. . . ." Baudrillard states, with typical insistence, about such implosions: "*this is where simulation begins*" (*Simulations* 57; original emphasis).

In the case of live and mediatized performance, the result of implosion is that a seemingly secure opposition is now a site of anxiety, an anxiety that infects all who have an interest in maintaining the distinction between the live and the mediatized. It is manifest in some performance theorists' assertions of the integrity of the live and the corrupt, coopted nature of the mediatized. Anxiety is also manifest in the response of capital to the collapse of this distinction. Simulation occurs at the moment a cultural economy is thoroughly saturated with repetitions. It threatens to undermine the economy of repetition by imploding oppositions on which that economy depends: in order to render performance in a repeatable form, there must be an "original" performance to reify.[13] In the remainder of this essay, I will analyze the crisis surrounding the implosion of the opposition between live and mediatized performance by examining an event that crystallizes the issues I have been discussing here. The event is the Milli Vanilli scandal of 1990, which occurred at the contentious intersection of discourses of liveness, mediatization, capital, and technology in the realm of popular music. I want also to suggest that Baudrillard's contention that the triumph of simulation means the end of power as it is has been traditionally understood is problematic. In Baudrillard's schema, when the binary implodes, when it is no longer possible to distinguish between the two terms, ideological opposition, indeed the whole concept of Ideology itself, is voided of meaning. While I find Baudrillard's paradigm of simulation persuasive as a description of the situation of performance (and many other) discourses in a mediatized culture, I am not convinced that the advent of simulation necessarily implies a voiding of the existing structures of power and ideology.

In the spring of 1990, the German pop singing and dancing duo Milli Vanilli was awarded the Best New Artist Grammy for 1989. The award preceded six months of speculation and commentary in the media concerning performers, including Milli Vanilli, who allegedly lip-synched to pre-recorded vocals in concert (Madonna, Michael Jackson, Paula Abdul, and many others were similarly accused).[14] Legislators in many states followed the lead of those in New York and New Jersey in introducing bills mandating that tickets and posters promoting concerts during which performers lip-synch state that fact;

stiff fines were to be levied against violators. The legislators claimed to see the lip-synch question as a consumer issue. In November, Milli Vanilli's producer admitted that the duo had not in fact sung on the recording for which they were awarded the Grammy, which was then rescinded, much to the embarassment of the National Academy of Recording Arts and Sciences (NARAS).

The whole lip-synching controversy inspired a great deal of commentary across the country, prompting a spate of newspaper articles with titles like "That Syncing [*sic*] Feeling" (*Detroit News* 31 July 1990). Most of the commentary was adamantly opposed to the practice, though virtually all of it also admitted that the main audiences for the performers in question, mostly young teenagers, did not seem to care whether their idols actually sing or not. (My own younger students, polled in the fall of 1990, felt precisely that way.)

Jon Pareles, a *New York Times* popular music journalist, inveighed against the use of both lip-synching and computer-programmed musical instruments in concert, upholding the value of traditional live performance. "I'm not ready for the new paradigm . . ." he wrote. "The spontaneity, uncertainty and ensemble coordination that automation eliminates are exactly what I go to concerts to see . . ." (25). The new paradigm to which Pareles refers is the paradigm of *simulation* which has usurped the paradigms of *representation* and *reproduction* in popular music and, arguably, in the culture at large. The performances he discusses are simulacra in the strict Baudrillardian sense: like the recordings they incorporate and the music videos they emulate, they are recreations of performances that never took place, representations without referents in the real.

Indeed, the historical progression of technologies of musical reproduction exactly recapitulates the three orders of simulacra and the three stages of the image Baudrillard identifies in the general movement from the dominance of reproduction to that of simulation. First-order simulacra are *counterfeits* that "never abolished difference" but suppose "an always detectable alteration between semblance and reality" (*Simulations* 94–5). Baudrillard's example is that of the automaton which counterfeits the human figure, but imperfectly, and thus defers to the human being as the referent of the real. In terms of musical technologies, the player piano is a first-order simulacrum, a device that counterfeits a human performance but clearly is not human. The second order is associated with an industrial economy in which the serial production of objects ultimately obliterates the unique object from which they were generated, Attali's economy of repetition. "In a series, objects become undefined simulacra one of the other" (*Simulations* 97). The phonograph record is a second-order simulacrum, a mass-produced object whose reference back to an original artifact has been rendered irrelevant.

The third stage of the image is what Baudrillard refers to as simulation proper, "the reigning scheme of the current phase that is controlled by the code" (*Simulations* 83).

And here it is a question of a reversal of origin and finality, for all the forms change once they are not so much mechanically reproduced but even *conceived from the point-of-view of their very reproducibility*, diffracted from a generating nucleus we call the model. . . . Here are the models from which proceed all forms according to the modulation of their differences.

(Simulations 100–1; original emphasis)

In terms of technologies of musical reproduction, the age of the compact disc is the age of simulation proper. The code and model to which Baudrillard refers is the binary code that defines all products of digital technology, products that differ from one another, as Baudrillard states, only according to different modulations of the common code from which they are all diffracted. There is no intrinsic difference between the binary code on a music disc and the code in the software that controls the launching of missiles: regardless of its purpose or destination, all digital information is generated from the same model and is, in that sense, of the same genetic stuff and, therefore, perfectly exchangeable with all other digital information. And since digital code is reproduced through a process of "cloning," the information on all compact discs and their sources is identical: all are "originals"; there is neither an originary referent nor a first in the series. (In a *reproductive* process, one can speak of a "parent." A clone, however, is a *simulation*, a replication of a model, not the offspring of a parent.) The performances to which Pareles refers indicate the form assumed by live performance in the age of simulation of which they, like the compact disc, are a manifestation.

With the award to Milli Vanilli, the Grammies could be said to have entered the age of simulation, an age the music industry itself had entered long before. The process of which Milli Vanilli had been a part is quite typical of the way popular music has been produced since at least the early 1960s: there are many well-known cases of groups' being formed by producers specifically to exploit recordings made using other voices.[15] It is also the case that rumors that Milli Vanilli did not sing live and had not sung on their album were in circulation as much as a year before the Grammy vote. In fact, one member of the NARAS voted for Milli Vanilli even though he had specific knowledge that they had not sung on the record (Britt G4). He knew this because he was their vocal coach (though exactly what he coached is not clear). The award to Milli Vanilli constituted the recognition of a particularly impressive simulation by an industry devoted to the creation of simulations. How, then, do we explain *l'affaire Milli Vanilli?*

I propose that we begin by recognizing, as Baudrillard says of Watergate, that the Milli Vanilli "scandal" was not a *real* scandal at all but rather a *scandal effect* used by agencies of power and capital to "regenerate a reality principle in distress" (*Simulations* 26–7). As Baudrillard points out, power requires for its working a matrix of significant oppositions and "capital, which is immoral and unscrupulous, can only function behind a moral superstructure . . ." (*Simulations* 27). Simulation threatens the structures on which power and capital depend by implying that moral, political, and other distinctions are no longer meaningful: the Right *is* the Left; the Mediatized *is* the Live. "When it is threatened today by simulation (the threat of vanishing in the play of signs), power risks the real, risks crisis . . ." (*Simulations* 44).

I am arguing that a scandal effect had to be created around Milli Vanilli because the music industry and the concentric rings of power that attend it (including music critics) could not afford to admit that it is an industry devoted to simulation. If the distinction between live and mediatized performance were to be revealed as empty, then the ability to sell the same material over and over again – as a studio recording, as a music video, as a live performance, as a video of the live performance, as a live album – would disappear. The Grammies' ideological procedure of awarding the prize to performers, as though they are the authors of their recordings and not merely, as Deyan Sudjic puts it, "the tip of an elaborate commercial network of investors, managers, agents, and publishers" (143), would be exposed. And what of critics like Pareles? On what basis will they discriminate amongst recordings and performances once it is acknowledged that all are simply different articulations of the same code, recombinant variations on the same genetic material?

More is at stake here than simply the survival of the music industry in its current form. As Baudrillard reminds us, "the denunciation of scandal always pays homage to the law" (*Simulations* 27). We have already seen that the law sought in this case to bring simulationist practices under the authority of existing legal structures. Because simulation *per se* is not illegal, even though it is the "crime" to which the power structure is responding in this case, the legislators recast the issue as a moral one easily addressed within existing legal categories. (Our youth are being duped! It's a matter for consumer law.) By scapegoating Milli Vanilli, the music industry could simultaneously render homage to the authority of law, thus subverting the need for legislation, and establish the appearance of a moral superstructure behind which to conduct business as usual. (Notice the chronology of events: it was only *after* legislation was proposed that the award to Milli Vanilli was rescinded.)

Baudrillard also points out that

> When the real is no longer what it used to be, nostalgia assumes its full meaning. There is a proliferation of myths of origin and signs of reality; of second-hand truth, objectivity and authenticity. There is an escalation of the true, of the lived experience. . . . And there is a panic-stricken reproduction of the real and the referential.
>
> (*Simulations* 12–13)

I believe we have witnessed these very phenomena in the wake of the challenge to the real posed by the near-legitimation of the simulation Milli Vanilli. I am thinking primarily of two such phenomena: the recently re-newed emphasis within pop music on acoustic performance, of which MTV's

"Unplugged" program is the apotheosis, and of the multiple awards given to Eric Clapton at the 1993 Grammy ceremony. These two phenomena overlap significantly, since the recording for which Clapton won his awards was the live album derived from his acoustic performance on "Unplugged."

That the lauds heaped on Clapton in the spring of 1993 were based in nostalgia for a pre-Milli Vanilli time when pop musicians could actually play and sing is obvious. Both Clapton's *Unplugged* album and the television series that generated it are overloaded with signs for reality and authenticity that are conventional within the realm of rock music. At least since the early 1960s, acoustic playing has stood for authenticity, sincerity, and rootsiness; hence, the dismay that greeted Bob Dylan's use of an electric guitar at the 1965 Newport Folk Festival. Live performance, too, has long been understood as the realm of the authentic, the true test of musicianship undisguised by studio trickery.[16] It is clear that the MTV show "Unplugged," which takes acoustic performance and liveness as its twin imperatives, ironically for consumption as television, is a veritable cornucopia of signs of the real as that category is articulated within the context of the rock and folk-rock music of the 1960s.

The fact that Clapton's *Unplugged* album is largely given over to performances of venerable blues numbers is another bid for authenticity and also an evocation of myths of origin: both rock music's ancestry in the blues and Clapton's own personal history as a rock music legend who launched his career in the mid-1960s as a faithful devotee of American blues guitar styles and who, despite various changes in his music over time, has never fully abandoned that original commitment to the bedrock of the music. These two strands intertwine in one of the most popular selections from the record, Clapton's new acoustic rendition of his song "Layla." Thus, both the myth of the blues as rock's progenitor (and rock's consequent mythological claim to authenticity as folk expression) and Clapton's own authenticity as a blues-educated rock legend are brought into play.

At the risk of seeming cynical, I will also suggest that the song singled out for particular Grammy recognition from Clapton's *Unplugged* album, "Tears in Heaven," itself contributes greatly to the real-effect sought by the music industry in the wake of Milli Vanilli. The song is a memorial to Clapton's young son, who died in a freak accident. Clearly, this corresponds to what Baudrillard calls "an escalation of the true, of the lived experience." As opposed to Milli Vanilli, who won an award for a song they neither composed nor sang, Clapton was rewarded for a song that he not only wrote and actually performed but that also alludes to his personal tragedy. Does it get any "realer" than this? The song's regret at the death of an individual reinstates the value of the unique that has lost ground in the current cultural moment. In this age of digital cloning, the model is infinitely replicable – death is no longer the ultimate limit, as can be seen from the posthumous performances by musicians and, now, actors cloned from their existing recordings and films.[17] Through the specificity of the personal experience it describes and the personal relationship of singer to song, Clapton's performance returns us to an economy of representation in which the singular event is valorized. By poignantly reinstating death as an unmitigable absence and, thus, apparently recovering the life/death opposition from implosion, the song valorizes living presence and underscores "Unplugged's" assertion of its own liveness and authenticity. All of this, however, is merely another diversionary tactic designed to mask the fact that the music industry is now fully given over to simulation. Clapton's song and performance took place *on television* and was designed from the start to occupy a position in the economy of repetition through its many lives as cable show, compact disc, and video cassette. If Milli Vanilli provided capital with the opportunity to stage a scandal-effect, Clapton's meditation on living presence and the abundance of signs insisting on "Unplugged's" status as live event themselves contribute to the simulation of liveness, the creation of a liveness-effect that also appears to denounce simulation while actually furthering its dominance.[18]

This excessive proliferation of signs of the real and the authentic constitutes the panic to which Baudrillard refers, the music industry's urgent program of damage control designed to rescue the reality principle and, hence, its own power, from the exposure of simulation. In place of Milli Vanilli we are given what Arthur Kroker might choose to call "Panic MTV" and "Panic Clapton," which reinstate the signs that signify the real in the context of pop music. Indeed, MTV's "Unplugged" has become a virtual clearinghouse for musical authenticity: even rap and hip-hop artists, whose musical idioms are directly linked with such simulationist technologies as digital sampling, feel the need to appear on "Unplugged" to legitimate themselves. Arrested Development, the hip-hop group chosen as the Best New Artist at the 1993 awards ceremony, certainly lost no time in doing so.

The psychic trope of Baudrillardian cultural analysis is paranoia. I will push my paranoid interpretation one step further to show that it ultimately rebounds on Baudrillard's own assertion that simulation is symptomatic of the undoing of the power structure on which capital depends. Surely it is important that MTV has been an active agent at almost every crucial point in the story I have been telling. It is through MTV that music videos have become the "reality" that music performance seeks to recreate. It was during an MTV-sponsored tour in 1988 that rumors about Milli Vanilli's inability to sing live first appeared. And, of course, the whole "unplugged" phenomenon that is so powerfully implicated in the restoration of the reality principle post-Milli Vanilli was institutionalized, if not actually created, by MTV.

Coincidence? I think not. Power, Baudrillard writes, requires a binary matrix in which to operate and will create the appearance of a binary system in response to the implosion of previously operational binaries. "[P]ower is absolute only if it is capable of diffraction into various equivalents, if it knows how to take off so as to put more on. This goes for brands of soap-suds as well as peaceful coexistence" (*Simulations* 134). This diffraction of power is clearly visible in the operation of MTV. Through its establishment of the music video as a form, MTV is responsible for bringing musical performance into the age of simulation. Through "Unplugged," MTV also proposes itself as the antidote to the regime of simulation. A truly paranoid reading of the fact that Milli Vanilli first came under suspicion during an MTV-sponsored tour would suggest that MTV actually engineered the whole scenario as a way of solidifying its own power, first by problematizing the reality principle through the promotion of simulation, then by creating a scandal-effect around Milli Vanilli, and finally by establishing itself as the champion of the reality principle through a seemingly panicked reassertion of reality and authenticity in popular music that was, in fact, merely the creation of a liveness-effect through a cynical merchandizing of Eric Clapton's personal loss. In the context of MTV's regime of simulated liveness, Clapton's touching memorial becomes a means of bringing the one realm that might seem to evade simulation under its thrall. It may be that, in a mediatized culture, live performance inevitably brings death into the economy of repetition. When its specificity is impinged upon through its entanglement with mediatization, the live asserts itself not as a triumph over death (it is *simulation* that represents such a triumph) but as a celebration of the unique, nonrepeatable event, of which death is the ultimate example.[19] Ironically, the effect of this attempt to recuperate death as a sign of the live results in the commodification of death itself, for the live finally cannot evade the economy of repetition. As Attali puts it, "repetition makes death exchangeable, in other words, it represents it, puts it on stage, and sells it as a spectacle" (126).

To put the matter more generally, it may be that the implosion of the opposition between live and mediatized performance in popular music from which this discussion departs was actually a *simulation* of implosion created by an agency of capital to consolidate and extend its power by *recuperating simulation itself as one of its strategies.* It seems to be just as possible to see simulation as the latest weapon in the arsenal of capital (or at least as a phenomenon coopted by capital) as to insist that it means the end of the entire system of real power within which capital operates. At the end of a passage I quoted earlier, Baudrillard claims that when power "is threatened today by simulation . . . [it] risks the real. . . . This is a question of life and death for it. But it is too late" (*Simulations* 44). But *is* it, in fact, too late? Or is it possible that simulation can be brought into the system of power to be used by capital to maintain its dominance, as I have suggested in my interpretation of the machinations of MTV?

At the very least, it would seem that the development that Baudrillard treats as a *fait accompli* is actually in the process of occurring. Assuming that we are currently living through such a transitional moment, the problem for cultural criticism is to find ways of identifying sites on which the crises and anxieties that mark this transition occur and to use them as footholds, however tenuous, for critique. This critique, however, must deal realistically with the cultural economy within which representation and reproduction occur, an economy that is, at least in the West and the technocratic East, thoroughly dominated by repetition and mediatization. Cultural criticism must walk a tightrope between uncritical acceptance or cynical celebration of new technologies and cultural configurations on the one hand, and a nostalgic commitment to categories that are very nearly obsolete on the other. I alluded earlier to the fact that the young audiences for Milli Vanilli and other acts are not concerned with their idols' liveness: simulation does not create anxiety for them in the way it does for the generation of Clapton's earliest fans and for performance theorists. In giving us both Clapton and Milli Vanilli, MTV may be working both sides of the generational street – placating rock's older fans with simulations of authenticity while simultaneously ushering in the new paradigm for the children of those fans.[20] When this latter generation assumes "power," the regime of simulation may be in full force, its expansion into the realms of the social and the political may be complete.

NOTES

1 The writing of this essay was supported in part by funding provided by the Fulton County Commission under the guidance of the Fulton County Arts Council, Fulton County, Atlanta, Georgia, USA. I would like to thank Fulton County for its support and Elin Diamond for her phenomenal editorial contributions.

2 I have taken the term "mediatized" from Baudrillard (see "Requiem"). It refers to a culture dominated by the presentations of the mass media. I also use it in reference to specific cultural representations that have been adapted or designed for dissemination by the mass media.

3 I realize that I am considering only a portion of Phelan's argument, which ultimately has to do with the specific relevance of the issues of reproduction and presence for a *feminist* performance practice. I am concerned here only with her fundamental ontological premises.

4 I have argued this position at length elsewhere. See Auslander, *Presence and Resistance*, especially ch. 2.

5 I am not suggesting that Phelan is presenting Festa's performance as an ontologically pure example. Phelan expresses significant doubts about several aspects of the performance.

6 Attali's perspective on the contemporary situation of music and the culture in which it takes place touches on many of the issues I address here and corresponds in many particulars to Baudrillard's overall perspective, on which I have drawn in greater detail. Baudrillard's schema is, as we shall see, a bit more developed than Attali's in that he identifies more stages of simulation and tends to treat representation and simulation as a smooth continuum rather than the strong dichotomy Attali sees. See also n. 13.

7 I extend the criticism I develop here to my own earlier formulation of these issues. See Auslander, "Live Performance."

8 I want to make clear that *reproduction* (recording) is the key issue. The Greek theater was technologically mediated in the sense that the actors' voices were

amplified. What concerns me here, however, is technological reproduction, not just technological mediation. Throughout history, performance has employed available technologies and has been mediated, in one sense or another. It is only since the advent of recording technologies, however, that performance has been mediatized.

9 My use of the term "popular music" throughout this essay requires some specification. What I have in mind is post-war, commercial music with roots in African-American idioms: rhythm and blues, rock and roll, rock, soul, etc. Most of the comments I make about performance conventions apply to any of the genres within this cluster. They also apply to other genres that have taken on the trappings of the ones in the cluster. The performance style and, increasingly, the music of many popular country (formerly "country and western") artists, for example, is taking on many of the characteristics formerly associated with rock music (e.g., Garth Brooks's arena antics and use of songs written by rock artists).

10 I have argued here that this assumption is invalid, that the live is always already defined by the possibility of mediatization. Nevertheless, the terms of this opposition are widely accepted and used; this is what I mean by the "traditional" assumption. My point is that this assumption was never theoretically valid and is now becoming harder to maintain in the face of contemporary developments in the relationship between technology and cultural discourses.

11 Kirby acknowledges that "the film actor may do very little, while the camera and the physical/informational context do the 'acting' for him" (107) and characterizes film acting as "simple acting" which, for him, is at the "matrixed" end of the spectrum between nonmatrixed and matrixed performing. Although I employ Kirby's vocabulary, my own characterization of film acting is somewhat different in emphasis.

12 For a more detailed discussion of cross-over performance artists, see Auslander, *Presence and Resistance*, ch. 4.

13 It should be evident that I am attempting in this passage to reconcile the two main theoretical vocabularies I am employing here, Baudrillard's and Attali's, by suggesting a relationship between Baudrillard's notion of simulation and Attali's of repetition.

14 I have been asked whether race was a factor in the singling out of Milli Vanilli. My own feeling is that their status as Europeans is probably more significant than their African heritage. The fact of their being German places them outside the American music establishment in a way that their being black does not and may account for why they rather than, say, Michael Jackson, were challenged.

15 As Attali observes, this practice is typical of but not exclusive to popular music: "Janis Joplin's backup band and the 'Chausettes noires' (Black Socks) were not composed of the same musicians on stage and in the studio. Elisabeth Schwartzkopf agreed to record in Kirsten Flagstad's name" (106).

16 What counts as "authentic" varies among musical genres and idioms, of course. Although every genre of popular music carries with it an implicit standard of authenticity, the specific semiotic markers of authenticity vary by genre. Whereas acoustic playing and live performance may be signs of authenticity for the blues-rock and folk-rock of the 1960s and1970s, they clearly do not function that way for rap or industrial noise.

17 For a discussion of performance in the age of digital technology that includes reference to the practice of posthumous cloning, see Auslander, "Intellectual Property Meets the Cyborg." An example of actor-cloning can be seen in the film *The Crow* (1994), in which Brandon Lee, who was killed during the making

of the film, is enabled to act in scenes he never shot through the intervention of digital technology.

18 The small audience that participated in the taping and for whom Clapton's "Unplugged" concert was a "real" live event was similarly packaged for repetition and becomes another sign of the event's liveness and authenticity. The experience of the audience present at a live musical event that has been designed for repetition is, as Attali points out, "to be totally reduced to the role of an extra in the record or film [or, in this case, television show] that finances it," to become part of a simulated, commodified audience (137).

19 A sad but pertinent example is the recent suicide of Kurt Cobain. According to published accounts, Cobain's self-murder was motivated by his sense that as his band, Nirvana, became more successful, their music was losing its spontaneity and authenticity. Rather than face the prospect of endlessly repeating his performances, Cobain sought refuge in what he seems to have thought of as the only authentic gesture left to him. It was, of course, a gesture that was instantly recuperated by the very economy that drove Cobain to self-destruction, as has been the case with all famous "rock and roll suicides" (David Bowie); witness the marketing of Jimi Hendrix and Jim Morrison, in particular, since (and because of) their respective demises.

20 I am indebted to my colleague Blake Leland for his insight here.

REFERENCES

Attali, Jacques, *Noise: The Political Economy of Music*, trans. Brian Massumi, Minneapolis: University of Minnesota Press, 1985.

Auslander, Philip, "Intellectual Property Meets the Cyborg: Performance and the Cultural Politics of Technology," *Performing Arts Journal* 14.1 (1992): 30–42.

—— "Live Performance in a Mediatized Culture," *Essays in Theatre* 11 (1992): 33–9.

—— *Presence and Resistance: Postmodernism and Cultural Politics in Contemporary American Performance*, Ann Arbor: University of Michigan Press, 1992.

—— "Task and Vision: Willem Dafoe in *L.S.D.*," *Tulane Drama Review* 29.2 (Summer 1985): 94–8.

Baudrillard, Jean. "Requiem for the Media." *For a Critique of the Political Economy of the Sign*, trans. Charles Levin, St. Louis: Telos Press, 1981. pp. 164–84.

—— *Simulations*, trans. P. Foss, P. Patton, P. Beitchman, New York: Semiotext(e), 1983.

Blau, Herbert. *To All Appearances: Ideology and Performance*, New York and London: Routledge, 1992.

Britt, Bruce, "Milli Vanilli's Pact with the Devil," Los Angeles *Daily News*, 21 Nov. 1990, *NewsBank Review of the Arts*, Performing Arts, 1990, fiche 173, grids G4–5.

Connor, Steven, *Postmodernist Culture: An Introduction to Theories of the Contemporary*, Oxford, England, and Cambridge, Mass.: Basil Blackwell, 1989.

Copeland, Roger, "The Presence of Mediation." *Tulane Drama Review 34.4 (1990): 28–44.*

Kirby, Michael, "On Acting and Not-Acting" *(1972), The Art of Performance.* eds. Gregory Battcock and Robert Nickas, New York: Dutton, 1984, pp. 97–117.

Newman, Charles, *The Post-Modern Aura: The Act of Fiction in an Age of Inflation*, Evanston, Ill.: Northwestern University Press, 1985.

Pareles, Jon, "The Midi Menace: Machine Perfection is far from Perfect," *New York Times*, 13 May 1990: H 25.

Pavis, Patrice, "Theatre and the Media: Specificity and Interference." *Theatre at the Crossroads of Culture*, trans. Loren Kruger. London, New York: Routledge, 1992, pp. 99–135.

Phelan, Peggy, *Unmarked: The Politics of Performance*, London and New York: Routledge, 1993.

Sudjic, Deyan, *Cult Heroes*, London and New York: Norton, 1989.

Williams, Bernard, ed. *Obscenity and Film Censorship: An Abridgement of the Williams Report*, Cambridge: Cambridge University Press, 1981.

Part IV

IDENTITY POLITICS
Law and performance

12

KINSHIP, INTELLIGENCE, AND MEMORY AS IMPROVISATION

Culture and performance in New Orleans

Joseph Roach

On 14 September 1874, an armed force under the direction of an organization called the Crescent City White League carried out a bloody *coup d'état* against Louisiana Governor William Pitt Kellogg and his racially integrated administration. The authors of the blueprint for the event, the "Platform of the Crescent City White League," included Fred Nash Ogden, the former Confederate officer who would lead over 8,000 paramilitary volunteers against the state government's Metropolitan Police and Negro Militia. The "Platform" proclaimed in advance the victory of what its authors called "that just and legitimate superiority in the administration of our State affairs to which we are entitled by superior responsibility, superior numbers and superior intelligence." Although Governor Kellogg survived to be reinstated by Federal troops several days later, Reconstruction in Louisiana was soon effectively aborted, and the era of Southern Redemption begun.

Phrased in the past tense, this account disguises a continuous reenactment of a deep cultural performance that many New Orleanians call the present. Over the past several years, as the city has contended with the legalities of integrating the "Old Line" Mardi Gras organizations, which date from the nineteenth century, another, closely related issue has festered in city council chambers, on editorial pages, and in the streets: the disposition of the "Liberty Monument," an obelisk erected to honor the perpetrators of the terrorist *coup* of 1874. On this stage of contested but collective memory, intensified by the political rise of former Klansman David Duke, the city of New Orleans has made a national spectacle of its cultural politics, going over some of the same ground it covered 100 years ago when *Plessy v. Ferguson*, the Louisiana public accommodations lawsuit that challenged Jim Crow, provided the United States Supreme Court with the occasion to establish "separate but equal" as the law of the land.

In writing this essay about a particularly volatile form of local knowledge – the rites and secular rituals of a performance-saturated interculture – I have two, more general goals.

First, without in any way diminishing the importance of any one of the more familiar categories of difference and exclusion that cultural studies surveys, I want to apply current trends in the emerging field of performance studies to suggest how categories of race, class, gender, and sexuality may be produced by (and remain imbedded in) complex networks of other measures of human difference. Based on my research into the local conditions of cultural performance in New Orleans, I have chosen kinship, intelligence, and memory to represent these other measures. They are no more or less constructed, no more or less essential, no more or less naturalized than other rubrics within human taxonomies, but they have remained far less prominent in discussions of alterity. Like other culturally encoded categories of difference, tradition insists on the rootedness of kinship, intelligence, and memory in "Nature," even – or perhaps especially – when the facts of their constructedness within cultural and social norms may be explicitly demonstrated. The secret history of Mardi Gras in New Orleans documents this process of naturalization by exposing putatively timeless annual rituals as contingent improvisations.

Second, I preface my account of this historical instance of culture as performance with a version of the development of performance studies as an interdisciplinary (or postdisciplinary) methodology. Not entirely by coincidence, this history also involves New Orleans. As a framework for my account, I am adopting Richard Schechner's definition of performance, set forth most comprehensively in *Between Theater and Anthropology* (1985), as "restored behavior" or "twice-behaved behavior" – (re)presentations that can be rehearsed, repeated, and, above all, recreated (35-116). The concept of restored behavior emerges from the cusp of the arts and human sciences as the process wherein cultures understand themselves reflexively and whereby they explain themselves to others. Theater, as a high-culture form, remains important in this formulation as a genre with a rich theoretical lexicon, in light of which the cultural significance of other performance modes may be interpreted (Beeman, Balme). The concept of the restoration of behavior extends performance to include what Brooks McNamara terms "invisible theater" and Michel de Certeau calls the "practice of everyday life." Looked at in this light, literature itself (and not just dramatic literature) may be understood as the historic archive of restored behavior, the repository and the medium of transmission of performative tropes like Mary Poovey's proper lady, say, or Karen Halttunen's confidence man.

I want further to limit my definition of performance, however, by adopting John J. MacAloon's restriction, proposed in the preface to *Rite, Drama, Festival, Spectacle: Rehearsals Toward a Theory of Cultural Performance* (1984). MacAloon argues that performance is a particular class or subset of restored behavior "in which one or more persons assume responsibility to an audience and to tradition as they understand it." This qualifier adds not only an element of self-consciousness (or "reflexivity") as an intensifying

218

precondition for the raising of restored behavior to the level of cultural performance, but it also introduces an element of risk and risk-taking. "Performances are anything but routine," MacAloon continues: "By acknowledging responsibility to one another and to the traditions condensed and objectified in the 'scripts,' agents and audiences acknowledge a risk that things might not go well. To agree to perform is to agree to take a chance" (9). Performance thus entails a compact between actors and audience (even when their roles are rapidly handed back and forth, as in carnival), a compact that promises the production of certain mutually anticipated effects, but the stipulations of the compact are often subject to negotiation, adjustment, and even transformation. The range of human interactions defined within these limits delineates the field of performance studies, to which institutional history I now turn.

I

Theoretically speaking, performance studies, like jazz, can claim its status as an American invention. The formation of the field in the 1960s – including its predilection for the comparative juxtaposition of matrixed and non-matrixed performances, its interest in street theater and non-scripted events, its valorization of popular entertainment and oral performance, and its methodological engagement with ethnographic, folkloric, and anthropological approaches – owes more than it has perhaps fully acknowledged to the Afro-Caribbean retentions and adaptations of New Orleans. My version of the disciplinary history of performance studies begins with the early years of *The Tulane Drama Review* (*TDR*), which, under Richard Schechner's editorship, "served as a sort of clearinghouse of the new ideas, seeking out and encouraging new theoreticians and practitioners in America and spreading news of work in Europe and elsewhere" (Carlson 254). Among those new ideas was an expanded notion of what constituted a performance event, including non-scripted Happenings and ritual practices from many cultural traditions.

Quite apart from *TDR*, however, theater and drama had maintained from its disciplinary inception a receptiveness to cultural anthropology, largely stemming from the influence of Sir James Frazer on the Cambridge Ritualists – Jane Harrison, Gilbert Murray, and F. M. Cornford – who stressed the origin of drama in rites of death and renewal. Although these Hellenists worked with the texts of Attic tragedy and comedy, they imagined between the lines a world of forgotten gestures, intonations, practices, and meanings that "evolved" from the primordial rituals of vegetation worship, regicide, and sympathetic magic. They carried into the study of pre-history their version of the old anthropological distinction between civilized and savage on the basis of literacy. Because many of Frazer's key examples in *The Golden Bough* come from Africa, inscribed by the Cambridge Ritualists as

219

"primitive" analogues to the origins of Greek theater, an interesting ligature developed in anticipation of Martin Bernal's *Black Athena: The Afroasiatic Roots of Classical Civilization* (1987), whereby the ritual fragments of African oral traditions re-oriented the received meaning of the most hallowed texts of the Eurocentric canon.

The Ritualist emphasis on the stasis and sacrificial conservatism of rites and rituals continued to inform the reigning teleology of theater history, which traced the evolutionary progress of drama in the West from "the sympathetic magic of 'primitive peoples' before the beginning of history to the Pisgah sights of European modernism at its end" (Reinelt and Roach 293). Most histories of the theater prefaced their accounts of the origins of the ancient theater with photographs of "tribal" rituals from around the world. These tribes presumably occupied a place in cultural evolution equivalent to that of the pre-history of Greece, or more precisely, they existed outside of time altogether as political nullities in a disconnected realm, untroubled by progress or even by history itself. Theater thus derived from anthropology one of the latter field's most troubling (and troubled) issues, what Johannes Fabian in *Time and the Other* calls the "denial of coevalness" between the anthropologist and his or her human "object" of study (31). Such chronopolitics of difference denied the cultural performances of traditional societies participation in history, while at the same time they accepted the products of the anthropologists' or historians' own tradition as the aesthetic consummation of a most satisfactory evolution. In theater studies, this ethnocentric mind-set segregated the study of canonical forms, such as Greek or Elizabethan drama, for instance, from many of the world's most prolific performance genres.

In New Orleans, however, the elitist bias and Eurocentrism of these influences encountered a uniquely countervailing alternative in the popular culture of carnival, especially in the simultaneous interpenetration of European and African-American festive traditions. The topical presentness of these forms in the streets of an American city disrupted the denial of coevalness. The ethnographic "field" was not on another continent but in the next block, a block likely to be peopled by the creolized descendants of most European, African, and American extractions, but still divided by segregationist violence in law and custom. Given its role as a polyglot entrepôt on the circum-Caribbean rim, the historic collision of cultures in New Orleans has customarily been marked by public performances. The eye-popping juxtaposition of these events has the surrealistic effect of defamiliarizing the forms of one culture (making the familiar strange) in the very process whereby it increases understanding of others (making the strange familiar). In *The Future of Ritual* (1993), Richard Schechner looks back on those "seething public processions," such as the famous African-American "Zulu" parade, which, when he last saw it in the 1960s, translated the turbulence of the Civil Rights era into "black and gold painted coconuts [hurled] like cannonballs at white spectators" (74–5). The real show is clearly in the streets, and the participants annually enact therein a local version of intercultural co-production, which insists that their histories and identities, though distinctive in their own ways, do in fact overlap in many others.

Memory and history do not always or even often agree (Le Goff), for differing conventions and technologies of retention shape the contents as well as the form of remembrance. In a passage that has great resonance for the performance culture of New Orleans, Kwame Anthony Appiah's *In My Father's House: Africa in the Philosophy of Culture* (1992) describes the contested terrain of literacy at the modern juncture of African and European languages, and he concludes: "On the other side [orality], there are many devices for supporting the transmission of a complex and nuanced body of practice and belief without writing" (132). Performance studies attempts to find not only a way of writing about these "devices" but also a way of researching them by participating in them. Performance offers itself as an alternative or a supplement to textual mediation. A shared belief in the possibility of such participation links a variety of otherwise autonomous practitioners, though they may differ widely over methodological particulars (Hymes, Bauman and Briggs, Conquergood).

To this configuration of the field of performance studies, the work of Victor Turner remains generative. Turner's formative experience in the field was with the Ndembu people of Africa, among whom he developed his idea of "social dramas," the stagings and resolutions of conflicts within a society, which afford "a limited area of transparency in the otherwise opaque surface of regular, uneventful social life" (*Schism and Continuity* 93). As performances of and by the community, they are "at once the distillation and typification of its corporate identity" (*Celebration* 16). Perhaps most important of all, Turner's development of the Van Gennepian concept of liminality, the "threshold" stage of "becoming" in rites of passage, theorized an entire area for performance research. In an oft-cited and oft-critiqued experiment at New York University, Richard Schechner and Turner adapted Ndembu initiation rituals for use in a co-led workshop on liminal experience (*From Ritual to Theatre* 89–101). I do not accept the dismissive characterization of such intercultural experiments as "naive and unexamined ethnocentricity" (Bharucha 14), but neither do I view them as unproblematic. Nor did Schechner and Turner. In such a transfer of ritual practices from their source, and in the particular cultural appropriation of African "corporate identity" that such an experiment performs, the anthropologist-directors re-enacted the secret history of the field that they were engaged in inventing: performance studies as the restoration of borrowed African behaviors in the radically re-defined contexts of the postmodern global interculture. They attempted the cross-cultural transfer of memory without writing, and in the proposed reflexivity of their embodiment, the Ndembu appeared only to disappear in the project of improvising somebody new.

That is one reason why the question of improvisation remains one of the pressing issues on the interdisciplinary agenda of performance studies today. The idea of improvisation adds the element of reflexive self-invention to the matrix of repetition described by the concept of restored behavior. It troubles the inherent conservatism attributed to ritual by Turner's concept of the "social drama." The importance of improvisation in ritual is elaborated by Margaret Thompson Drewal in her important book on West African performance, *Yoruba Ritual: Performers, Play, Agency* (1992, with video supplement). Drawing upon Linda Hutcheon's theory of parody as repetition with a critical distance (and difference) and Henry Louis Gates, Jr.'s analysis of Jelly Roll Morton's riff on Scott Joplin ("Maple Leaf Rag [A Transformation]"), Drewal examines the importance of transformational improvisation in Yoruba ritual praxis "as *repetition with revision*" (2–6, her emphasis). Improvisation introduces a space for play within memory itself and, as Drewal's title suggests, for agency within the performative compact of traditions and conventions of restored behavior.

Outside of Afrocentric traditions of "signifying" – which foreground the signifier to dramatize both the presence and the adaptability of remembered affiliations (Gates; cf. Berliner 257) – the most intriguing point about the ubiquity of improvisation in performance, especially Eurocentric performance, is that its memory is so often erased by its very success. The present stabilizes the past by representing itself as the inevitable consummation of deliberate steps, but to do this it must smooth over the unbidden eruptions necessary to its own creation. Not only are African forms forgotten, but also effaced are the traces of the process whereby improvisation celebrates (not negates) memory. This retroactive solemnification of the marriage between ritual and amnesia is elegantly summarized in Franz Kafka's miniature parable: "Leopards break into the temple and drink the sacrificial chalices dry; this occurs repeatedly, again and again: finally it can reckoned on beforehand and becomes part of the ceremony" (qtd. States 40). Improvisation and its erasure figure prominently in the struggle between the intertwined performance traditions of New Orleans, as I hope to demonstrate. In so doing, I offer the disclosure of suppressed improvisations as a method of cultural critique.

II

The carnival krewes originated among English-speaking New Orleanians in the mid-nineteenth century in order to establish a more socially regulated alternative to promiscuous masking of Creole Mardi Gras (Young). Formed along with exclusive men's clubs, such ostensibly festive organizations as the Mistick Krewe of Comus and the subsequent krewes of Momus, Proteus, and Rex have set the social tone for New Orleans since the post-Reconstruction era (Kinser, Mitchell, O'Brien). Their rites of passage offer a rich array of ethnographic and historical materials that highlight performance as the principal mode whereby elite cultures produce themselves by contrast with the excluded.

One informative document is a privately printed, first-person account by William J. Behan, wholesale grocer and sugar factor, later mayor of the city of New Orleans, of his 1871 initiation into the original and most exclusive krewe, the Mistick Krewe of Comus, whose membership was and is secret, and its co-extensive social arm, the Pickwick Club. Behan recalls:

> At that time, when a duly elected member was presented to the Pickwick Club, he was met by the Sergeant-at-Arms, booted and spurred, and equipped with the largest and fiercest-looking saber which could be found. The position of Sergeant-at-Arms was filled by the most robust member of the Krewe, and one whom nature had endowed with the most sonorous basso-profundo voice to be heard on the operatic stage. He was an awe-inspiring figure, and the spirit of the new-comer quailed within him, as he was led blindfolded, into the darkened and mysterious chamber where the ceremony of initiation was to take place. The room was draped with sable curtains, and ornamented (if such a word can apply) with owls, death's heads, cross-bones and similar blood-curdling devices. Behind the curtains, the merry Krewe of Comus was concealed, but never was this reassuring fact suspected until having administered the oath to the aspirant, the President asked in a loud and solemn voice: "Are you willing that this stranger be admitted," and then a mighty and unanimous roar burst forth from behind the curtains: "We are," and the curtains were drawn back, disclosing the merrymakers. Now, the room was flooded with light, solemnity yielded to hilarity, and the evening waxed merrier and merrier, for the "Big Mug" had been discovered, filled with the wine of the gods, for Comus and his Krewe. (2)

It is perhaps challenging to keep in mind that the performers in this social drama are not boys, in possession of a tree house, but grown men – social, commercial, and civic leaders of a city that was then reconstituting itself as an Anglo-American version of a Latin-Caribbean capital. By Behan's account, the Comus initiation follows the classic pattern of rites of passage – separation, liminality, and reincorporation – and his hearty effort to take the whole affair lightly conceals neither the serious purposes of homosocial affiliation that the rite reaffirms, nor the oligarchical entitlements afforded by membership in the community that it secretly and selectively enlarges.

The Pickwick Club and the Krewe of Comus exerted social discipline over the families of the New Orleans elite by a system of rigorous black-balling in which fathers controlled the marriageability of one another's daughters – and hence the uppercrust's densely endogamous kinship networks – by minutely regulating both club membership and the annual invitations to the coming-out balls of the Mardi Gras social season (Ryan). In the useful *Hand-Book of Carnival*, furnished by J. Curtis Waldo in 1873, the secret rites of social selection of the Mistick Krewe of Comus are explained in relationship to its public parades at Mardi Gras:

Not only have the gorgeous and fantastic processions been the occasion of an out-door demonstration on the part of almost the entire population, but the tableaux and ball which terminate the evening's festivities have ever been a subject of the deepest anxiety with a certain class of our population. The beautiful and costly cards of invitation and the mysterious manner of their distribution, combine with the social position of those selected, to invest this part of the entertainment with a still deeper interest. It has grown to be a recognized evidence of caste to be the recipient of one of these mysterious biddings, and here is sole clue we have to the character of the organization.

(6–7)

Waldo's choice of the word *ever* to describe a practice that had been instituted fourteen years earlier (and had been interrupted by the Civil War) shows how by 1873 the intruding leopards had established themselves in the memory of some as eternal consumers at the ritual chalices of Mardi Gras.

William J. Behan's initiation to the Krewe of Comus and the Club of Pickwick in 1871 and Waldo's sycophantic *Hand-Book* of 1873 offer revelatory insights into the self-creation (out of little more than their supposed intelligence, really) of a dominant social elite. As fictive kin, they invented themselves through restored behavior – repetition with revision – the improvisatory quality of which has since receded from the living memory of their descendants, but not from their family memoirs. In the mid-nineteenth century, their records disclose, they underwent a kind of collective puberty, a self-dramatizing and even violent quest for identity and position. Victor Turner's elaboration of Van Gennep's classic study of tribal rites of passage led him to the crucial concept of liminality, a "betwixt and betweenness," the vulnerable state that precedes (yet is indispensable to) full acceptance by the group. The word *liminal* well describes many of the Anglo-American New Orleanians of mid-century, as they invented their own traditions of social selection amidst the failing memories of the creolized interculture they appropriated and then replaced (Hirsch and Logsdon).

William J. Behan, the vulnerable "new-comer" whose spirit "quailed" before the awe-inspiring paraphernalia of the threshold between inclusion and exclusion, stands in symbolically for many others. I have found the names and addresses of twenty-seven of the original Comus members of 1857, their homes and offices, and all are representative of an ill-defined assortment of American opportunists, a number from Mobile, Alabama, drawn to New Orleans between the Louisiana Purchase and the Civil War, to seek their fortunes. A memorandum from the daughter of the first president of the Pickwick Club records the addresses as well as the professions of the founders – steamboat agents, accountants, lawyers, produce wholesalers, and a "cotton pickery" – in all eighteen merchants, four professionals, three bankers, and two unknowns (Werlein Memorandum, Churchill Family Papers). Most have distinctly English-sounding names (there is an Addison, a Pope, and a Newton

Figure 12.1 The Mistick Krewe of Comus, "The Classic Pantheon," *London Illustrated News*, May 8, 1858 (The Historic New Orleans Collection, Museum/Research Center. 1959.172.12)

among the founders), but others, like Behan, who joined after the Civil War, are Irish or Scottish.

In antebellum New Orleans, such American fortune-hunters, once contemptuously sneered at as "Kaintucks" and "Riverboatmen," countered the old lineage and established caste system of the francophone Creoles by advertising frequently and shrilly their intrinsic merit based on intelligence. They contrasted Yankee ingenuity – in manufacturing and marketing goods, in draining swamps and digging canals, in building houses and laying down trolley lines – with what they took to be Creole decadence, sloth, and stupidity. The self-inventing, improvisatory rhetoric of the period still resonates in a privately printed history of the Mistick Krewe of Comus, compiled to celebrate its centenary year: "The people of New Orleans are under three influences – the French, the Spanish, and the Anglo-Saxon. The Spanish influence is especially shown in the early architecture of the city, the French influence by the manner and customs of the people, the Anglo-Saxon by aggressive-ness in developing the commercial and business growth of the city" (Herndon 6). The strong signifier of superior aggression and superior industry sets apart the category pompously labeled Anglo-Saxon, concealing its rag-tag origins, the teeming refuse of several distant shores.

The collective rite of passage for this ill-defined group – and the demon-stration of its supposed intelligence – was an improvisation on a borrowed theme. In the 1850s, the Anglo-Americans reinvented "Mardi Gras": Comus

225

began the tradition (unbroken except by war and police-strikes until 1992) of elaborate float parades and tableau balls, which resembled royal entries and masques of Renaissance princes, to supplant the willy-nilly bacchanal of Latin carnival (Figure 12.1). Early on, this was a very fluid kind of association of fictive kin – mostly young men, mostly wholesalers, who met regularly "Uptown" at John Pope's drug store on the corner of Jackson and Prytania streets – as yet neither a class nor a caste, but rather an imagined kinship network founded upon mutual appreciation for one another's industry, invention, and powers of organization. The founding president's daughter sets the scene:

> New Orleans in 1857 was but a comparatively small place spread over a very considerable area and divided into a number of small districts, each of the latter being either under separate administrations or were recently become a part of the City. It was not an unusual thing then, as it is now in small cities, for the better element of young business and professional men to gather of an evening at the leading drug store and to sit or stand around, smoke a cigar and pass a few words with one another before returning to their work or going elsewhere. . . . At that time this neighborhood was the centre of the then new residential district; there resided the well-to-do American (as opposed to the French) residents of the City. . . . [At John Pope's drug store] the early affairs of the Mystic Krewe of Comus were doubtless frequently discussed; and it was here that the inception of the Pickwick Club was made.
>
> (Werlein Memorandum 2–3)

Reinventing Creole carnival prior to and immediately following the Civil War was an improvisation, a repetition with revision, a space for play, in which the homosocial kin, hanging out together at the local drug store, decided to transform their world by building a club house and conspicuously over-spending on party hats and *papier-mâché*.

One strong proof for this assertion resides, I believe, in the privileged role of English literature in the krewe's early attempts to accumulate cultural capital to assert anglophone pre-eminence. The name "Comus" derives from the stately masque of the same name by John Milton. The first procession of the Mistick Krewe of Comus in 1857 impersonated "The Demon Actors in Milton's *Paradise Lost*." Another early Comus parade took up Spenser's *Faerie Queene*, and, according to J. Curtis Waldo, in his later *History of the Carnival in New Orleans* (1882), "illustrated in appropriate groupings the principal episode of that delicate and fanciful creation, which, in the centuries that have elapsed since its birth, has lost no beauty or splendor by comparison" (12). Without completely ruling out the possibility that Spenser's epic romance spoke urgently to the hearts of New Orleans dry-goods merchants, the more likely explanation is that they were claiming kin, performing their intelligence with learned citations. The "Pickwick Club," of course, quoted Charles Dickens, suggesting its generous openness to the good-hearted members of a motley krewe. The by-laws of the club explain that it was formed by Comus members "to give continuity to comradeship born under the mask" and to "conceal the secrets of their other identity" (*The Pickwick Club* 3).

That "other identity," like the ritual staging of Behan's initiation, mixes menace with mirth. Underneath the veneer of boyish self-invention seethed a deep capacity for violence, soon to be tested: "Most of the membership exchanged billiard cue for the musket and offered their lives for the Southern Cause" (*The Pickwick Club* 4). They returned in bitter defeat to find the city of New Orleans occupied by Federal troops, with blacks and creoles of color soon thereafter seeking important public offices and the reconstructionist Republicans able to remain at least nominally in charge. The response of the club and krewe membership to this state of affairs was a campaign of armed terrorism, culminating in the *coup* of 1874. My research has confirmed in detail what many native New Orleanians generally know as a commonplace: that the officer corps of the White League (and a not insignificant number of its rank and file) formed an interlocking directorship with the secret membership of the exclusive Mardi Gras krewes and men's clubs, especially Comus-Pickwick. Like the Ku Klux Klan elsewhere in the South, the carnival krewes took advantage of their "comradeship under the mask" to assert the entitlements of their group, most obviously against blacks, but eventually against others with whom they made temporary alliances of convenience: the Crescent City White League had a separate regiment into which Italians were segregated, for instance, and another for the Irish. Unlike the Klan, the krewes have ever since maintained a strict standard of exclusion by caste. By confirming the roster of White Leaguers in Augusto Miceli's *The Pickwick Club of New Orleans*, privately printed in 1964, with *The Roll of Honor: Roster of the Citizen Soldiery Who Saved Louisiana*, compiled in 1877 by carnival historian J. Curtis Waldo, I have confirmed a list of over 120 names of Comus-Pickwickians who took up arms to fight "The Battle of Liberty Place" in 1874.

First on Waldo's *Roll of Honor* is Major General Fred Nash Ogden, the hemp merchant and member of the Pickwick Club (Miceli Appendix "J"). Ogden was a Confederate veteran, cited for valor at Vicksburg, and the co-author of the "Platform of the Crescent City White League," which denounced the "stupid Africanization" of Reconstruction, whereby "the negro has proved himself as destitute of common gratitude as of common sense." Next on the list of heroes is Brigadier General William J. Behan, the wholesale grocer, also a wounded veteran of Gettysburg, whose brother was killed at Antietam on his eighteenth birthday, and whose Van Gennepian rite of passage into Comus and the Pickwick Club has already been cited. Most ominously, however, in terms of the history of American race relations in the twentieth century, was the armed service of a young lawyer in Company E of the Second Regiment, "Louisiana's Own" (*Roll of Honor* 24): Edward Douglas White, later Justice and ultimately Chief Justice of the Supreme Court of

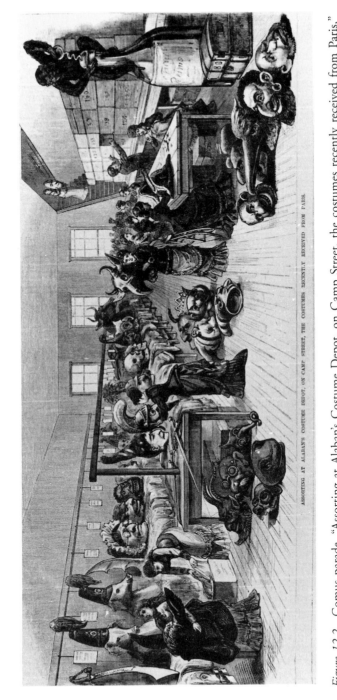

ASSORTING AT ALABAN'S COSTUME DEPOT, ON CAMP STREET, THE COSTUMES RECENTLY RECEIVED FROM PARIS.

Figure 12.2 Comus parade. "Assorting at Alaban's Costume Depot, on Camp Street, the costumes recently received from Paris," *Frank Leslie's Illustrated Newspaper*, March 16, 1878 (The Historic New Orleans Collection, Museum/Research Center. 1980.38ii)

the United States, who joined the majority opinion in *Plessy v. Ferguson*. Justice White was also a member of the Pickwick Club and perforce the Mistick Krewe (Miceli Appendix "J").

To historians of cultural performance, the most fascinating phenomenon to emerge from this juncture of *coup* and carnival is the way in which Comus rehearsed the former by improvising the latter. At Mardi Gras in 1873, eighteen months prior to the "The Battle of Liberty Place," the theme for the Krewe of Comus parade and ball was "The Missing Links to Darwin's *Origin of Species*." It presented animal-like caricatures of hated public figures from Reconstruction, such as Ulysses S. Grant as a verminous potato bug or the "Radical" J. R. Pitkin as "The Cunning Fox [carrying a carpetbag] which joins the Coon" (Figure 12.2). This taxonomy, arranged by phyla in a parodic version of "survival of the fittest," culminated in the mock crowning of the "The Gorilla," a caricature of the Negro Lt. Governor of Louisiana, strumming a banjo with hairy paws, as the "Missing Link of Darwin's Eden" (Figure 12.3). In the tradition of carnivalesque inversion, the lowest changed places with the highest, but this "topsy-turvydom" mocked the regime that supposedly had created its own Lords of Misrule by placing black people in positions of power over whites in the first place. The White League's "Platform" denounced Reconstruction as "the most absurd inversion of the relations of race," and its members volunteered to set the State of Louisiana right-side up again by turning it up-side down.

The sense of doubleness provoked by this inversion, however, played itself out in the form of a weird kind of identification through disguise. White carnival during Reconstruction took on the mask of blackness to protest what it saw as the injustice of its postwar abjection and exclusion from power. The Krewe of Momus, for instance, representing a mounted battalion of Moors in blackface, performed such a drama of protest in their street parade for Mardi Gras of 1873: "Trooping down the streets of an American City, between rows of stately modern edifices, came the dusky battalions of the race who could not be conquered, and who fought with blind savagery for things they only prized because the hated Christians desired it. Their swarthy faces and barbaric splendour of their trappings recalled the vanished centuries" (Waldo, *Hand-Book* 60). In the collective memory of both blacks and whites under slavery, the historic license of carnival had provided a locus in which rebellions in the name of Liberty could at least be imagined, if not implemented. In Martin Delany's abolitionist novel, *Blake; or, the Huts of America* (1859), the threat of a slave revolt flickers amidst the "games, shows, exhibitions, theatrical performances, festivals, masquerade balls, and numerous entertainments and gatherings" on the eve of Mardi Gras in New Orleans: "It was on this account that the Negroes had been allowed such unlimited privileges this evening. Nor were they remiss to the utmost extent of its advantages" (98–9). Delany evokes the memory of the best-organized slave revolt in North American history, the Louisiana rising of 1811, when, during

Figure 12.3   Comus ball. Charles Darwin, the "Sapient Ass" (left) and the "Missing Link" (right), *Scribner's Monthly*, November 1873 (The Louisiana Collection, Howard-Tilton Memorial Library, Tulane University)

carnival season, a force of over 500 freedom fighters marched on New Orleans under Haitian officers with flags unfurled and drums beating (Hofstadter and Wallace 190). The restoration of behavior that such an adventure inspires reappears through the doublings and inversions of white carnival: the face of the "fittest" behind the black mask of the gorilla representing Darwin's "Missing Link" certainly belonged to a member of the Mistick Krewe of Comus, perhaps to Brigadier General Behan himself, who was known to have taken a masked role in the parade (Miceli Appendix "H").

There is no question that the insanity of American racial politics dominated this event, but there also flourished at its heart an invented and symbolic kinship, performed in the rites of fraternal initiation of New Orleanian krewes, performed again in the streets as Mardi Gras parades, rehearsed as acts of homosocial bonding in carnival disguise, and then restored as behavior in storming the gates of the statehouse. In their own words, they forged their bond on the strength of their "superior intelligence." In their own imagery, they took the risks implicit in the compact of performance, the rite of passage, the admission behind the curtains into social power. In their own lethal festival, they enacted the rites of kinship through violence. Back from

Gettysburg and Vicksburg, but still playing war, these boy-men and their sons and younger brothers occupied New Orleans, reinvented it, and re-enacted it annually. In the expansion of restored behavior to the level of reflexive cultural performance, in the mystifying production of social identity and difference, one initiation ceremony may inquire for thousands, "Are you willing that this stranger be admitted?" – to which an invisible chorus may or may not then answer, "We are."

III

On 15 June 1993, the Advisory Committee on Human Relations, which reports to the New Orleans City Council, held a hearing on the disposition of the "Liberty Place Monument." Erected at the height of Jim Crow and Southern Redemption in the 1890s, the monument lionized the White League and elevated to martyrdom the handful who lost their lives in its cause. In connection with street improvements in 1989, the monument had been removed and placed in storage, where it remained until a lawsuit by "historic preservationists" forced the city reluctantly to re-erect it (Eggler B–1). Contemplating its removal for the second time on the grounds that it represented a "nuisance" and that it honored those who had shot dead a number of city and state policemen, the New Orleans City Council asked its Advisory Committee on Human Relations to render an opinion on memories evoked by the monument and their impact on the city's "great cosmopolitan population consisting of large numbers of people of every race, color, creed, religion, age, physical condition, national origin and ancestry" ("Scope of the HRC Hearings"). As carnival itself was the subject of a heated integration controversy, the monument became the scene of a number of demonstrations, counter-demonstrations, and confrontations.

As a study in the performance of memory, the hearing of 15 June, which was chaired by Rabbi Edward P. Cohn, provided moments of breath-taking improvisation that coagulated, before the eyes of the onlookers, into law and history. Speaking in support of the preservationist Friends of the Liberty Monument was David Duke, former Klansman and Nazi enthusiast, who celebrated Adolph Hitler's birthday as recently as 1988 and whose run for the U.S. Senate and then the Louisiana Governorship attracted a majority of the white votes cast in both elections. Duke's testimony touched only indirectly on the White League and not at all on the carnival krewes, whose members, in any case, have despised white-trash opportunists since the days of John Pope's drug store. Speaking of what he called "the true meaning of the monument," Duke cited the battles of Lexington and Concord as the real precedents invoked by the Battle of Liberty Place and its cenotaph: there the patriotic "Minutemen" fought and died for their freedom against the occupying forces of "tyranny." Removing the Liberty Monument would be tantamount to desecrating statues of Washington and Jefferson, he continued, which would be defacing public property symbolizing "Liberty" itself, an act with dire consequences. To remove the Monument would be to rewrite history, argued Duke, who denies the Holocaust: "Then we don't have a civilization any more. We have a jungle."

The slippage that conjured the "Founding Fathers" out of the self-congratulatory erection honoring silk-stockinged rioters starkly illustrates the convenience of Eurocentric memory, which serves to erase the troubling evidence of intervening improvisations by direct appeal to origins. To Duke this distinction suggested a choice between the alternatives of "civilization" and "jungle." Carried away by his defense of American civilization against a rising tide of barbarism, he likened the opponents of the monument to "book-burning Nazis." Rabbi Cohn interrupted the testimony at this point to ask with perfect chairmanly decorum, as if clarifying an obscure phrase for the record, "Nazis, Mr. Duke? Pardon me, but did I hear you say 'Nazis'?" Duke nodded affirmatively but with apparent confusion; then he continued his eulogy, paraphrasing, without attribution and perhaps accidentally, the "mystic chords of memory" passage from Lincoln's First Inaugural Address.

A silent witness to the 15 June hearing was city council member-at-large Dorothy Mae Taylor, who was instrumental in framing and passing the 1991 civil rights ordinance that prompted Comus, Momus, and Proteus to end their Mardi Gras parades, even though the intent of council's legislation was to end segregation, not celebration. Her silence was eloquent. Taylor's leadership, which was visited by more denunciations and ridicule than support, even from some of the other council members who had voted for the ordinance (Vennman, "Boundary Face-Off" 89–104), was forged in the crucible in New Orleans racial politics in the 1960s (Hirsch and Logsdon 262–319). Taylor's record in this regard seemed to fall prey to collective amnesia. The 1991 ordinance developed logically from the civil rights legislation of the 1960s, and indeed from the historic argument of fair and equal access to public accommodations. Even before the final and softened version of the ordinance had been made law, however, the krewes of Comus, Momus, and Proteus cancelled their 1992 parades, and many New Orleanians blamed Taylor for trashing carnival tradition. The Mardi Gras festivities of the three krewes continue now only in private as debutante balls behind closed doors (and here and there in the form of some guerrilla-style street parading, lampooning city council members and others).

The society pages of the local paper report on the symbolism and iconography of these festivities, however. In the 1993–4 season, the Harlequins, a youth Mardi Gras affiliate of the Old-Line krewes, staged a most pointed pageant. On the surface, the film *Jurassic Park* seemed to provide a theme for the preliminary training-debut of the Harlequin Queen and the Maids of her Court. Underneath the surface, an explicit restoration of behavior evoked the local creation myths of race and caste:

As the tableau began, several Jurassic species, including the Comusaurus, the Proteadactyl and Momusraptor, were seen meandering through the primeval forests. They were being watched by "modern man," who was confident that his science, his culture, his civilization, were superior to that of these ancient beasts. Man's confidence led him to believe that times were changing, that ancient species should die off and be replaced, and that the dinosaurs must go. Darwin's ghost looked down upon the scene with a wry grin, and the end of the reign of the dinosaurs was proclaimed. But then something went awry. The dinosaurs refused to accept their fate and rose up in rebellion, proclaiming that they too had rights. Modern man was unable to dominate them and in the end, the dinosaurs were left to themselves.

("Primeval partying" E–3)

On the liminal occasion of a rite of passage that serves to mark acceptance of its initiates into society and announce their availability for exchange within its patriarchal kinship network, the soon-to-be marriageable daughters of the krewes performed a most precise embodiment of selective cultural memory. The Darwinian anxiety about being replaced by another "species" directly quotes the Mistick Krewe of Comus 1873 parade and grand tableau: "The Missing Links to Darwin's *Origin of Species*." The "rebellion" of the dinosaurs, justified by a proclamation of their "rights," makes a clear reference to the coup of 1874 and its enactment of "the survival of the fittest" at the expense of the racially mixed Kellogg government.

There are no trivial rituals. In the service of memory, or in its betrayal, performances have powerful, if often unpredictable consequences. Knowing nothing of the Mistick Krewe of Comus Mardi Gras parade and ball of 1873, historians of constitutional law stress the importance of the almost magical sway of "Social Darwinism" over the Supreme Court of the United States at the turn of the century (Highshaw 64–5), particularly in the opinions rendered by Justice Edward Douglas White, Pickwickian, formerly Private White, Company E, Crescent City White League. Many other influences, no doubt, shaped the Justice White's reasoning in *Plessy v. Ferguson*, but probably none more exhilarating to one who regarded himself as speaking for the "fittest" than the overthrow of Reconstruction in Louisiana by Carnival in New Orleans.

Of the persistence of memory about "The Battle of Liberty Place" among the descendants of the White Leaguers, historian Lawrence N. Powell has written: "For decades to come, their sons and grandsons – even grand-daughters – felt compelled to measure themselves against the legend born that humid September afternoon" (Powell B-7). From the intense dialogue between the illusion of rote repetition, which erases the memory of impro-visation, and repetition with revision, which foregrounds it, performance studies gets a critical edge. The future of ritual, however, remains uncertain and deeply contested. As of this writing, the Liberty Monument still stands in New Orleans, a shrine not only to the Pyrrhic re-enactment of "comradeship born under the mask," but also to the implacable erasure of improvisation that occurs when memory turns to stone.

REFERENCES AND SELECT BIBLIOGRAPHY

Primary Sources

Behan, William J., "Pickwick Club Reminiscences," New Orleans: privately printed, 1912. Louisiana Collection, Tulane University Library.

Delany, Martin R., *Blake; or, The Huts of America* (1859–61), Boston: Beacon Press, 1970.

Eggler, Bruce, "Barthelemy: Monument will be re-erected," New Orleans *Time-Picayune*, 22 Sept 1992, B-1-2.

Herndon, Thomas C., "One Hundred Years of Comus: Report of the Historical Committee of the M. K. C," 1956–7, Rogers Family Papers, Manuscripts Division, Tulane University Library.

Miceli, Augusto P., *The Pickwick Club of New Orleans*, New Orleans: The Pickwick Press, 1964. Historic New Orleans Collection.

The Pickwick Club: Historical Summary, Act of Incorporation, By-Laws and Roster of Membership, New Orleans: privately printed, 1929. Churchill Family Papers, Manuscripts Division, Tulane University Library.

"Platform of the Crescent City White League of New Orleans," New Orleans, 27 June 1874. Fred Nash Ogden Papers, Manuscripts Division, Tulane University Library.

"Primeval partying for Harlequins," New Orleans *Times-Picayune*, 29 Dec. 1993, E-3.

"Scope of the HRC 'Liberty Monument' Hearings," Human Relations Commission, Advisory Committee on Human Relations, City of New Orleans, 15 June 1993.

Waldo, J. Curtis, *Hand-Book of Carnival, containing Mardi Gras, its Ancient and Modern Observance, History of the Mistick Krewe of Comus, Twelfth Night Revelers and Knights of Momus, With Annals of the Reign of His Majesty, the King of Carnival in New Orleans*, New Orleans: W. E. Seebold, 1873. Historic New Orleans Collection.

—— *History of the Carnival in New Orleans, 1857–1882*, New Orleans: L. Graham & Son, 1882. Louisiana Collection, Tulane University Library.

—— *The Roll of Honor of the Citizen Soldiery Who Saved Louisiana*, revised and complete, New Orleans: privately printed, 1877. Louisiana Collection, Tulane University Library.

Werlein Memorandum. Letter dated 18 June 1915 to Philip Werlein, President, Pickwick Club (unsigned) from the daughter of Charles H. Churchill, founding president. Churchill Family Papers, Manuscripts Division, Tulane University Library.

Secondary Sources

Appiah, Kwame Anthony, *In My Father's House: Africa in the Philosophy of Culture*, New York and Oxford: Oxford University Press, 1992.

Balme, Christopher B., "Cultural Anthropology and Theatre Historiography: Notes on a Methodological Rapprochement," *Theatre Survey* 35 (1994): 33–52.

Bauman, Richard and Charles Briggs, "Poetics and Performance as Critical Perspectives on Language and Social Life," *Annual Review of Anthropology* 19 (1990): 59–88.

Beeman, William O, "The Anthropology of Theater and Spectacle," *Annual Review of Anthropology* 22 (1993): 369–93.

Berliner, Paul, *Thinking in Jazz: The Infinite Art of Improvisation*, Chicago and London: University of Chicago Press, 1994.

Bernal, Martin, *Black Athena: The Afroasiatic Roots of Classical Civilization*, 2 vols., New Brunswick, NJ: Rutgers University Press, 1987–91.

Bharucha, Rustom, *Theatre and the World: Performance and the Politics of Culture*, London and New York: Routledge, 1993.

Carlson, Marvin, *Theories of the Theatre: A Historical and Critical Survey, from the Greeks to the Present*, expanded edn. Ithaca, NY and London: Cornell University Press, 1993.

Conquergood, Dwight, "Rethinking Ethnography: Towards a Critical Cultural Politics," *Communication Monographs* 58 (1991): 179–94.

de Certeau, Michel, *The Practice of Everyday Life*, trans. Stephen F. Rendall, Berkeley and Los Angeles: University of California Press, 1984.

Drewal, Margaret Thompson, *Yoruba Ritual: Performers, Play, Agency*, Bloomington and Indianapolis: Indiana University Press, 1992.

Fabian, Johannes, *Time and the Other: How Anthropology Makes Its Object*, New York: Columbia University Press, 1983.

Gates, Henry Louis, Jr., *The Signifying Monkey: A Theory of Afro-American Literary Criticism*, New York: Oxford University Press, 1988.

Halttunen, Karen, *Confidence Men and Painted Women: A Study of Middle-class Culture in America, 1830–1870*, New Haven and London: Yale University Press, 1982.

Highshaw, Robert B., *Edward Douglas White: Defender of the Conservative Faith*, Baton Rouge and London: Louisiana State University Press, 1981.

Hirsch, Arnold and Joseph Logsdon, *Creole New Orleans: Race and Americanization*, Baton Rouge and London: Louisiana State University Press, 1992.

Hofstadter, Richard and Michael Wallace (eds), *American Violence: A Documentary History*, New York: Alfred Knopf, 1970.

Hymes, Dell, *Foundations in Sociolinguistics: An Ethnographic Perspective*, Philadelphia: University of Pennsylvania Press, 1975.

Kinser, Samuel, *Carnival, American Style: Mardi Gras at New Orleans and Mobile*, Chicago and London: University of Chicago Press, 1990.

Le Goff, Jacques, *History and Memory*, trans. Steven Rendall and Elizabeth Claman, New York: Columbia University Press, 1992.

MacAloon, John J., *Rite, Drama, Festival, Spectacle: Rehearsals Toward a Theory of Cultural Performance*, Philadelphia: Institute for the Study of the Human Issues, 1984.

McNamara, Brooks, "Invisible Theatre: Folk and Festival Tradition in America," in *Theatre Byways: Essays in Honor of Claude L. Shaver*, eds C. J. Stevens and Joseph Aurbach, New Orleans: Polyanthos, 1978, pp. 6–16.

Mitchell, Reid, *All on a Mardi Gras Day: Episodes in the History of New Orleans Carnival*, Cambridge, Mass. and London: Harvard University Press, 1995.

Myerhoff, Barbara, "The Transformation of Consciousness in Ritual Performance: Some Thoughts and Questions," in *By Means of Performance: Intercultural Studies of Theatre and Ritual*, eds Richard Schechner and Willa Appel, Cambridge and New York: Cambridge University Press, 1990, pp. 245–9.

O'Brien, Rosary Hartel, "The New Orleans Carnival Organizations: Theatre of Prestige," dissertation: UCLA, 1973.

Powell, Lawrence N., "Put Liberty Monument in proper setting: a museum," New Orleans *Times Picayune*, 17 March 1993, B–7.

Poovey, Mary, *The Proper Lady and the Woman Writer: Ideology as Style in the Works of Mary Wollstoncraft, Mary Shelley, and Jane Austen*, Chicago: University of Chicago Press, 1984.

Reinelt, Janelle and Joseph Roach (eds), *Critical Theory and Performance*, Ann Arbor: University of Michigan Press, 1992.

Roach, Joseph R., "Carnival and the Law in New Orleans," *The Drama Review: A Journal of Performance Studies* 37 (1993): 42–75.

Ryan, Mary, *Women in Public: Between Banners and Ballots, 1825–1880*, Baltimore and London: Johns Hopkins University Press, 1990.

Schechner, Richard, *Between Theater and Anthropology*, Philadelphia: University of Pennsylvania Press, 1985.

—— *The Future of Ritual: Writings on Culture and Performance*, London and New York: Routledge, 1993.

States, Bert O., *Great Reckonings in Little Rooms: On the Phenomenology of Theater*, Berkeley and Los Angeles: University of California Press, 1985.

Turner, Victor, ed., *Celebration: Studies in Festivity and Ritual*, Washington, DC: Smithsonian Institution Press, 1982.

—— *From Ritual to Theatre: The Human Seriousness of Play*, New York: PAJ Publications, 1982.

—— *Schism and Continuity: A Study of Ndembu Village Life*, Manchester: Manchester University Press, 1957.

Vennman, Barbara, "Boundary Face Off: New Orleans Civil Rights Law and Carnival Tradition," *The Drama Review: A Journal of Performance Studies* 37 (1993): 76–109.

—— "New Orleans 1993 Carnival: Tradition at Play in *Papier-Mâché* and Stone," *Theatre Insight* 5 (1993): 5–14.

Young, Perry, *The Mistick Krewe: Chronicles of Comus and his Kin*, 1931. Rpt. New Orleans: Louisiana Heritage Press, 1969.

13

FORMS OF APPEARANCE OF VALUE

Homer Plessy and the politics of privacy

Amy Robinson

In an academic milieu where identity and identity politics remain at the forefront of a battle over legitimate critical and/or political acts, the subject of passing has received increasing attention. But too often this attention claims the performative logic of passing as a troubling solution to the problem of identity. In this formulation, the pass reiterates the process of identity formation itself; the passer's performance chronicles the becoming of a self that cannot, by definition, lay claim to a fiction of natural essence. Violating the sturdy boundaries of ontology, the passer throws the logic of social hierarchies into disarray. While I am sympathetic to this reading, it's important to note that the logic of performativity cannot "solve" the problem of institutional subversion or recuperation. Rather, the field of performance studies brings with it the wisdom of contingent identities that, almost by virtue of this contingency, recommend the taking up of positions on necessarily unstable ground.

I would suggest, therefore, that the seemingly endless critical debates about performance that Eve Sedgwick has characterized as concluding with the refrain, "kinda subversive, kinda hegemonic,"[1] are frankly less interesting and more self-indulgent than the contentious politics of identity that continue to inform daily practice. In contrast to those who would claim the pass as a liberating rejection of natural essence – an appealing analytic structure of indeterminacy – this essay poses the proximate relation between passing and appropriation as a necessary starting-point of investigation, rather than as a culminating riposte. As a strategy of entrance into a field of representation, the social practice of passing is thoroughly invested in the logic of the system it attempts to subvert. As such, the subject of passing has much to teach us about the possibilities and problematics of resistance in a performative culture. While it is far from my purpose to recommend passing as a political strategy, the continued relevance of the subject of passing lies precisely in its thoroughgoing complicity with those institutions that we daily negotiate in an ongoing attempt to imagine a political context in which structural change is not merely a fantasy relegated to the theatrical frame. Despite the false promise of authenticity, it is still necessary, if not politically imperative, to theorize the body that performs in the place of an/other.

The particular body I have in mind belongs to Homer Plessy, whose performance as a white subject in a whites-only railroad car provoked the Supreme Court in 1896 to establish "separate but equal" as the justifying foundation of segregation in the United States. Homer Plessy's act of strategic passing, ironically dedicated to the demise of racial discrimination, was read by the Supreme Court as an act of appropriation, as an unqualified theft of an identity imagined as property – as that which is properly and privately owned by a "legitimate" white subject. The Supreme Court's decision, while reprehensible and historically unforgivable, was by no means merely idiosyncratic; it was precisely in the name of identity *as* property that the Plessy case waged its battle against segregation and in the name of "natural" ownership that the Plessy claim was denied. In this sense, it is not surprising that *Plessy v. Ferguson* holds a central place in the history of American privacy law; for, as I will argue, privacy is a zone produced by and about a discourse of property. Defined by the *Oxford English Dictionary* as the "making of a thing *private property*, whether another's or one's own," appropriation stands at the very center of the problem of passing and social performativity.[2]

Rather than merely summarizing *Plessy v. Ferguson* for its own sake, therefore, I am most interested in the kinds of questions that can be asked as a consequence of the decision to construct the case as a passing narrative. What was it about passing that endeared it as a strategy to the seeming opponents of segregation? What can we learn about passing by examining its historical relationship to the rhetoric of the propertied self? What role should a discourse of ownership have in contemporary struggles to achieve full political recognition under the law? Are all such attempts to earn the fundamental right of self-definition and self-determination always gained at the cost of a discourse of natural ownership which seems ultimately to undermine the very progressive project for which it has been invoked?

Nowhere are these difficult questions so clearly dramatized as in recent public debates ranging from gays in the military, abortion, and affirmative action, to white rappers and stylish lesbians appearing on the covers of America's most popular magazines. In each of these cases, attempts to prevent, or at least frustrate, the center's parasitic infatuations with the margins often take the form of a claim to "own" the identities that are so unrelentingly performed on prime-time television, the covers of *Vanity Fair* or *New York Magazine*, and in the hallowed halls of the Senate Judiciary Committee. And yet this claim to self-ownership, when enacted in the legal sphere, fails to gain access to the very institutions of the social that construct many of us as unnatural subjects and therefore unqualified for the "right to privacy."

The consequences of *Plessy v. Ferguson* extend far beyond the parameters of 1896 and the particularities of passing as a strategy of cultural performance. In a culture in which the division between private and public comes to be figured as the battleground of identity itself, the Plessy case is an instructive and well-documented attempt to expose passing as the "threat" against which "protected spheres" of identity are both enacted and justified – in the service of either domination *or* resistance. For all of us whose identities and social practices are determined by the institutional framework of privacy and self-ownership, *Plessy v. Ferguson* continues to be a critical topic of conversation.

I

> But the Conductor, the autocrat of caste, armed with the power of the State conferred by this statute, will listen neither to denial or protest. "In you go or out you go," is his ultimatum.[3]

In 1890 the Louisiana State legislature passed an act entitled, "An Act to Promote the Comfort of Passengers," requiring that all Louisiana railway companies carrying passengers in their coaches provide "equal but separate accommodations for the white, and colored races."[4] In response to the passage of Louisiana Act 111, the African American journalist and activist, Louis Martinet, formed "A Citizens Committee to Test the Constitutionality of the Separate Car Law."[5] Enlisting the aid of the white liberal "carpetbagger" lawyer Albion Tourgée, Martinet and the Citizens' Committee proposed to test the constitutionality of the Louisiana law by engineering a violation of the law. Devising a strategy that would allow a black subject to successfully occupy a seat in a whites-only car, Tourgée proposed that a "nearly white" Negro be used to test the "equal but separate" legislation approved by the Louisiana State Senate.[6]

After one unsuccessful attempt to test the law in February 1892,[7] Tourgée and Martinet enlisted the services of Homer Adelph Plessy who, on 7 June 1892, boarded a train in New Orleans and took a seat in a coach reserved for white passengers. While there are numerous versions of this particular historical performance of passing, the most convincing accounts report that immediately after claiming his seat Plessy "announced himself a Negro to the Conductor"[8] and refused to accede to the conductor's demands that he relocate to the train's blacks-only car. According to a pre-arranged plan, a detective appeared as if by magic to arrest Plessy for having criminally violated the Louisiana law. Plessy was immediately removed from the train and placed in jail under the jurisdiction of Judge John H. Ferguson. The following day, Plessy was released on a bond of $500 and soon after retained the free legal services of Albion Tourgée and Associates. The case then appeared before the Louisiana State Supreme Court and on appeal before the Supreme Court. Denying the centerpiece of Tourgée's argument – that the statute violated

Plessy's right to property and equal protection under the law – the Supreme Court in 1896 transformed the Louisiana law into the legal justification for segregation.[9]

While, in retrospect, the Supreme Court fulfilled the prosecution's worst nightmare by establishing what Judge Leon Higginbotham has called "a venal precedent"[10] that would not fully be overturned *in the law* until the Voting Rights Act of 1964, the chosen strategy was not entirely without its own justifying logic. In order to actually violate the law, rather than merely stage an exercise of the law, Martinet and Tourgée reasoned that a black subject who could "pass" would be more useful to their cause than a visibly black subject who would, from the outset, be "refused admission."[11] To be refused admission to a whites-only car would merely produce an embarrassing public spectacle,[12] whereas to successfully inhabit a whites-only car would constitute a wholesale violation of both the spirit and the letter of the Louisiana law.

In essence, Tourgée and Martinet's strategy was designed to demonstrate that the law requiring segregation was illegal because segregation itself was an impossible social project. Using Plessy's ability to pass undetected into a whites-only car as "evidence" of the unreliability of segregated boundaries, Tourgée hoped to prove that the very possibility of passing undermined the railroad's ability to enforce and maintain "separate" cars. As he argued in his brief before the Supreme Court:

> The gist of our case is the unconstitutionality of the *assortment*; not the question of equal accommodation; that much, the decisions of the Court give without doubt. We insist that the State has no right to compel us to ride in a car "set apart" for a particular race, whether it is as good as another or not.

(97)

In a decision that would haunt civil rights activists for the next sixty years, Tourgée refused to engage with the question of whether "equal but separate" cars were in fact inherently inequitable. Instead, Tourgée claimed that the Court had confirmed "without doubt" the principle of "equal but separate" and that what could be overturned was the very premise of "separate" cars altogether.

In order to narrow in on the very principle of "assortment" by which the railroad "set apart" discrete cars for black and white passengers, Tourgée asked the court to determine whether "The officer of a railroad [was] competent to decide the question of race?" (81). Centering his case around the actions of the conductor who was empowered by the statute "to distinguish between citizens according to race," Tourgée maintained that the statute "was an act of race discrimination pure and simple."[13] But by the word "discrimination," Tourgée did not mean to refer to the unequal accommodations provided to Louisiana's black passengers. On the contrary, Tourgée's brief explicitly defers

240

to Supreme Court precedent in the matter of "equal but separate" and uses the word discrimination to refer to the social practice of reading identity:

> The state has no power to authorize the officers of railway trains to determine the question of race without testimony, to make the rights and privileges of citizens to depend on such decision, or to compel the citizen to accept and submit to such decision.
>
> (76)

In effect, Tourgée employs an argument familiar to most students of contemporary critical theory. His analysis locates the "truth" of identity in the conductor's act of visual apprehension rather than in the substance of a passenger's blackness or whiteness. While Tourgée does not agree with this reading – proposing the right of "testimony" as an antidote to the state's mistake – his reasoning jeopardizes the very notion of race as a biological essence, foregrounding the social contexts of vision by calling into question the "truth" of the object in question. In this context, "race" is exposed as a construct, an arbitrary principle of classification that produces the "racial" subject in the very act of social categorization.

Tourgée's prophetic divination of poststructuralist academic theories of "race" can be traced to yet another rather earthbound letter he received from Louis Martinet.[14] Martinet's letter furnishes Tourgée with the building blocks of his brief by relating the most rudimentary lesson of passing:

> There are the strangest white people you ever saw here [Louisiana]. Walking up & down our principal thoroughfare- Canal Street- you would [be] surprised to have persons pointed out to you, some as white & others as colored, and if you were not informed you would be sure to pick out the white for colored & the colored for white.
>
> (56–7)

Martinet's anecdote testifies to Tourgée's illiteracy – his (not uncommon) unreliability as a reader of racial texts.[15] In so doing, Martinet introduces Tourgée to the very visual economy that produces passing as a systemic possibility. As he confidently asserts that Tourgée "would be sure to pick out the white for colored & the colored for white," he chronicles the process by which passing functions in the social field. Only when a spectator adopts the presumptive mechanisms that "read" a racially indeterminate subject as a legible social identity can a subject truly be said to pass. Calling attention to the hypothetical act of reading by which Tourgée would establish the "race" of Louisiana's diverse citizenry, Martinet discloses the social practice of reading identity as the enabling machinery of the pass. In an economy of presumed legibility (you are what you look like), the successful passer only disappears from view insofar as s/he appears (to her reader) to be the category into which s/he has passed. Martinet's letter reminds Tourgée that it is the spectator who manufactures a successful pass, whose act of reading (or misreading) constitutes the performance of the passing subject.

Relying as it does on the learned wisdom of the pass, the content of Tourgée's argument is inextricably tied to the structural qualities of passing itself. In 1892, the precise details of Martinet's passing scenario were replayed by Homer Plessy on the train bound for New Orleans. While it was Plessy himself who "pointed out" to the conductor his own racial identity, the conductor proved to be the perfect dupe, for his initial mis-reading of Homer Plessy allowed Tourgée to establish that "the question of race . . . [was] very often impossible of determination" (81). It is only in the context of passing that Tourgée could use the conductor as the center of an argument about the constitutionality of "assortment" and thus shift the entire focus of the case away from the injustice of "equal but separate" accommodations and towards the feasibility of a system of segregation. Repeatedly stressing the irrelevance of Plessy's racial identity (a point I will return to later), Tourgée insists that the illegality of segregation lies in the arbitrary process of reading by which race is determined in the United States.

It is remarkable, therefore, but not entirely unbelievable that the legal foundation of segregation can be traced to a case of passing *as* performance. Indelibly marked by its affiliation with the social practice of passing, the ultimate failure of Tourgée's argument is the failure of passing to emerge as a viable political strategy.[16] While passing will indeed throw the logic of cultural hierarchy into disarray, such a philosophical revolution relies on the very terms of the system it is intended to subvert. Like many contemporary theorists of passing, Tourgée disregarded the limited subversion of passing in favor of a more romantic vision of its political consequences. In order to anticipate that the conductor would "misread" Plessy as a white man in whites-only car, Tourgée relied on the same conventional fictions of racial difference that would ultimately prove to be the case's demise. Assuming that the institutional binaries of black and white would limit the conductor's decision-making process, Tourgée was able to correctly prophesize that the conductor would presume that Plessy was not-black and "read" him as a white man. The case therefore depends on the very presence of structures of racial difference to prove that such structures are untenable, or at best, impossible to administer. In other words, the very tactic that animates Tourgée's case against segregation *is the logic of segregation itself.*

Although the inadequacy of Tourgée's challenge to the Louisiana statute lies partly in the inadequacy of passing itself as a political tactic, Tourgée also, and perhaps more importantly, did not fully understand how passing operates in a social field. And by failing adequately to understand the performative logic of passing that stood at the center of his case, Tourgée failed to anticipate the Supreme Court's verdict: in response to the newly exposed threat of infiltration, they merely tightened the temporarily unstable borders of "race."[17] For Tourgée forgot (or never knew) that to focus on the spectator of passing one must account for *what* and *how* that spectator will read – literally the apparatus enabling the performance. Crucially, Homer

Plessy's act of passing had to be intelligible to the Court as *an act of passing*; had Plessy merely passed and not told anyone of his black identity, then his pass would surely have "happened" but the mark of its success would have been precisely in its inconspicuousness. The fact that Plessy's pass is available to be understood as a calculated performance is, after all, the justification for staging a violation, rather than a mere exercise of the Louisiana Statute.[18] As a passing subject, Plessy's presence in a whites-only car could *only be recognized* as an act of appropriation and not as a "legitimate" pursuit of entitlement.

Tourgée's disregard for the logic of passing in the visual field brings him to a peculiar and problematic crossroads. For it is precisely in the antithetical relationship between appropriation and private property that Tourgée's case unravels before the Supreme Court. Arguing that the statute was "an invasion and deprivation of the natural and absolute rights of citizens in the United States" (75), Tourgée invoked the "protected sphere" of property as Plessy's right to own his white identity:

> We shall . . . contend that, in any mixed community, the reputation of belonging to the dominant race, in this instance the white race, is *property*, in the same sense that a right of action or of inheritance is property; and that the provisions of the act in question which authorize an officer of a railroad company to ask a person to a car set apart for a particular race, enable such officer to deprive him, to a certain extent at least, of this property – this reputation which has an actual pecuniary value "without due process of law," and are therefore in violation of the Second restrictive clause of the XIVth Amendment of the Constitution of the United States.
>
> (83)

Naming the reputation of whiteness *as* property, and the right to property as a natural right, Tourgée invokes a rhetoric of "possessive individualism" as Plessy's right to own property under the Fourteenth Amendment. In a remarkable articulation of the drama of appropriation, Tourgée claims that the conductor's misreading of Plessy deprives him of his property.

It is precisely in the terms of property, however, that Justice Brown denies that Plessy has a right to this particular identity:

> Conceding this [that Plessy's whiteness is property] for the purposes of this case, we are unable to see how this statute deprives him of, or in any way affects his right to, such property. If he be a white man and assigned to a colored coach, he may have his action for damages . . . Upon the other hand, if he be a colored man and be so assigned he has been deprived of no property, since he is not lawfully entitled to the reputation of being a white man.
>
> (110–11)

In a rare display of retaliatory wit, Brown responds to Tourgée by reminding the lawyer for the defense that Homer Plessy was "in fact" *passing* in a whites-only car. As such, Plessy does not properly "own" his whiteness, since it is only the pass that allows him to enter the "wrong" car. Brown expressly rules that the social practice of passing is tantamount to an abdication of the rights of ownership. As a passing subject, Plessy is not "lawfully entitled" to own his whiteness.

While Tourgée expends tremendous energy on the identity of the reader of passing (the white conductor), it is the performance of Plessy's blackness *as* whiteness that returns to sabotage his defense. In the context of a passing scenario, Tourgée's claim that Plessy's whiteness was in fact property, could only have elicited the response that it did: the court responded that Plessy was the bearer of stolen property. But regardless of the court's predictable response, Tourgée's argument makes explicit the Fourteenth Amendment's equivalence between the "private" citizen and those spheres of identity recast as the "private domain." While the "right to privacy" does not appear in Supreme Court opinion until the mid-twentieth century, the Plessy case dramatically exposes the foundational terms of property and identity on which the concept of privacy rests.

II

"No one has an inherent or constitutional right to pass himself off for what he is not"[19]

While the word "privacy" does not appear in the text of the Declaration of Independence, the Constitution, or any of its affiliated amendments, the word "property" does appear in the preamble of the Declaration of Independence, in the Fifth Amendment of the Constitution, and in the first section of the Fourteenth Amendment. The right to own property and the consequent privileges of possession have conventionally been understood as one of the few enumerated rights "protected" by the American legal system. But it is not until the Fourteenth Amendment that the Constitution makes explicit the relationship between citizenship and the right to property:

> All persons born or naturalized in the United States, and subject to the jurisdiction there of, are citizens of the United States and of the State wherein they reside. No State shall make or enforce any law which shall abridge the privileges or immunities of citizens of the United States; nor shall any State deprive any person of life, liberty, or property, without due process of law; nor deny to any person within its jurisdiction the equal protection of the laws.

Historically, the Fourteenth Amendment offered the mantle of citizenship to a set of social subjects who had been considered as "chattel personal" and thus property by the American legal system. While the "right to property" is only one of the "natural rights" enumerated by the Fourteenth Amendment, in 1868 I would argue that it is the most important "right" defining citizenship for all Americans, and in particular, for newly self-possessing African American subjects.

The right of self-possession is not accidentally the legal foundation of American citizenship. For it is the most primary of a series of "natural rights" considered by liberal political theory as the inheritance of the bona fide social subject. According to John Locke, "every man [*sic*] has a property in his own person,"[20] and thus qualifies for other "natural rights" insofar as he initially and primarily possesses himself. While Locke calls "the great foundation of property" contained within the individual a universal human right, the right of self-ownership has historically been dispensed only to certain individuals as a gauge of their political and cultural legitimacy. In the economic framework constructed by the Fourteenth Amendment one is licensed as a legitimate subject precisely to the extent to which "the body" in question qualifies as a paradigmatic "private" dominion. Only in this context were those slaves already freed by the Thirteenth Amendment entitled to the "equal protection of the laws." In short, the rhetoric of "possessive individualism" that subsidizes the Fourteenth Amendment's legal definition of citizenship rewards the "private" social subject with a protected sphere of cultural activity.

For those readers familiar with the classical legal arguments on privacy, my analysis may seem counterintuitive at best. In traditional legal theory, the private is understood as an insular sphere, free from government intrusion. But this is precisely where I depart from classical legal theory, arguing instead that privacy functions as a zone that creates that which it protects and constructs.[21] Although traditionally the right to privacy is seen as placing certain subjects beyond the purview of government interference, such subjects are simultaneously rewarded with a sphere in which they and they alone can do whatever they would like. It is my contention that the criterion for such a reward is the "natural" right of self-ownership, which a history of colonization, enslavement, and general disentitlement would seem to suggest has been anything but a natural right. The constitutive relationship between property and privacy thus emerges as the missing step that makes sense of the importance of identity in the articulation of American privacy law.

If, as Justice Robert Jackson wrote in 1943, "the very purpose of a Bill of Rights was to withdraw certain subjects from the vicissitudes of political controversy,"[22] then the very concept of the "private" citizen includes the formulation of a "private" arena in which "certain subjects" are considered prior to or separate from the unqualified burden of the social.[23] Collapsing the distinction between the social subject and the space he or she inhabits, the rhetoric of possessive individualism contains within itself the promise of a space and a subject withdrawn from the antagonism of surrounding difference.

While Jackson's language is actually meant to refer to "subjects" as "rights" (such as life, liberty, and property, free speech, free press, freedom of worship and assembly, etc.), the slippery double meaning of subject has historically positioned the court to intrude on those individuals or groups whose identities deny them the "right" of equal protection. The legal umbrella of "equal protection" that takes the discursive form of the "right" to "life, liberty and property," makes such rights relevant only in the terms of a perceived intrusion or incursion from "outside" that social subject. As an identification and documentation of a sphere of permissible intrusion, privacy paradoxically functions as a zone that in fact increases the sphere of government regulation even as it positions certain subjects to be intruded upon, or more importantly, *as* the "intrusion" on which the concept of privacy rests.

Although, in the twentieth century, the "right to privacy" has been most famously defined by Louis Brandeis as the "right to be left alone," the less famous words of Justice Jackson remind us that only "certain subjects" are endowed with the legal privilege of an "inside" protected from ideological and political contestation.[24] Creating a sanctuary of identity, the "zone of privacy" which protects the "private" citizen relies on an illusory ground of purity to define both the social subject and the social space he or she will inhabit. Characterized by exclusivity and discrete boundaries, the "private" sphere reiterates the promise of the "private" citizen whose right to "life, liberty, and property" is defined against the threat of infiltration and contamination.

What Lauren Berlant has aptly christened this enabling fiction of a "prophylactic private sphere"[25] is a logic, like Locke's "great foundation of property," contained within the individual who is an owner of property in his own person. For only when identity is considered to be a form of property can the exclusivity of certain kinds of identities be redeployed as the prerogative of social space. As the legal scholar Patricia Williams contends, those social spaces that enact the problematic of privacy are spaces envisioned as "protected" spheres of identity:

> "Black," "female," "male" and "white" are every bit as much properties as the buses, private clubs, neighborhoods, and schools that provide the extracorporeal battleground of their expression.[26]

Staging the "right to privacy" as the right to associate with one's "own kind," these social spaces – be they public toilets or private clubs – are defined against the threat of intrusion produced by the difference of certain kinds of social subjects. It is finally the prerogative of both the "private" subject and "private" space to prohibit anything other than the "same" identity from inhabiting its exclusive borders.[27]

It is in this context that Homer Plessy's act of strategic passing can be seen as a paradigmatic invasion of privacy. Enacting the scenario of "infiltration" which subtends the legal concept of the "private," the Plessy in *Plessy v. Ferguson* acts out the very possibility of intrusion on which the law is founded.

What is unusual about Tourgée's defense is that he names the identity protected by the "private" as Plessy's literal property. That is, rather than merely designating the sphere in which Plessy's identity operates as the "private" – a much more typical phenomenon we have witnessed in debates over private clubs, neighborhoods, schools, bathrooms, etc. – Tourgée specifically labels that identity as a protected sphere. Tourgée's uncommon approach thereby anticipates the development of privacy law in the United States: it will develop precisely as an implicit relationship between the protected sphere (the private) and the identity so protected. This pattern emerges in the series of cases that define the right to privacy: forced sterilization, interracial marriage, contraception, abortion, and homosexuality.[28] In each of these cases, debates over a "private" zone (to coin a current military phrase) are in fact debates about the legitimacy of certain kinds of identities.

Tourgée's argument thus makes manifest the unstated logic of what will later appear as the "right to privacy" by submitting the criterion of social legitimacy as an enabling qualification for equal protection. In Tourgée's brief, Plessy's right to whiteness is clearly expressed as the right to "own" an identity that is considered in the terms of the dominant culture to be more valuable than his unmarked and unremarkable blackness:

> How much would it be *worth* to a young man entering upon the practice of law, to be regarded as a *white* man rather than a colored one? Six-sevenths of the population is white. Nineteen-twentieths of the property of the country is owned by white people. Ninety-nine hundredths of the business opportunities are in the control of white people . . . Probably most white persons if given a choice, would prefer death to life in the United States *as colored persons.* Under these conditions, is it possible to conclude that the *reputation of being white* is not property? Indeed, is it not the most valuable sort of property, being the master-key that unlocks the golden door of opportunity?
>
> (83)

Plessy's whiteness, argues Tourgée, is valuable precisely because whiteness "unlocks the golden door of opportunity." Granting Plessy unobstructed access to the pursuit of property and employment, whiteness qualifies for the protection of the private insofar as it entitles Plessy to a superior social position. The unparalleled social legitimacy of whiteness is precisely the reason Tourgée can claim Plessy's whiteness *as* property. And it is only when identity is understood *as* property that the "right to privacy" can be understood as the right to practice certain kinds of identities.

With this in mind, it is useful to return to the earlier wording of Justice Brown's decision in order to apprehend the extraordinary move the Plessy case represents in the history of American privacy law. Although Brown's ruling denies that Plessy has a right to *whiteness* as property, he importantly does *not deny* that identity is property, he merely suggests that Plessy is not entitled to it. In this sense, Tourgée failed to account for the kind of property that Plessy now owned: the act of passing casts him as the bearer of stolen property. By granting Plessy's identity as property, Brown writes into Supreme Court precedent the Lockean formula for the "natural rights" of citizenship. Such "natural rights," however, are expressly rescinded for the passing subject whose identity represents a threat to the very notion of a propertied self. As a self-named passer, Plessy stages the "right" to whiteness as an exercise in appropriation and not in self-ownership.

The hostility that emerges between Homer Plessy and the very concept of "natural" ownership is an old and seasoned antagonism. If identity is to be considered as property – as what belongs to me and what makes me belong – then it is not altogether irrelevant that commodification operates as one of the earliest interpretive frameworks associated with passing. Although private property can be understood as one potential form the commodity takes under capitalism, I will contend that the process of commodification is itself inimical to the very idea of identity as private property. In fact, it is here that the social practice of passing repays an historical debt to the role of the commodity in commercial culture. Infiltrating the sacred domain of whites-only car, the passer stages his identity by manipulating the logic of a culture of exchange. This logic is exactly what consistently eludes Albion Tourgée. While thus far I have considered the question of property in the terms of privacy, in the following pages I will consider both property and privacy in the illustrative terms of passing. Such an approach will help me to map out Plessy's predicament by more fully addressing Tourgée's mistake.

III

This *Belong To Me* Aspect of Representations So Reminiscent of Property[29]

Two of the earliest written notices of passing occur in the context of commodification in works respectively by Thomas Middleton and Randle Holmes: "I might make my bond pass for a hundred pound in the city" (1607), and "The Double Rose Noble . . . passes for thirty-nine or Forty shillings" (1688). These proto and early capitalist examples of passing refer to the exchange of money – soon to be paper money – and thus the elaborate system of government debt and credit that arose in the late seventeenth and eighteenth centuries. While much more remains to be said about the complex phenomenon of early capitalism, even these rarified citations suggest that, in order to signify as a verb of commodification, passing requires a culture in which exchange functions as the primary distributive mechanism. In fact, I would go so far as to argue that *only* in the context of a culture of exchange can the commodity rehearse the social logic of passing.

As I have suggested, the question of passing cannot be posed outside the terms of a visual culture – the system of power relations that constructs the meaning of what we see. Similarly, I would suggest that an exchange-based economy is, above all, an economy which poses the question of social value as a problematic of visuality – a term that Hal Foster defines as "sight as a social fact" or that Elin Diamond might describe as "the ideological nature of the seeable ... what can, and more importantly what cannot be seen."[30] In order to make this claim, I would like to isolate a very particular moment in the history of the commodity that Marx identifies as the tension between the "plain, homely, natural form" of use-value and the "mode of expression," the "form of appearance" of exchange value.[31] As Marx painstakingly documents in the first chapter of *Capital,* the form of appearance of value of linen is to be found in the physical body of the coat it will become.[32] "As a use-value," writes Marx "the linen is something palpably different from the coat; as value, it is identical with the coat, and therefore *looks like* the coat"(143). In this example, the linen only acquires social value insofar as it assumes the visual form of the coat. While the linen retains its "own" value (in labor) it does not retain its own visual form. As Marx insists,

> Nevertheless the coat cannot represent value towards the linen unless value, for the latter, simultaneously assumes the form of a coat. An individual, A, for instance, cannot be "your majesty" to another individual, B, unless majesty in B's eyes assumes the physical shape of A, and moreover changes facial features, hair and many other things, with every new "father of his people."
>
> (143)

In this passage, Marx articulates the relation between use-value and exchange-value as a relation that literally produces an economy of the visible. His consideration of the value of the commodity in tandem with the value of majesty suggests, that in an exchange-based economy, adequacy for representation (be it political, social, or economic) is measured in the terms of visual paradigms of value.

It is this expressed alliance with an economy of visuality that endears the commodity to the interpretive framework of passing. For while passing has often been used as an unspecified euphemism for impersonation and general acts of cultural misrepresentation, it is most useful I would argue to maintain the enriching specificity of its historic relation to visuality. From its earliest appearances as a verb of gender performance and commodification to its most sophisticated enunciation as a strategy of racial impersonation, the success of the "pass" has always depended on its faithful reenactment of what Luce Irigaray has called "the photological metaphor system of the West."[33] In the case of Homer Plessy, for example, his ability to "pass" as white hinges on the entrenched conventions of racial difference which assume that the appearance of blackness and whiteness always signifies the stable contours of a white and black identity. The preconditions for the pass always concern its proximity to a model of identity: a social taxonomy of designation which, since Plato, has been dominated by a vocabulary of the visual subject. As the devoted analogue of an economy of visuality, passing is particularly suited to an exchange-based economy. As Marx keenly notes in the above passage, an exchange-based economy places a premium on the form of appearance of value, and as such, considers the *appearance* of the commodity (however mystified and fetishized) to be a crucial gauge of social value.

A strategy such as passing that explicitly manipulates the "form of appearance of value" (in this case "race") as a means of gaining access to systemic representation, is at the very least indebted to (and perhaps requested by) a culture that considers certain kinds of appearances to be a requirement for systemic representation. And precisely because appearance is the site of mystification and fetishization in the commodity-form, it is uniquely qualified to bear the weight of identity in a culture of legibility. In other words, when appearance is assumed to bear a mimetic relation to identity, but in fact does not and can not, it is easy to bypass the rules of representation and claim an identity by virtue of a "misleading" appearance. Ironically, the logic of readable identity – that you are what you look like – is precisely the precondition for the subject who passes – who appears as what he or she is not. In this sense, passing emerges as a challenge to the very notion of the visual as an epistemological guarantee. Calling into the question the relationship between insides and outside, truth and appearance, identity and identity politics, passing documents the false promise of the visual that underwrites a culture of legibility.

Although identity is often posed as private property – somehow protected from the possibility that appearance could misconstrue or violate the identity it is assumed to represent – the very concept of commodification is at odds with Locke's notion of "possessive individualism." Despite the claim that self-ownership is a "natural" and "universal" right that exists prior to, and is unmediated by, the social, even the propertied self becomes "visible" only in terms of the value it is accorded in the commercial culture. To consider the individual as an owner of property in his own personal identity is to attach a fixed and "pure" meaning to a *relation* that is constitutively social and necessarily "infected" with contingent formulations of social value.

This is the indispensable insight contained in Marx's analogy between the commodity form and the form of appearance of majesty. For if majesty must be invested with the "physical shape" of a particular "father of the people" in order to signify *as* majesty, then the social practice of identity (as distinguished from its status as a philosophical ideal) rehearses the logic of the commodity-form. In other words, the idea of majesty cannot be detached from its particular embodiment; although the particular body may be purely arbitrary, materiality itself manufactures the concept of majesty. As a social practice, identity cannot be divested from a body that is unrelentingly invested with the value of appearance.[34]

Following Marx's lead, many contemporary critics have found a useful paradigm for the "problem" of identity in the tension between use-value and exchange-value enacted in the literal body of the commodity.[35] Taking seriously the hazardous implications of the propertied self, some of these scholars view the discrepancy between use-value and exchange-value as a critical gauge of social appropriation. In this framework, the value of marginal peoples is refracted (like "the plain, homely, natural form" of use-value) only through the distorting lens of the dominant culture. Exchanged between men, between white men and women, between heterosexual white men and women, between proprietors and possessors of any and every ilk, marginal peoples take on the characteristics of the commodity whose value is only relative to that of another.[36] As Marx writes, "By means of the value relation ... the natural form of commodity B becomes the value-form of commodity A; in other words, the physical body of commodity B becomes a mirror for the value of commodity A" (144). Considered as a system of identity-relations, use-value and exchange-value stage a drama of exploitation. For certain readers, the process by which exchange refigures the form of appearance of use-value stands in for a pervasive paradigm of social dispossession.

While I agree that the literal body of the commodity rehearses the problematic of appropriation, I must announce from the outset my skepticism concerning the conclusions such an analysis often generates. As a remedy to the exploitative foundations of commodity culture, many critics of exchange-value recommend a return to use-value.[37] Protesting the "transformation" of natural form into the artificial form of the commodity, such advocates of use-value hope to combat a pervasive system of appropriation by reclaiming the prerogative of "natural value" denied by a culture of exchange. But too often, such important political work collapses the distinction between use-value and the "natural" so that requests for the return of use-value deteriorate into a renewed rhetoric of "real" identity, "a permanent fixed self."[38] Claiming use-value as an antidote to exchange-value, this strategy too often functions as an "alibi"[39] for the oppositional reclamation of authenticity and natural essence.

Making a claim to the "natural," the ardent critic of exchange-value perceives the institutions of cultural domination as agents of cultural theft. For in the name of exchange-value, the state-sponsored institutions of racism, sexism, colonialism, and homophobia (to name only a few) are authorized to confiscate the principal signs of an/other's identity. In this context, the relation between the center and the margins reiterates the relations of power implicit in the commodity form itself. Only relevant or valuable in the terms of exchange, the "natural" body of the commodity is dispossessed of its "own" meaning in order to signify as an object of exchange.[40]

At the risk of alienating critics whose politics seem to be commensurate with my own, I would suggest that the claim to "natural" identity is always subsidized by the troublesome logic of the propertied self. For in order to reclaim the prerogative of self-definition denied by a culture of exchange, the critic of exchange-value reasserts the "natural" right of the commodity to control its "own" cultural signification. Rescuing the "natural" form of use-value from its artificial manipulation at the hands of exchange-value, the "right" of self-definition is gained at the cost of a discourse of "natural" ownership which cannot, and should not, be divorced from a rhetoric of the "natural" in whose name marginal peoples have always been relegated to the working materials of culture itself. Rehearsing the utopian logic of the "private" sphere, the champion of use-value claims a boundary of the "real" as insulation from the seeming artifice of cultural manipulation. Such well-intentioned grounds of resistance merely substitute the perils of exchange-value for the dangers of use-value, replacing the fluidity of identity with the faithful stability of the propertied self. As my reading of Locke's enlightenment formula suggests, the concept of "natural" ownership poses a pure and inviolate ground of identity as a *defense* against the very difference represented by the so-called marginal subject. As such, the problem with the Lockean formula of identity as property is precisely the "politics of value"[41] implicit in the concept of "possessive individualism": the space of ownership, privacy, and use-value is almost always constructed as a space prior to social mediation, prior to politics, and prior to difference.

This is the fatal flaw of Tourgée's defense. By deploying a passer in the service of a discourse of natural ownership, Tourgée profoundly misunderstood the threat of passing to any notion of the propertied self. The claim to "own" one's identity is finally little more than a claim to belong within and to a "natural" order that excludes and is in fact hostile to many of us whose identities are (like Homer Plessy's) considered to lie outside the zone "in which he properly belongs" (110). As a passing subject, Plessy's virtue lies precisely in his rejection of the "natural" order. While it is not my purpose here to recommend passing as a political strategy, its hostile relation to the "natural" order *could have been* its utility to Tourgée's case. Instead, Tourgée yoked the social practice passing to the propertied self – a pure space of imagined identity incommensurate with the social logic of passing and the mechanics of performance on which it relies.

And indeed, this inhospitable field of the natural is finally what marks the place of *Plessy v. Ferguson* in the history of American privacy law. In each of the rulings delivered against Homer Plessy, it was precisely the "natural, legal, and customary difference between the white and black races"[42] that emerged as a self-evident justification for "equal but separate accommodations." Stripped of its origins in a discourse of private property, the question of "natural" ownership is recast as the purely "natural" character of protected spheres of identity. In his 1896 Supreme Court ruling Justice Brown wrote,

> The legislature is at liberty to act with reference to the established usages, customs, and traditions of the people, and with a view to the promotion of their comfort, and the preservation of the public peace and good order. Gauged by this standard, we cannot say that the law which authorizes or even requires the separating of the two races in public conveyances is unreasonable.[43]

Converting the earlier and bolder language of the "natural" into the seemingly more benign "established usages, customs, and traditions of the people," Justice Brown betrays what was at stake, from the outset, in the Louisiana law entitled, "An Act to Promote the Comfort of Passengers." Denying Homer Plessy his right to equal protection under the law allows Justice Brown to construct a zone of comfort protected from the threat of a Homer Plessy.

It is thus not accidental that *Plessy v. Ferguson* holds a central place in a history of American privacy law. For privacy has historically been used as a gauge of cultural legitimacy, buttressing the legal exclusion of those subjects deemed somehow unfit for juridical representation. Forever marrying the legal questions of property and privacy to the character of the identity in question, *Plessy v. Ferguson* has made an indelible mark on American legal discourse. As a paradigmatic invasion of privacy, Homer Plessy's act of strategic passing exposes the normative logic by which "protected spheres" of identity are both constructed and preserved.

Although *Plessy v. Ferguson* is never cited by name in the collection of cases that establish the modern notion of the "right to privacy," its enduring logic of "natural" identity appears in many of the most famous "social issue" privacy cases of the twentieth century. While in retrospect, the majority opinion in Plessy has been repudiated from all sides of the political spectrum as "a compound of bad logic, bad sociology, and bad constitutional law,"[44] discrete portions of Justice Brown's decision have been cited as precedent when the plaintiffs in question have been considered (like Homer Plessy) to be a threat to the very notion of privacy itself as a protected sphere of "natural" identity.

In *Bowers v. Hardwick*, for example, the Supreme Court upheld a Georgia anti-sodomy statute, judging homosexuality a threat to the very notion of privacy as a protected sphere. Not surprisingly, Justice Scalia's decision (the basis for the majority opinion in Bowers) uncannily echoes the court's 1896 ruling in *Plessy v. Ferguson*:

> As we have put it, the Due Process Clause affords only those protections "so rooted in the traditions and conscience of our people so as to be ranked as fundamental." Our cases reflect continual insistence upon respect for the teachings of history [and] solid recognition of the basic values that underlie our society.[45]

Invoking Plessy implicitly by citing a contemporaneous 1989 case in which the Plessy text appears,[46] Scalia's ruling is unabashedly a function of the normative. His citational formula – "those protections 'so rooted in the traditions and conscience of our people so as to be ranked as fundamental – ' " surreptitiously attaches his decision to a particular tradition of privacy law in which (to quote the Plessy ruling) "the established usages, customs, and traditions of the people" stand as the sole justification for denying certain subjects the equal protection of the private sphere.

Plessy v. Ferguson, a case Scalia himself has publicly renounced, thus stands at the conceptual center of *Bowers v. Hardwick*, as well as the court's limitation of abortion rights in *Webster v. Reproductive Services*. In each of these cases, the private is a function of the "usages, conventions and customs of the people," and not as some would claim a "natural" space prior to political negotiation. Perhaps this is why our efforts to secure gay and lesbian rights, civil rights, and reproductive freedom in the name of the "right to privacy" seem destined to fail. For we inevitably collapse a quest for human rights with a humanist discourse which pretends to offer safe havens of privacy in an effort to naturalize the very "standards of decency" which exclude us.

As a means of extending the "rights of man" to an increasingly wider set of social subjects, privacy is one of a larger set of general liberal principles that have been "universalized" in the name of an oppositional political humanism. But as many critics have suggested, the danger of the universal as an erstwhile container of identity lies precisely in its reproduction of a disembodied politic, disengaged from the sphere of difference that constitutes the social field.[47] Rather than privacy, therefore, many legal scholars suggest that we pursue legal redress under the Fourteenth Amendment's equal protection clause.[48] Although the premise of equal protection cannot be entirely divorced from the problematic of privacy, the rubric of equal protection does not require that its subjects be "real" or "natural," and thus may provide a more substantive basis from which to challenge discriminatory legislation. In Boulder Colorado, for example, lawyers who filed briefs for a stay against Amendment Two were successful in my estimation, because they argued that Amendment Two violated equal protection and not the right to privacy. Unfortunately these same lawyers are now arguing for the biological basis of homosexuality in order to establish queers as a "suspect" class.[49] In my opinion, this is a mistake tantamount to using the right to privacy for it relies on a notion of the natural for which I suspect gays and lesbians will never, and perhaps ought never want to, qualify.[50]

In this context, it is interesting to note that Tourgée's faith in a "natural" field of vision, instead of a performative one, represents his greatest analytic failure. In my estimation, the wisdom of performance studies lies in its abandonment of an "outside"; as an exemplary theory of material iteration it rejects master narratives of truth and ontology on the one hand, and the possibility of absolute liberation on the other. Indeed, it was Tourgée's faith in both the former and the latter that had dire consequences for his client. Perhaps we should remember *Plessy v. Ferguson*, rather than merely reenacting its problematics of resistance.

Simply to accuse Albion Tourgée, however, is to participate in the seemingly endless refrain of "kinda subversive, kinda hegemonic" that from the outset I announced as antithetical to my project. Is the alternative to munificently acknowledge the authorizing vocabulary of the master's tools and apologetically leave the house intact? Is the alternative a kind of hapless relativism, in which the contradictory nature of identity formations prohibits the very possibility of political activism? While these questions must seem naive in their simplicity and almost interminable familiarity, perhaps their endless repetition in our conferences, classrooms, bedrooms, and meeting halls suggests that the answer is worth repeating as well. I would be in good company to suggest that if truths are constructed, and contingency is the *only* domain of value, then there is little alternative but performance, imagined as an explicit ethical intervention into a necessarily contentious social field.[51]

While it is easy and in fact irresistible to find fault with Tourgée, his brief posed a question to the Court that has never been quite so boldly posed: what is the relationship between property and social normativity? In an era in which the "problem" of identity is more often than not the problem of "appropriation," the value of Tourgée's brief lies in what we can learn from the court's equally blunt reply. Reasserting the fidelity of those "natural" boundaries we construct to alleviate the tensions of our own differences, the court responded to Tourgée by defining the private as a space of "natural, legal, and customary difference." Such a space is understandably hostile to the legal claims of the passer. But it is not the passer alone who is barred from a zone of privacy.[52] In an era of anti-gay legislation that takes the form of dismantling "protected" rights for gays and lesbians where no such "protected spheres" exist, in a time when abortion rights are increasingly (despite Bill Clinton) under duress, in a political arena in which affirmative action is more often than not staged as an attack on white male entitlement, in an age such as this when this list is seemingly infinite, Tourgée's brief asks us to consider how we resist – how we pursue our demands for equitable treatment.

Is there ever a politics to passing? I don't think so, but perhaps there is a lesson. In the cautionary words of two unfortunate characters in Maureen Duffy's play, *Rites*:

> Why can't we unlock the stall door? Because it's bolted from the inside; they call it privacy. You could die in there in private.[53]

NOTES

I would like to thank Miranda Joseph for her friendship as well as for her meticulous reading of, and generous comments on, an earlier draft of this essay.

1 "Queer Performativity: Henry James's *The Art of the Novel*," *GLQ: A Journal of Lesbian and Gay Studies* 1.1., p. 15.
2 Please note that this essay represents an adumbrated version of a much larger project.
3 Tourgée's brief as cited in Otto H. Olsen, *The Thin Disguise: Plessy v. Ferguson, A Documentary Presentation* (New York: Humanities Press, 1967), p. 103. Hereafter all references to *The Thin Disguise* will be indicated by page number.

4 Preamble of Act No. 111, the Laws of Louisiana, 10 July 1980. I am most grateful for the extensive information about *Plessy v. Ferguson* that appears in the following places. Eric Sundquist, "Mark Twain and Homer Plessy" *Representations* 21 (Fall 1998): 102–28; Olsen, *The Thin Disguise*; Otto H. Olsen, *The Carpetbagger's Crusade: A Life of Albion Winegar Tourgée* (Baltimore: John Hopkins University Press); Richard Kluger, *Simple Justice: The History of Brown v. Board of Eduction and Black America's Struggle for Equality* (New York: Vintage Books, 1975); Derek Bell, *Race, Racism and American Law* (Boston: Little, Brown & Company, 1980); Lerone Bennett, Jr., *Before the Mayflower: A History of the Negro in America 1619–1964* (Baltimore: Penguin Books, 1962); C. Vann Woodward, *The Strange Career of Jim Crow* (New York: Oxford University Press, 1955). Paul Oberst, "The Strange Career of *Plessy v. Ferguson*," *Arizona Law Review* 389 (1973).

5 As cited in Olsen, *Carpetbagger's Crusade*, p. 310.

6 Correspondence from Martinet to Tourgée, 5 Oct. 1891 as cited in Olsen, *Thin Disguise*, p.56.

7 In the first attempt they also used a light-skinned black man named Daniel Desdunes, but the train chosen was interstate, and in the meantime, the state supreme court had ruled that the commerce clause prohibited Jim Crow regulation of interstate travel.

8 I am in agreement with this account provided by Eric Sundquist.

9 Although the arguments I will entail in this essay are the basis of Tourgée's brief, and I believe the basis on which his claimed was denied, more official chroniclers of the case place it within in a history of assaults on the Fourteenth Amendment in the tradition of the *Slaughterhouse Cases*. See, Sundquist "Mark Twain and Homer Plessy" essay for the implications of this argument.

10 A. Leon Higginbotham, Jr., "An Open Letter to Justice Clarence Thomas from a Federal Judicial Colleague," *Race-ing Justice, En-gendering Power*, ed. Toni Morrison (New York: Pantheon Books, 1992), p. 8. It is important to remember that in 1890, the Louisiana statute was one of a handful of state ordinances that actually *required* segregation in public accommodations. While discrimination and segregation were certainly practiced in the United States prior to 1890, only three states had approved similar legislation prior to the Louisiana statute. After the 1896 Supreme Court ruling in *Plessy v. Ferguson*, however, North Carolina, Virginia, Arkansas, South Carolina, Tennessee, Mississippi, Maryland, Florida, and Oklahoma soon adopted similar provisions. By 1920, almost every Southern state had approved Jim Crow legislation that required "equal but separate" facilities for black and white subjects.

11 In response to Tourgée's suggestion that a "nearly white" Negro be used to test the Louisiana statute, Martinet wrote his approval of the plan into a 1891 letter to Tourgée. "It would be quite difficult," he agreed, "to have a lady too nearly white refused admission to a 'white' car" (56). While Martinet's reply seems cryptic at best, leading some critics to the conclusion that he did not entirely agree with Tourgée's proposal, I would suggest that Martinet's letter both records the logic of the decision to stage the test case as a passing event and provides Tourgée with a literal blueprint on how to do so. Although the "lady" disappears (I suspect it would not have been as effortless to get a black "lady" in only to be kicked out), Martinet and Tourgée did engineer a strategy that would allow a black male subject to successfully occupy a seat in a whites-only car.

12 Some fifty years later it was precisely such embarrassing public spectacles that would be staged as sit-ins by the Civil Rights movement. Authorizing demonstrations that required the presence of the visibly black subject, the NAACP (National Assocation for the Advancement of Colored People) not only explic-

itly rejected the strategic value of passing but the very logic of passing that informed Tourgée's case. When, in 1952, *Brown v. Board of Education* appeared before the Supreme Court, the NAACP refused even to mention *Plessy v. Ferguson* as a relevant case. See Kluger, *Simple Justice*.

13 Olsen, *Thin Disguise*, p. 95. Although Tourgée's decision to focus on the conductor seems rather idiosyncratic, the law itself is mostly concerned with outlining the conductor's new duties – at least three-fourths of the actual statute is devoted to the conductor's obligations under the new statute.

14 My irony is purposeful here. Many of the central tenets of theory have not needed the language of theory to interrogate the truth claims of the dominant culture. As Tourgée and Martinet demonstrate, poststructuralist theory is often a formulation of insights previously understood in, by, and through the social practice of the larger "non-academic" culture.

15 In this context, Tourgée's whiteness functions as a key aspect of his racial illiteracy, although Martinet's anecdote testifies to the more expansive failure of the visual as an epistemological guarantee. For a more detailed discussion of the role of spectatorship and the relationship between passing and practices of reading identity please see my, "It Takes One to Know One: Passing and Communities of Common Interest," *Critical Inquiry* 20 (Summer 1994): 715–36.

16 Walter White represents another interesting attempt to pass in the name of politics. During his tenure as the first black executive director of the NAACP, White struggled to no avail to pass a federal anti-lynching bill. Without any "evidence" of lynching, the NAACP found it impossible. Subsidized by his white skin, blue eyes, and blond hair, White went down south and passed as a white man after lynchings to amass "evidence." He then wrote publicly about his experiences, in the form of popular essays, a novel, and a critical study of lynching.

17 In this sense, the Supreme Court decision fulfilled the expectations of much of the black community of Louisiana who took issue with Tourgée and Martinet's proposed case of strategic passing. Arguing that Tourgée's strategy (if successful) would only garner equal rights for light-skinned blacks, the case (when unsuccessful) only proved that light-skinned blacks could and would travel undetected in whites-only cars.

18 In this sense, Tourgee ignores the very thing that makes this case one of the rare examples of passing in legal discourse. That is, the "truly" successful pass is not available to history, since it must remain undetected by the law to be successful. It is only at the moment of encounter with institutional prohibition (Jim Crow) that passing becomes available to be narrativized. By staging the case as a passing scenario the pass enters narrativity and historical visibility. Without some concession to the peculiarly literary formulation of passing, "the problem of evidence," warns Winthrop Jordan, "is insurmountable." *White Over Black* (New York: W. W. Norton & Co., 1968), p. 174.

19 Judge Greenfield as cited in Jane Gaines's fascinating and provocative article, "Dead Ringer: Jacqueline Onassis and the Look-Alike," *The South Atlantic Quarterly* 88.2 (Spring 1989): 477.

20 John Locke, "Of Property," *Two Treatises of Government*, ed. Thomas I. Cook (New York: Hafner Publishing Co., 1947), p. 134.

21 In many senses, this is a classically Foucauldian argument (that prohibition is productive of the very social subjects it seeks to enjoin), as he articulates it in both *Discipline and Punish* and *A History of Sexuality Volume I*.

22 As cited in Lawrence Tribe, *Abortion: The Clash of Absolutes* (New York: W. W. Norton & Co., 1990), p. 81. My thinking on the subject of privacy is indebted to Tribe's reading.

23 Jane Gaines writes, "The branch of United States Law referred to as 'privacy' has its historical origins in a particular right of seclusion from the public eye" (472).

24 Justice Louis Brandeis, dissenting in *Olmstead v. United States*, 277 U.S. 438, 478 (1928) as cited in Tribe, *Abortion*, p. 92.

25 Lauren Berlant, "National Brands/National Body: *Imitation of Life*," *Comparative American Identities: Race, Sex, and Nationality in the Modern Text*. Essays From the English Institute, ed. Hortense Spillers (London: Routledge, 1991), p. 139. In a vastly different context, she claims that there is "no prophylactic private sphere, no space safe from performance or imitation."

26 Patricia Williams, *The Alchemy of Race and Rights* (Cambridge, Mass.: Harvard University Press, 1991), p. 124. Williams makes this comment in reference to a white transsexual student who comes to her in desperation after being barred from every bathroom on campus after her sex-change operation. As "private" space, the bathroom rehearses the logic of property. Please see my "Musing on Toilets: The Bathroom as Boundary line of Identity and Performance" (ATHE conference paper, 1990), "The Architecture of Identity: Bathrooms and the Politics of Privacy" (unpublished manuscript, 1992).

27 A condensed version of my thoughts on privacy has previously appeared in "Is She or Isn't She: Madonna and the Erotics of Appropriation," *Acting Out: Feminist Performances*, ed. Peggy Phelan and Lynda Hart (Michigan: University of Michigan Press, 1993). In addition to the texts already cited, my thinking on the public/private divide is particularly indebted to Carol Pateman, *Disorder of Women: Democracy, Feminism and Political Theory* (Cambridge: Polity Press, 1989). Nancy Fraser, "Rethinking the Public Sphere: A Contribution to the Critique of Actually Existing Democracy," *Social Text* 25/26 (1990): 56–80. J. G. A. Pocock, *The Machiavellian Moment: Florentine Political Thought and the Atlantic Republic Tradition* (New Jersey: Princeton University Press, 1975) and *Virtue, Commerce and History: Essays on Political Thought and History* (New York: Cambridge University Press, 1985). Robert L. Caserio, "Supreme Court Discourse vs. Homosexual Fiction," *South Atlantic Quarterly* 88.1 (Winter 1989): 267–99. This is only a partial listing of the extensive literature on the general issues of privacy, property, and the public sphere.

28 Please see Tribe, *Abortion*, pp. 77–112.

29 Jacques Lacan, *Four Fundamental Concepts of Psychoanalysis*, trans. Alan Sheridan (New York: W. W. Norton & Company, 1981), p. 81. Lacan makes this observation in the context of a larger discussion about the gaze and the constitution of a Cartesian subject in contrast to which he poses his own theories.

30 Hal Foster, Introduction, in *Vision and Visuality* (Seattle: Bay Press, 1988), p. ix and Elin Diamond, "(In)Visible Bodies in Churchill's Theatre," in *Making a Spectacle: Feminist Essays on Contemporary Women's Theatre*, ed. Lynda Hart (Ann Arbor: Michigan, 1989), pp. 261–2.

31 Karl Marx, *Capital, Vol. I*, trans. Ernest Mandel (New York: Vintage Books, 1977), p. 138, 127. Hereafter all references to Marx will be indicated by page number. Although such an isolated reading of the commodity may seem to artificially frame the question of exchange-value by disregarding the importance of questions of labor, production, distribution, and consumption, I think this particular moment in Marx (when exchange-value rides on use-value through the process of "equivalence") offers a productive moment to consider the relation between commodification and the social practice of passing.

32 It is important to recognize that the example of the linen and the coat is, to some extent, an arbitrary one. Not only could Marx have easily chosen another illustrative pair, but also the linen by no means *has* to become a coat. Although,

in this example, it is important that it will *become*, surely it can also become something else besides a coat.

33 Luce Irigaray, *Speculum of the Other Woman*, trans. Gillian Gill (Ithaca, NY: Cornell University Press, 1985), p. 345

34 This is why performance studies is such a useful tool of analysis, for it refuses to consider the body outside the terms of its social signification. The distinction I'm making between an "idea" of majesty and the way majesty works in a social context is in many ways an anti-Platonic idea, for unlike Plato, Marx suggests that an idea of majesty cannot be divested from the particular body that performs it; in fact such bodies produce the actual concept. In this sense, current debates about the importance of role models are informed by a anti-Platonic credo, for the idea that certain bodies must be in positions of authority in order to encourage others to pursue such positions is based on the assumption that these bodies construct the job itself and therefore the sense of possible access to positions of authority. I am indebted to my students at Georgetown University in our class, "Appropriation and Cultural Style" (Fall 1993) for helping me to articulate this idea.

35 The following represents a necessarily partial list of those critics who have used the concept of the commodity form itself as a rubric under which to consider the questions of identity and appropriation. By lumping together these critics, I do not mean to suggest any similarity in their arguments; in fact many of these critics are diametrically opposed in both form and analysis. Please see subsequent footnotes for my specification of which critics deploy use-value as an antidote to exchange-value – a strategy about which I (as well as many of the critics below) have strong reservations. Please see Mary Anne Doane, "The Economy of Desire; The Commodity Form in/of the Cinema," *Quarterly Review of Film and Video*, Vol. 11 (1989): 22-33. Luce Irigaray, *This Sex Which Is Not One*, trans. Catherine Porter (Ithaca, NY: Cornell University Press, 1985). Abdul JanMohamed, *Manichean Aesthetics: The Politics of Literature in Colonial Africa* (Amherst; University of Massachusetts Press, 1983). Susan Willis, *A Primer For Daily Life* (London: Routledge, 1991). Fredric Jameson, "Postmodernism, or the Cultural Logic of Late Capitalism," *New Left Review* 146 (July–Aug. 1984): 53–92. Danae Clark, "Commodity Lesbianism," *Camera Obscura* 25–6 (Jan.–May 1991): 181–201. Arjun Appadurai, ed., *The Social Life of Things: Commodities in Cultural Perspective* (Cambridge: Cambridge University Press, 1986). Gayatri Chakravorty Spivak, "Scattered Speculations on the Question of Value," in *Other Worlds: Essays in Cultural Politics* (New York: Methuen, 1987). Jean Baudrillard, "For A Critique of the Political Economy of the Sign," *Selected Writings*, ed., Mark Poster (Stanford: Stanford University Press, 1988). Guy Dubord, *Society of the Spectacle* (Detroit: Black and Red, 1977). Stuart Hall, "Notes on Deconstructing 'the popular,'" *People's History and Socialist Theory*, ed. Ralph Samuel (London: Routledge & Kegan Paul, 1981). Gayle Rubin, "The Traffic In Women," *Towards An Anthropology of Women*, ed. Rayna Reiter (New York: Monthly Review Press, 1975), pp. 157–210. Nancy Hartsock, *Money, Sex and Power: Toward a Feminist Historical Materialism* (New York: Longman, 1983).

36 As Mary Anne Doane phrases it in "The Economy of Desire: The Commodity Form in/of the Cinema," "Much of feminist theory tends to envisage the woman's relation to the commodity in terms of 'being' rather than 'having;' she is the object of exchange rather than its subject" (22–3).

37 Susan Willis, for example, envisions a world in which gender is "free" from the commodity form. "Such a conceptualization of gender," she argues "would be analogous to conceiving and creating objects in terms of use-value alone,"

p. 23. Another approach imagines a world in which use-value and exchange-value are indistinguishable, for example Irigaray, *This Sex Which Is Not One*. In my estimation, this argument ends up as an argument about the endless poly-sexuality and ambiguity of identity which may in fact characterize desire, but to me, do not have anything to do with politics and identity which is about fixed (though provisional) positions.

38 In the work of Abdul JanMohamed, for instance, the wrongs of colonialism are attributed to the pursuit of exchange-value, and in reaction, he promotes an appreciation for "a permanent fixed self" which he maintains "is essential if one is going to understand and appreciate a racial or cultural alterity." In "The Economy of Manichean Allegory: The Function of Racial Difference in Colonialist Literature," *"Race," Writing, and Difference*, ed. Henry Louis Gates, Jr. (Chicago: University of Chicago Press, 1985), p. 97.

39 Baudrillard, "For A Critique of the Political Economy of the Sign," p. 70.

40 As Luce Irigaray phrases it in *This Sex Which is Not One*, "Woman is divided into two irreconcilable 'bodies': her 'natural' body and her socially valued, exchangeable body, which is a particularly mimetic expression of masculine values" (180). As Abdul JanMohamed phrases it in "The Economy of Manichean Allegory," "Exchange value remains the central motivating force of both colonialist material practice and colonialist literary representation" (87).

41 I take this term from Appadurai, *Social Life of Things*, i.

42 Justice Fenner's decision in the Louisiana Supreme Court as cited in Olsen, *Thin Disguise*, p. 73. He writes, "Law and custom having sanctioned a separation of the races, it is not the province of the judiciary to legislate it away. Following these guides, we are compelled to declare that, at the time of the alleged inquiry, there was that natural, legal, and customary difference between the white and black races in this state which made their separation as passengers in a public conveyance the subject of a sound regulation to secure order, promote comfort, preserve the peace and maintain the rights, both of carriers and passengers." The crux of his decision is recycled by Justice Brown in the United States Supreme Court.

43 As cited in Kluger, *Simple Justice*, p. 79.

44 Robert Harris as cited in Sundquist "Mark Twain and Homer Plessy," p. 108.

45 Cited in Tribe, 92.

46 *Michael H. vs. Gerald D.* 109 Supreme Ct. 2333, 2341 (1989).

47 Although it is possible to trace one kind of political history that has gradually effected social change by reinhabiting the category of the "natural," I suspect that such an approach unavoidably reproduces the category of "man," despite a best intention to include and protect those "others" intentionally excluded from its original parameters. The problem with an oppositional humanism, as Anne Cubilié argues, is that it "constructs the very subject that it is meant to protect, thereby initiating its entrance into the very system that is responsible for the subject's abuse." "Performing Anti-Violence Intervention: Human Rights and the Body in Representation," unpublished Ph.D. Dissertation, University of Pennsylvania (Summer 1995), p. 7. In political and legal theory, this question has been take up in the form of debates about the role of "rights" and the efficacy of rights discourse in the pursuit of justice.

48 Please see, for example, Rhonda Copelon, "From Privacy to Autonomy: The Conditions for Sexual and Reproductive Freedom," *From Abortion to Reproductive Freedom: Transforming A Movement*, ed. Marlene Gerber (Boston: South End Press, 1990), pp. 27–43.

49 See Janet Haley, "The Construction of Heterosexuality," *Fear of A Queer Planet: Queer Politics and Social Theory*, ed. Michael Warner (Minneapolis: University

of Minnesota Press, 1993), pp. 82-102 for a more nuanced engagement with the problem of "suspect class" and a way out of a biological justification for equitable treatment.

50 As Lynda Hart suggests, perhaps we do even not want to try and qualify for the mantle of social purity and the consequent burden of the natural. Please see her "Karen Finley's Dirty Work: Censorship, Homophobia, and the NEA," *Genders* 14 (Fall 1992): 2–15.

51 Here, I am obviously making reference to Barbara Hernstein Smith's *Contingencies of Value: alterative perspectives for critical theory* (Cambridge, Mass.: Harvard University Press, 1988). Although it is impossible to reference the entire field of performance and cultural studies and indicate my debt, candidates for inclusion consist of those already clearly cited in this essay as well as the work of Judith Butler, Peggy Phelan, Valerie Smith, Lynda Hart, Hortense Spillers, Patricia Williams, Gayatri Spivak, Peter Stallybrass, Kobena Mercer, Marcos Becquer, Donna Haraway, Homi Bhabha, James Scott, Douglas Crimp, etc. The list is necessarily partial, but the mere presence of the "etc" indicates that I situate myself and my work as part and product of a large group of scholars committed to the political consequences of intellectual work.

52 In one particularly blatant expression of who exactly is barred from the zone of privacy and why, Charles Fried explicitly defined the right of privacy as self-ownership when he appeared before the Supreme Court to *defend* the Reagan administration's interest in *limiting* abortion rights. He wrote, "The subject of personal privacy rest[s] squarely on the moral fact that a person belongs to himself and not to others nor to society as a whole" (as cited in *Abortion*, Tribe, p. 101). In the name of privacy, the Reagan administration determined that women in general, and women of color in particular, were unsuitable for self-ownership and thus the consequent "right" to safe, respectful, and affordable abortions. Dare I repeat myself: considered as a form of property, the problem of privacy is the problem of identity itself.

53 Maureen Duffy, *Rites* in *Plays By and About Women*, eds. Victoria Sullivan and James Hatch (New York: Vintage Books, 1972), p. 370.

Part V

PERFORMER/ PERFORMANCE

14

THOUGHTS ON MY CAREER, *THE OTHER WEAPON*, AND OTHER PROJECTS

Robbie McCauley

> Sometimes I feel I'm walking on three feet,
> one in survival, one in rebellion,
> and a third one for balance.
>
> from *San Juan Hill*/ The Father Parts

One day in New York

I saw some men working, making a delivery of walls to a storefront space. Men from inside came out. They were all intending to carry the walls into the store. First they greeted each other. One had a cup of coffee. They all seemed uncomfortable. When one started to pull a wall from a flatbed truck, another approached him and asked, "Why are you doing it like that?" The first man turned the wall on its long edge, stooped under, and began to walk his hands along it. The other guy got in front of the first and let the wall land on his shoulder. When they stood up the sight was spectacular. It reminded me of actors working together.

The performance theater work I have been doing for the last many years has involved a conscious process wherein I sought to address certain assumptions about art, history, community, the personal and the political. Those assumptions had seemed to me to be an official attitude in this society, mouthed by numerous people educated in the United States – the idea that art about social issues and community either must be done a certain way and must say certain things in order to be relevant, or that such art is doomed to "preach to the converted" and is not good work. I wanted to do a kind of theater I felt I remembered from before I was born.

I think perhaps

It came through my mother's memory of the wagon shows. Or maybe it was that there was always live music at the house parties Mother and 'em went to. The house would come alive with perfume, shiny jewels, cigarette smoke, and whiskey smells as she and her sisters slipped themselves into magnificent dresses and splendid shoes. There was good food, a pecan tree, chickens, a fig tree, and the dirt. There was no talk of struggle or freedom. I thought we were already free. Memories that faded too soon.

I've been

Always concerned about power and control, being on the bottom of the heap, fighting, rising, no time to be tired, concerned about the big invisible thing, tight people, tiny streams of light and hidden terror. Scarier still are monsters that smile in the bright day and steal from us.

I'm shy and struggle with a problem of low self-esteem. The problem has puzzled me because I was brought up to advance myself, think for myself, be proud. Well, what your family teaches you is so full of contradictions. I knew very young that I am not only the people I come from, but the world I was born into. As a black girl in the United States in the mid-1940s and 1950s, I felt the contradictions of life in this country were brutal and confusing. What I internalized out of the situation was that I was not all right, but if I got all right, I could be accepted. That is why I think the fault for my problem lies not entirely in myself or in my family but in the government. Government as idea, reality, metaphor. The people my mother called THEY.

Like diabetes

Low self-esteem may be a condition that has no cure. Like diabetes it may be something you have to control in order to function. Like diabetes, I'm sure there are many biographical reasons for the condition. Like diabetes, I believe the condition also has political reasons. The triangular slave trade in the Americas was largely based on sugar.

A politically conscious woman shared this anecdote with me: I was once at a party with members of an old rich family. Their money had been made from sugar. The waiter put sugar on the table for coffee. One of them pushed it away and laughed. "Poison," another of them said, and they all laughed even harder. Hearsay probably, but I like gossip. Stories that reflect feelings of the insiders and outsiders. Personal stories are usually political. "My father was in the war when I was born." Causes and effects are stated passionately. "My mother wanted to be a lady, but had to work." Despite the general belief in individual choices, people are affected probably more by the wars they are born into than anything. Talking about wars one gets a sense of her own power or lack of it.

People often ask, "Do you eat a lot of sugar?" when they discover I have diabetes. I sometimes answer, "Well . . . partly." Diabetes is not a result of eating too much sugar. The causes for it are a combination of genetic, psychological, and dietary things, and each case is individual. Its cure may lie in the recognition of it as a condition of imbalance, of each person learning how her whole body ought to be nurtured. Yet, I've become dependent on western medicine to maintain my life, and though I am in good shape, I do have annoying problems. Even the excellent internist with whom I'm finally working is puzzled by the extremes of my case. I'd have questions about balance if I did not have diabetes. The tightrope image for me catalyzes clear thinking and change.

I want to continue in the tradition of performance art which encourages people to learn from the past and to challenge the stories. I want to follow a tradition that heightens the connection of art to life. I have particular obsessive urges to analyze the world I was born into. I've had certain key, gut artistic influences. I call myself an artist to demystify the term. I always imagine my mother in the audience. Art is work. I'm also a mother, which is extraordinary. I want to build on a form of performance as discourse. The first Last Poets, whom I saw in 1969 in a loft on downtown 2nd Avenue, New York, who consisted of Gylan Kain, Felipe Luciano, and David Nelson, initially inspired me to create my own work.

As luck would have it, with my interest in charged form and content, I arrived in New York City in 1965 at a time when experimental theater and Black theater were present up and down the city. By '79, I had gained some reputation as a "good actress," had received an Audelco Award in 1974. I worked at the Judson Church on Washington Square, Circle in the Square on Bleecker Street, the Cafe Cino, a crowded bar, and sometimes theater, on Cornelia Street all in the West Village; La Mama, E.T.C., when it was the experimental theater club in a second floor loft on 2nd Avenue catty-cornered southeast of Gem's Spa and later in a basement on East 9th Street; the Negro Ensemble Company then on the northwest corner across from Gem's Spa; and the Public Theater at Lafayette and Astor all in the East Village. I lived first at 3rd and MacDougal and later on East 9th Street. The fire of change and rebellion in the world at that time was reflected in the theater. Downtown. Uptown. I had a chance to observe work by the Open Theater under the direction of Joseph Chaiken and the New Lafayette in Harlem under the direction of Robert Macbeth.

I would have been dead or crazy years ago had I not become an actor. A bewildered young black woman with a do-gooder attitude, I crossed into a world where I saw that one's talent helped to define one's identity, a world where I felt encouraged to follow my impulses to find beautiful ways to express hard feelings. I came to New York in my early twenties to seek new experiences, but had been brought up well enough not to fall all the way off the edge. I literally tuned in to my insides, as was the mode of the day, and seized upon the stirrings inside me as raw material.

Performance theater work fulfills my desire to make a contribution to the world of culture. In 1979, with composer Ed Montgomery and his musical group, Sedition Ensemble, I began to create musical performance theater pieces. Since then, I've concentrated on engaging the audience and performers to face charged issues. I do have concern for the essentials of time, money, and status in work, but I've often felt immobilized by the majority of well-meant advice offered over the years on how to be successful in the theater.

In my family

> ... a passion for history, a sense of connection with the past.
> No great scholars in the family, but stories survived from the time
> of slavery told in snatches around the breakfast table,
> as answers to mine and Sister's constant questions,
> and even as declarations in my father's drinking rages.
> "We fought for this country for you to be free,
> so don't be giving me no lip." Things like that.

Ed Montgomery and I felt almost the same way about the drama inherent in political text. He had already started a collection of startling passages from pamphlets, rallies, and news reports from which we selected tellable stories. Avowed anti-imperialists, we followed the events of political prisoners in current U.S. history including Geronimo Pratt, Leonard Peltier, Assata Shakur, and Lolita Lebron as protagonists with Uncle Sam, the FBI/CIA, and several right-wingers as antagonists. We worked with several musicians and performers in the New York area. Even with a range of political and spiritual beliefs among us, and very little money, nobody was turned off from the views of history Ed and I espoused. Bern Nicks, Martin Aubert, Bob De Meo, Valois Mickens, Verna Hampton, April Green, Crystal Joy, the late Jay Oliver, Jaribu Hill and Ngoma Hill, Sharita Hunt, a host of dedicated artists ... affirmed my belief that what is performed *about* is essential.

Back then in Georgia

Dr. B. was the best-educated, nicest man. He made house calls. A black man to look up to. He got killed, downtown, stepping in between the police and another black man they say the police were getting ready to shoot on Broad Street, or something like that. They say white folks came to his funeral. Not much was said about what happened downtown, and no justice was done. After that, not much foolishness was tolerated. My Aunt Jessie started using the phrase, "do like the white folks do".

Sedition Ensemble terminated from natural causes. Groups get to the end of their time. I now miss the uncompromising politics as the source of the work, but then I missed the personal stirrings. I continued to seek a way to balance both. Ed and I worked with the late performer, Bob Carroll, from 1982 to 1984. In a piece of his called *Dirt*, I began to create *San Juan Hill*. This became the basis of a series about my family's survival since the nineteenth century, "Confessions of a Working Class Black Woman" and included *My Father And The Wars, Indian Blood*, and *Sally's Rape*. I was revved up by the stories my family had told me. My imagination kicked in. I began to see possibilities of teaching history in a non-academic way.

Buffalo

I did this series out of the obsession for examining my feelings about survival. The work was structured like jazz music with black and white players. In 1988 we played at Hallwalls, an art center in Buffalo, with *Indian Blood*. By then I was already impressed with how audiences of many races identified with this work. Riding around in the town, I observed the racial separations of neighborhoods, as usual in U.S. cities.

I was influenced to open up the connection with the audience by a conversation with Ron Ehmke who curated the work at Hallwalls. I asked him if there were any stories in Buffalo concerning race that the community shared. Ehmke told me about the "riots" there in 1967, and told me about a sociological study of it based on interviews with people in the town. The concept of working with actors was my own. Having taught for several years, I was anxious to share some of the work I'd been doing with students, how one's personal biography is part of history and how that affects the actor's voice. Ehmke applied for and received a grant from the New York State Council on the Arts for such a project. *The Buffalo Project* was the first work I did with text from local witnesses.

There is always a personal and political investment in work. Having grown up in the southern United States and having moved to the north later, I was affected by the out-and-out all-day-long racism in both areas. I wondered how events I was told about, known as "the riot" in Buffalo in 1967, reflected racial attitudes in a northern industrial city. Ed Montgomery, who I had by then married and who is the father of my daughter, is a second-generation member of an Italian working-class family of Buffalo. This intensified my curiosity about the place.

The assignment for each actor was to interview one or more people in Buffalo about the riots. This would include a variety of people, whether or not they experienced it. For instance, the actors themselves, who either grew up in the community or had come later and heard stories, were witnesses. The script would be a basis for talking about racial relations in Buffalo today. I knew that the performance would include choral passages. I like the idea of modern events having the choral voice. In Buffalo the cast consisted of ten people from age 70 to age 22, with several stated identities – men and women, black, Jewish, Protestant, Catholic, mothers, fathers, Italian. Thus began a way of working that became basic for subsequent projects. The actors and I declared a safe space in which to express thoughts and feelings about the subject matter, and to listen to each other.

Some have asked me about the relationship of my "histories" work to that of Anna Deavere Smith (author and performer of *Fires in the Mirror* and *Twilight: Los Angeles 1992*). The recognition of the way people talk about the charged issues in the United States is something I think we're both exploring. We also share a certain intelligence about acting and, of course, blackness. Aside from feeling naturally jealous of her fame, I like the similarities. Her particular talent and work is so fine-tuned that mine does not compare. The truth is I have neither the skill nor the interest in being so precise. Working with actors in the places I am investigating, the personal response of the actors to the content of the witnesses' interviews, the mirror reflecting the community back on itself and dialogue about it are my priorities. I am eternally grateful to the actors who engaged with me in exploring their towns, so many actors on various levels willing to learn, give up other work, take risks to succeed or not. Unlike Smith, I seldom identify witnesses in the piece. They are given the option as to whether they want to be indentified even on the program. I enjoy the question that has emerged about Smith's work. Is it writing? I think that her ability to hear, script, and sculpt what people say is indeed legitimate, possibly great, new writing. My work, though, developed quite separately from hers.

I select an event that stirs me, like the riot in Buffalo, and work with the producer or curator to seek out people in local community and artistic organizations and request meetings with them to talk about collaborating on a project. When we first get together I usually describe my intentions with the image of the Trojan War. It was an event of real and mythical weight that affected not only the participants but also people way beyond that time. These meetings are best when they result in the exchange of images, stories, and philosophical comments. The potential co-sponsors actually get a taste of how the performance allows different points of view to be talked about while retaining passion. Here is where I get the first suggestions for actors and witnesses.

Primary Sources

A series of work, "Primary Sources" produced by Marie Cieri (The Arts Company) from 1991 to 1994 followed *The Buffalo Project. Mississippi Freedom*, about the freedom rides and the voting rights struggle in Mississippi in 1964; *Turf*, about court-enforced busing in Boston in 1974; and *The Other Weapon*, about law enforcement and the Black Panther Party in Los Angeles in 1969 resulted. The event itself, not necessarily as factual history, but as witnessed by people in the place is the clay for the work.

With producer Cieri, there were hours in cars talking about our own likenesses and differences. Once in a Mississippi motel room I badgered her to tell me what it is that white people want. One of the choicest bits of information she told me was that white people have the power and don't intend to give it up. What a relief that was! That made working with her

Figure 14.1 Robbie McCauley in *Indian Blood* at The Kitchen, November 1987
(Photograph: Vivian Selto)

271

much easier. I have not made up my mind about the role of the producer in performance theater. I know part of her work involves the creative aspect. That was the uneasiest part for me, because I've always been nervous about holding on to what belongs to everyone. What guided me in these projects was to stick to what I wanted to accomplish in the work. The work is valuable in so many ways. Ownership in this work is uncomfortable. I put my name on it to take responsibility for and identify myself as the gatherer and shaper.

Making the transition from the dialogues to the performances is always shocking. The task of the actor is to identify and try to work through resistances and see how material plays from the inside out. The key is the material itself. I try to be fair. I try to be honest. The work is to get actors to be present with information and their own vulnerability in the face of it. As much work as possible must be done to play the material with one's intellect, voice, body, and sense of connection to others. Here is a process by which the actors can learn and teach history.

In a Mississippi meeting two community leaders actually flinched when I described the way I work. Why work with actors rather than "real people?" I felt that question was an insult to the work of an actor, but I understood the prejudice because of how actors are often perceived. Implied in that question is the discomfort about bringing up painful subject matter and ownership of experience. I explained that I identify myself as the outsider and try to share my passion for the subject matter of each work to help cut through people's resistance to the outsider. I explained that I felt the work of artists was to connect to the community and try to interpret and reveal history. I explained that I wanted to find among them, perhaps, people who may want to act, and to support the proposition that storytelling is real work. Later both of these leaders welcomed the final project. Theirs were two of the most responsive audiences. The assumption seems to be that actors are some strange creatures that do not walk among regular folks. I assume that actors are everywhere, like musicians.

One might say

My family is conservative. This takes many forms among black people. It often has to do with words. African American is a conservative name. Negro capitalized. I like language. I like black uncapitalized. I lean to the left politically. Brought up in a reasonably well functioning, reasonably intact black family in the U.S., I saw later in life what a prized condition that was. Still, angry and rebellious impulses began to inhabit my persona.

I still get bitter

Exhaustion from too much humiliation. Rage is healthy, more active. As an actor, I'm interested in the range of emotions that emanate from anger.

Jean Paul Sartre, the French philosopher, once wrote that love and fear were the only emotions. Maybe. I work with emotion as if it is energetic material at the source of my being. Moving through it is a journey that is sometimes beautiful, can keep one from sinking into it.

Acting is basic to work I create. Intelligence is a valuable element of the craft. It is an element that ought to be identified and nurtured. I believe it is an element that is, especially in the anti-intellectual culture of the United States, systematically undervalued. The best teaching of acting too often impedes the thinking process. "Don't think," is a common admonition to the actor. This makes sense in many cases where tension and judgement are inhibiting her. The question, "What are you thinking?", whether answered or not, may be more useful. However, in eliciting the actor's presence, I find it valuable to explore what is being thought. Uncharted dialogue, daring talk, not humiliation, but fiery personal analysis of ideas, is raw material for work.

Becoming intellectually engaged with new details can be an empowering for actors. In the Los Angeles project, there was a lot of resistance from the performers, especially the men. I usually welcome resistance, especially from men. I have a talent to recognize, name, open up, and explore the information inside of the resistance. Resistance is information. Perhaps bitterness too is information to be picked apart and used.

I use what people already know, what they may not know, surprising details, strong images, a sense of the absurd, and that we are all a part of different stories. I aim to neither bash, nor to forgive the privileged, neither to praise nor blame the underprivileged, but to simply include more stories. I do have a prejudice in favor of those who've been systematically denied. How history is taught continues to be challenged. The powers that be in the academy, who naturally fear change, still stifle stories, and isolate contributions of those not in the official versions. In the new theater performers are teaching history. This work need not diminish academic versions, but it may include more people, more life and more sense of continuity from one time to another.

Actors can rather safely explore the painful, the sad, the fearful, the so-called negative conditions and be able to perform them with energy, joy, beauty, power. Recognition of blocks and belief in the ability to penetrate them are craft elements. For instance, you may visualize a stone block and imagine you have a hammer and chisel. The block is full of things you are resisting – learning lines, feeling the emotions that the words bring up, listening to the director, whatever. Your will to move toward what you are resisting is the hammer and chisel. Moving or pounding at the block can transform one's resistance to a meeting with what's inside the block. From inside there, something new may be made. This work, basic to acting, is useful for audiences as well – to see examples of people grappling to think clearly.

I've been fortunate to work with master directors. Lloyd Richards persuaded me to say to myself "I am an actor." To admit that felt scary and strangely powerful.

Gilbert Moses, who'd trained directly with Viola Spolin (author of *Improvisation for the Theater*), spoke the language of animal imagery in a down-to-earth tone that my body repsonded to. "You're like a goat," he told me one day, rehearsing Ed Bullins's *The Taking of Miss Janie*. Right away I began to move more freely.

Bill Duke, for DREAM at the Negro Ensemble Company, gave the actors situations that put such a demand on our imaginations that we learned to perform a piece that was never written down. I still remember the lines from it.

Carl Weber, who directed the original Ed Bullins's *Jo Anne!*, one day called me over and described how he was making the story move. Whether he sensed that I needed to feel part of the creation of the play, I don't know, but I could feel my resistance move away, and thought he was very clever.

Joseph Chaiken some years after, said to me, "You have many voices inside you," and gave me a tape of Marian Anderson singing spirtuals to listen to, not to sing he said, just to hear.

Conversational music, choruses, dialogue, poetry, monologues are new and old forms at my disposal. This work is endemic to the poetry, politics, and music of the 1960s black cultural movement.

It requires a willingness and some technique in involving oneself personally with the content of text. I am still experimenting with how to articulate it. The mystery of it has to do with the commitment to explore the subject matter. These projects work more or less on that basis. Giving voice to the range and subtlety of feelings about charged issues is the task here. Mainly educated in western culture I use all I can, including a visceral imagination out of my blackness. Certain images emerge consistently. The human heartbeat and color are basic. Jazz is the major inspiration. Each actor is an instrument whose keys when played resonate her experience and imagination. Being willing to tune her instrument to the material (or score), to enter a time and space to play herself with others is basic to acting. I experience jazz and theater as a source of infinite manifestations with an African American center.

A change in motion

I miss dancing for the hell of it. Except for my Aunt T. who drank too much and was great fun, my family tightened up so much in Georgia that it became hard to let go. My confessions come from that. I had to admit the murderous jobs people take in order to survive. My grandfather and my father were soldiers for the government. I hate that I was the one born with the bad pancreas and so many sad feelings. I inherited my father's wars. Men are little gods propped up to play the role of savior. I have never been able to just jump up and down. It would make me cry so uncontrollably to be happy that I'd miss it anyhow. I've been diagnosed as irritable. Still, the sources of my rage are political. I will not rest until confessions of privilege come from all sides.

White supremacy is a better term for the kind of racism I'm dealing with. The idea that white people are something special and that to identify with the white condition is a good thing has been so much a part of European colonial thinking that so-called white people and colonized people all over the world have internalized the thought for centuries. People easily bristle at these statements. People who consider themselves white may be tired of being put in the role of oppressor, and may feel there's nothing they can do about it anyhow.

We know that black slavery and Indian land were the reasons for the success of U.S. and European capitalism. If we all have ancestors who somehow gained or lost from that story, we may be able to continue with less irrational prejudice. I am amazed at how much in denial people in the U.S. are. It makes the general population, black and white, seem hopelessly ignorant. We relate to one another in a reactive mode. We seem terrified of facing the truth about class. Whites seem as if they may disappear if they had to admit they're nothing special in relation to other peoples. Native American people seem to have withdrawn (which may save us all), and other populations, especially blacks, seem exhausted and desperate.

I encourage white actors to take the material of how their families participated in, or received privileges from, the horrors of racism and take time to think about it. I announce at the start of all these projects that I will not try to be objective. Black people by necessity are smart about social conditions. I encourage black actors to look for and admit what they don't know. Certain recognitions about craft come up in this work. There needs to be a healthy arrogance about one's ability to dialogue about the subject matter. Coupled with that arrogance is the recognition that vulnerability is the source of strength for the actor. The ability to grapple with vulnerability and arrogance comes as a result of extensive dialogue between us.

The Other Weapon

February, 1994. It is the day I hand out the first few pages of *The Other Weapon*. It is the day the actors see their names as characters. It is the day the group resistance seems impenetrable. However, I trust that such resistance is full of energy. It is shocking, I know, to see one's name in print, especially connected to words stated out of context. It shocked the actors in Buffalo, Boston, and Mississippi too. That I had explained before that this was the way I would write means nothing at this moment. Almost to a person, the actors feel somehow ripped off, betrayed, or unrewarded for their contributions. I do not take time to defend or explain the script pages. I literally have to pry people from the walls in order to lead a warm-up. A sullenness permeates, but the warm-up is effective. Then I assign the actors to tell personal stories with elements related to the charged subject matter of race. We were working in a dusty, dark alternative theater space on Venice Boulevard called Beyond Baroque. "Barely," I say, looking around, reaching for a cheap laugh. No takers. I take a deep breath. The personal story, I think, is the best way to go today. We'll get back to the script later. The actors are thrown back on their ability to listen to each other, to remember, to tell the truth, and/or lie compellingly.

I immediately choose some of those stories for the performance. I consider bebop, the jazz form, popular in the 1940s and '50s, characterized by improvisation, as a direct source for putting a performance together. The melody may be just a fragment. Push through, I tell myself. Familiar forms can be a way to chip at the block of resistance. Trusting the actor's ability is a craft element for the director, I think grandly. In other words I am desperate to keep on playing. What a day!

In *The Other Weapon* we were concerned with three dramatic events about law enforcement and the Black Panther Party in Los Angeles, 1969–71. The story from that time is that the police attacked a BPP headquarters at 41st and Central Avenue and the Panthers held the police off without anyone getting killed, unlike what happened in Chicago a few days earlier with the infamous police murder of Fred Hampton and Mark Clark. The story resonates the idea that Los Angeles had a strong black community and that these events signified a victorious moment. A strong point of the story for me was that when the Panthers finally surrendered and emerged from the headquarters, numbers of people from the community were there bearing witness. At the end of this performance, the actors improvise an interview with one of the original women in the headquarters, Sister Somayah "Peaches" Moore-Kambui, who happens to be a performer and agreed to work in the project. The interview segues to the dialogue with the audience. A delightful woman, Sister Somayah helped me to deal with the absurdities and realities of trying to do the work in this way now.

I have had such good experiences working in theater that I tend to expect them. As a director, my struggle for personal strength has been put to the test. I've discovered for myself that the director is not a position of power. It is more Zen than that. The director is a guide and an actor. She has a sense of the world in which she is working. She lets the material and the actors guide her. Sometimes, in order to get things done, she acts like the powerful one. This is the most risky part. The energy of actors comes from so many sources. I continue to aim for processes wherein trust, nuturance, and imagination are basic and effective. Clearly stating what you need to happen inspires actors to be creative.

Figure 14.2 The Other Weapon by Robbie McCauley, produced by The Arts Company, 1994 (Photograph: Martin Cox. Courtesy The Arts Company)

Kristin Linklater, author of *Freeing the Natural Voice*, received a Ford Foundation grant in 1968 to train people in the United States to teach. As a member of the apprentice company in the early years of Negro Ensemble Company, I had already fallen in love with her work. She had stated that she wanted particularly to work with black people. She had identified something I understood. It was that American actors – especially black American actors – exhibited a good ability to connect with passionate impulses, but not so good an ability to transmit the full power and range of such connections through their voices. She felt that the British actors were more articulate but not so passionately connected. Of course, this was general, and possibly reflected a cultural metaphor. At any rate, it made sense to me. Without question, I responded to her handwritten note on the wall for anyone interested in teacher training with her to write their name and number. The grant allowed me to quit my day job and change my life. The teacher training taught me how to teach how to learn.

L.A. Lessons

There are more screaming matches than I would have wanted in this project. In the script I use testimony of one of the actors referring to Rodney King and the killing of a young black woman by a Korean shopkeeper. When the Asian woman protests against the passage, on the grounds that many Asians had responded constructively to that incident, the young black man states his point of view that Asians don't work hard enough against the model minority status they enjoy. I was, as usual, cutting off the white man in the group whenever I felt he was trying to have the last word. In a previous exercise wherein we admitted prejudices I had not admitted that particular one – white men getting the last word – and don't know if I was aware of it then. The older black woman sighs to the young black man that he's being too hard on the Asian woman. The two Latino women complain that again their issues are being ignored. The white man keeps trying to give *the* solution. The older black man agrees with the older black woman that the younger black man is being too hard. The two of them and the two Latino women begin to do a physical manifestation of what is going on, one climbing on top of the other, trying to be the winner. I yell over and over, "L.A. is fucked up!" My losing it lightens things up just a bit.

Until this day

Black people get caught into behaving – acting – in order to get along. I met an intelligent, mature black woman painter in Mississippi who had a few white friends. Their affection and support for each other seemed genuine. However, I noticed that the black woman's behavior was full of bad acting, using bad white grammar, as opposed to good black English, all in all an unconvincing portrayal of southern earthiness. After she saw the show and discussion there, she walked up to me with her face discontorted, breathing easily, and simply said, "Thank you." I hoped we had given her permission to relax. I hoped she would begin to be more honestly present with her friends.

Rather than avoid stereotypes, I study them. Stereotypes are based on how people perceive others. People are also consciously or unconsciously driven to act out them out. Stereotypes of white people include the idea that they are all extremely self-involved, uneducated about people other than themselves, are unable to understand complicated ways in which people who are not white survive, and are in deep denial about racism. Some of that is sometimes true. Black people are seen as angry, hostile, finding racists behind every bush. There's some truth in some of that. Down south until quite recently it was often a matter of life and death for black people to behave in a prescribed manner. Blacks could not express arrogance, anger, or hostility without risking a violent death.

In the early days

The signs that told you where you could not go. WHITES ONLY. Black people down south who say they did not adhere to that are lying, or they came along when official apartheid was over. We had to. It left a deep mark on my psyche. If there is a collective memory of slavery, harassment, and humiliation among black people, I certainly got my share. My folks worked against the signs by striving to be better. Not so strictly Christian, but strictly patriarchial. Internal ambiguities ... good Negroes ... military values ... southern food ... bad nigger in there somewhere ... better not come out. The class and race strivings, that I believed were required, and my rebellion against them, the contradictions remain.

Actors can be effective collectors and transmitters of the meaning of history. The aim is not "to tell real stories from real people" but to create something that emerged from the process of the actor's examination of, and ability to give voice to, the essence of events. Organized Improvisation is how I describe the connection between that theater art and bebop. The actor herself is the instrument. Her act of thinking becomes physical. She plays herself. She is committed to and has a heightened consciousness of the theme. This work like bebop depends upon the mind as an important element of the playing. Each instrument is alone, but is present with all that is being played. Bebop reflects the art of black survival.

> The oppressor is smarter than we thought.
> He's made it passé to be oppressed
> Out of style to be emotional about injustice
> Absolutely boring to wish for his death,
> So we pull ourselves by fashionable boots,

And try to get over with a hustle or two
In a world turning backwards, in a world
turning backwards, in a world turning . . .

from *My Father and the Wars*

In Mississippi the history of the freedom riders who came from outside the state to help stir up change was the material of the piece. It was an obvious metaphor for my relation to the community. This work, of course, is in no way the same as the politcal action of the freedom riders. I do not call the telling of stories and making a place for dialogue a political act. Some would say it is. The aim of the work is providing continuity from one generation to the next. The aim of the work is not to gain power for a particular people. The fact that I create work from my black experience is what makes it universal. Many people of all races have internalized the idea that blackness is a limitation. People are able to get beyond that idea.

L.A. Again

If this city were a character, it might reveal quite clearly the political reality of how the police are used to perpetuate racism and class prejudice in American cities. Black people are definitely targeted as criminals. I, a rather mild-mannered artiste (well, somewhat mild), found myself in a screaming match in a Santa Monica drugstore with a white store manager who physically handled me and accused me of stealing. Most black people I talked to there, no matter what their lifestyle, had had a variety of such occurrences with or without the police. Many felt the attitude of business people reflected that of the police. A Los Angeles Police Department former officer, a white man, gave testimony that young black men are targeted as gang members, are murdered indiscriminately, and that the average police officer has "more respect for a dog" than he has for a young black man.

According to other testimony, many Latino people also had hard times with the police. Asians generally had not. A Japanese man I interviewed told me that he grew up in an L.A. with many Latino hangout buddies. They were periodically picked up by the police, as often happened with young men, especially blacks and Latinos. He said if he were picked up with his Latino friends, he would be dropped off and told to go home whereas the Latino guys would be taken to headquarters and harassed. One of the most volatile exchanges in the work was an ongoing dialogue between an Asian and a black performer about Asians being seen as, and getting privileges from, being the model minority. The young Asian woman did not like being stuck in this role. The young black man saw her as being in denial of that role. I know it was frustrating to both of them that neither of them won the fight. I hoped that eventually the two got the point, that a lesson from the Panthers is that the class struggle continues, and that more people are becoming consciously affected by it.

The new right wing shows little movement away from the basic position of white supremacy in the United States, or the denial and distortion about it that Malcolm X made plain.

At The Vision Complex, after the first performance of *The Other Weapon* in L.A.'s Leimert Park area, a black community, a 14-year-old girl with a pen and pad in her hand stood up and told us how grateful she was about what she was learning. How could she learn more? A woman in that same audience said it brought back parts of her life she never talked about, when she worked in the Black Panther Party programs. A sophisticated black male artist was disappointed because for him the form was nostalgic.

The organized improvisational form took another route in a later perform- ance at the Southland Cultural Center in Inglewood. Included in the piece was a personal story by the Asian woman. She told how her white employer had made a racist remark about Rodney King. She first ended the story by saying how hard it was to say something back to the person who hands out the paycheck. For some reason, she began ending the story by saying that she quit the job. I had told her I thought the first telling was strongest because black and other people could identify with having to keep a job. Well, on one night when she did the revised version, the young black man went at her verbally about revising the story, about not admitting to the model minority status. She went back at him about not hearing the whole story. It played like a good fight scene. In the moment I remembered that he'd warned me he might do this. Maybe my forgetting was convenient. I liked thinking that both actors were in on a possible improvisation. The moment was live and fresh. The performance went on. Another actor jokingly accused me of beaming when it happened.

The L.A. project was by then not what I wanted. My exhaustion made me impatient. Patience is part of the process, and I tried to hold on to it. One actor told me privately that their careers, their images were always on the line. At Hollywood Moguls during the audience talkback, a white male audience member complained about the portrayal of whites in the piece whom he perceived as negative characters. I pointed out that there was plenty of okay stuff about white people, but the piece was more about the brutality of the L.A.P.D. against black people. Well, I probably was not that clear. The white male actor stated that he'd never left the company no matter how hard it got for him. Clearer.

The best parts of this project for me happened during audience discus- sions. Many people have asked how this is done. I started this work before I knew what interactive theater was. Having been around a long time, I often have the feeling that I invented something that others caught on to. The truth is that things are in the air. Serious conversations happen often now in public. Talk shows on television, however maddening, are a part of this. I try not to get hung up on who came first, but it is a sensitive thing for me, being black and getting credit. We are all reshaping material, catching things from out of the air. It has been difficult for me to own and then to release ownership. Perhaps generosity is a craft element. The more one shares the work, the more one learns, I keep telling myself.

In L.A. the talkbacks often went on as long as the show, which was about an hour and twenty minutes. At the University of California Los Angeles, several students expressed dismay that they knew few, if any, facts about the 1969 shooting there that was dramatized in the piece. In Hollywood, previous members of the B.P.P. came and talked back with enthusiasm about how useful the work was in being specific about the Los Angeles Black Panthers. Still others criticized that fact that we did not tell the whole story, or parts they would have liked to tell. I feel there is a balancing act in the work between the artist/outsider and the local artists, the witnesses and the audiences. The tightrope sways also between the parameters of the personal, the aesthetic, the political, the scholarly, and the hearsay. All these elements spill over into each other and surprising things happen. Sometimes the artist has to compromise her aesthetic concerns for the sensitivity of community members.

Learning from mistakes was almost a cliché with the L.A. project. How personal is one able to get without messing up? Personalizing frees the actor's voice. That is the purpose of it. It is not the same as substituting one's own personal experience for one in the performance. It is the work of exercising one's imagination and giving voice to what comes up in response to the issues of the work. This process can weed out what is irrelevant. Artists need to make unique connections with the issues.

A Mexican American woman in the cast had a story about confronting the insults of so-called society women in Beverly Hills. Her story was strong because it was honest and repeatable and because it allowed her imagination to respond to the humor in it. In the performance it was placed as a moment of contemplation, the passing of refreshments to the audience and a transition to one of the more tragic stories in the piece. The balance of all those elements was my favorite moment.

One night in the aftershow talk a black man started to speak and broke into tears. "Take your time," we echoed from the stage like folks do in church. He thanked us for showing what he said he no longer heard people speak of. The end of the work is often the beginning. The L.A. project was not what I wanted it to be. Maybe that is better.

INDEX

283